D1204138

International Perspectives on Teacher Stress

A volume in
Stress and Coping in Education
Gordon Gates, *Series Editor*

International Perspectives on Teacher Stress

edited by

Christopher J. McCarthy
The University of Texas at Austin

Richard G. Lambert
UNC Charlotte

Annette Ullrich
Baden-Württemberg Cooperative State University

INFORMATION AGE PUBLISHING, INC.
Charlotte, NC • www.infoagepub.com

Library of Congress Cataloging-in-Publication Data

International perspectives on teacher stress / edited by Christopher J. McCarthy, Richard G. Lambert, Annette Ullrich.
    p. cm. – (Research on stress and coping in education)
 ISBN 978-1-61735-915-6 (pbk.) – ISBN 978-1-61735-916-3 (hardcover) – ISBN 978-1-61735-917-0 (ebook) 1. Teachers–Job stress–Cross-cultural studies. I. McCarthy, Christopher J. II. Lambert, Richard G. III. Ullrich, Annette.
 LB2840.2.I68 2012
 371.1001'9–dc23

                                                      2012020708

Printed in the United States of America

CONTENTS

PART I

UNDERSTANDING INTERNATIONAL TEACHER STRESS
USING A MULTI-METHOD, MULTI-CONTEXT APPROACH

PART II

UNDERSTANDING INTERNATIONAL TEACHER STRESS
USING A MONO-METHOD, MULTI-CONTEXT APPROACH

ACKNOWLEDGEMENTS

First, we would like to acknowledge the leadership, direction, and editorial reviews provided by the series editor, Gordon Gates. We also wish to acknowledge the sustained energy and enthusiasm for this book series generated by the members of the Stress and Coping Special Interest Group of the American Educational Research Association. The editors of this volume also acknowledge the contributions of Huub A. Everaert Kees Van der Wolf, and Rob Roesser for their editorial contributions to the second section of this book. Doctoral students at the University of Texas at Austin provided invaluable assistance as reviewers for the contributions of this volume, under the supervision of the volume editors: Nicolina Calfa, Elizabeth Crowe, Ryan Douglas, Sonia Hart, Minda Markle, Sara Gilbert, and Lauren Yadley. Finally, we wish to thank George Johnson, publisher of Information Age Publishing, for his continued support of this books series.

International Perspectives on Teacher Stress, page ix
Copyright © 2012 by Information Age Publishing

INTRODUCTION

As intended by Gordon Gates, the series editor of *Research on Stress and Coping in Education,* in this seventh volume, *International Perspectives on Teacher Stress,* we have assembled the work of scholars affiliated with Stress and Anxiety Research society (STAR) as well as papers presented in Stress and Coping in Education Special Interest Group (SIG) sessions at annual conferences of the American Educational Research Association (AERA). It contains research on teacher stress in the Netherlands, Italy, Russia, China, Germany, and the United States. We decided to organize the chapters into two sections. The first one contains papers with a multi-method, multi-context approach. The second one presents work related to teacher stress using a mono-method, multi-context approach. In other words, the first part studies using different measures in different countries, and the second part provides studies in different countries using a common measure (the standard questionnaire).

Teacher stress is an international phenomenon, and it is widely know that teachers face a multitude of stressors in their day-to-day lives. These factors are multidimensional in nature. They can originate from a political, social, ethical, professional, or economic level. An international perspective on teacher stress offers possibilities to deepen our understanding not only of the impact of stressors on teachers but also on differences in stress and coping. Similarities were found between the countries with respect to dealing with challenging student or parent behavior.

The first section has 12 chapters. The first chapter by Mette Baran is on the "Impact of Cultural Values, Country Characteristics, and Educational Reform on Teacher Stress Levels in Norway," where high rates of teacher

International Perspectives on Teacher Stress, pages xi–xvi
Copyright © 2012 by Information Age Publishing

attrition have been reported. This chapter presents a model of five factors leading to burnout, namely leadership values, geographic characteristics leading to many small schools, demographic changes (some schools have thirty different nationalities), educational reforms, and Europe-wide student assessments such as PISA. All of those factors put stress on teachers, which the paper discusses in detail followed by suggestions of how to support teachers to cope with the challenges they face.

The second chapter by Emine Erktin and Zahid Kısa is titled "Elementary Level Mathematics Teachers' Stress at a Time of Curriculum Reform in Turkey." Erktin and Kisa surveyed 395 Turkish elementary mathematics teachers. Based on transactional models of stress, they examined the relationships of efficacy, readiness, resources, appraisal of a new mathematics curriculum reform (threat or challenge), anxiety, and attitude. They found that teachers with high efficacy beliefs, who were ready to implement the new curriculum, and who indicated a perception of sufficient resources saw the reform implementation as a challenge rather than a threat. These teachers had also lower levels of anxiety during the reform implementation period and therefore more positive attitudes towards it. In addition, the authors compared the impacts of personal and situational variables on anxiety level and attitude using the correlation coefficients. The results were that readiness and efficacy (personal variables) were associated more strongly with anxiety and attitude than perceived resources (situational variable). Erktin and Kisa conclude that this result is in accordance with research on self-efficacy in supporting the notion that teachers with higher self-efficacy are more ready to set higher goals and to meet challenges.

The third chapter is titled "Student Teachers' Epistemological Beliefs, Conceptions about Teaching and Learning and Perceived Stress During Practicum: Are They Related?" Kokkinos, Stavropoulos, and Davazoglou investigated the link between student teachers' epistemologies about knowledge acquisition and conceptions about teaching and learning with perceived stress during their teaching practicum. They conducted a survey of 138 Greek elementary student teachers, who participated in this study at the end of a four-week teaching practicum. They found that conceptions about teaching and learning contribute to the understanding of student teachers' perceived stress after controlling for the effects of gender and epistemological beliefs about knowledge and knowledge acquisition. Correlational analyses confirmed a relationship between student teachers' epistemologies and their conceptions of teaching and learning. This supports previous research that suggests the impact of beliefs on conceptions of teaching and learning. In addition, an association was found between stress for issues directly related to actual teaching (i.e., meeting students' needs) and epistemological beliefs about teaching and learning, but not for administrative and assessment issues. A factor analysis provided evidence for the stability of the Epistemological Beliefs Questionnaire, which has so far only been used in Asian countries.

The fourth chapter "Effects of Stress on Teacher Decision Making" by Gokalp examined the effects of four variables: stress, years of experience, amount of behavior management training, and type of challenging behavior on teachers' strategies to handle problematic student behavior. Eighty-four elementary school teachers were surveyed using three vignettes that described students with behavior problems. Using regression analysis, Gokalp found that the use of effective strategies decreased when stress level increased. Years of experience and amount of behavior management training were not found to impact strategy selection, but type of behavior problem did.

The fifth chapter by Lambert, Ullrich, and McCarthy "Mixed Methods Study of Stress, Coping, and Burnout among Kindergarten and Elementary Teachers in Germany" replicated previous research that examined the relationship of teachers' stress levels and coping resources to burnout symptoms in the United States. Based on data from classroom observations and qualitative interviews with eleven randomly selected participants from four groups (high self-acceptance/R > D, high self-acceptance/D > R, low self-acceptance/R > D, and low self-acceptance/D > R), they were classified into four groups (reactive, detached, engaged, and reflective). Distinct patterns of interaction between the subgroups of teachers and their students emerged with regard to attitudes towards teaching and values.

In the sixth chapter, titled "Early Childhood Teachers' Experiences with Challenging Student Behavior in Germany," Ullrich, Lambert, and McCarthy used qualitative data from a sample of 186 German kindergarten teachers in Baden-Württemberg, Germany. Open-ended questions about problematic student behavior and teachers' strategies were coded in four categories (disruptive behaviors, disrespectful behaviors, lack of engagement, and difficulty communicating). Findings confirm previous research suggesting that more support is needed for professionals in order to effectively cope with challenging student behaviors.

In the seventh chapter, Gates and Dean present a study in which they replicated a study on the impact of personality factors on stress by Jepson and Forrest (2006), "Washington State Elementary Teachers' Stress: The Importance of Occupational Commitment." Using a sample of 90 elementary teachers from 61 schools in Washington State, they examined the relationship between stress and personality traits. They found elevated stress levels in elementary teachers in Washington. Teachers who participated reported high levels of commitment and internal locus of control. Both of these personality factors were observed to moderate stress. Female teachers reported more stress than male teachers.

The eighth chapter provides a study by Lambert, McCarthy, McCarthy, Crowe, and Fisher: "Assessment of Teacher Demands and Resources: Relationship to Stress, Classroom Structural Characteristics, Job Satisfaction, and Turnover." It builds on a previous analysis of data collected from 158 high school statistics teachers. Teachers' demands and resources for stress prevention, job satisfaction, structural aspects of the classroom, and intention to leave the field were examined. Teachers who were classified as having higher demands were different from teachers classified as having higher resources in terms of classroom size and structural characteristics such as percentages of students with attendance and behavior problems. Higher resourced teachers reported more job satisfaction and less of an intention to leave the field. Teachers who indicated specific plans to leave the field also reported higher demands and lower classroom resources. These findings suggest that understanding teacher perceptions of demands and resources in the classroom could be an important component of teacher satisfaction and retention.

Chapter 9, "Assessing Multicultural Competence and Stress with Teachers," by McCarthy, Hart, McCarthy, Crowe, Guzmán, Lambert, and Reiser, describes the results of an intervention aimed at helping teachers dismantle stereotypes held by students about other students. Similar to the fourth chapter by Gokalp, the authors used vignettes about students demonstrating stereotyping behavior to evaluate the effectiveness of a stereotype dismantling workshop. Replicating analyses by Lambert, McCarthy et al. (this volume), they used a shortened version of the CARD and in addition developed a Diversity Experiences Questionnaire (DEQ). Self-acceptance, job satisfaction, and intention to leave were also measured. Based on the Appraisal Index (see Lambert, McCarthy et al., this volume), they categorized teachers into a resourced, a balanced, and a demand group and compared the three groups on stress outcomes (stress related to diversity/ intention to leave, and job satisfaction).

Carson, Tsouloupas, and Barber found that there is a paucity of research that examines differences in coping strategies and burnout in primary and secondary teachers. In the tenth chapter, "Burnout and Coping Strategies across Primary and Secondary Public Schoolteachers," they investigated whether the use of specific coping strategies (active or defensive) and levels of burnout differed based on teaching level in a sample of 645 full-time primary (n=302) and secondary (n=344) teachers in the U.S. The results indicated that the coping–burnout relationship can vary across teaching levels. One possible interpretation for this result may be individual differences between teachers who choose to teach at the primary versus the secondary level.

The eleventh chapter by Singleton, Shue, and Smith, "Effects of Collaborative Problem Solving on Stress, Burnout, and Coping Resources in Early Childhood Special Educators," used a mixed-method design in order to collect data on teachers' levels of stress, burnout, and coping resources before and after a six-week collaborative problem solving (CPS) intervention. Qualitative data were collected with regard to stress and coping resources. Findings showed that the intervention had positive effects on all three participants: a decrease of stress and burnout and an increase of coping resources.

A transition between the two parts of the book is provided in Chapter 12 by Lambert and Ullrich. The second part of the book has five chapters. Huub Everaert's study, titled "Measuring the Perceived Incidence of Challenging Student Behavior: The Development of the Utrecht Challenging Student Questionnaire for Teachers (UCSQT)," focuses on teacher perceptions of student behavior using the UCSQT, which measures two dimensions of challenging students' behavior, namely externalizing and internalizing behaviors. It also provides an overview of the development of the UCSQT (three studies) as well as results from a fourth study on the internal consistency of th UCSQT.

Chapter 14, "A Mixed Methods Study of the Responses to Two Open-Ended Questions Regarding Stress in the Classroom from a Sample of Italian Teachers" by Castelli, Pepe, and Addimando discusses research on the construct validity of the UCSQT. Using a mixed-method design, the authors collected data from a sample of 518 teachers. They found that teachers' qualitative responses accurately reflected statistical results, thus providing evidence for the overall validity of the underlying theoretical constructs of the UCSQT.

Volochkov and Popov's "Stress in Teacher–Student Interactions and Teacher Activeness as a Positive Coping Resource" explore the relationship of teacher stress due to challenging student behavior measured by the standard questionnaire (SQ) and teacher activeness measured by the Teacher Professional Activeness Questionnaire (TAQ). The concept of teacher activeness is a coping resource related to how teachers respond to stressful situations. The authors found that levels of stress decreased if teacher activeness increased. Thus, teacher activeness plays an important role in the stress equation. Therefore, they recommend the inclusion of the concept of teacher activeness in teacher training in order to help teachers to become effective and socially–emotionally balanced professionals.

Chapter 16 is by Pang and Tao, titled "Teacher Stress in Working with Behavioral Problems of Students in Hong Kong." They report the results of a study of 1,210 elementary teachers in Hong Kong and compare their results to findings from seven other countries (Italy, the Netherlands, Russia, South Africa, Surinam, and the United States). Similar to the results from the study in Russia as well as to the results from a study conducted in the Netherlands, Chinese teachers rated behaviors coded as "full of activity/easily distractible" as among the most challenging student behaviors. They also concluded that teacher beliefs (namely self-efficacy, negative affect, self-critical attitude) may be seen as moderating the effects of challenging student behaviors on teachers. Teacher beliefs were more strongly associated with teacher stress than school characteristics were.

Chapter 17, "Predictors of Elementary Teachers' Burnout Symptoms: The Role of Teachers' Personal Resources, Perceptions of Classroom Stress, and Disruption of Teaching" is by McCarthy, Lambert, O'Donnell, Villarreal, and Melendres. In an effort to better understand teacher perceptions of resources and demands they tested disruption of teaching and classroom demands as possible mediators between preventive resources and burnout symptom using structural equation modeling. The hypothesis could not be confirmed; however, all independent variables were associated with the dependent variable (burnout symptoms) in the predicted direction.

This volume concludes with a chapter by McCarthy, Douglas, and Shah overviewing perspectives on stress and coping and how they fit with the perspectives contained in *International Perspectives on Teacher Stress*. This chapter also provides thoughts about teacher stress in a global economy and future directions for this area of inquiry.

During the process of editing this volume, the complexity of teacher stress and coping became evident, especially with regard to cultural differences. Nevertheless, this deepened our understanding of the underlying issues; for example, differences in job-related demands resulting in differences in stress levels may be due to a variety of variables such as parental expectations, teacher workload, class size, or educational system. We discovered that most of those differences can only be interpreted on the basis of in-depth cultural context and system knowledge. The value of this volume lies in its insights into what is relevant to finding ways to support teachers individually and structurally. In the end, reducing teacher stress not only is a goal in itself, but at the same it results in improving children's learning environments. Finally, we want to thank all contributing authors of this volume *International Perspectives on Teacher Stress*.

REFERENCE

Jepson, E., & Forrest, S. (2006). Individual contributory factors in teacher stress: The role of achievement . *British Journal of Educational Psychology, 76*, 183–196.

PART I

UNDERSTANDING INTERNATIONAL TEACHER STRESS
USING A MULTI-METHOD, MULTI-CONTEXT
APPROACH

CHAPTER 1

THE IMPACT OF CULTURAL VALUES, COUNTRY CHARACTERISTICS, AND EDUCATIONAL REFORM ON TEACHER STRESS LEVELS IN NORWAY

Mette Baran
Cardinal Stritch University

ABSTRACT

Recent research in Norway shows that many teachers feel a high level of stress and exhaustion and that many opt to exit the profession before they reach retirement age. This chapter proposes a model delineating forces leading to teacher burnout. While the focus is on Norway, similar forces may contribute to teacher burnout elsewhere. Five factors are seen as important. First are Norwegian leadership values characterized by modesty and little power distinction between administrators and employees. Second are the geographic and population characteristics of Norway, which have resulted in many small schools. Responsible for instructing multiple subjects to students of various

International Perspectives on Teacher Stress, pages 3–20
Copyright © 2012 by Information Age Publishing

ages, teachers in small schools have tended to be generalists but, due to educational reform, are now required to become specialists. Third are the demographic changes in the country with a tremendous influx of foreigners—many seeking political asylum—resulting in some school districts having to deal with thirty spoken languages and immense cultural differences. Fourth are the government-prescribed educational reforms including new curricula and mandated tests. Finally, the diminishing attainment of educational goals by Norwegian students as measured by a variety of European assessments is putting pressure on Norwegian teachers at all levels. Each of these factors will be discussed in further detail, and suggestions are made regarding practices to help teachers cope with these major changes in the Norwegian educational environment today.

THE IMPACT OF CULTURAL VALUES, COUNTRY CHARACTERISTICS, AND EDUCATIONAL REFORM ON TEACHER STRESS LEVELS IN NORWAY

In recent years, the issues of occupational stress and its consequences have become major research topics in education. Being a teacher is often regarded as a stressful occupation. Much international research supports the relationship between stress and teacher health problems (DeFrank & Stroup, 1989; Kyriacou, 1987; Mykletun, 1984; Travers & Cooper, 1993, 1994).

The many changes and demands placed on Norway's schools over the last two decades have reduced the quality of work life for teachers. One sign of this negative development has been an increased level of job stress. Teacher stress is defined as a state of negative affect experienced by educators that is attributable to their perception of work demands (Kyriacou & Sutcliffe, 1978). Recent research in Norway shows that many teachers feel high levels of stress and exhaustion, and many are opting to exit the profession before they reach retirement age—even though many also report a high level of job satisfaction (Ellingsen, 2009; Mykletun & Mykletun, 1999).

Sources of teacher stress identified in the literature include, among others: workload, poor student attitudes and behaviors, lack of promotional prospects, unsatisfactory working conditions, poor relationships with colleagues and superiors (Travers & Cooper, 1994), poor interactions with students (Mykletun & Mykletun, 1999), advances in technology (Kniveton, 1991), changes in the working environment (Cox, Kuk, & Leiter, 1993), and organizational climate—including poor administration (Michela, Lukaszewski, & Allegrante, 1995; Smith & Bourke, 1992; Travers & Cooper, 1993). A high level of job-related stress over a long period of time is associated with burnout symptoms typically identified as including feelings of emotional exhaustion, depersonalization, and reduced sense of personal accomplishment/achievement (Cordes & Dougherty, 1993; Jennett, Harris, & Mesibov, 2003; Maslach & Jackson, 1986). Emotional exhaustion is the experience of feeling drained of energy or all used up. People experiencing emotional exhaustion may begin to maintain an emotional distance from others (Maslach, 1982). Most teachers cope successfully with their work-related stress, for instance, through active problem solving, gaining social and emotional support from colleagues, reorganizing the teaching situation, cooperating with parents, or changing their teaching strategy (Skaalvik & Skaalvik, 2007). However, burnout may be the endpoint of coping unsuccessfully with chronic stress (Jennett et al., 2003).

The following chapter discusses the conditions and changes present in Norway and its system of public education that can be seen as contributing to early exit of Norwegian teachers from their chosen profession. The chapter is divided into several sections. The first section offers a brief introduction to Norway and its system of public education. The second describes the education reform underway in the nation, as preparation for research shared on teacher stress in Norway. The fourth section describes school leadership reform. The chapter closes with a summary and recommendations.

NORWAY AND ITS SCHOOLS

Located in Northern Europe, Norway is a small monarchy, similar in size to Britain, but with a highly homogeneous population of 4.8 million people, making its population density one of the lowest in Europe. Norway is well known for its high standard of living and extensive welfare system. The country consistently ranks highly in United Nations studies as one of the best places in the world to live based on income, life expectancy, and education levels (Smith, 2010). Norway has the second highest gross national product (GNP) per capita among the Organization for Economic Co-operation & Development (OECD) countries with a stable economy based on its rich resources in oil, natural gas, fishing, and forestry. The country boasts the lowest unemployment rate in Europe at 3.0%.

Government regulations have been enacted that place high priority on protecting the Norwegian workforce. An important example of this philosophy is evidenced in the Norwegian Working Environment Act that parliament passed in January 2006, which protects people by identifying the following labor policies:

1. Ensuring sound conditions of employment and equality of treatment at work
2. Facilitating adaptations of the individual employees' working situation in relation to his or her capabilities and life circumstances

3. Providing a basis whereby the employer and the employees may themselves safeguard and develop their working environment in cooperation with the employers' and employees' organizations, as well as with the requisite guidance and supervision of the public authorities.
4. Fostering inclusive working conditions (EWCO, n.d., para. 2)

Another example can be seen when the Research Council of Norway in 2007 launched the Sickness Absence Research Program in response to a request from the Ministry of Labor and Inclusion. The program is a long-term initiative that will span a period of 10 years (2007–2016) with the aim to increase knowledge on causes that lead to sickness, absence, disability, and exclusion from working life.

Norway's populace also receives the benefit of a generously supported system of public schools. Indeed, Norway is among a handful of countries worldwide that spend a high percentage of its budget on education (i.e., 9% of total public expenditure in 2005) (Statistics Norway, 2007). Adjusted for purchasing power, Norway spends 42% more per student in primary and lower secondary schools than the OECD average, amounting to approximately $10,000 per student (Norwegian Directorate for Education and Training, 2007). The Norwegian educational system is predominantly public. Only 2.3% of students at the elementary level and about 5.2% at the secondary level attend private schools (Norwegian Directorate for Education and Training, 2007).

Students start school at the age of 6. The elementary and lower secondary school is divided into an elementary level (grades 1–7) and a lower secondary level (grades 8–10). Students have the right and obligation to attend school until they complete the tenth grade. Students then have a choice to complete an application for entrance to upper secondary education (3 years) or vocational training consisting of two years of schooling followed by two years of apprenticeship. A total of 25% of the Norwegian population over the age of 16 has attended higher education institutions. This is almost twice as many as 20 years ago (Norwegian Directorate for Education and Training, 2007).

The national educational policy is to provide educational opportunities where people live. As a result, a large number of schools—40% of primary and lower secondary schools, serving 8.7% of the student body—are quite small (i.e., less than a hundred students), and in these schools children of different ages are often taught in the same classroom (Norwegian Directorate for Education and Training, 2007). The number of leadership positions in a school is dependent on the number of students. In small schools, it is often the principal who is given the entire leadership allocation, and at these schools he or she often has teaching duties. At larger schools it is common for resources and responsibilities to be divided between the principal and one or more assistant principals. In upper secondary schools, the assistant principal is often responsible for school finances or personnel management (Norwegian Directorate for Education and Training, 2007).

In Norwegian schools, principals are responsible for the quality of teaching, learning, and assessment (Almås & Nilsen, 2006). There are common national strategies concerning elementary and secondary education to guide decision making and practice, but school authorities at the municipal and county levels (there are 431 municipalities and 19 counties), as well as private school owners, are responsible for how educational policies are reflected in school procedures. Each municipality and county authority decides the powers that are to be delegated to the school level. As a result, there is great diversity and variation in how local authorities set priorities and the ways schools are managed. This state of affairs impacts both the content and the empowerment of administrators and teachers to embrace or accomplish the objectives presented in educational reform.

Educational Reform in Norway

Many changes have been implemented within the Norwegian school system over the last two decades. In 1985, the National Norwegian Curriculum emphasized that education should be adapted to individual students' needs (*Mønsterplan for grunnskolen*, 1985). More recently, in 2006, *The Knowledge Promotion Reform—From Words to Action* (KPR), provided all grades with new curricula and clearly stated competency objectives. The new set of curricula for the entire basic school program identified certain basic skills and knowledge as being especially important for students' and apprentices' professional and personal development. These basic skills are: (1) oral expression, (2) reading, (3) writing, (4) arithmetic, and (5) the use of digital tools. Other competencies or skills are also expressed in the curricula as principles for schooling in Norway and include social and cultural competencies, motivation, and learning strategies (Norwegian Directorate for Education and Training, 2007). The reform, as such, involved overhauling lower and upper secondary education curriculum, working to make smoother the transition between elementary and upper secondary education, and increasing cooperation between basic education and local commerce and industry (Ministry of Education and Research, 2004). The intention of this comprehensive reform was to create a national coherent school system covering grades 1 through 13.

The KPR required several modifications in substance, structure, and organization of Norwegian schools (Norwegian Directorate for Education and Training, 2007). One change relates to the "generalist" versus the "specialist" teacher. Norwegian primary and lower secondary education has been, and still is, adapted to the scattered population discussed earlier. Teachers as generalists have been trained to possess a solid basic and broad competence and have not been required to attain specialized in-depth subject expertise (Lagerstrøm, 2000). As a consequence, the profile and requirements of Norwegian teacher competence has been more general than those in other OECD countries where most teachers may be subject specialists even at the lower elementary levels. However, educational stakeholders are making a case for doing away with the generalist teacher. They argue the need for in-depth and specialized subject competence, even among teachers at lower levels, in order to successfully accomplish the reform objectives. The new national curriculum requires teachers who were trained as generalists to learn new competencies in order to help students reach standard (Norwegian Directorate for Education and Training, 2007). In contrast, arguments against specialization of teachers portray the change as jeopardizing the formation of long-term relationships between teachers and students in Norway's schools, which helped to create what many see as a positive learning environment with many social benefits (Baran, 2008). Additionally, the recruitment and retention of teacher specialists for small and remote schools has been argued to place these schools at a disadvantage as compared to their urban counterparts.

The KPR also articulated the responsibility of schools for ensuring that students develop skills in the use of digital tools—requiring teachers to gain expertise in this subject area as well. The oversight for this work is often delegated from the municipal and county levels to local schools, which in practice makes it the building administrator's responsibility. The increasing power of school principals to decide instructional methods, which may vary both among and within schools, places a demand on teachers trying to cope with all these changes (Skaalvik & Skaalvik, 2007).

In a related reform, the white paper *Culture for Learning* (2003–2004) pointed to the necessity of developing schools into learning organizations (Almås & Nilsen, 2006). Senge's (1990) concepts were adopted as the model for implementation. He defined a learning organization as one in which "people continually expand their capacity to create the results they truly desire, where new and expansive patterns of thinking are nurtured, where collective aspiration is set free, and where people are continually learning how to learn together" (p. 3). Most schools have gradually organized teachers into teams. It is not uncommon for some of the school's leadership resources to be divided among the team leaders, who are often also members of an extended leader/planning group. In addition, most upper secondary schools have a variety of areas of study where the leaders for each area are part of the school's leadership team.

The various reforms implemented through policy or championed in position papers can be seen as responding to growing public concern about the quality of Norway's schools. Surveys show that parents, while reasonably satisfied with the school(s) that their child(ren) attend, have become increasingly critical of the overall education system (Senge, 1990, p. 18). Encouraging the concern of both the public and policymakers was the fact that Norwegian students' test scores were falling below scores from neighboring countries with similar socioeconomic cultures on, for example, the Programme for International Student Assessment (PISA). Initiated by OECD, Norwegian students first joined the PISA study in 2000. The PISA study is an international comparative survey of the educational school systems in different countries. The PISA measures 15-year-olds' competencies in reading, mathematics, and scientific literacy every three years. According to the 2006 PISA results, 8.4% of Norwegian 15-year-olds scored below the proficiency level in reading and 7.3% were below in math. Tables 1.1 and 1.2 compare the 2006 results in reading and math for Norway, Finland and Sweden (OECD, n.d.).

Not only have Norwegian students consistently performed lowest of the Nordic countries and significantly below the OECD average in all three subjects, there has been a consistent decrease in performance in all three subject areas from 2000 to 2006 (Kjærnsli, Lie, Olsen, & Roe, 2007). The Norwegian results in science, reading, and math are worrisome, and teachers and school leaders as such have come under increasing pressure from the government to improve national rankings (Norwegian Directorate for Education and Training, 2007). Although external demands for results-driven curricula and other forms of bureaucratic accountability can be seen

TABLE 1.1 PISA Reading Scores for 15 Year Olds

	Mean	Below proficiency	Above proficiency
Norway	484	8.4	7.7
Finland	547	0.8	16.7
Sweden	507	5.0	10.6

Source: (OECD, n.d.)

TABLE 1.2 PISA Math Scores for 15 Year Olds

	Mean	Below proficiency	Above Proficiency
Norway	490	7.3	2.1
Finland	548	1.1	6.3
Sweden	502	5.4	2.9

Source: (OECD, n.d.)

as having increased in Norway over recent years, a national survey among school leaders in Norway conducted in 2005 demonstrated that they are not yet at the same level of intensity as those observed in the U.S. and UK (Møller, Sivesind, Skedsmo, & Aas, 2006).

In addition to the PISA results, the academic achievement of Norwegian students as assessed on national tests has given rise to concern. In 2004, mandatory testing began to ensure that all schools successfully developed student competencies in reading, math, and English in 5th and 8th grades. The results of these national tests are disturbing, revealing that many students do not develop reading ability during their compulsory schooling. Poor student performance has increased support for accountability. Educational accountability can be seen as keeping teachers to ethical and professional standards (Møller, 2006). One argument that surfaces is that "teachers' performance should be controlled and judged according to criteria established outside the profession" (Norwegian Directorate for Education and Training, 2007, p. 30). Examples of this are wage negotiations and negotiations of working time agreements. The Norwegian government has recently launched a campaign for accountability by implementing a system of quality control for schools where schools' average results on national tests in reading, mathematics, and English are published on a website. The government's rationale for such publication was to improve schools, but the newspapers immediately started ranking the schools through informal league tables (Norwegian Directorate for Education and Training, 2007). The analyses of the national tests also revealed systematic differences in achievement among students in relation to gender, social, and ethnic background (Ministry of Education and Research, 2004). Many students who were born outside the country or whose parents immigrated do not perform well on these academic assessments.

The steady immigration of people from non-western countries during the past 30 years has begun to transform Norway. Norway is increasingly a multicultural nation. At the beginning of 2006, the immigrant population was approximately 390,000 or 8.3% of the population (Norwegian Directorate for Education and Training, 2007). Immigrants to Norway come from 208 different nations, making it a highly heterogeneous group (Norwegian Directorate for Education and Training, 2007). The largest numbers of immigrants come from Pakistan (7.9%), Sweden, (7.3%), and Denmark (6.2%). Norway's schools reflect the changing demographics, as 8.3% of students in elementary schools have a mother tongue other than Norwegian.

In some districts in the capital, Oslo, schools have a clear immigrant majority representing 20–30 different nationalities. The immigrant population in Oslo has increased by 40% in the past few years, and in seven of the city districts over 20% of the population have a non-Western background. Consequently, Norwegian schools are becoming increasingly multicultural and multilingual. Instructing students and cooperating with parents from diverse backgrounds has brought teacher cultural competence, or lack thereof, to the attention of policymakers. Research in Norwegian schools has shown that teachers perceive this aspect of their work as extremely demanding, and many educators report not knowing how to address the diversity of students' needs and abilities (Skaalvik & Fossen, 1995). Teachers are struggling to cope with these demands at the same time that they are being required to differentiate instruction for students with disabilities, who are now being integrated into the regular education classroom (Norwegian Directorate for Education and Training, 2007).

The combination of social change and educational reform expose the various contextual features contributing to increasing demands and job stress for Norwegian teachers. In summary, there is the tremendous influx of nontraditional students (foreign speaking and with disabilities) into regular classrooms. Then, there is the government-prescribed educational reform requiring teachers to become specialists as opposed to generalists and learn new skills in the digital realm, which can also be seen as stress producing. The diminishing attainment of educational outcomes by Norwegian students as measured by a variety of European assessment measures puts further pressure on Norwegian teachers at all levels to attend to their students' performance and improve their instructional practice. Related to this are the new national testing mandates and competency objectives coupled with the new curricula for all grade levels.

NORWEGIAN TEACHERS AND STRESS

Before discussing the particulars of what is known about teacher stress in Norway, the following statistics and background provide some insight on the problem. In 2005, the total number of teachers in grades 1–10 was 62,200 (73% women). The total number of teachers in grades 10–13 was 23,100 (47% women) (Norwegian Directorate for Education and Training, 2007). Norwegian teachers are well educated. About 65% of the teachers at the elementary level have three or four years of general teacher training from a university college (namely, the four-year general teacher training program) (Norwegian Directorate for Education and Training, 2007).

In 2005, 48 percent of teachers in grades 1–10 were older than 45, as were 65% of teachers in grades 10–13. Over 50% of teachers are above the age of 50, while only a little more than 25% are younger than the age of 40. There is an increased concern that as the teaching population has aged, there has been a lack of recruitment into the profession. In addition, according to recent research, many of the younger teachers do not foresee working as teachers until they reach retirement age. Lastly, there are relatively few teachers above the age of 60, indicating that many are exiting the profession before they reach retirement age (Ellingsen, 2009; Norwegian Directorate for Education and Training, 2007).

Mykletun and Mykletun (1999) concluded that early exit from work is a sign of burnout. They sampled a group of 2,800 Norwegian school teachers. Teachers completed an instrument consisting of three combined inventories: (1) The General Burnout Scale (GPS; 16 items) with subscales for exhaustion, cynicism, and professional efficacy; (2) Mykletun's Sense of Competency Scale (SCS, 28 items); and (3) the Teacher's Stress Ratings Scale (TSRS, 88 items) focusing on main areas of stress for teachers. Results show that 185 individuals scored high on the exhaustion scale, 179 on the professional efficacy scale, and 175 on the cynicism scales. Factor analysis on the SCS revealed five factors accounted for 53% of total variance. Categories were named: classroom-processes competence, relations-to-students competence, teaching-plan competence, organizational factors competence, and relations-to-parents competence. Factor analysis on the TSRS revealed that 12 factors accounted for 61% of total variance. Categories were named: leadership problems, work-overload, over-concern about students, change stress, lack of critical competence, conflict with students' parents, conflict with colleagues, conflict with students, lack of infrastructure, stand-in procedures stress, wasting time on meetings stress, and fear of redundancy. According to the authors, work-overload constituted variables expressing perceptions of role conflict and ambiguity, difficult social relations at work, discontent with social standing and financial rewards and work responsibilities infringing on teachers' own spare time.

The findings from Mykletun and Mykletun's (1999) study revealed age is a critical variable for predicting early exit from teaching. The authors suggested that the number of working hours be reduced as teachers age to reduce overload stress and stress related to student conflict. In addition, the authors found that a low sense of competence, the "subjective feeling of being able to cope," was associated with early exit from the profession (p. 364) and that it was similar in its effect to the perceived stress variables. These findings receive support from other research on teacher self-efficacy and teacher burnout. Bandura (1997) found that low teacher self-efficacy may result in feelings of burnout.

A more recent study was conducted in Norway measuring the levels of stress among 2,200 teachers. Tiredness and exhaustion were problems for one out of four teachers. Prolonged exposure to such problems may mean that 25% or more of Norwegian teachers may be suffering from burnout or, at the very least, major job-related stress symptoms (Mykletun, 2002). According to the author, there is no doubt that teachers are at high risk of suffering from burnout. It is interesting to note that this research took place prior to the introduction of the Knowledge Reform in 2006, which placed additional demands on teachers. In addition, there is now more student diversity than ever in Norway's schools.

In 2008, 2,300 middle school teachers, representing 156 schools, participated in the Teaching and Learning International Survey (TALIS), an OECD survey focusing on teaching and learning in 23 countries. The results revealed that Norwegian teachers in general are satisfied with their positions with relatively high self-beliefs in their abilities to handle their teaching jobs.

One of the main challenges facing Norwegian schools, according to TALIS results, however, is a weak appraisal and feedback culture. Results indicated a low level of subject-matter feedback from teachers to their students. This may be linked to the low student scores on international tests (Vibe, Aamodt, & Carlsten, 2009) as compared to students in other countries. In addition, Norwegian teachers received less mentoring and support from their principals than their European counterparts. Seventeen percent of all teachers reported that they had never received feedback or evaluation. Teachers also rated their principals very low on providing constructive feedback that informed and contributed to their pedagogical practice. The feedback, evaluation, and appraisal system in Norway's schools can be seen as hampering teacher competence. It is research findings like these that are drawing attention to reform of school leadership. Change in school leadership has come to be identified as key to improvement for both student academic outcomes and teacher competence and coping.

SCHOOL LEADERSHIP REFORM

In order to better address the challenges facing the nation's schools, Norway participated in research that culminated in the 2007 OECD report, *Improving School Leadership*. As part of the process, stakeholders within the Norwegian educational system, namely researchers, school owners' representatives, school leaders, union organizations' representatives, and representatives from the authorities, produced Norway's Country Background Report (CBR). The overall purpose of the activity was to provide policymakers with information and analysis to assist them in formulating and implementing initiatives to support the development of school leaders who can systematically guide the improvement of teaching and learning and to facilitate the exchange of experience, knowledge, and policies among countries. The guidelines for school leadership to emerge from the study have been adopted (Norwegian Directorate for Education and Training, 2007). Part of the justification for such guidelines is evident in the finding that 40% of school leaders had no formal education in management or organizational skills and only 18.5% had taken coursework on leadership equivalent to one year's study (Møller et al., 2006). School leadership in Norway was found lacking. Simply put, many school administrators lacked training.

Efforts have been underway to bring about improvement. Indeed, the Directorate for Education and Training reported that by 2008, it had spent $3.5 billion focused on training school leaders, teachers, and others to help facilitate reform adoption and implementation. For example, universities, colleges, and other professional organizations have provided assistance and expertise to develop schools into learning organizations and professional learning communities as set forth in the *Culture for Learning* (2003–2004). There are few who have not heard that all stakeholders have an obligation to work towards common goals and engage in "continuous reflection over whether the objectives set and the decisions taken are the right ones for the organization. These are essential characteristics of learning organizations as well as necessary skills for schools as organizations" (Norwegian Directorate for Education and Training, 2007, p. 30). The educational philosophy practiced in Norway's schools is undergoing significant change.

Research by Møller et al. (2005) on successful school leadership in Norway has supported reform. Møller et al. describe the team organization among teachers and cooperation between the principal and assistant principals in buildings:

> Principal and deputy (assistant principal) walked in and out of each other's offices during the day, discussing concrete matters that had to be solved, or shared ideas about the school's long-term development. These are clear examples of informal co-principalship. In this way school leadership can be understood as a network of relationships among people, structures and cultures rather than merely a role-based function assigned to one person. (2005, p. 19)

Møller (2006) posited that leadership practice is relational; that is, it is distributed through the *interactions* of people and their situations. Elsewhere, Møller (2009) discussed heads of schools as "first among equals." The model of leadership being championed places great demands on principals and their faculty.

Hofstede's (1978) analysis of leadership practices based on cultural characteristics offers some hopeful insights for those advancing reform. His analysis linking national culture and dimensions of leadership shows that Norway differs from the norms found in other countries in two particular ways. First, there is little power distance, namely little distance between the leader and the employee. Second, Norwegian leadership culture is characterized by femininity (Hofstede's term, which includes modesty) and the "Scandinavian leadership model" involving little hierarchy, a flat structure, powerful labor unions, decentralized governance, few industrial disputes, and good social welfare schemes (Hofstede & Hofstede, 2005).

SUMMARY, RECOMMENDATIONS, AND NEED
FOR FUTURE RESEARCH

Recent research in Norway shows that many teachers feel a high level of stress and exhaustion, and one out of four teachers may be suffering from burnout or, at the very least, major job-related stress symptoms (Mykletun, 2002). A major effort is needed immediately regarding the equitable distribution of resources to better meet the needs of individual students. This would address the diversity among students in Norway today and perhaps result in the necessity for differential treatment in order to meet individual learning abilities (namely greater resources for greater needs). At present, there is a lack of knowledge about factors in the educational system that are of importance for social equality. There are moderate to large differences in performance, measured by grades, between ethnic Norwegian and non-Western immigrant students. In addition, immigrant students tend to drop out of school at a greater rate than ethnic Norwegian students (Støren, 2005). School leaders as well as teachers need to address these issues.

While Norwegian teachers have a great deal of autonomy in their daily work, the majority of teachers would like more professional development opportunities. The number of teachers participating in professional development is greatly lower than the TALIS average, and over 60% of Norwegian teachers would prefer additional development opportunities. The findings also show that Norway is one of the countries with the lowest degree of formal induction processes or mentoring programs for new teachers. According to the report, new teachers are, to a great extent, left to themselves when meeting their students from their first day on the job. The fact that teachers reported a desire for additional training is a concern and may result in unfavorable consequences, such as the fact that the majority of Norwegian middle school teachers report that unsatisfactory professional work is tolerated over time (Vibe et al., 2009). Currently, there are no formal requirements for evaluating teachers in Norway, but the results reveal that Norwegian teachers wish for more formal appraisals, feedback, and opportunities for professional development.

As mentioned previously, the Research Council of Norway is continuing research on teacher stress in the country. While a certain level of stress will always be unavoidable for teachers, future research should focus on how teachers can be best trained to manage stress. Teachers need to be proactive and learn how to control their work environment. Research needs to target what main factors this training should consist of in order to keep productive and effective teachers committed to the profession for the duration of their career. This chapter proposed a model delineating five forces that have led to teacher burnout in Norway. The first is school leadership. While there are national educational strategies, the local schools are responsible for implementing them as they see fit. Norwegian leadership values recognize little power distinction between leaders and employees, and decisions are discussed collectively as opposed to decisions being made by single leaders who direct the schools. Consequently, teachers oftentimes bear major responsibilities in planning and implementing school strategy for which they are ill-equipped.

Recommendations include efforts to better prepare future school administrators for their role and to ensure a steady line of recruits entering leadership positions. School owners need to invest more in leadership preparation programs. The curriculum for teacher education programs needs to be revisited, and more leadership training should be added to the program. There should also be an investment in mentoring programs for new principals and assistant principals similar to the Principal Induction Programs (PIP) in the United States. The PIP assists public school districts in providing support and professional development for first-year principals. This could encourage teachers to aspire to new positions within the school or district. In addition, due to the collaborative decision-making style, administrators and teachers alike need to commit to creating professional learning communities (PLCs). The continuous social changes taking place in Norway also necessitate that administrators and teachers commit themselves to a lifelong, collaborative learning process. The collaborative culture in Norwegian schools also requires that administrators focus on developing overall potential in teachers to better prepare them for decision making. By enhancing the overall capacity of everyone in the organization, the organization is better equipped to reach its goals.

Second, with a very small population scattered over a very large geography, many schools have few students, requiring teachers to be generalists; however, government mandates require them to become specialists in the future. The recommendation is that teachers need ongoing professional development so that they can make the switch to become more specialized within their field. Similarly, teacher preparation programs need to change the curriculum to better prepare teachers for their future roles. The 2008 TALIS results showed that Norwegian teachers received less feedback and mentoring from their principals than most of their European counterparts. School administrators need to ensure that a feedback and mentoring culture becomes the norm in their organizations.

Third are the demographic changes in the country with a tremendous influx of foreigners—many seeking political asylum—resulting in some school districts having to deal with thirty spoken languages and immense cultural differences. Teachers find it stressful to deal with students, parents, and guardians who speak many different languages and whose culture and religion differ significantly from their own. Most classrooms in Norway today are far from being homogeneous. Currently, 8% of the population in

Norway represents other cultures, and the blending of various cultures is becoming commonplace. This author urges that teachers need to become culturally competent. This should be part of the ongoing effort to create PLCs within schools. In addition, teacher preparation programs need to address this issue.

Fourth are the government-prescribed educational reforms resulting in teachers being required to become specialists as opposed to generalists in addition to learning new skills in the digital realm and focusing on team-teaching entire grade levels. Again, the recommendation is that schools develop a culture of learning that focuses on addressing the skills in which teachers feel they have deficiencies. In addition, the curriculum in school preparation programs needs to reflect the new requirements of teachers' knowledge base and skills.

Finally, the diminishing attainment of educational goals by Norwegian students, as measured by a variety of European assessment measures, is putting pressure on Norwegian teachers at all levels to increase their standards of performance in the classroom. The recommendation is that teachers pay attention to the 2008 TALIS results, which indicated that Norwegian teachers did not provide sufficient feedback to students on their performance. Teachers need to appreciate the fact that students may invest more in their own learning if they feel that teachers take the time to provide feedback. In addition, this may provide them with better knowledge of what is expected of them. Further, school owners need to develop a climate that values teachers and that pays attention to factors leading to teacher stress. The recommendation is to ensure that all school districts in Norway have specific practices in place that put focus on stress reduction and programs that may alleviate the stress factors for teachers and administrators. Suggestions include using in-service days to teach or reinforce skills that will have a positive impact on school climate and stress management. All the above efforts may have an aggregate effect in reducing stress levels among teachers and administrators in Norwegian schools.

REFERENCES

Almäs, A. G., & Nilsen, A. G. (2006). ICT competencies for the next generation of teachers. Retrieved from http://www.formatex.org/micte2006/pdf/468-472.pdf

Bandura, A. (1997). *Bandura's instrument teacher self-efficacy scale.* Retrieved from http://www.coe.ohio-state.edu/ahoy/Bandura%20Instr.pdf

Baran, M. L. (2008). Assessing the effects of a middle school looping program. *International Journal of Learning, 15*(7), 3–8.

Cordes, C. L., & Dougherty, T. W. (1993). A review and an integration of research on job burnout. *Academy of Management Review, 18*(4), 621–656.

Cox, T., Kuk, G., & Leiter, M. P. (1993). Burnout, health, work stress, and organizational healthiness. In W. B. Schaufeli, C. Maslach, & T. Marek (Eds.), *Professional burnout: Recent developments in theory and research. Series in applied psychology: Social issues and questions* (pp. 177–193). Philadelphia, PA: Taylor & Francis.

Culture for Learning. (2003–2004). Report no. 30 to the Norwegian Parliament. Retrieved from http://odin.dep.no/ufd/engelsk/publ/veiledninger/045071-120012/dok-bn.html

DeFrank, R. S., & Stroup, C. A. (1989). Teacher stress and health: Examination of a model. *Journal of Psychosomatic Research, 33,* 99–109.

Ellingsen, B. (2009). En av tre lærere vurderer å slutte. Retrieved from http://www.forskning.no/artikler/2009/juni/223721

EWCO. (n.d.) Norwegian Working Environment Act of January 2006. Retrieved from http://www.eurofound.europa.eu/ewco/studies/tn0612036s/no0612039q.htm

Forskningsradet. (n.d.). Programme on Sickness Absence Research (SYKEFRAVAER). Retrieved from http://www.forskningsradet.no/servlet/Satellite?c=Page&cid=1226993895606&pagename=sykefravaer%2FHovedsidemal

Hofstede, G. (July, 1978). The poverty of management control philosophy. *Academy of Management Review, 3*(3), 450–461.

Hofstede, G., & Hofstede, G. J. (2005). *Cultures and organizations: software of the mind.* New York: McGraw-Hill.

Jennett, H. K., Harris, S. L., & Mesibov, G. B. (2003). Commitment to philosophy, teacher efficacy, and burnout among teachers of children with autism. *Journal of Autism & Developmental Disorders, 33,* 583–593.

Kniveton, B. H. (1991). An investigation of factors contributing to teachers' job satisfaction. *School Psychology International, 12,* 361–371.

Kjærnsli, M., Lie, S., Olsen, R. V., & Roe, A. (2007). *Tid for tunge løft. Norske elevers kompetanse i naturfag, lesing og matematikk.* Oslo, Norway: Universitetsforlaget.

Kyriacou, C. (1987). Teacher stress and burnout: An international review. *Educational Research, 29,* 89–96.

Kyriacou, C., & Sutclilffe, J. (1978). Teacher stress. Prevalence, sources and symptoms. *British Journal of Educational Psychology, 48,* 159–167.

Lagerstrøm, B. O. (2000). *Kompetanse i grunnskolen: Hovedresultater 1999/2000. (Competence in primary and lower secondary schools: Main results 1999/2000)* Oslo, Norway: Statistisk sentralbyrå, Avdeling for personstatistikk/Seksjon for intervjuundersøkelser.

Maslach, C. (1982). *Burnout: The cost of caring.* Englewood Cliff, NJ: Prentice-Hall.

Maslach, C., & Jackson, S. E. (1986). *Maslach burnout inventory manual* (2nd ed.). Palo Alto, CA: Consulting Psychologists Press.

Michela, J. L., Lukaszewski, M. P., & Allegrante, J. (1995). Organisational climate and work stress: A general framework applied to inner-city schoolteachers. In S. L. Sauter & L. R. Murphy, (Eds.), *Organizational risk factors for job stress* (pp. 61–80). Washington, DC: American Psychologists Association.

Mykletun, R. J. (1984). Teacher stress: Perceived and objective sources, and quality of life. *Scandinavian Journal of Educational Research, 28,* 17–45.

Mykletun, R. J. (2002). *Utbrent. Krevende jobber—gode liv?* Bergen, Norway: Fagbok-forlaget.

Mykletun, R. J., & Mykletun, A. (1999). Comprehensive schoolteachers at risk of early exit from work. *Experimental Ageing Research, 25,* 359–366.

Møller, J. (2006). Democratic schooling in Norway: Implications for leadership in practice. Leadership and policy in Schools. *Special issue on International Perspectives on Leadership for Social Justice, 5*(1), 53–69.

Møller, J. (2009). Approaches to school leadership in Scandinavia. *Journal of Educational Administration and History, 41*(2), 165–177.

Møller, J., Eggen, A., Fuglestad, O. L., Langfeldt, G., Presthus, A. M., Skrøvset, S., Stjernstrøm, E., & Vedøy, G. (2005): Successful school leadership: The Norwegian case. *Journal of Educational Administration, 43*(6), 584–594.

Møller, J., Sivesind, K., Skedsmo, G., & Aas, M. (2006). Skolelederundersøkelsen 2005. Om arbeidsforhold, evalueringspraksis og ledelse i skolen. (The school leader survey 2005. Working conditions, evaluation and leadership in school). *Acta Didactica, 1.* Institutt for lærerutdanning og skoleutvikling. Universitetet i Oslo.

Mønsterplan for grunnskolen. (1985). Kirke og undervisningsdepartementet. Oslo, Norway: Aschehoug.

Norwegian Directorate for Education and Training. (2007). Improving school leadership: Country background report for Norway. Retrieved from http://www.oecd.org/edu/schoolleadership

Norwegian Working Environment Act. (2006). Retrieved from http://www.eurofound.europa.eu/ewco/studies/tn0612036s/no0612039q.htm

OECD (2007, March). *Improving school leadership.* Retrieved from http://www.oecd.org/dataoecd/35/44/38574871.pdf

OECD. (n.d.). Pisa 2006 Results. Retrieved from http://www.oecd.org/document/2/0,3746,en_21571361_44315115_39718850_1_1_1_1,00.html

Senge, P. M. (1990). *The fifth discipline: The art and practice of the learning organization.* New York, NY: Currency/Doubleday.

Skaalvik, E. M., & Fossen, I. (1995). *Tilpassing og differensiering. Idealer og realiteter i norsk grunnskole* [Adapting education to individual needs: Ideals and realities in Norwegian Schools]. Trondheim, Norway: Tapir.

Skaalvik, E., & Skaalvik, S. (2007). Dimensions of teacher self-efficacy and relations with strain factors, perceived collective teacher efficacy, and teacher burnout. *Journal of Educational Psychology, 99*(3), 611–625. DOI: 10.1037/0022-0663.99.3.611

Smith, A. (2010). *Norway: Best place to live, but why?* Retrieved from http://news.gather.com/viewArticle.action?articleId=281474978674515

Smith, M., & Bourke, S. (1992). Teacher stress: examining a model based on context, workload, and satisfaction. *Teaching and Teacher Education, 8,* 31–46.

Statistics Norway. (2007). Facts about education in Norway—Key Figures. Retrieved from http://www.ssb.no/english/subjects/04/02/facts/arkiv/2007/facts2007.pdf

Støren, L.A. (2005). *Ungdom med innvandrerbakgrunn i norsk utdanning: et dokumentasjonsnotat.* (Adolescents from immigrant backgrounds in Norwegian schools. A documentation memo) Oslo, Norway: NIFU STEP.

Travers, C. J., & Cooper, C. L. (1993). Mental health, job satisfaction and occupational stress among UK teachers. *Work and Stress, 7,* 203–219.

Travers, C. J., & Cooper, C. L. (1994). Psychophysiological responses to teacher stress: a move toward more objective methodologies. Special Issue. Stress research in Europe. *European Review of Applied Psychology, 44,* 137–146.

Utdanningsdirektoratet (n.d.). *TALIS 2008 – Norske resultater 2009.* Retrieved from http://www.udir.no/Rapporter/TALIS-2008—norske-resultater-2009/

Vibe, N., Aamodt, P. O., & Carlsten, T. C. (2009). Å være ungdomsskolelærer i Norge. *Resultater fra OECDs internasjonale studie av undervisning og læring (TALIS).* Retrieved from http://www.udir.no/upload/Rapporter/2009/TALIS_2008.pdf

CHAPTER 2

ELEMENTARY LEVEL MATHEMATICS TEACHERS' STRESS AT A TIME OF CURRICULUM REFORM IN TURKEY

Emine Erktin and Zahid Kısa
Bogazici University

ABSTRACT

Educational innovations can lead to teacher stress, but the actual impact of reform on teachers' stress levels is a source of controversy. This study examined elementary level mathematics teachers' stress during a time of mathematics curriculum reform in Turkey. Following transactional models of stress, the relationships among the following constructs were examined: teachers' perceived resources, teachers' feelings of readiness and efficacy about the reform, their appraisals of the reform, coping patterns, and adaptive outcomes. Participants were 395 teachers of elementary level mathematics. The variables within the framework of the proposed model were found to be significantly related to each other. It was concluded that teachers have lower anxiety and more positive attitudes when they perceive curricular changes as a challenge rather than a threat.

International Perspectives on Teacher Stress, pages 21–43
Copyright © 2012 by Information Age Publishing

Research on teacher stress published during the past twenty years indicates that between 20% and 25% of teachers frequently experience a great deal of stress and that most teachers experience some stress from time to time (Kyriacou, 1998). It is said that teaching is more stressful than any other job in the public sector, including those in health services (Antoniou, Polychroni, & Vlachakis, 2006; Borg, Riding, & Falzon, 1991; Chaplain, 2008; Finlayson, 2005; Johnson, Cooper, Cartwright, Donald, Taylor, & Millet, 2005; Richter, 2003).

Studies investigating sources of teachers' stress have identified educational reform as a major factor in contributing to demands on teachers. Based on the findings of numerous studies, Kyriacou (1998) grouped the most commonly identified sources of stress into six categories: pupil misbehavior; negative work environment; time pressure and work overload; inadequate prospects concerning pay, promotion, and career development; poor school ethos; and change (Brown, Ralph, & Brember, 2002; Cox, Boot, & Cox, 1989; Jepson & Forrest, 2006; Kiziltepe, 2007; Ransford, 2007; Troman & Woods, 2001). Change as a source of stress is most relevant to the present study, which focuses on the stress experienced by elementary level mathematics teachers at a time of a curriculum reform in Turkish elementary schools, which extend from grade 1 through grade 8.

CHANGE AS A SOURCE OF STRESS

Educational innovations require change, which brings uncertainty, accompanied by stress (Fullan, 1993; Gibbons, 2002). Smylie (2006) suggested that change intensifies already stressful conditions related to teaching.

One explanation for the stress is that change imposed from the outside reduces a teacher's range of control (Hinton & Rotheiler, 1998). Hall and Hord (1987) claimed that when faced with change, teachers are concerned about how new practices will affect them personally and professionally. Since it diminishes respect for the status quo, change changes the nature of the job and threatens job security (Travers & Cooper, 2006). Further, change almost always means loss, as it threatens teachers' sense of competence and frustrates their wish to be effective and to feel valued, replacing job satisfaction with confusion, unpredictability, and conflict (Evans, 2001).

The present study set out to investigate the stress experienced by teachers of mathematics during the implementation of a new mathematics curriculum in elementary schools in Turkey. There are three main components involved in implementing any new program: new materials, new teaching methods, and alteration of beliefs (Fullan & Stiegelbauer, 1991). In curriculum reform efforts, teachers are required to use new materials, including new course books and recent technology. They have to learn a new approach and employ new methods of teaching, and they have to adopt the ideology of a reform that challenges current beliefs. Hence, teachers tend to experience high levels of stress during educational reforms (Brown et al., 2002; Chakravorty, 1989; Cosgrove, 2000; Dunham, 1992; Gibbons, 2002; Kyriacou, 2001; McCormick & Ayres, 2009; McCormick, Ayres, & Beechey, 2006; Travers & Cooper, 2006; Zembylas, 2009). Brown et al. (2002) suggested that the factors that intensify stress during reform movements include a lack of rationale behind demands for change, lack of resources and information to facilitate change, lack of role and goal clarity, and feelings of powerlessness and failure. These factors were apparent in the complaints of many teachers during recent reform of the mathematics curriculum in Turkey. This was our reason for investigating teachers' stress and related variables.

CURRICULUM REFORM IN TURKEY

Beginning in 2003, the Ministry of National Education implemented a series of new programs for grades 1–8 (Ministry of National Education, 2005). The reform mandated substantial revisions in five school subjects: mathematics, science, social science, life science, and Turkish. The purpose was to develop a curriculum consistent with international standards of education implemented in Europe, North America, and East Asia. The new curriculum was intended to instigate active learning environments, to relate various disciplines to one another, and to support new teaching methods (Koc, Isiksal, & Bulut, 2007; MNE, 2005). Structurally, the reform would shift schools from a teacher-centered didactic model to a student-centered constructivist model, reduce the content and number of concepts taught, arrange instructional units thematically, develop core competencies across the curriculum, incorporate educational technologies, change assessments from tests of factual recall to more authentic assessments, enhance citizenship education, introduce a system of student representation, and engage students in community service (Aksit, 2007; Board of Education, 2005).

To guide teachers into new patterns of teaching, the Ministry defined two new sets of competencies for teachers: a set of core competencies and a set of subject-specific competencies. The core competencies addressed students' needs, interests, and wants; the process of teaching and learning; monitoring progress; and relationships with parents and community. These core competencies made teachers responsible for the personal and academic development of students, establishing a democratic social environment, and promoting tolerance and diversity (General Directorate of Teacher Training, 2003).

The most influential component of the reform for all the teachers, including the mathematics teachers, was a major shift from a behaviorist to a constructivist teaching philosophy and from teacher-centered to student-centered instruction. A study to evaluate the new curriculum indicated that the qualities of the mathematics curriculum matched those of a constructivist curriculum as described in the literature, thus requiring teachers to develop a new set of skills (Sahin, 2010). Whereas the behaviorist approach had expected teachers as transmit knowledge to their students, the constructivist approach expected them to facilitate their students' construction of knowledge (Aksit, 2007).

In 2003, the new curriculum for grades 1 to 5 was implemented as a pilot study in 120 schools in nine cities. After some revision, a nationwide implementation began in 2005–2006. Since then, a new curriculum for grades 6 to 8 has been developed and implemented gradually: grade 6 in 2006–2007, grade 7 in 2007–2908, and grade 8, after a trial in 2007–2008, nationwide implementation in 2008–2009.

Considering the literature on teachers' stress at times of change (e.g., Schmidt, 2000; Schmidt & Datnow, 2005), the hypothesis that teachers in Turkey would experience stress as a result of change seemed reasonable. This study set out to examine teachers' responses to the new mathematics curriculum.

In 1998, the duration of compulsory education in Turkey was changed from five years to eight years (grades 1–8) of elementary education. Mathematics lessons are taught by classroom teachers in grades 1–5, and by mathematics teachers in grades 6–8. Both of these groups were affected by reform of the mathematics curriculum. The present study set out to investigate the stress experienced by these mathematics teachers during the period of implementation. While several studies have investigated the curriculum reform in Turkey from various perspectives (Aksit, 2007; Aypay & Kalayci, 2008; Isikoglu, Basturk, & Karaca, 2009; Koc et al., 2007; Sahin, 2010), none has specifically studied the relationship between the reform and teachers' stress.

THEORETICAL MODEL OF TEACHER STRESS

Lazarus and Folkman's (1984) transactional model of stress provided the framework for identifying the variables to be used in this study. The degree of stress experienced by an individual depends on objective, personal, and subjective factors of an evaluative situation. The model conceptualizes the phenomenon of stress as a dynamic process of interaction among the evaluative situation, individual differences, perceptions of the evaluation situation, coping patterns, and adaptive outcomes. An evaluative situation is defined as a situation in which a person is judged or assessed with respect to some standard of performance. It implies chances for either success or failure. Consequences of the evaluation are relevant and meaningful to the person's life goals and values. Appraisal is a process in which the person perceives the evaluative situation as threatening, harmful, or challenging. Coping has been claimed to moderate the effects of evaluative stress on adaptation outcomes. The degree of stress experienced depends on objective, personal, and subjective factors of the evaluative situation (Lazarus & Folkman, 1984).

We used Lazarus and Folkman's transactional stress model (1984) to describe teachers' stress during the implementation of the new curriculum. We considered anxiety to be a pertinent issue largely because it has been considered as an indicator of stress in the literature (Lazarus, 1991; Sarason, 1986). Anxiety appears when an event is appraised as being a threat and hence its presence is an indicator of perceived threat. Additionally, test anxiety has been conceptualized as a self-control process or as a form of self-handicapping employed to preserve one's merit in the face of potential failure. It refers to the set of phenomenological, physiological, and behavioral reactions that accompanies apprehension about possible negative consequences or failure in an evaluative situation. Based on prior discussions of anxiety in the literature from a transactional perspective (Spielberger & Vagg, 1995), Zeidner (1998) proposed an integrative transactional model of test anxiety, conceptualizing the anxiety phenomenon as a dynamic process involving the interaction of a number of elements in the stressful encounter between a person and an evaluative situation.

MODEL OF TEACHER STRESS IN THE PRESENT STUDY

We adopted the test anxiety model to explain the stress felt by teachers during the period of curriculum reform because teaching mathematics according to the requirements of the new curriculum was an evaluative situation. Complexity, novelty, ambiguity, and difficulty brought about by the application of the new curriculum all contributed to the evaluative situation. We hypothesized that teachers were judged with respect to their prior teaching experience by students, principals, families, and even by themselves. The model is presented in Figure 2.1.

The evaluative situation that leads to appraisal is found in the first part of the model. We investigated the teachers' appraisals of the reform as an evaluative situation taking personal and situational variables as predictor variables. Personal variables indicated teachers' characteristics. Situational variables pertain to the characteristics of the conditions. In this study, the personal variables were readiness and efficacy. Perceived resources were the situational variable.

The second part of the model involves appraisals of events that have the potential to impact the individual. The evaluative situation of implement-

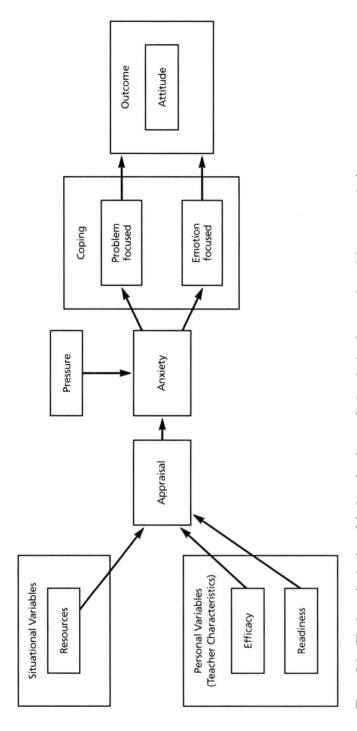

Figure 2.1 The hypothesized model of teachers' stress during the implementation of the new curriculum.

ing the new curriculum meant that teachers could be judged as either effectively or ineffectively implementing the new curriculum. The consequences of such an evaluation were relevant and meaningful to teachers' goals and values in the teaching profession.

Lazarus and Folkman's (1984) model suggests that teachers could perceive this evaluative situation as threatening, harmful, or as a challenging opportunity. Teachers who were used to teaching in traditional ways would need to change their way of teaching and use new materials and textbooks that were different from the ones they were accustomed to using. Such requirements could be perceived as threatening or even harmful. Teachers who appraised the new curriculum as a threat would be predicted to experience more stress during its implementation. Alternatively, some teachers might have perceived such changes as a challenge that could improve their teaching skills through the adoption of new methods and materials. If they perceived the implementation of the reform as a challenge, teachers would be predicted to experience less stress (Lazarus & Folkman, 1984).

The third component of the model presented in Figure 2.1 includes anxiety. In this study, teachers' stress during the implementation of the new curriculum was operationalized as anxiety. In order to investigate the relationship between appraisal and anxiety, we felt the need to include another variable: perceived pressure. We have frequently encountered teachers who complain about being subject to direct pressure from administrators, parents, colleagues, and students to implement or ignore the new curriculum. Interviews with two teachers led us to believe that perceived pressure would have a significant influence on teachers' stress during the implementation Therefore, it was hypothesized that in addition to appraisals of the evaluative situation of implementing the new curriculum, this perceived outside pressure could also lead to anxiety.

The fourth component of the model, presented in Figure 2.1, is coping. Coping is hypothesized to be a mediating variable between stress and the outcome variable. Transactional models suggest that person–environment transactions are mediated first by a person's judgment about the significance of an event (stressful, positive, controllable, challenging, or irrelevant) and second on the social and cultural resources at their disposal. Actual coping efforts aimed at regulation of the situation give rise to the outcomes of the coping process. A discrimination between problem-focused and emotion-focused coping has been put forward within the transactional model (Lazarus & Folkman, 1984). Problem-focused strategies are aimed at actually managing or dealing with the stressor, while the emotion-focused strategies are directed at dealing with the emotion caused by the stressor.

In the test anxiety model (Zeidner, 1998), the final outcome is adaptive behavior, but in this study the final outcome is the teachers' attitudes towards implementation of the new curriculum. The true adaptive behavior, which could be effective teaching, is unfortunately very difficult to assess in an educational reform. Since studies often call attention to the need to examine the implementation of reform in relation to the teachers' attitudes (Maskit, 2011), it was assumed that teachers with more positive attitudes towards change would be more supportive of the reform and would, in consequence, teach more effectively (Sparks, 1988).

Based on the model, we arrived at the following hypothesis: If teachers perceive the implementation of the new curriculum as a challenge and feel they can cope with the problems of implementation, the outcomes may be positive. If teachers perceive the implementation of the new curriculum as a threat and cannot cope with the problems of implementation, the outcomes may be negative.

The aim of this study was to explain teachers' stress during the implementation of a new mathematics curriculum and to investigate the relationships between the variables within an anxiety framework based on transactional models of stress (Lazarus & Folkman, 1984). The model included personal and situational, appraisal, anxiety, coping, and outcome variables. In the hypothesized model, readiness and efficacy were the personal variables and perceived resources was the situational variable. Appraisal was regressed upon the situational and personal variables. Appraisal was modeling as having a direct effect on stress. Coping was hypothesized to be the variable between stress and attitude. In addition to these variables, although not present in the anxiety model, the role of perceived pressure on anxiety was added to the model. Attitude towards the new curriculum was taken to be the outcome of the model. It was thought that teachers with a more positive attitude towards the new curriculum would be more willing to implement it.

Since a literature review indicated a lack of Turkish instruments for measuring specific constructs for teachers' stress, we decided to develop new instruments rather than translating existing instruments into Turkish. We needed to assess variables that were based on a transactional anxiety model and a correlational analysis between the variables in question. We arrived at operational definitions for the variables, which included stress levels for the mathematics teachers, their appraisals of the curriculum change, their efficacy beliefs for the implementation of the new curriculum, their readiness to implement the new curriculum, perceived resources for the implementation, the pressures they felt during the change, their means of coping with stress caused by the change, and their attitudes toward the new curriculum. Before generating items for the instruments, we conducted in-depth interviews with two mathematics teachers. Thus, we had an opportunity to create culturally relevant scales, drawing on closely related research reports and the teacher interviews as we composed the items.

The interrelationships between these variables were examined separately through regression and correlation analyses. We hypothesized that readiness and efficacy, the personal variables, and perceived resources, the situational variable, would have a role in teachers' appraisal. Perceived pressure as well as appraisal would be related to anxiety. Regression analyses were planned to investigate the first two parts of the model. Coping was modeled as between anxiety and attitude towards the new curriculum, which was taken as the outcome of the model.

METHOD

Participants

Three groups of participants took part in the study sequentially as the instruments were developed, their psychometric qualities were tested, and the main study was carried out. The participants in all three groups were teaching mathematics in elementary schools (grades 1–8). Grades 1 to 8 are considered as part of elementary school in Turkey since 1998 when compulsory education was raised from five years to eight years. In the first five years of elementary school, classroom teachers teach all subjects, including mathematics. In grades 6–8, mathematics is taught by subject specialists. In this study, therefore, unless otherwise noted, both the classroom teachers and the subject specialists may be referred to as "mathematics teachers" or just "the teachers." Data were collected through convenience sampling. Most of the participating teachers worked in schools cooperating with Boğaziçi University in our teacher education program. While most of the data were collected in Istanbul, the teachers in the sample for assessing the psychometric qualities of the instruments came from three cities in the same region of Turkey. The average age of all participating teachers was 36, with a standard deviation of 7.3.

The sample for the development of the instruments consisted of 44 teachers from Istanbul. Of these, 97.7% were female and 2.3% were male; 68.2% were elementary classroom teachers and 31.8% were mathematics teachers; 72.7% taught in public schools and 27.3% taught in private schools.

The sample for the assessment of the psychometric qualities of the instruments consisted of 157 elementary classroom teachers and mathematics teachers from three cities in Turkey. Of these, 59.6% were female and 40.4% were male; 82.5% were elementary classroom teachers and 17.5% were mathematics teachers; 81.3% taught in public schools and 18.7% taught in private schools.

The sample for the main study consisted of 395 elementary classroom teachers and mathematics teachers from 32 elementary schools in Istanbul.

Of these, 68.6% were female and 31.4% were male; 80.1% were elementary classroom teachers and 19.9% were mathematics teachers; 71.3% taught in public schools and 28.7% taught in private schools.

Procedure

As was noted above, the study was conducted in three parts. First, after the items were developed, we tried the instruments with a mixed group of elementary classroom and mathematics teachers. Based on the results and psychometric analyses of the data, we revised or removed problematic items. As a next step, we invited an expert to check the items for accuracy and appropriateness of the Turkish.

Then we conducted a pilot study with a second group of classroom and mathematics teachers from three different cities to evaluate the psychometric qualities of the instruments. Once we were satisfied with their content and psychometric qualities, we applied to the Ministry of Education for permission to conduct the study in state schools and likewise to the principals of selected private schools. To gather data for the final part of the study, we administered the instruments to 395 teachers in 32 schools.

Instruments

The scales correspond to the variables derived from the model: situational and personal variables, appraisal, pressure, stress, coping, and attitude. The operational definitions for the first part of the model were Readiness to Implement the New Curriculum Scale (RINCS), Efficacy Beliefs for the Implementation of the New Curriculum Scale (EINCS), and Perceived Resources During the Implementation of the New Curriculum Scale (PRDINCS). Appraisals of the evaluative situation were assessed by Appraisal of Implementation of the New Curriculum Scale (AINCS). Both appraisal and perceived pressure to implement the new curriculum, which was operationally defined as the score from Pressure During the Implementation of the New Curriculum Scale (PDINCS), led to stress, which was defined as anxiety as measured by the New Mathematics Curriculum Anxiety Scale (NMCAS). The next part of the model pertained to coping, which was assessed by Coping with the New Curriculum Scale (CNCS). Attitude, as assessed by Attitude towards the New Mathematics Curriculum Scale (ATNMCS), was the outcome variable of the study.

Readiness to Implement the New Curriculum Scale (RINCS)

In this scale, teachers' perceived knowledge of constructivism, perceived knowledge of mathematics as a subject, perceived knowledge about the implementation of the new curriculum, and effectiveness of in-service training were assessed by an item for each perception. The scale included four Likert-type items ranging from 1, "not at all," to 5, "totally informed." As was noted, the items were generated using formative data from interviews with two teachers. The teachers' greatest concerns were about constructivism, the theoretical backdrop to changes in the curriculum, and about corresponding instructional methods. They were also worried about their competence pertaining to new mathematical topics in the curriculum. Thus, items in the scale asked how confident the teachers were after being informed about the constructivist approach, related instructional methods, and new mathematical topics. Another item asked about the effectiveness of the in-service training they received. High scores indicated that the teachers felt fully equipped to implement the new curriculum, and low scores that they did not feel equipped. A sample item: "How competent do you think you are on math topics in the new math curriculum?"

Efficacy Beliefs for the Implementation of the New Curriculum Scale (EINCS)

The EINCS used twelve Likert-type items to assess the mathematics teachers' efficacy beliefs. Respondents were asked to indicate how strongly they agreed with statements about their ability to teach mathematics according to the new methods and techniques that were expected of them. High scores indicated strong efficacy beliefs, and low scores weak efficacy beliefs. The items were based on a previously used scale (McCormick et al., 2006). A sample item: "I can apply the activities required by the new curriculum successfully in my classes."

Perceived Resources During the Implementation of the New Curriculum Scale (PRDINCS)

In this scale, the average number of students present in a teacher's classroom, education level of the students' families, economic level of the students' families, and adequacy of the school for maintaining necessary materials were assessed by one item for each category. High scores indicated teachers' perceptions of high levels of resources during the implementation of the new curriculum, and low scores indicated perceptions of low levels of resources.

Pressure During the Implementation of the New Curriculum Scale (PDINCS)

The PDINCS assessed the teachers' perceptions of pressure from parents, administrators, colleagues, students, and inspectors during the implementation of the new curriculum. The scale consisted of eight items. Each item pertained to pressure from a single source. As was noted, to help generate PDICS items, we used information gathered from the interviews with two teachers.

Appraisal of Implementation of the New Curriculum Scale (AINCS)

This scale consisted of five Likert-type items. Each item asked if the teachers agreed with a statement regarding their opinions about the implementation. A high score indicated that a participating teacher perceived the implementation of the new curriculum as a challenge, a low score that he or she perceived the implementation as a threat. A sample item: "I think the new curriculum brings a new opportunity for the teachers to improve professionally."

The New Mathematics Curriculum Anxiety Scale (NMCAS)

We used the NMCAS to measure the anxiety levels of teachers. Twenty-two Likert-type items reflect the anxieties that teachers might have felt during the implementation of the new mathematics curriculum. High scores indicate high levels of anxiety, low scores low levels. The items were based on items in the Modified Teachers' Attribution of Responsibility for Stress Questionnaire (TARSQ) (McCormick et al., 2006). The alpha coefficients for the domains of the TARSQ ranged from .72 to .86, and the validity was assessed through the factor structure (McCormick et al., 2006). For the current study, we generated new items with different wording. A sample item: "Uncertainties about how the new curriculum will be applied disturb me."

Coping with the New Curriculum Scale (CNCS)

The coping scale has eleven items. When developing the CNCS, we consulted the Pullis Inventory of Teacher Stress (Pullis, 1983, as cited in Pack, 2000). The coping part of that questionnaire included fifteen strategies that teachers could use to manage their stress, each rated on a Likert-type scale. The Cronbach alpha coefficients and test retest reliability indicators for the Pullis Inventory were reported to be satisfactory (Pack, 2000). Items in our CNCS asked teachers to indicate their level of agreement with statements about their use of coping strategies.

Two types of coping are addressed in the CNCS: problem-focused coping and emotion-focused coping (Dewe, 1991; Folkman & Lazarus, 1980; Lazarus & Folkman, 1984). Problem-focused coping items refer to actions in response to problems that arose during implementation of the new curriculum. Out of eleven items, six represent problem-focused coping strategies and five represent emotion-focused coping strategies. To investigate the construct validity of the scale, we ran an exploratory factor analysis based on eigenvalues over one and varimax rotation, which produced three factors. Upon examination, we found that each factor consisted of items representing one of the coping strategies, either problem-focused or emotion-focused. This result was accepted as evidence for construct validity. A sample item for problem-focused coping: "I am reading everything I can find about the new curriculum." A sample item for emotion-focused coping: "Taking a walk seems to take my mind off my concerns about the new curriculum."

Attitude towards the New Mathematics Curriculum Scale (ATNMCS)

The attitude questionnaire has 28 Likert-type items for collecting data about the teachers' personal opinions about the new mathematics curriculum. Most of the ATNMC items are adapted from "A Study of Intermediate School-Teachers and their Attitudes toward the California Mathematics Content Standards Questionnaire" (Jones, 2005). Jones (2005) reported the Cronbach's alpha coefficient calculated on 256 participants to be .90 in her study. Higher scores indicate more positive attitudes towards the new curriculum, lower scores less positive or negative attitudes. A sample item: "The new curriculum is helpful in preparing students for mathematics at higher levels."

Analyses

The first part of the teacher stress model refers to the relationship between teachers' appraisals of the curriculum reform and personal and situational variables. The first regression analysis was carried out taking appraisal as the dependent variable and the situational and personal characteristics as the independent variables. In the next part of the model, the relationship between anxiety appraisal and perceived pressure is examined. Anxiety was the dependent variable in the second regression analysis where the independent variables were appraisal and perceived pressure. At the last part of the model relating to anxiety, coping and attitude correlations were calculated to investigate the proposed relations.

RESULTS

Reliability coefficients for the instruments that were obtained from 157 teachers in the trial administration are presented in Table 2.1, which shows Cronbach alpha coefficients and the minimum and maximum values of the item total correlations. The correlation between the teachers' scores from the Attitude towards the New Mathematics Curriculum Scale (ATNMCS) and the New Mathematics Curriculum Anxiety Scale (NMCAS) was calculated to be -0.63 (p<.001). This was accepted as evidence for the construct

TABLE 2.1   Cronbach Alpha Coefficients, the Minimum and Maximum Values of the Item Total Correlations, Means and Standard Deviations of the Scores

		Cronbach alpha	Range for item-total Correlation	Possible Range	Mean	Standard Deviation
Readiness to Implement the New Curriculum	RINCS	0.72	.27 – .60	3 – 20	13.61	3.21
Efficacy Beliefs for the Implementation of the New Curriculum	EINCS	0.96	.56 – .79	12 – 60	47	9.1
Perceived Resources during the Implementation of the New Curriculum	PRDINCS	0.88	.61 – .70	4 – 18	11.49	3.53
Appraisal of Implementation of the New Curriculum	AINCS	0.56	.18 – .53	5 – 25	17.4	4.05
Perceived pressure	PDINCS	0.89	.34 – .78	8 – 40	18.06	7.21
Anxiety Related to New Curriculum	NMCAS	0.90	.30 – .72	22 – 88	47.67	11.6
Problem-focused coping	CNCS-1	0.76	.41 – .59	6 – 24	17.79	3.5
Emotion-focused coping	CNCS-2	0.80	.53 – .61	5 – 20	8.9	3.03
Attitude Toward the New Curriculum	ATNMCS	0.90	.42 – .71	28 – 140	91.03	19.32

validity of both scales. The results indicated that the instruments had satisfactory psychometric attributes and could be used in the study.

The means and standard deviations of scores from the scales that were used in the study are presented in Table 2.1. The distribution of the scores on most of the variables showed normal distribution except for measures of efficacy and pressure. Although the mean was calculated to be 47 on the Efficacy Beliefs for the Implementation of the New Curriculum Scale (EINCS), the mode of the distribution was 60, the highest possible score. The distribution of scores on the Pressure During the Implementation of the New Curriculum Scale (PDINCS), on the other hand, displayed a positively skewed curve. We interpreted these two distributions to mean that the teachers' self-efficacy levels were higher than expected and that the pressure they felt was not as much as expected. When we separated results from the PDINCS, which identified various sources of pressure to implement the new curriculum, we observed that although the teachers perceived moderate levels of pressure in general, they perceived more pressure from the inspectors, their colleagues, and their principals than from parents and students.

Anxiety scores were distributed almost normally, with a mean of 47 out of 88 and a standard deviation of 11.6. This result indicated that, on average, teachers experienced a moderate level of anxiety during the implementation of the new curriculum. Approximately 22% of the teachers reported that they never or only occasionally experienced anxiety; 38% reported moderate levels of anxiety; and 16% reported moderate to high levels of anxiety. In most of the research studies of teacher stress, teachers mostly reported that they were experiencing high levels of stress (Borg et al., 1991; Chaplain, 2008; Finlayson, 2005; Kyriacou, 1998; Ricther, 2003). This study is more in line with other studies in which teachers reported moderate or low levels of stress (Griffith, Steptoe, & Cropley, 1999; Jepson & Forest, 2006; Stevenson & Harper, 2006).

The coping scores of the problem-focused subscale of the CNCS were distributed normally. The distribution of the scores of the emotion-focused subscale displayed a positively skewed curve. Frequency distributions indicated that most of the teachers preferred to use problem-focused strategies rather than emotion-focused strategies to cope with problems related to the implementation of the new curriculum.

The attitude scores obtained from the ATNMCS were distributed almost normally with a mean of 91.03 out of a possible score of 140 and a standard deviation of 19.32. The frequency distributions showed that 14% of the teachers had scores below 72, indicating negative to strongly negative attitudes towards the new curriculum; 68% had scores between 72 and 110, indicating moderately positive attitudes; and 18% had scores higher than 110, indicating positive to strongly positive attitudes.

The hypothesized model explaining the relationship among the various components of teachers' stress is shown in Figure 2.1. In this model, readiness and efficacy, the teachers' personal variables, and perceived resources, the situational variable, precede appraisal of the implementation as a challenge or a threat (or a neutral response). Appraisal precedes anxiety. Based on views obtained through an interview with two teachers prior to data collection, we thought that perceived pressure from outside would also have a direct bearing on anxiety. Coping was hypothesized to be in between anxiety and the outcome, which was measured as attitude towards the new curriculum. The correlation coefficients between variables in the model are given in Table 2.2.

The first part of the teacher stress model refers to the relationship between teachers' appraisals of the curriculum reform and personal and situational variables. The correlation coefficient between readiness and appraisal was calculated to be .37 ($p < .01$), and the correlation coefficient between efficacy and appraisal was calculated to be .38 ($p < .01$), which indicated that as the teachers felt more equipped and ready and more self-confident to teach the new curriculum, they perceived the implementation of the new curriculum more as a challenging opportunity rather than a

TABLE 2.2   Intercorrelations Between the Variables Related with Teacher Stress

	2	3	4	5	6	7	8	9
Attitude	−.63**	.61**	.40**	.32**	.47**	−.23**	.19**	−.04
Anxiety	—	−.57**	−.52**	−.36**	−.60**	.33**	−.25**	.11*
Appraisal		—	.37**	.35**	.38**	−.25**	.20**	−.09
Readiness			—	.43**	.53**	−.15**	.36**	.11*
Resources				—	.42**	−.18**	.18**	.18**
Efficacy					—	−.18**	.40**	.02
Emotion-focused coping						—	.05	.14**
Problem-focused coping							—	.14**
Pressure								—

*$p < .05.$ ** $p < .01.$ ($n = 395$)

threat. The correlation coefficient between perceived resources, the situational variable, and appraisal was found to be .35 ($p < .01$). This finding showed that as the teachers perceived the resources to be more adequate, they perceived the implementation of the new curriculum more as a challenging opportunity rather than a threat. The results of these correlations were also supported by the regression results as well. A regression analysis of appraisal as the dependent variable indicated a model with $r^2 = .20$ and beta values of .20 ($p < .01$), .19 ($p < .01$), and .18 ($p < .01$) for efficacy, readiness, and perceived resources, respectively.

In the next part of the model, the relationship between anxiety, appraisal, and perceived pressure is examined. The correlation coefficient between anxiety and appraisal was calculated to be −.57 ($p < .01$). This result shows that teachers who scored high on the appraisal scale and perceived the implementation of the new curriculum as a challenging opportunity had lower levels of anxiety during the implementation, as opposed to the teachers who scored low on the appraisal scale and perceived the change as a threat. The correlation coefficient between anxiety and perceived pressure was found to be .11 ($p < .05$). This result suggests the possibility that teachers who were subjected to more pressure to implement the new curriculum may have had higher levels of anxiety during the implementation. A stepwise regression analysis in which anxiety was dependent variable while appraisal and perceived outside pressure were independent variables indicated a model where $r^2 = .32$ and beta value of −.57 ($p < .01$) for appraisal. Perceived pressure was excluded from the regression model, indicating the role of appraisal to be more apparent on anxiety than perceived pressure from parents, administrators, students, and colleagues.

The correlation coefficient for the relationship between anxiety and readiness, one of the personal variables, was found to be $r = -.52$ ($p < .01$).

Teaching efficacy beliefs, the other personal variable, was also highly correlated to anxiety, $r = -.60$ ($p < .01$). These results indicate that as readiness and teaching efficacy beliefs increased teacher stress during the implementation decreased. The correlation coefficient between anxiety and perceived resources was calculated to be $-.36$ ($p < .01$).

In the last part of the model, coping is hypothesized to be situated between stress and outcome. Examination of the relationship between teachers' anxiety levels and coping revealed that the coping strategies, both problem-focused and emotion-focused, were significantly related to the stress that teachers experience during the implementation of the new curriculum. The positive correlation between anxiety and emotion-focused coping was found to be .33 ($p < .01$), and the negative correlation between anxiety and problem-focused coping was found to be $-.25$ ($p < .01$). These findings suggest the likelihood that teachers with high levels of anxiety tended to use problem-focused rather than emotion-focused coping strategies. The correlation coefficients between the outcome variable attitude and emotion-focused coping was found to be $-.23$ ($p < .01$) and between attitude and problem-focused coping to be .19 ($p < .01$). We interpreted these findings to mean that teachers who used problem-focused coping strategies had more positive attitudes towards the new curriculum, and teachers who used emotion-focused coping strategies had more negative attitudes towards the new curriculum.

The correlation coefficient between teachers' anxiety during the implementation and teachers' attitude towards the new curriculum was $r = -.63$ ($p < .01$). This negative correlation indicated evidence for a relationship where as feelings of stress became more intense, teachers' attitudes towards the new curriculum were more negative.

Attitudes towards the new curriculum, the outcome variable in the stress model, were related significantly to all other variables that we investigated, except pressure felt by the teachers. The correlation coefficient between attitude towards the new curriculum and readiness, one of the personal variables, was found to be $r = .40$ ($p < .01$). Efficacy beliefs, the other personal variable, was also found to be related to attitude towards the new curriculum, $r = .47$ ($p < .01$). The correlation coefficient between attitude towards the new curriculum and appraisal of the implementation was $r = .61$ ($p < .01$). The variable of perceived pressure from parents, administrators, and colleagues was not significantly related to attitudes towards the new curriculum.

DISCUSSION

The hypothesis of the model was that teachers with higher efficacy beliefs, higher readiness, higher perceived resources, but lower perceived pressure and lower anxiety, who perceived the situation as a challenge, would be associated with a willingness to implement the new curriculum. The results of the study show that readiness, efficacy, appraisal, anxiety, perceived pressure, availability of resources, and attitude were related to one another. These results indicated that teachers who had high efficacy beliefs, who were ready to implement the new curriculum, and who perceived their resources to be adequate, saw the implementation of the new mathematics curriculum as a challenge rather than a threat. These teachers had relatively lower levels of anxiety during the implementation and thus had more positive attitudes towards the new curriculum. Teachers who had low efficacy beliefs, who did not feel as ready to implement the curriculum, and who did not perceive their resources to be adequate perceived the implementation of the new curriculum as a threat. These teachers had higher anxiety levels, and their attitudes toward the implementation were not so positive.

Although not represented in the test anxiety model (Zeidner, 1998), we tested the possible relationship of perceived pressure to anxiety in our initial hypothesized model. The hypothesis that teachers who perceived high pressure from outside sources like administrators and parents during the implementation of the new curriculum would also feel high levels of anxiety was not as strongly supported as we had expected.

Apart from its statistically significant high negative correlation with anxiety, appraisal was also found to be positively correlated with teachers' attitude towards the new curriculum (see Table 2.2). When we compared the impacts of the personal and situational variables on anxiety and attitude based on the correlation coefficients between the personal and situational variables and anxiety and attitude, we observed that readiness and efficacy, the personal variables, were slightly more associated with anxiety and attitude than perceived resources, the situational variable. These findings might suggest that personal factors are related to teachers' stress and attitudes about the implementation of the new curriculum. These findings are consistent with the findings of earlier research supporting the claim that teachers with a higher sense of self-efficacy set more challenging goals for themselves and are more persistent when facing challenging tasks (Ransford, 2007). Some teachers, depending on their personality, prior experience, and stage of career have a relatively strong sense of self-efficacy, which leads them to take action and persist in the sort of effort required to bring about successful implementation of challenging new programs (Fullan & Stiegelbauer, 1991).

In the hypothesized model, coping was situated between anxiety and attitude. Correlation coefficients revealed that there was a positive relationship between anxiety and emotion-focused coping, and there was a negative relationship between anxiety and problem-focused coping. These findings are consistent with the findings of other studies on teacher stress (Zeidner, 1998) in which a negative relationship between problem-focused coping and anxiety and a positive relationship between emotion-focused coping and anxiety was observed. Similarly, the results revealed a positive relationship between problem-focused coping and attitude and a negative relationship between emotion-focused coping and attitude. Given the findings reported above, we conclude that the transactional model could be instrumental in explaining teachers' stress.

LIMITATIONS AND SUGGESTIONS FOR FURTHER RESEARCH

This study set out to explain the stress of teachers of mathematics at a time of a curriculum reform. The basis for the study was the transactional stress framework proposed by Lazarus and Folkman (1984) as well as Zeidner's (1998) test anxiety model. Although the proposed model representing the relationships among situational and personal variables, appraisal, stress, and outcome was supported through the correlation analyses, the present study should be considered preliminary due to the presence of several limitations.

One limitation is the use of data based on single-source self-reports. Furthermore, since this study involved the development of eight instruments, a more thorough investigation of the psychometric qualities of each scale is necessary in further studies.

Another suggestion might involve the operational definition of the outcome variable in the model. Teachers' attitudes towards the implementation of the new curriculum was accepted to be the outcome variable mostly for practical purposes in this study. A more desirable outcome would be successful implementation of the new curriculum. For each individual teacher this could be translated into a favorable external assessment of their achievement or an evaluation of their adaptive behaviors, since it has been shown that in some cases when teachers believe they have changed the way they teach, performance data reflect otherwise (Obara & Sloan, 2009). In subsequent research, a more direct outcome could be tested, such as performance in the classroom. On the other hand, since teachers' attitudes have been shown to be an important variable in educational reform, a different model could include the attitudes of teachers at different stages of professional development (Maskit, 2011).

The assessment of coping could be reconsidered in future studies. As we developed the coping scales, we were aware of the cognitive appraisal model, which makes use of the two-part distinction between problem-focused and emotion-focused coping (Dewe, 1991; McCormick et al., 2006). Different theories and models of coping could be used in similar models where coping could be reconsidered from different perspectives. Conceptualizing coping as the conservation of resources would be a good example (Hobfoll,

1988) since perceived resources did seem to come up to be a relevant variable in this study. Also, the mediating role of coping between anxiety and the outcome variable can be statistically tested in another study.

Once the constructs have been operationally well defined through further validity and reliability studies, the interrelationships between the relevant variables of this study can be examined in a more holistic way. We feel that testing the proposed model using structural equation modeling should be the next step. Furthermore, the statistical testing of a proposed model using longitudinal data might provide deeper understanding of teacher stress as a result of an innovation such as a curriculum reform.

REFERENCES

Aksit, N. (2007). Educational reform in Turkey. *International Journal of Educational Development, 27*, 129–137.

Antoniou, A. S., Polychroni, F., & Vlachakis, A. N. (2006). Gender and age differences in occupational stress and professional burnout between primary and high-school teachers in Greece. *Journal of Managerial Psychology, 21*, 682–690.

Aypay, A., & Kalayci, S. S. (2008). Assessing institutionalization of educational reforms. *International Journal of Educational Development, 28*, 723–736.

Board of Education [Talim Terbiye Kurulu]. (2005). Ilkogretim 1–5. sinif programlari tanitim el kitabi. Ankara, Turkey: Milli Eğitim Bakanlığı.

Borg, M. G., Riding, R. J., & Falzon, J. M. (1991). Stress in teaching: A study of occupational stress and its determinants, job satisfaction and career commitment among primary school teachers. *Educational Psychology, 11*, 59–75.

Brown, M., Ralph, S., & Brember, I. (2002). Change-linked work-related stress in British teachers. *Research in Education, 67*, 1–12.

Chakravorty, B. (1989). Mental health among school teachers. In M. Cole & S. Walker (Eds.), *Teaching and stress* (pp. 68–82). Milton Keynes, UK: Open University Press.

Chaplain, R. P. (2008). Stress and psychological distress among trainee secondary teachers in England. *Educational Psychology, 28*, 195–209.

Cosgrove, J. (2000). *Breakdown: The facts about stress in teaching.* London, UK: Routledge Falmer.

Cox, T., Boot, N., & Cox, S. (1989). Stress in schools: A problem solving approach. In M. Cole & S. Walker (Eds.), *Stress and teaching.* Milton Keynes, UK: Open University Press.

Dewe, P. (1991). Primary appraisal, secondary appraisal and coping: their role in stressful work encounters. *Journal of Occupational Psychology, 64*, 31–51.

Dunham, J. (1992). *Stress in teaching.* London, UK: Routledge.

Evans, R. (2001). *The human side of school change: Reform, resistance, and the real-life problems of innovation.* San Francisco, CA: Jossey-Bass.

Finlayson, M. (2005). Teacher stress in Scotland. *Education Journal, 83*, 7-7.

Folkman, S. & Lazarus, R. S. (1980). An analysis of coping in a middle-aged community sample. *Journal of Health and Social Behaviour, 2*, 219–239.

Fullan, G. M., & Stiegelbauer, S. (1991). *The new meaning of educational change.* New York, NY: Teachers College Press.

Fullan, M. (1993). *Change forces: Probing the depths of educational reform.* London, UK: Falmer Press.

General Directorate of Teacher Training. (2003). *Teacher competencies* [Ogretmen yeterlilikleri]. Retrieved from /http://oyegm.meb.gov.tr/yetS. Access date: 1 July 2005.

Gibbons, S. J. (2002). *Urban elementary and middle school teachers' perception of stress associated with standards based curriculum reforms and mandated statewide testing.* Unpublished doctoral dissertation, Rutgers University, New Brunswick, NJ.

Griffith, J., Steptoe, A., & Cropley, M. (1999). An investigation of coping strategies associated with job stress in teachers. *British Journal of Educational Psychology, 69,* 517–531.

Hall, G. E., & Hord, S. M. (1987). *Change in schools. Facilitating the process.* Albany: State University of New York Press.

Hinton, J. W., & Rotheiler, E. (1998). Teacher support teams. In J. Dunham & V. Varma (Eds.), *Stress in teachers: Past, present, and future* (pp. 95–119). London, UK: Whurr Publishers.

Hobfoll, S. E. (1988). Conservation of resources: A new attempt at conceptualizing stress. *American Psychologist, 44,* 513–524.

Isikoglu, N., Basturk, R., & Karaca, F. (2009). Assessing in-service teachers instructional beliefs about student-centered education: A Turkish perspective. *Teaching and Teacher Education, 25,* 350–356.

Jepson, E., & Forrest, S. (2006). Individual contributory factors in teacher stress: The role of achievement striving and occupational commitment. *British Journal of Educational Psychology, 76,* 183–197.

Johnson, S., Cooper, C., Cartwright, S., Donald, I., Taylor, P., & Millet, C. (2005). The experience of work-related stress across occupations. *Journal of Managerial Psychology, 20,* 178–187.

Jones, M. C. (2005). *The attitudes of intermediate school teachers toward the California Mathematics Content Standards.* Unpublished doctoral dissertation, University of San Francisco, CA.

Kiziltepe, Z. (2007). Teacher occupational stress in Istanbul. In G. S. Gates (Ed.), *Emerging thought and research on student, teacher, and administrator stress and coping* (pp. 131–144). Charlotte, NC: Information Age Publishing.

Koc, Y., Isiksal, M., & Bulut, S. (2007). Elementary school curriculum reform in Turkey. *International Education Journal, 8*(1), 30–39.

Kyriacou, C. (1998). Teacher stress: Past and present. In J. Dunham & V. Varma (Eds.), *Stress in teachers: Past, present, and future* (pp. 1–13). London: Whurr Publishers.

Kyriacou, C. (2001). Teacher stress: Directions for future research. *Educational Review, 53,* 27–35.

Lazarus, R. S. (1991). *Emotion and adaptation.* Oxford, UK: Oxford University Press.

Lazarus, R. S., & Folkman, S. (1984). *Stress, appraisal and coping.* New York, NY: Springer.

Maskit, D. (2011). Teachers' attitudes toward pedagogical changes during various stages of professional development. *Teaching and Teacher Education, 27*, 851–860.

McCormick, J., & Ayres, P. (2009). Teacher self efficacy and occupational stress: A major Australian curriculum reform revisited. *Journal of Educational Administration, 47*, 463–476.

McCormick, J., Ayres, P., & Beechey, B. (2006). Teaching self-efficacy, stress and coping in a major curriculum reform: Apply theory to context. *Journal of Educational Administration, 44*, 53–70.

Ministry of National Education [MNE]. (2005). *Ilkogretim Matematik Dersi (1–5 siniflar) Ogretim Programi Taslagi* [Elementary School Mathematics Curriculum Draft (grades 1–5)]. Ankara, Turkey: MNE.

Obara, S., & Sloan, M. (2009). Classroom experiences with new curriculum materials during the implementation of performance standards in mathematics: A case study of teachers coping with change. *International Journal of Science and Mathematics Education, 8*, 349–372.

Pack, G. (2000). *Stress, its effects, and coping strategies employed by teachers in a small rural Saskatchewan school division.* Unpublished doctoral dissertation, The University of Regina, Istanbul, Turkey.

Ransford, C. R. (2007). *The role of school and teacher characteristics on teacher burnout and implementation quality of social-emotional learning curriculum.* Unpublished doctoral dissertation, Pennsylvania State University, University Park, PA.

Richter, A. (2003). Teacher stress rising, but venting helps. *District Administration, 39*, 12–15.

Sahin, I. (2010). Curriculum assessment: Constructivist primary mathematics curriculum in Turkey. *International Journal of Science and Mathematics Education, 8*, 51–72.

Sarason, I. G. (1986). Test anxiety, worry and cognitive interference. In R. Schwarzer (Ed.), *Self related cognitions in anxiety and motivation* (pp. 19–35). Hillsdale, NJ: Erlbaum.

Schmidt, M. (2000). Role theory, emotions and identity in the department headship of secondary schooling. *Teaching and Teacher Education, 16*, 827–842.

Schmidt, M., & Datnow, A. (2005). Teachers' sense-making about comprehensive school reform: The influence of emotions. *Teaching and Teacher Education, 21*, 949–965.

Smylie, M. A. (2006). Teacher stress in a time of reform. In R. Vandenberghe, & A. M. Huberman (Eds.) *Understanding and preventing teacher burnout: A sourcebook of international research and practice* (pp. 59–84). Cambridge: Cambridge University Press.

Sparks, G. (1988). Teachers' attitudes towards change and subsequent improvements in classroom teaching. *Journal of Educational Psychology, 80*(1), 111–117.

Spielberger, C. D. & Vagg, P. R. (1995). Test anxiety: A transactional process. In C. D. Spielberger & P. R. Vagg (Eds.), *Test anxiety: Theory, assessment and treatment* (pp. 3–14). Washington, DC: Taylor & Francis.

Stevenson, A., & Harper, S. (2006). Workplace stress and the student learning experience. *Quality Assurance in Education, 14*, 167–178.

Travers, J., & Cooper, C. L. (2006). *Teachers under pressure: Stress in the teaching profession.* London, UK: Routledge.

Troman, G., & Woods, P. (2001). *Primary teachers' stress.* London, UK: Routledge Falmer.

Zeidner, M. (1998). *Test anxiety: The state of the art.* New York, NY: Plenum Press

Zembylas, M. (2009). Teacher emotions in the context of educational reforms. In A. Hargreaves, A. Lieberman, M. Fullan, & D. Hopkins (Eds.), *Second international handbook of educational change* (pp. 221–236). Dordrecht, The Netherlands: Springer.

CHAPTER 3

STUDENT TEACHERS' EPISTEMOLOGICAL BELIEFS, CONCEPTIONS ABOUT TEACHING AND LEARNING AND PERCEIVED STRESS DURING PRACTICUM

Are They Related?

Constantinos M. Kokkinos, George Stavropoulos, and Aggeliki Davazoglou
Democritus University of Thrace, Greece

ABSTRACT

The study investigated the ways student teachers' epistemologies about knowledge acquisition and conceptions about teaching and learning are linked with perceived stress during the practicum. One hundred and thirty eight Greek primary school student teachers participated in the investigation. Subjects' stress levels were also assessed at the end of a four-week practicum. Factor

International Perspectives on Teacher Stress, pages 45–68
Copyright © 2012 by Information Age Publishing
All rights of reproduction in any form reserved.

analysis confirmed the structure of epistemological beliefs identified in previous research. Overall, the results suggest that conceptions about teaching and learning help to predict student teachers' perceived practicum-related stress both before (to a greater extent) and after (to a lesser extent) the practicum, after student teachers' gender and epistemological beliefs were controlled for.

It is during the teaching practicum that student teachers must negotiate situations which require them to be a "student" and "teacher" at the same time (Fives, Hamman, & Olivarez, 2006). Rickinson (1998) views the practicum as a crisis point for vulnerable preservice teachers. For example, student teachers are required to contain their anxiety well enough to adapt to their supervising teacher's instructional approach, particularly when it differs from their preferred teaching style or contradicts expectations promoted in their undergraduate degree program. Research has found multiple sources of stress in the practicum, including pupil misbehaviors or lack of motivation, inadequate training, lack of clearly defined expectations, professional isolation, communication issues, practicum assessment methods, perceived lack of support, and grade level to which the student teacher has been assigned (e.g., Fives et al., 2006).

Participation in the practicum is one of several requirements for most teacher training programs. Studies have shown it to be a valuable time for promoting changes in preservice teachers' thinking, particularly in relation to beliefs about knowledge and its acquisition. Researchers argue that teacher educators can assist student teachers in changing their beliefs about knowledge and learning and focusing more on knowledge processes than knowledge products. Among other things, teacher educators can help preservice teachers to refine their approaches to studying, improve their thinking and problem-solving skills, assist them to make more informed decisions in their personal and professional lives, and develop greater appreciation of the perspectives of others (Schommer-Aikins & Easter, 2006).

Student teachers' beliefs about knowledge and knowledge acquisition are viewed as being shaped by those experiences that occurred prior to entering the profession. Most salient to how preservice teachers conceptualize teaching and learning in classrooms are their experiences of being a student. These beliefs constitute an individual's personal epistemology and, according to Hofer (2001), include some or all of the following aspects: beliefs about the meaning of knowledge, the way knowledge is constructed and evaluated, where knowledge resides, and how knowing (processing of knowledge) occurs.

In addition, student teachers' epistemological beliefs are connected to prospective classroom teaching practices (Lawrence, 1992; Pajares, 1992), such as curriculum implementation and instructional approaches (Hofer & Pintrich, 1997). The practicum is a stage during initial teacher training where student teachers are confronted with situations where they have to adapt. In this case, their epistemological beliefs and conceptions about teaching may come into play and interfere with their emotional state, which may give rise to feelings of heightened stress. In order to better understand this hypothetical interplay, this study set out to investigate the way student teachers' epistemologies about knowledge acquisition and conceptions about teaching and learning are linked with perceived stress during the practicum.

THEORETICAL FOUNDATIONS

The study of personal epistemology originated in the work of Perry (1968) on the understanding of college students' epistemological beliefs. Perry (1970) found that as students progressed through their studies, they progressively developed more sophisticated ways of perceiving the world. He described the epistemological developmental stages among Harvard male graduates as beginning with dualism (i.e., knowledge is perceived as simple and certain, and the world to be dichotomous—that is, only black and white, good and bad, right and wrong). Hard work and adherence to authority is the way dualistic people feel that they achieve things. The second stage is multiplism (i.e., individuals feel uncertain about the decisions they make since they believe that there are many different choices or answers). People in this stage often feel that authority figures are not the only ones with answers since everyone "has a right to his or her own opinion." The third stage is relativism (i.e., knowledge becomes viewed as qualitative and complex). As individuals gain more information on a subject, they acquire a new perspective. They also believe that something is not good or bad, but rather one answer is better or worse than another answer. Metacognition (thinking about thinking) also seems to be present in this stage. The final stage is commitment with relativism (i.e., relativistic thinking appears to be a feature of this stage, but particular beliefs are more valued than others and tend to be held in a flexible manner). Despite Perry's proposal that college students pass through a predictable sequence of epistemological growth stages, further research has challenged the assumption "that personal epistemology is one-dimensional and develops in a fixed progression of stages" (Schommer, 1990, p. 498). Nevertheless, Perry's seminal work continues to function as the primary reference point in discussions on epistemological growth in adult learners.

Many researchers have been inspired by Perry's work on personal epistemology, focusing on different aspects or alternatives to his arguments. Among these, Schommer (1990, 1994) proposed a multidimensional model based on how students' epistemological beliefs are related to their academic cognition and performance. She described personal epistemology as a system of more or less independent beliefs, which are not inborn, unchanging characteristics of the individual. Further, she claimed that they evolve over time due largely to educational experiences. These beliefs concern the simplicity, certainty, and source of knowledge, as well as the control and speed of knowledge acquisition, and are conceptualized as varying along a continuum, from naïve to sophisticated.

To examine her proposed system of epistemological beliefs, Schommer (1990) developed the Epistemological Beliefs Questionnaire (EBQ), which taps five dimensions of beliefs according to (1) the structure of knowledge (ranging from isolated bits and pieces to integrated concepts), (2) the stability of knowledge (ranging from unchanging to continually changing), (3) the source of knowledge[1] (ranging from handed down by authority to derived through empirical evidence and reasoning), (4) the speed of knowledge acquisition (ranging from quick all-or-none to gradual), and (5) the control of knowledge acquisition (ranging from genetically predetermined ability to learn to learning through experience). Schommer was the first researcher who applied quantitative methodology to the investigation of epistemological beliefs. Previous studies relied on qualitative or mixed methodology and were unidimensional and developmental in nature.

EPISTEMOLOGICAL BELIEFS, LEARNING, AND TEACHING

A growing body of research has examined the association between epistemological beliefs and teaching. The belief systems about teaching and learning that are held by teachers can be seen as influencing their practice. For example, teachers who hold naïve epistemologies believe that knowledge is simple, clear, and specific; rests in authorities; and is certain and stable. Naïve epistemologies support a view that learning ability is innate and fixed and concepts are learned either quickly or not at all. Conversely, teachers who hold sophisticated epistemologies believe that knowledge is complex, uncertain, and tentative, and that there is no absolutely true knowledge. With such a view, learning tends to be seen as gradual and based largely on reasoning processes (Howard, McGee, Schwartz, & Purcell, 2000; Schommer, 1994).

Chan and Elliott's (2004a) study confirmed that teachers' conceptions about teaching are beliefs-driven. In this line of inquiry, teachers' beliefs about teaching tend to be classified as either knowledge transmission (i.e., traditional/teacher-centered) or knowledge construction (i.e., constructivist-oriented/student-centered) (Lim & Chai, 2008). Van Driel, Bulte, and Verloop (2005) found, however, that the teaching repertoire of teachers may possess elements that reflect both. Chan and Elliott's (2004a) documented that authority/expert knowledge (i.e., knowledge being handed down by experts) and certainty of knowledge (i.e., whether knowledge is certain, permanent, and unchanged at one end or tentative and ever-changing at the other) were positively related to beliefs in innate ability. Thus, beliefs in innate ability are likely to be negatively associated with constructivist teaching, which promotes the facilitation of the learning process rather than the transmission of knowledge.

The relationship between epistemological beliefs and teaching should be no less salient for prospective teachers given how it affects curriculum implementation and instructional approaches in the classroom (Hofer & Pintrich, 1997) and hence influences student learning outcomes. Indeed, evidence from empirical studies seems to suggest that student teachers who believe that knowledge is simple and stable are also less likely to consider learning as a result of effort (i.e., hard work and effort to understand) and process (Ravindran, Greene, & Debacker, 2005). Yet when preservice teachers respect their teacher educators and are strongly challenged and attracted by ideas that better explain their experiences, they are able to modify these beliefs (Austin & Reinhardt, 1999). Currently, questions remain as to the extent to which these beliefs may be altered by training and experience. Stanton (1996) found that interventions during teacher training programs may lead to more sophisticated epistemologies, whereas Davis (1997) failed to report significant changes in student teachers' epistemological beliefs after an intervention. While there has been plenty of empirical work on teachers' personal epistemology, research on preservice teachers and the particulars needed for effective preparation is in need of attention (Chai, Teo, & Lee, 2009).

THE PRESENT STUDY

Research so far has identified many potentially stressful situations which can be encountered by student teachers during the practicum. These could be classified in four general categories: administrative (i.e., work overload, time management), classroom-based (i.e., disruptive behavior and lack of student discipline), personal (i.e., successful performance, personal competency), and assessment issues (i.e., being evaluated) (Cambell & Uusimaki, 2006; Costin, Fogarty, & Yarrow, 1992; Priyadharshini & Robinson-Point, 2003). The present study set out to explore the way student teachers' epistemologies about knowledge and knowledge acquisition as well as conceptions about teaching and learning were linked with perceived stress during the practicum. Four hypotheses were formulated and empirically investigated. First, it was assumed that perceived stress for those issues related to teaching during the practicum were likely to be associated with student teachers' epistemological beliefs and conceptions about teaching and learning, which appear to be directly related to teaching practice (H1). However, for those issues related to other aspects of the practicum, such as administrative and evaluative components, it was hypothesised that there will be a weak or no association (H2; Ravindran et al., 2005). Third, it was hypothesized that student teachers who hold naïve epistemologies would adhere to more traditional teaching practices (H3), whereas those who held more sophisticated epistemologies would engage in more constructivist instruction (H4; Chan & Elliot, 2004a).

Second, the study explored the structure of the Epistemological Beliefs Questionnaire and the Teaching and Learning Conceptions Subscale (TLCS, Chan & Elliot, 2004a). The EBQ is a widely used instrument for the measurement of epistemological beliefs (Duell & Schommer-Aikins, 2001) despite the fact that research has shown that epistemologies are culture-specific and that there exist different dimensions of beliefs across cultural groups (Arredondo, & Rucinski, 1996; Chan & Elliott, 2004a). The scale has been systematically used with samples from Western countries and the Asia-Pacific region (Hofer, 2000; Schommer, 1990, 1993), but never with Greek-speaking samples. Similarly, in the case of the TLCS, most previous research was conducted in Asian educational contexts (Chan & Elliott, 2004b; Teo & Chai, 2008), and therefore the investigation of the structure of TLCS will provide evidence regarding the stability of the scale's structure across cultures.

Finally, the present study explored the potential predictive utility of epistemological beliefs about knowledge and knowledge acquisition and conceptions about teaching and learning on student teachers' perceived as well as experienced practicum-related stressors. The model tested relationships among student teachers' epistemological beliefs, conceptions about teaching and learning and practicum-related stressors since the latter emerge during the teaching process. More specifically, since personal epistemologies precede conceptions about teaching and learning, the present study investigated the extent to which the latter contribute to the understanding of student teachers' perceived stress after controlling for the effects of their personal epistemologies.

METHOD

Participants

A convenient sample of 312 student teachers participated in the study and completed a paper-and-pencil questionnaire. Forty-five respondents were male (14.4%) and 267 were female (85.6%), aged between 20 and 43 years old. They were all enrolled in the final year of a four-year preservice teacher training program for primary school teachers at the Department of Primary Education, Democritus University of Thrace in north-eastern Greece. A sub-sample of those participants, consisting of 138 student teachers (27 males—19.6%, and 111 females—80.4%), 20–43 years old, also completed an inventory about their perceived practicum-related stressors before and after the practicum. No participant attrition was observed for this sub-sample or for the total sample.

The Context of the Study

The teaching profession in Greece has been considered as a job with a relatively high degree of security, since public school teachers are civil servants and therefore benefit from tenure, set salary structures, automatic promotion, and good overall working conditions. Teacher selection takes place centrally and thus allows a great degree of control over the number and quality of teachers appointed to the profession. Despite the considerable unemployment among qualified teachers in the 1990s, the profession regained its attractiveness recently, and thus more able student teachers have begun university teacher programs, since the prospect of recruitment as permanent or temporary substitute teachers appears to be increasing (Hellenic Statistical Authority, 2010).

Teacher preparation programs in Greek universities take four years or eight semesters of course credits. In the Department of Primary Education, University of Thrace, the practicum takes place during the last semester. The purpose of the practicum is to connect theory and practice, familiarize student teachers' with school realities, introduce them to daily teaching activities (i.e., the analysis, design, application, and evaluation of teaching and learning processes), and assist them in forming a professional identity entailing comprehensive understanding and development of critical skills regarding the real conditions and prerequisites of being a teacher.

The practicum consists of two phases: a series of three-week seminars on issues relevant to classroom realities, as well as in-service teacher observations during actual teaching. The second phase consists of another two-week seminar and four-week teaching in classrooms.

Student teachers' performance during the practicum is evaluated in terms of their ability (1) to plan and implement a lesson, (2) to analyze and evaluate their own teaching, and (3) to reflect upon their teaching experiences. In addition, qualities such as responsibility, consistency, communication, and interpersonal skills are also evaluated. Evaluation is accomplished by means of a series of report writing, questionnaire completion, and formal and informal discussions with the supervising teachers, classroom in-service teachers, and university professors.

Materials

The Epistemological Beliefs Questionnaire (EBQ)

The 30-item version of the Epistemological Beliefs Questionnaire (EBQ) developed by Chan and Elliot (2002) was used in this study. It was adapted from Schommer's 63-item questionnaire that was created to measure five dimensions of epistemological beliefs, which are: Innate/Fixed Ability (the ability to learn is innate rather than acquired), Omniscient Authority (knowledge is handed down by authority rather than derived from reason), Certain Knowledge (knowledge is certain rather than tentative), Simple Knowledge (knowledge is simple rather than complex), and Quick Learning (learning is quick or not at all) (Schommer, 1994). Although the Epistemological Beliefs Questionnaire has undergone many adaptations, its structure has been in the center of debate about whether it captures the dimensions of epistemological beliefs suggested by the scale's developer. For example, although Chan and Elliott (2002) found a similar structure to that reported by Schommer (1994) with a sample of Hong Kong student teachers, the nature of the factors was different. Thus, they proposed a shorter instrument measuring four dimensions—that is, Innate/Fixed Ability, Learning Effort/Process, Authority/Expert Knowledge, and Certainty Knowledge. Reliability statistics (Cronbach's alphas) were not very promising and ranged from .58 to .69.

The Greek translation of the EBQ was developed using the method of front and back translation by two bilingual educational psychologists. Differences in translation were resolved through consensus.

Teaching and Learning Conceptions Subscale (TLCS)

The 30-item version of the original 35-item Teaching and Learning Conceptions Subscale (TLCS; Chan & Elliot, 2004a) was used in the present study to measure student teachers' conceptions about teaching and learning (i.e., beliefs held by teachers about their preferred ways of teaching and learning). The instrument is based on the literature review of prevailing conceptions about teaching and learning and dialogues with Hong Kong students before the practicum. It measures two basic dimensions: Traditional (knowledge transmission/teacher-centered) and Constructivist (knowledge construction/student-centered). Chan and Elliot (2004a) conducted pilot studies across 12 months, with repeated processes of factor analysis, item identification/clarification, and interviews with students. The result was the development of a 35-item questionnaire. Exploratory factor analysis of item responses yielded two factors or subscales, totaling 30 items. The Cronbach's alpha values for the two subscales were .86 and .84 respectively. Front and back translation methods were used to achieve the Greek translation of the instrument.

Stressors about Practicum Inventory (SPI)

A 94-item questionnaire was used to measure student teachers' potential stressors during the practicum. These stressors have been either documented in previous national (Kokkinos & Stavropoulos, 2009) and international (e.g., Allison, 2004) research or emerged from either informal or formal pre-survey interviews conducted with student teachers. The factor structure of the scale has been explored elsewhere (Kokkinos, Stavropoulos, & Davazoglou, 2010). The scale consists of four general categories of stressors: *professional interactions* (e.g., with university and school personnel), *student teachers' assessment* (supervising, in-service, university teachers' and pupils' opinions about student teachers' professional and personal competency), *the practicum workload and required skills* (e.g., time constraints, effective lesson planning, familiarization with the curriculum), and *meeting pupils' needs during the practicum* (e.g., effective class management, pupils' disruptive behavior, motivating pupils). Participants were asked to indicate the level of stress they think that the particular condition would cause on a 5-point scale ranging from 1 (*no stress*) to 5 (*extreme stress*). Reliability coefficients (Cronbach's alpha) were .97 for the total scale before and .98 after the practicum. Internal reliabilities for the four factors ranged from .87 to .94 for the pre test and from .90 to .94 for the post test.

Procedure

The study took place at two points in time: a week before the practicum (May, 2007), and 4 weeks immediately after its completion (June, 2007). Participants were informed about the purpose of the study, gave their consent. No course credits were assigned to the students. Before the practicum participants were requested to provide their demographics—gender, age, and semester of studies—and to complete the EBQ, the TLCS, and practicum-related stressors scale. In order to protect participants' identity, each was provided with a numerical code during the first administration, which was used to match their responses with those gathered during the second administration. A sub-sample of student teachers (i.e., 138 subjects) completed the practicum-related stressors inventory after the practicum. The questionnaires were completed in the presence of the second author during a seminar, after permission was granted by the lecturer. The first administration of the questionnaires took less than half an hour to complete and no more than a quarter of an hour for the second. No sample attrition was recorded.

Methods of Analysis

The examination of EPQ's and TLCS's psychometric characteristics was performed on the data provided by the whole sample (N = 312) and included exploratory factor analyses and reliability analysis using the Cronbach's alpha internal reliability coefficient. For all exploratory factor analyses, items with factor loadings ≥ .4 were used for interpretation.

Means and standard deviations were generated for each subscale of the measures used in the study. Associations between epistemological beliefs, conceptions about teaching and learning, and perceived practicum-related stressors were calculated using Pearson's correlation. Student teachers' gender effects on their perceived practicum-related stressors, epistemological beliefs, and conceptions about teaching and learning were estimated using independent samples t-tests.

Finally, four hierarchical multiple regression analyses were performed to determine the amount of variance in student teachers' perceived practicum-related stress explained by participants' gender, epistemological beliefs, and conceptions about teaching and learning. Each stressor was used as a criterion variable, whereas dimensions of epistemological beliefs and perceptions about teaching and learning were used as predictors. These were added to the regression equations in three steps: first, student teachers' gender was examined; in the second step, epistemological beliefs about knowledge and knowledge acquisition (Innate and Fixed Ability, Learning Effort/Process, Authority/Expert Knowledge, and Certainty Knowledge) entered the equation; in the third step, student teachers' conceptions about teaching and learning (constructivist, traditional) were included. Hierarchical models determine, step by step, the independent contribution of each set of predictor variables on the criterion variable over and above the effect of the other independent variables entered first; each set of independent predicting variables is relevant for the model if they significantly increase the variance (ΔR^2). It should be noted that the latter analyses were performed only for the 138 participants who completed the inventory on perceived practicum-related stressors both before and after the practicum.

RESULTS

Factor structure of the EBQ and the TLCS

EBQ

Since the EBQ scale has not been factor analyzed with a Greek sample, it was deemed appropriate to explore its factor structure. Thus, the 30 items were submitted to factor analysis using Principal Components Analysis (PCA) with varimax rotation. Nine factors with eigenvalues over 1 were generated, accounting for a total of 57.36% of variance. Consecutive PCAs were run and the nine factors were reduced to six, based on the following criteria: (1) Item classification was not theoretically possible to any of

TABLE 3.1   Factor Labels, Number and Sample of Items for the EBQ (N = 312)

Factor label	No. of Items	Sample item
Innate Ability	5	Some people are born good learners, others are just stuck with limited abilities
Learning Effort	6	Learning something really well takes a long time or much effort
Authority/Expert Knowledge	3	I still believe in what the experts say even though it differs from what I know'
Learning Process	4	Everyone needs to learn how to learn
Certainty Knowledge	2	Scientists will ultimately get to the truth if they keep searching for it
Fixed Ability	2	Our abilities to learn are fixed at birth'

the emerged components, (2) Cronbach' s alpha reliability coefficient for the emerged factors, was less than .50, and (3) factor loadings were insignificant ($\leq .4$). Items loaded on each one of the six factors were summed to form subscales (Table 3.1). Thus, although the factors of Innate/ Fixed Ability and Learning Effort/Process were supported by the data of the present study, they split into two dimensions each. Internal reliabilities, using the Cronbach's alpha coefficient ranged from .63 to .69, and were higher than those reported in the Chan and Elliot's (2004a) study.

TLCS

In order to explore the TLCS's factor structure, the 30 items were factor analyzed using PCA with varimax rotation. Eight factors with eigenvalues over 1 were generated, accounting for a total of 55.08 % of variance. Consecutive PCAs were run but did not succeed in generating the original two dimensions of the scale. Thus, a two-factor constrained PCA with varimax rotation was performed. Items loaded on the emerged factors were summed to form two subscales (Table 3.2). Internal reliabilities, using the Cronbach's alpha coefficient, were .81 for both scales.

TABLE 3.2   Factor Labels, Number and Sample of Items for the TLCS (N = 312)

Factor label	No. of Items	Sample item
Constructivist conception	10	It is important that a teacher understands the feelings of the students
Traditional conception	14	A teacher's major task is to give student knowledge/information, assign them drill and practice, and test their recall

Descriptive Statistics

Means and standard deviations for the whole sample for each subscale of the EBQ, TLCS, and SPI are shown in Table 3.3. Learning Effort, Learning Process, and Certainty Knowledge dimension scores were above the midpoint (based on sample means) with Fixed Ability, Innate Ability, and Authority/Expert Knowledge achieving the lowest means. Student teachers appeared to hold more constructivist perceptions regarding teaching than traditional ones. In terms of the perceived practicum-related stressors, before the practicum participants found more stressful the issue regarding meeting pupils' needs, followed by their assessment and practicum workload/required skills, whereas professional interactions during the practicum were perceived as less stressful. After the practicum, participants felt more stressed about their assessment, followed by meeting pupils' needs as well as the practicum workload/required skills, and professional interactions during the practicum.

Gender Differences

In order to examine the effects of gender on student teachers' epistemological beliefs, conceptions about learning and teaching, and practicum-

TABLE 3.3   Descriptive Statistics and Internal Consistency Coefficients for the EBQ, TLSC, and SPI Subscales[a]

	Alpha	M	SD	Range
EBQ subscales (*N* = 312)				
Innate Ability	.69	2.50	.64	1–5
Learning Effort	.66	3.62	.52	1–5
Learning Process	.65	3.96	.59	1–5
Authority/Expert Knowledge	.64	2.30	.65	1–5
Certainty Knowledge	.63	3.24	.72	1–5
Fixed Ability	.65	1.75	.74	1–5
TLCS subscales (*N* = 312)				
Constructivist conception	.81	4.29	.43	1–5
Traditional conception	.81	2.42	.49	1–5
SPI subscales (*N* = 138)				
Professional interactions	.91 (.91)	2.16 (1.99)	.66 (.58)	1–5
Student teachers' assessment	.94 (.94)	2.81 (2.84)	.77 (.79)	1–5
Practicum workload/required skills	.90 (.92)	2.75 (2.59)	.65 (.65)	1–5
Meeting Pupils's needs during practicum	.87 (.90)	3.01 (2.79)	.70 (.73)	1–5

[a] Latter post-test scores are in parentheses.

related stressors, a series of independent samples t-tests were performed. Male student teachers ($M = 2.72$, $SD = .74$ and $M = 1.95$, $SD = .89$ respectively) scored higher than female ($M = 2.46$, $SD = .61$ and $M = 1.71$, $SD = .70$ respectively) in Innate, $t(310) = 2.61$, $p = .009$, and Fixed Ability, $t(309) = 2.08$, $p = .04$. Furthermore, male student teachers ($M = 2.62$, $SD = .55$) seemed to hold more traditional conceptions about teaching and learning than females ($M = 2.39$, $SD = .48$), $t(310) = 2.94$, $p = .004$, who scored higher ($M = 4.33$, $SD = .38$) than males ($M = 4.04$, $SD = .56$) on constructivist conceptions, $t(310) = -3.37$, $p = .001$.

Lastly, no statistically significant differences were found in mean scale scores between male and female student teachers regarding the practicum-related stressors both before and after the practicum.

Correlation Analyses

Pearson correlations were computed between epistemological beliefs, conceptions about teaching and learning and perceived practicum-related stressors. The results are presented in Table 3.4. The effect sizes of the obtained correlations[2] were mainly considered small to moderate before the practicum, and moderate to large after the practicum.

Specifically, perceived practicum-related stressors, in both conditions (pre- and post-practicum), were all positively intercorrelated with coefficients ranging from $r = .57$ to $r = .82$ before and $r = .65$ to $r = .87$ after the practicum. All dimensions of epistemological beliefs were positively intercorrelated except for Learning Process with Innate ($r = -.25$, $p < .01$) and Fixed Abilities ($r = -.35$, $p < .01$), which showed negative correlations. In addition, Constructivist and Traditional conceptions about teaching and learning were negatively correlated ($r = -.40$, $p < .01$).

When considering the correlations between epistemological beliefs and student teachers' conceptions about teaching and learning, both Innate Ability and Authority Knowledge (naïve epistemologies) were found to correlate positively with the Traditional conception ($r = .50$, $p < .01$, and $r = .44$, $p < .01$ respectively), whereas Learning Effort and Learning Process (sophisticated epistemologies) correlated positively with the Constructivist conception about teaching and learning ($r = .40$, $p < .01$ and $r = .55$, $p < .01$ respectively). Conversely, Innate Ability, Authority/Expert Knowledge and Fixed Ability was negatively correlated with the Constructivist conception (coefficients ranged from $r = -.44$ to $r = -.25$). What is more, the Traditional conception of teaching and learning was correlated negatively with Learning Process ($r = -.33$, $p < .01$), and Fixed Ability ($r = -.44$, $p < .01$).

Before the practicum, perceived stress about the practicum workload/required skills was positively correlated with Innate Ability; stress about

TABLE 3.4 Correlation Among EBQ, TLSC, and SPI Subscales Before the Practicum[a]

	Practicum workload/required skills	Pupils's needs during the practicum	Professional interactions	Student teachers' assessment	Innate ability	Learning effort	Authority/expert knowledge	Learning process	Certainty Knowledge	Fixed Ability	Constructivist conception
Pupils' needs during practicum	.82** (.87**)										
Professional interactions	.67** (.82**)	.60** (.70**)									
Student teachers' assessment	.73** (.73**)	.68** (.65**)	.57** (.66**)								
Innate ability	.21* (.25**)	.08 (.16)	.24** (.16)	.14 (.17)							
Learning effort	.06 (.06)	.02 (.05)	-.12 (-.01)	.06 (-.13)	.01						
Authority/expert knowledge	.08 (.10)	.01 (.01)	.23* (.13)	-.01 (.07)	.13	.10					
Learning Process	.09 (.05)	.24** (.13)	-.02 (.01)	.07 (-.07)	-.25**	.22*	-.16				
Certainty Knowledge	-.08 (-.14)	-.05 (-.09)	-.06 (-.14)	-.06 (-.06)	-.02	.24*	-.01	.15			
Fixed Ability	-.03 (-.09)	-.13 (-.12)	.25** (-.04)	-.08 -.14	.40**	-.13	.19*	-.35**	-.12		
Constructivist conception	-.08 (.05)	.10 (.06)	-.45** (-.04)	-.06 (-.08)	-.26**	.40**	-.25**	.55**	.15	-.44**	
Traditional conception	.13 (.06)	.03 (-.03)	.28** (.1)	.08 (.05)	.50**	.08	.44**	-.33**	.00	.44**	-.40**

[a] correlations after the practicum are in parentheses (n = 138)

** p < .01; * p < .05

meeting pupils' needs with the Learning Process; perceived stress about professional interactions with Innate Ability, Authority/Expert Knowledge, Fixed Ability, and Traditional conception about teaching and learning (coefficients ranged from $r = .21$ to $r = .82$). Perceived stress about professional interactions was negatively correlated with the Constructivist conception ($r = -.45$, $p < .01$). However, after the practicum, only the correlation between perceived stress about the practicum workload/required skills and Innate Ability ($r = .25$, $p < .01$) remained statistically significant.

Regression Analyses

A series of hierarchical stepwise multiple regressions were run using each of the student teachers' perceived practicum-related stressors as the dependent variable in order to examine the predictive utility of student teachers' epistemological beliefs and perceptions about teaching and learning. Gender was entered at step one, epistemological beliefs at step two, and finally, at step three, perceptions about teaching and learning. It should be noted that the most relevant to the criterion variable predictors were entered in the model last to establish the extent to which practicum-related stressors can be predicted by student teachers' perceptions about teaching and learning over and beyond gender and epistemological beliefs, which were entered in the model first. Results from the regression analyses are shown in Table 3.5.

The analysis was significant for the prediction of three out of four practicum-related stressors before the practicum and only for one out of four after the practicum. Thus, the results with the before the practicum data showed that perceived stress about the practicum workload/required skills was predicted only by Innate Ability, which accounted for 5% of the variance [$R^2 = .047$, $F(1,136) = 6.16$, $p < .05$]. For the post-practicum data, practicum workload/required skills was predicted by Innate and Fixed Ability, which accounted for 10% of the explained variance, [$R^2 = .103$, $F(2,128) = 7.31$, $p < .001$], with the best predictor being the former ($\beta = .32$, $p < .001$). Perceived stress about professional interactions (before the practicum) was predicted by Authority/Expert Knowledge, Fixed Ability and by the Constructivist conception about teaching and learning, which all together accounted for the 23% of the variance [$R^2 = .226$, $F(3,134) = 12.88$, $p < .0001$], with the best predictor being the second ($\beta = .04$, $p > .05$).

Finally, perceived stress about meeting pupils' needs during practicum (before the practicum) was predicted by Learning Process, which explained 6% of the variance [$R^2 = .059$, $F(1,136) = 8.49$, $p < .004$].

TABLE 3.5 Hierarchical Multiple Regression for Student Teachers' Gender, Dimensions of Epistemological Beliefs, and Conceptions About Teaching and Learning Predicting Perceived Practicum Related Stressors Before and After the Practicum (n = 138)

Predictor variables	Practicum workload/required skills (Pre)			Practicum workload/required skills (Post)			Professional interactions (Pre)			Pupils during practicum (Pre)		
	B	SE	Beta	B	SE	Beta	B	SE	Beta	B	SE	Beta
Step 1	($R^2 = .05$)			($R^2 = .10$)			($R^2 = .23$)			($R^2 = .06$)		
Gender												
Step 2												
Innate Ability	.20	.08	.21	.32	.09	.33						
Learning Effort												
Learning Process										.26	.09	.24
Certainty Knowledge												
Authority/Expert Knowledge							.12	.08	.13			
Fixed Ability				−.19	.07	−.23	.04	.07	.05			
Step 3												
Constructivist Conception							−.55	.12	−.41			
Traditional Conception												

** $p < .01$; * $p < .05$

DISCUSSION

The present study sought to empirically examine the link between student teachers' perceived teaching practicum related stressors, their epistemological beliefs about knowledge and knowledge acquisition, as well as the conceptions about teaching and learning in a sample of Greek student teachers. In addition, the study investigated the best predictive combination of the studied variables on each perceived practicum-related stressor before and after the practicum. Overall, the results suggest that conceptions about teaching and learning help to predict student teachers' perceived practicum-related stressors both before (to a greater extent) and after (to a lesser extent) the practicum, after student teachers' gender and epistemological beliefs were controlled for.

One of the purposes of the study was to examine the factor structure of the Epistemological Beliefs Questionnaire and the Teaching and Learning Conceptions Subscale with a Greek-speaking sample. With regards to the EBQ, the findings suggested the existence of six (instead of four) interpretable factors of epistemological beliefs. This factor structure is quite similar to that proposed by Chan and Elliot (2004a) with the only exception that the Innate/Fixed ability and the Learning Effort/Process dimensions were broken into two factors each, namely, Innate and Fixed Ability and Learning Effort and Process. It should be also noted that, for the final analyses, eight items were removed from the original instrument due to low factor loadings. The internal consistency of the emerged factors was moderate and ranged from .63 to .69. Student teachers in the present sample tended to believe that knowledge is created through learning process and effort, and that knowledge is tentative and ever-changing. The latter finding is in agreement with previous research suggesting that as students grow older and develop, they tend to adopt a more sophisticated viewpoint towards knowledge (Schommer, 1993). The low mean score of the dimension of Fixed Ability indicates the belief that knowledge is acquired and is changeable. Similarly, student teachers tended to disagree that knowledge is handed down by authorities or experts but rather is a result of personal experience.

Two dimensions of conceptions about teaching and learning were identified for the sample of the present study. Statistical analysis of the TLCS data showed that, on the whole, student teachers almost exclusively hold constructivist conceptions about teaching. Despite some other research findings that showed student teachers to be more ambiguous regarding their conceptions about teaching and learning (Chan & Elliot, 2004a), the present study revealed that Greek student teachers are more likely to apply constructivist teaching practices as future teachers. It is common practice in the Greek educational system, which is highly centralized, for teachers to use more traditional teaching practices. However, prospective student teachers seem to prefer more active ways of learning by constructing knowledge from experiences and showing respect for learners' ideas. To this end, one can assume that participants' responses may be due to their training, but further research is needed to confirm this finding.

Correlational analyses showed that student teachers' epistemologies were related to their conceptions about teaching and learning, thus supporting previous research suggesting that the latter are beliefs-driven (Chan & Elliot, 2004a). Specifically, Innate Ability, Fixed Ability, and Authority/Expert Knowledge were positively related to Traditional Conceptions, whereas Learning Process was negatively associated with Traditional Conceptions, a finding similar to that of Ravindran et al. (2005), suggesting that individuals who think that learning occurs as a result of process are less likely to endorse traditional teaching, which precludes active participation of students in the construction of knowledge. These findings confirm H3.

Constructivist conceptions about teaching and learning were negatively correlated with Innate ability, Authority/expert knowledge and Fixed ability, a finding consistent to that of Chan and Elliott (2004a). On the other hand, Learning Effort and Learning Process were positively associated with Constructivist conceptions, a finding that confirms H4. Thus, student teachers who hold naïve epistemologies are more likely to adhere to more traditional teaching practices, whereas those who hold more sophisticated ones engage in more constructivist instruction, a finding that confirms one of the hypotheses of the study.

Perceived stress for issues related to actual teaching during the practicum (i.e., meeting pupils' needs) was more likely to be associated with student teachers' epistemological beliefs and conceptions about teaching and learning, whereas for those issues related to administrative and evaluative components, there was a weak or no association. These findings confirm H1 and H2. However, the correlations between stressors, epistemological beliefs, and conceptions about learning and teaching were weak and in all but one case involved naïve rather than sophisticated epistemologies. Perceived stress about the interpersonal relations of student teachers and those involved in the practicum was associated with student teachers' belief that knowledge is being handed down by authority figures or experts and by the fact that ability is fixed and unchangeable. Those who believed that learning is a process were more stressed about meeting students' needs and managing their behavior during the practicum. In terms of student teachers' conceptions about teaching and learning and the association with perceived stressors, those who held conceptions of traditional teaching tended to perceive more stress about their interpersonal relations with those involved in the practicum, but those who were in favor of constructivist approaches in classroom teaching were significantly less stressed about their relations with others.

In all, it appears that student teachers' epistemologies and conceptions about teaching and learning were related to perceived stressors both before and after the practicum, although to a lesser extent (Table 3.4). However, the obtained significant correlations were more and stronger before than after the practicum. In order to elucidate this finding, a series of repeated-measures ANOVAs was used to compare the means of the four practicum-related stressors before and after the practicum. In all cases, except for the perceived stress about student teachers' assessment, mean scores before the practicum were significantly higher than after the practicum. This result, which has been supported by similar findings (e.g., Morton, Vesco, Williams, & Awender, 1997; Murray-Harvey, Slee, Lawson, & Silins, 2000), suggests that although the potential experience with the classroom reality during the practicum may constitute a source of stress, the actual teaching experience itself seems to act as an effective coping strategy against stress (Kokkinos et al., 2010). However, after the practicum, only the correlation between perceived stress about the practicum workload/required skills and Innate Ability remained statistically significant. It seems that those student teachers who believed that ability is fixed and unchangeable still perceive time constraints, effective lesson planning, and familiarization with the curriculum as stressful even after this short teaching experience. This finding is rather awkward and unexpected and needs further investigation by future research, since beliefs in innate ability are related to traditional/teacher-centered conceptions about teaching (Chan & Elliot, 2004a).

The study findings have implications for teacher educators who design and develop teacher training programs. Pedagogy in higher education should be informed by personal epistemology rather than by the mere implementation of teaching strategies. Teacher education programs should aim at developing an inquiring attitude among student teachers, based on learning by analysis and reflection and not on beliefs grounded on knowledge delivered by authority figures. The development of constructivist novice teachers who should learn to cope with the problems in their interpersonal relations and who will be able to effectively meet students' needs and manage their behavior during the practicum should be among the priorities of training programs. In turn, teachers should inspire such learning attitudes and beliefs within the pupils they teach in order to promote critical thinking in class. In addition, teacher educators should take student teachers' prior beliefs and conceptions into consideration while planning and providing teaching experiences in the course of their training if they wish to bring about changes within student teachers.

Regression analyses showed that student teachers' perceived stress about the practicum workload and required skills was more likely to be predicted by Innate Ability, both before and after the practicum, and by Fixed Ability only after the practicum (Table 3.5). Again, these results require cautious interpretation since they are somewhat unexpected. One would expect that a teacher who believes in innate ability is more likely to endorse traditional teaching methods, since she is driven by beliefs that concepts, for example, are quickly learned or not at all. Thus, the levels of stress may not be elevated since teaching does not require hard work and effort from the teacher's part. However, in the case of pupils' limited ability, things may be more complicated. Thus, engaging those pupils in the learning process may require additional teaching skills, which student teachers probably do not possess, and therefore are more likely to perceive more stress about this situation. In addition, since the teacher should be in the center of the classroom as an infallible authority on whom pupils' learning entirely depends (i.e., naïve epistemology), by the time they believe that pupils' characteristics to failure are innate, they believe that they cannot do many things to enhance their academic performance and therefore may feel more stressed.

Interestingly enough, almost all perceived practicum-related stressors before the practicum were predicted by naïve epistemologies and by low constructivist conceptions about teaching and learning, except in the case of perceived stress about meeting pupils' needs. This stressor was predicted by beliefs regarding the process of learning (sophisticated epistemology), a finding that was no longer valid after the experience of the practicum. Similarly, all the naïve epistemology predictors no longer predicted practicum-related stressors after the practicum.

Although it cannot be concluded from the present findings, it seems possible that the experience of the practicum on student teachers' perceptions appears to have an effect on these beliefs and therefore on the way the practicum is perceived. Perceived stress regarding professional interactions was predicted by low constructivist perceptions about teaching and learning, as well as by naïve epistemologies (Authority/Expert Knowledge, and Fixed Ability), suggesting that those student teachers who believe that knowledge is handed down by experts and pupils' ability to learn is unchangeable and not improvable are more likely to perceive interactions with in-service teachers, fellow students, and university and school personnel as stressful probably because they are less likely to criticize the authority of experts. Furthermore, it is possible that student teachers who hold naïve epistemologies push themselves to apply other teachers' methods despite the expected disagreement between their ideas and style and that of their supervising teachers. This situation may lead to frustration, which in turn affects their stress levels (Costin et al., 1992). Nonetheless, the experience of the practicum may have acted as a coping mechanism since none of the predictor variables seemed to predict stress for professional interactions after the practicum.

Perceived stress about meeting pupils' needs during the practicum was predicted by the dimension of Learning Process. The finding suggests that student teachers who believe that learning is a process that needs effort to be achieved (constructivist view) are more likely to feel more stressed about meeting pupils' needs. A possible explanation of this finding is that those student teachers who hold a constructivist view about teaching and learning may set higher standards for students' success and put more effort to meet these expectations, which may be related to higher levels of perceived stress (Dangel & Guyton, 2004). The fact that none of the studied variables predicted this stressor after the practicum may be explained by the fact that either student teachers were well prepared to meet pupils' needs or these needs were not as demanding as were initially perceived.

Finally, none of the variables predicted student teachers' perceived stress about their assessment, both before and after the practicum. Therefore, it is obvious that perceived stress that arises from issues related to actual teaching during the practicum is associated mainly with student teachers' epistemological beliefs, while for those conditions related to other aspects of the practicum, such as evaluative (i.e., student teacher's assessment), and administrative (i.e., practicum workload/required skills), there was little or no association.

There are limitations of the present research that pose questions about the generalizability of the findings. Apart from the fact that the results are based on cross-sectional data, collected by a convenient sample, the use of self-report measures of practicum-related stressors may have posed threats to internal validity. Such threats include exaggerated answers, social desirability bias, and the respondents' emotional state during the completion of the questionnaire. Nevertheless, since stress is a subjective experience, student teachers' reports are assumed to be authentic, and it is assumed that they have expressed the reality as they perceive it. Despite the consistency and stability of the teaching system in Greece, different university departments have different terms and conditions regarding the organization and the delivery of the practicum, and therefore the findings apply only to those who participated in the current research. Finally, the present study conceptualized epistemological beliefs as multidimensional and independent rather than stage-like, an issue that may have affected the hypothesized relationship with perceived practicum-related stressors. Of course, replication of the results is deemed necessary since this study is probably the first in its kind.

In all, the findings suggest that student teachers' epistemologies and conceptions about teaching and learning may be taken into consideration in understanding student teachers' perceived practicum-related stressors, and thus should become more significant in future conceptualizations of teacher education. There remains much to be uncovered in the domain of epistemological beliefs, conceptions about teaching and learning, and their relations with practicum-related stressors. By understanding student teachers' practicum-related stressors and the associated variables, teacher educators will be better informed about the ways to improve teacher education programs.

NOTES

1 This dimension was not supported by the empirical work conducted on the instrument.
2. The standard measure of effect size for correlations is the coefficient of determination (r^2), which is interpreted as the proportion of variance in the dependent variable that can be accounted for by the relationship between the dependent and the independent variables. According to Cohen (1988), when the effect accounts for: 25% of the variance ($r = .50$) is considered large; 9% ($r = .30$) moderate and 1% ($r = .10$) small.

REFERENCES

Allison, G. J. (2004). *Perceived and reported occupational stressors and coping strategies of selected community college business faculty members in Texas*. Unpublished PhD Thesis, Texas A & M University, College Station, TX.

Arredondo, D. E., & Rucinski, T. T. (1996, November). *Epistemological beliefs of Chilean educators and school reform efforts*. Paper presented at the Tercer Encuentro National de Enfoques Cognitivos Actuales en Educacion, Santiago, Chile.

Austin, J. R., & Reinhardt, D. (1999). Philosophy and advocacy: An examination of preservice music teachers' beliefs. *Journal of Research in Music Education, 47*, 18–30.

Cambell, M. A., & Uusimaki, L. S. (2006). Teaching with confidence: A pilot study of an intervention challenging pre-service education students' field experience anxieties. *International Journal of Practical Experiences in Professional Education, 9*, 20–32.

Chai, C. S., Teo, T., & Lee B. L. (2009). The change in epistemological beliefs and beliefs about teaching and learning: a study among pre-service teachers. *Asia-Pacific Journal of Teacher Education, 37*, 351–362.

Chan, K. W., & Elliott, R. G. (2002). Exploratory study of Hong Kong teacher education students' epistemological beliefs: Cultural perspectives and implications on beliefs research. *Contemporary Educational Psychology, 27*, 392–414.

Chan, K. W., & Elliott, R. G. (2004a). Relational analysis of personal epistemology and conceptions about teaching and learning. *Teaching and Teacher Education, 20*, 817–831.

Chan, K., & Elliott, R. G. (2004b). Epistemological beliefs across cultures: Critique and analysis of beliefs structure studies. *Educational Psychology, 24*, 123–142.

Cohen, J. (1988). *Statistical power analysis for the behavioral sciences* (2nd ed.). Mahwah, NJ: Erlbaum.

Costin, G., Fogarty, M., & Yarrow, A. (1992). *Student teacher stress in practice teaching.* Retrieved from http://www.swin.edu.au/aare/conf92/COSTG92.400.

Dangel, J. R., & Guyton, E. (2004). An emerging picture of constructivist teacher education. *The Constructivist, 15*, 1–35.

Davis, E. A. (1997, April). *Students' epistemological beliefs about science and learning.* Paper presented at the Annual Meeting of the American Educational Research Association, Chicago.

Duell, O. K., & Schommer-Aikins, M. (2001). Measures of people's beliefs about knowledge and learning. *Educational Psychology Review, 13*, 419–449.

Fives, H., Hamman, D. & Olivarez, A. (2006). Does burnout begin with student-teaching? Analyzing efficacy, burnout, and support during the student-teaching semester. *Teaching and Teacher Education, 6*, 916–934.

Hellenic Statistical Authority. (2010). *Concise statistical yearbook 2009.* Athens, Greece: Author.

Hofer, B. K. (2000). Dimensionality and disciplinary differences in personal epistemology. *Contemporary Educational Psychology, 25*, 378–405.

Hofer, B. K. (2001). Personal epistemology research: implications for learning and teaching. *Journal of Educational Psychology Review, 13*, 353–383.

Hofer, B. K., & Pintrich, P. R. (1997). The development of epistemological theories: beliefs about knowledge and knowing and their relation to learning. *Review of Educational Research, 67*, 88–140.

Howard, B., McGee, S., Schwartz, N., & Purcell, S. (2000). The experience of constructivism: Transforming teacher epistemology. *Journal of Research on Computing in Education, 32*, 455–465.

Kokkinos, C. M., & Stavropoulos, G. (2009, July). *Potential stressors in teaching: Student teachers' future occupational concerns.* Paper presented at the 11th European Congress of Psychology, Oslo, Norway.

Kokkinos, C. M., Stavropoulos, G., & Davazoglou, A. (2010, April/May). *Student teachers' perceived stress about the teaching practicum: the role of dispositional anxiety, gender and academic achievement.* Paper presented at the Annual Meeting of the American Educational Research Association, Denver, CO.

Lawrence, C. L. (1992, April). *Preservice teachers' development of pedagogical understandings and epistemological frameworks.* Paper presented at the Annual Meeting of the Educational Research Association. San Francisco, CA.

Lim, C. P. & Chai, C. S. (2008). Teachers' pedagogical beliefs and their planning and conduct of computer-mediated classroom lessons. *British Journal of Educational Technology, 39*, 807–828.

Morton, L. L., Vesco, R., Williams, N. H. & Awender, M.A. (1997). Student teacher anxieties related to class management, pedagogy, evaluation, and staff relations. *British Journal of Educational Psychology, 67*, 69–89.

Murray-Harvey, R., Slee, P. T., Lawson, M. J. & Silins, H. (2000). Under stress: the concerns and coping strategies of teacher education students. *European Journal of Teacher Education, 23*, 19–30.

Pajares, M. F. (1992). Teachers' beliefs and educational research: Cleaning up a messy construct. *Review of Educational Research, 62*(3), 307–332.

Perry, W. G., Jr. (1968). *Patterns of development in thought and values of students in a liberal arts college: a validation of a scheme.* Cambridge, MA: Bureau of Study Counsel, Harvard University. (ERIC Document Reproduction Service No. ED 024315).

Perry, W. G. (1970). *Forms of intellectual and ethical development in the college years.* New York, NY: Holt, Rinehart and Winston.

Priyadarshini, E., & Robinson-Pant, A. (2003). The attractions of teaching: an investigation into why people change careers to teach. *Journal of Education for Teaching, 29,* 95–112.

Ravindran, B., Greene, B. A., & DeBacker, T. K. (2005). Predicting preservice teachers' cognitive engagement with goals and epistemological beliefs. *Journal of Educational Research, 98,* 222–232.

Rickinson, B. (1998). The relationship between undergraduate student counselling and successful degree completion. *Studies in Higher Education, 23,* 95–102.

Schommer, M. A. (1990). Effects of beliefs about the nature of knowledge on comprehension. *Journal of Educational Psychology, 82,* 498–504.

Schommer, M. A. (1993). Comparisons of beliefs about the nature of knowledge and learning among postsecondary students. *Research in Higher Education, 34,* 355–370.

Schommer, M. A. (1994). Synthesizing epistemological belief of research: Tentative understandings and provocative confusions. *Educational Psychology Review, 6,* 293–319.

Schommer-Aikins, M., & Easter, M. (2006). Ways of knowing and epistemological beliefs' combined effect on academic performance. *Educational Psychology, 26,* 411–423

Stanton, A. (1996). Reconfiguring teaching and knowing in the college classroom. In N. R. Goldberger, J. M. Tarule, B. M. Clinchy, & M. F. Belenky (Eds.), *Knowledge, difference, and power: Essays inspired by 'women's ways of knowing'* (pp. 25–56). New York, NY: Basic Books.

Teo, T. & Chai, C.S. (2008). Conformatory factor analysis of the Conception for Teaching and Learning Questionnaire (CTLQ). *The Asian Pacific Education Researcher, 17,* 215–224.

Van Driel, J. H., Bulte, A. M. W., & Verloop, N. (2005). The conceptions of chemistry teachers about teaching and learning in the context of curriculum innovation. *International Journal of Science Education, 27,* 303–322.

CHAPTER 4

EFFECTS OF STRESS ON TEACHER DECISION MAKING

Gokce Gokalp
University of Southern California

ABSTRACT

This study explored the effects of stress on the strategies teachers choose to deal with pupil behavior problems. Years of teaching experience and amount of behavior management training were also examined. Finally, the impact of different types of behavior problems on teachers' strategy selection was examined. Eighty-four elementary school teachers completed two questionnaires and responded to three vignettes describing student behavior problems. The results indicated that as stress level increased, likelihood of using effective strategies decreased, and likelihood of using ineffective strategies increased. Years of experience and amount of behavior management training received did not lead to more effective strategy selection. Finally, it was found that the type of behavior problem described in the vignettes impacted the type of strategies teachers selected to deal with the misbehavior.

Research on teachers' cognitive processes highlights the importance of decision making (such as student placement decisions, planning decisions, classroom management decisions, and interactive in-class decisions) in the task of teaching (Borko, Cone, Russo, & Shavelson, 1979; Clark, 1988;

International Perspectives on Teacher Stress, pages 69–94
Copyright © 2012 by Information Age Publishing
All rights of reproduction in any form reserved.

Copeland, Birmingham, DeMeulle, D'Emilio-Caston, & Natal, 1994; Shavelson, 1983; Shavelson & Stern, 1981; Stern & Shavelson, 1983). In fact, teaching is described as a process of decision making by many of the researchers in the field (Anderson, 2003; Clark, 1988; Copeland et al., 1994; Rea-Dickins, 2001; Shavelson, 1983; Shulman 1987). This is validated by the finding that teachers are faced with a decision situation every two minutes while teaching, and their decisions have a direct impact on their students (Clark, 1988), making it important that teachers make accurate decisions. Accurate decisions are reasonable choices made with the intent of optimizing student outcomes (Shavelson, 1983). Although research on teacher decision making has demonstrated that for the most part teachers' judgments and decisions are fairly accurate (Shavelson, Cadwell, & Izu, 1977), there are several factors that could influence the accuracy of the decisions.

One factor found to influence decision making in teachers is stress. Stress is defined as any demand on the body that leads to sympathetic nervous system arousal, and the resultant attempts to remove it (Mandler, 1993). A more comprehensive definition of stress offered by Folkman and Lazarus (1984) suggests that stress is based on a person's appraisal of the relationship between environmental and personal demands and the resources the person has to deal with these demands. The general perception among teachers and researchers is that teachers are faced with occupational stress daily due to interpersonal demands that accompany the job and heavy task demands and expectations (Brown & Nagel, 2004; Kerlin, 2002; Kyriacou, 2001; Pithers, 1995). Furthermore, high levels of stress among teachers have important implications for work performance, health, and psychological status (Pithers, 1995). This, coupled with the fact that teachers are often required to make important decisions under very stressful conditions (Brown & Nagel, 2004; Kerlin, 2002; Kyriacou, 2001; Pithers, 1995), shows the importance of exploring the effects of stress on teacher decision making.

Although early work on teacher decision making introduced comprehensive models of teachers' cognitive processes, such as decision making and problem solving (Shavelson, 1983; Snow, 1972), more recent research has made little use of these models and is often without ties to any theoretical perspectives. Therefore, the theoretical perspective of this study is based on the older models of teacher decision making and their more current counterparts from cognitive psychology, such as the cognitive load theory (Sweller, 1988, 1994) and conflict theory models (Janis, 1993), which are described in detail below.

Teaching is described as a process of decision making where teachers make reasonable judgments and decisions in an uncertain and complex environment (Borko et al., 1979). Shavelson's (1983) model of teachers' judgments, plans, and interactive decisions is based on this description. The model identifies factors that are expected to affect teachers' decisions.

It takes into consideration that teachers have to deal with a large amount of information about their students from different sources, and it suggests that to handle this overload of information, teachers integrate the information into a few best estimates about students' learning, behavior, and feelings. This integration helps reduce the working memory capacity required (Sweller, 1988). This decision-making model of teachers aligns well with the more recent cognitive load theory (Sweller, 1988, 1994), which assumes a working memory limited in capacity and duration, and an unlimited long-term memory. From the cognitive load theory perspective, the integration of information into a few best categories is *schema development*, and having schemas helps to organize and store knowledge, which significantly reduces working memory load (van Merrienboer & Sweller, 2005). In fact, Borko et al. (1979) indicated that all of the factors identified above—such as teacher estimates of student learning, feelings, and behavior; teacher educational beliefs; the nature of the instructional tasks; and the availability of strategies and materials—may influence decisions by limiting or expanding the number of alternatives from which the teacher can choose.

As indicated previously, stress is defined as any demand on the body leading to sympathetic nervous system arousal and the resultant attempts to remove it (Mandler, 1993). Researchers have shown that there is a strong covariation between increased levels of stress and a reduction in cognitive performance (Bar-Tal, Raviv, & Spitzer, 1999). This reduction in cognitive performance can manifest itself in such actions as premature reaction and closure (i.e., making a decision too soon), restricted use of relevant cues (i.e., not considering all the available cues), use of cruder categories (use of very general categories), more errors on cognitive tasks, and increased use of schematic or stereotyped judgments (Bar-Tal et al., 1999).

In the same vein, the conflict theory model of Janis (1993) states that high levels of stress reduce problem-solving capabilities, especially in dealing with a complicated decision-making task. Impairment of the decision maker's attention and perception results in narrowing of perceived alternatives, not taking into account long-term consequences, ineffective searching for information, inaccurately assessing outcomes, and using oversimplified decision rules (heuristics). Teachers have also been found to suffer from reduced cognitive performance due to stress (Anderson, 2003; Chan, 2003; Chinn & Brewer, 1993; Kishor, 1994), leading to the decision-making impairments identified above.

One factor that has been shown to mediate the effect of stress on teacher decision making is the years of experience teachers have (Copeland et al., 1994; Keavney & Sinclair, 1978; Parsons, 1973). As teachers gain experience, they establish routines that are automated; because their cognitive resources aren't overtaxed they are able to engage in systematic scanning of alternatives before they make a decision (Blessing & Anderson, 1996).

For example, it was found that teachers who were experienced were more likely than novices to select effective strategies to deal with misbehavior in the classroom (Swanson, O'Connor, & Cooney, 1990).

In summary, literature on the effects of stress on cognitive processes shows that under high levels of stress, cognitive performance is reduced (Baradell & Klein, 1993; Bar-Tal et al., 1999; Janis, 1993). Research on teacher stress reaffirms the impact of stress on teachers' performance. Researchers like Pithers (1995), Chan (2003), and Wiley (2000) indicate that stress leads to poor teaching performance. It has also been shown that teachers often work in very stressful circumstances, and literature on teaching suggests that teaching is a process of making decisions in the face of this stress. However, very few studies have explored the effects of stress on teacher decision making. Specifically, there is a lack of studies on teachers' interactive decision making. Interactive decision making refers to the decisions teachers have to make as they are teaching and interacting with students in their classrooms. Such decisions are also referred to as "real-time" or "in-flight" decisions, since teachers have to react to events they have no control over, without the opportunity to reflect or to seek additional information (Shavelson, 1983). Yet in the comprehensive review of literature Shavelson and Stern (1981) provided on teacher decision making, it was shown that only nine out of 32 studies on teacher decision making examined interactive decisions. Keeping these findings in mind, the current study explores the impact of stress on teachers' interactive decisions in the classroom.

This study examined the strategies teachers choose in dealing with pupil behavior problems and what influence, if any, their level of stress has on these choices in K–12 settings. The effect on teachers' decisions of their experience, and the amount of behavior management training they have had, was also explored. Finally, the impact of different vignettes on strategy selection was examined. The research questions explored by this study are: (1) Do levels of reported teacher stress and years of teaching experience influence teachers' strategy selection? (2) Do the different behavior problems exhibited by students influence probability ratings for using each of the strategies? (3) Does reported teacher stress influence the kind of information teachers use to choose a strategy to deal with the disruptive behavior? (4) Does amount of behavior management training influence the types of strategies teachers choose?

METHOD

Participants

Eighty-four elementary school teachers with varying years of teaching experience were recruited from elementary schools in a large urban city in southern California and from a teacher education program at a university in southern California. The researchers recruited teachers by visiting the schools and describing the study to teachers after school on a day identified by each school's administrators. Those who volunteered to participate in the study completed the questionnaire after school hours. The participants from the teacher education program were recruited by researchers visiting classrooms in the university and administering the questionnaires to those who volunteered to participate in the study.

All participants were included in a drawing for four $50 gift certificates from a bookstore. The mean age of participants was 36, with the youngest participant being 21 years old and oldest participant being 64 years old. Seventy-two percent of the participants were female. Thirty-one percent of the participants were first-grade teachers, 23% were second-grade teachers, 19% were fourth-grade teachers, 14% were fifth-grade teachers, and 13% were third-grade teachers (see Table 4.1). Age was significantly correlated with years of experience ($r = .83$, $p < .001$) and with amount of behavior management training received ($r = .24$, $p < .05$).

The sample size was determined based on Van Voorhis and Morgan's (2001) recommendations of how to determine sample size when conducting regression analysis. They indicate that having approximately 30 participants per predictor variable provides better power to detect small effect sizes. A sample size calculator for multiple regression (Soper, 2008) was also used to determine sample size for a multiple regression analysis with three predictors, a medium effect size ($f^2 = .15$) and 80% power. The calculation indicated that the minimum sample size for such an analysis is 76. A medium effect size was used based on findings that sources of stress, such as interruptions, had a medium effect size (effect size $r = .20$) on accuracy of decisions for complex tasks (Speier, Vessey, & Valacich, 2003), and the finding that a threat stress appraisal had a medium effect size (effect size $r = .29$) on a complex cognitive task (Space Fortress task) (Gildea, Schneider, & Shebilske, 2007). Although these studies did not report effect sizes in their articles, the effect sizes were calculated using the means and standard

TABLE 4.1 Descriptive Statistics for Demographic Information

	n	M	SD
Gender	Male: 26 Female: 58		0.45
Age		36.27	11.31
Grade Level		2.63	1.45
Years of Experience		10.00	9.21
Behavior Management Training		1.84	1.93

Note: N = 84

deviations they provided. It is important to note here that only 70 of the 84 participants responded to the last question of the survey, regarding what information they used in deciding what strategy to use. Since the response rate for this question was below the required sample size, only correlational analysis was conducted on this variable.

Measures

The study examined the relationship between teacher stress and the decisions teachers make about how to deal with disruptive behavior (classroom management problems). Teacher stress is conceptualized here as environmental (outside of the person).

Demographic Questionnaire

This questionnaire consisted of five open-ended questions which were: (1) gender, (2) age, (3) grade level they teach, (4) years of experience teaching, and (5) number of behavior management training classes they have taken and how recently they were taken (see Table 4.2).

Teacher Stress Inventory (TSI) (Fimian, 1984)

This inventory is composed of five stress sources and five stress manifestation factors. Stress manifestations are behavioral and physical symptoms that are indicative of high levels of stress. It was developed to measure the perceived strength of different sources of stress related to teaching by teachers. TSI was used to assess teacher stress, as "discipline and motivation" is included in this measure as one of the source of stress factors. Since this study is concerned with dealing with misbehavior in the classroom, a teacher stress measure that assesses discipline and motivation issues as a possible source of stress was used.

TABLE 4.2   Correlations Between the Independent Variables

	Age	Grade Level	Years of Experience	Behavior Management Training
Age	1			
Grade Level	0.08	1		
Years of Experience	0.83**	−0.03	1	
Behavior Management Training	0.24*	0.03	0.18	1

Note: N = 84
*$p < .05$; **$p < .01$

TSI has been demonstrated to be a highly reliable measure of teacher stress, with a whole scale alpha of 0.93 (Fimian & Fastenau, 1990), based on an administration of the measure to 3,401 teachers representing 21 samples from seven eastern states in the United States. The test–retest reliability of the inventory for this sample was 0.76 (reliability value for the total scale). It has 49 items. Response items are used with a strength-rating scale of 1 to 5, with 1 representing no strength, and 5 representing major strength. Strength refers to the degree to which different stress experiences related to teaching roles impact the teacher's stress level (Fimian & Fastenau, 1990). The aggregate TSI score was used in this study because the alpha for the overall measure of this instrument is higher than the alphas for each of the subscales. The total score assesses the perceived stress levels of teachers (measures 10 stress-related problems for teachers) (Mearns & Cain, 2003). Furthermore, while the subscales are all significantly correlated with each other, they were even more strongly correlated with the total strength of stress. For this measure, a score of 3.29 or above is indicative of a significantly strong stress level, a score between 1.91 and 3.28 indicates mild to medium strength, while a score at or below 1.9 indicates significantly weak strength (Fimian, 2008).

Vignette Instrument of Brophy and McCaslin (1992)

Of the 24 vignettes Brophy and McCaslin generated, three were selected—with some modifications, described below—that describe the behavior problems identified by several researchers as the most frequently encountered in the classroom (Geiger, 2000; Houghton, Wheldall, & Merrett, 1988; Lawrence & Steed, 1986; Merrett & Wheldall, 1984). The first vignette describes an act of inattention by a hyperactive student, who gets in and out of his seat frequently during the lesson and bothers his classmate (accidently knocking down his friend's sculpture). The second and third vignettes describe acts of disruption; however, the student described in the second vignette generally exhibits excessive and nearly constant movement, even when he is sitting, while the student described in the third vignette is not motivated and contributes minimal work output in class. In the second vignette, the student disrupts the class by fidgeting in his seat and making a lot of noise, while in the third vignette the student disrupts the class by talking to her classmates.

Unlike the original vignette instrument, in which participants were asked to indicate what strategy they would use for each vignette, for the purposes of this study, after reading each vignette participants were provided with seven possible strategies that have been identified in the literature as the types of strategies teachers tend to use often (Grubaugh, 1989; Ringer, Doerr, Hollenshead, & Wills, 1993; Tulley & Chiu, 1995). They were asked to indicate the probability that they would use each of the strategies, on a

1–100 scale. From the seven strategies, "praising other students who are exhibiting appropriate behavior" and "ignoring" strategies were included because they have been identified as effective strategies for dealing with a disruption problem (Tulley & Chui, 1995), which is the problem exhibited by the students in Vignettes 2 and 3. The "moving closer and cueing appropriate behavior" strategy was included because it has been identified as an effective strategy for dealing with an inattention problem (Kher, Lacina-Gifford, & Yandell, 2000; Lacina-Gifford, Kher, & Besant, 2002; Lacina-Gifford, Kher, & Besant, 2003; Tulley & Chui, 1995), which is the problem exhibited by the student in Vignette 1. "Isolation by giving time-out" and "punishment" strategies were included because they have been identified as ineffective strategies for any type of behavior problem (Tulley & Chui, 1995). Finally, the "passing the problem to the parents" and "passing the problem to the principal" strategies were included because they are typical strategies teachers use when they are stressed, and are somewhat ineffective (Martin, Linfoot, & Stephenson, 1999). As was noted, the effective strategy for Vignette 1 is "moving closer to the student and cueing appropriate behavior," and the effective strategy for Vignettes 2 and 3 is "praising others who are exhibiting appropriate behavior." These strategies were determined to be the most effective for the behavior problems described in the three vignettes, based on previous research on effective strategies for eliminating behavior problems of inattention and disruption (Geiger, 2000; Martin et al., 1999; Ringer et al., 1993; Tulley & Chui, 1995) (see Table 4.3).

Participants were also asked to indicate what information they took into account when making a decision about what strategy to use. Each piece of information participants provided in their answer was coded as relevant if the information was specific to the behavior that was described in the vignette and to the student in the vignette (if the participant provided five pieces of information and two pieces were relevant and the other three pieces were irrelevant, that meant they received a score of 2 for relevant information and a score of 3 for irrelevant information), and irrelevant if it was general information about teachers' past experiences with situations and students like those described in the vignette and other generalizations, since it was found that high levels of stress are highly correlated with reduction in cognitive performance, which restricts the use of relevant cues while increasing the use of schematic, stereotyped generalizations (Bar-Tal et al., 1999).

Procedures

All participants were given the questionnaire booklet, which included the three measures described above. Participants were instructed to complete the entire booklet in one sitting at their own pace. It took approxi-

TABLE 4.3 Effective and Ineffective Strategies for the Vignettes

				Strategies			
	Praising	Ignoring	Moving Closer	Isolation	Punishment	Passing Problem to Parent	Passing Problem to Principal
Vignette 1	Ineffective	Ineffective	Effective	Ineffective	Ineffective	Ineffective	Ineffective
Vignette 2	Effective	Ineffective	Ineffective	Ineffective	Ineffective	Ineffective	Ineffective
Vignette 3	Effective	Ineffective	Ineffective	Ineffective	Ineffective	Ineffective	Ineffective

mately 20–25 minutes to complete the questionnaires. Anonymity and confidentiality were achieved by not asking for any identifying information and by assigning each package a number. The booklets were then collected by the researcher.

Data Analysis

The first independent variable is teacher stress (trait stress), which was measured by the Teacher Stress Inventory (TSI) (Fimian, 1984). The second and third independent variables are the participants' years of experience teaching and the amount of behavior management training they have received. The dependent variables are the probability that the participants would use each of the seven strategies for each of the three vignettes to deal with the misbehavior described, and the types of information they took into account in deciding what strategy to use.

This study employed a non-experimental research design. For research question 1, descriptive, correlational, and multiple regression analyses were conducted to examine the relationship between years of teaching experience, stress, and strategy selection. Logistic regression analysis was also conducted to examine the impact of the independent variables on selecting the effective strategy for each of the vignettes. The distribution of responses for the effective strategy for each of the three vignettes was highly and negatively skewed (Skewness = −1.70 for Vignette 1; Skewness = −1.13 for Vignette 2; Skewness = −1.22 for Vignette 3). This justifies the use of logistic regression analysis with these variables; Streiner (2002) indicates that continuous variables should be dichotomized only when the distribution of the variable is highly skewed. The use of logistic regression analysis served the purpose of understanding how the three predictor variables contributed to the probability of using the effective strategy for each of the three vignettes, with the assumption that out of the seven strategies given, only one strategy was correct for each vignette.

For research question 2, a within-subjects repeated measures ANOVA was conducted to examine the impact of the type of behavior problem exhibited on teachers' strategy selection. The repeated measure in this case was the set of seven strategies, since each participant had to rate the probability of use of the same seven strategies for each of the three vignettes. Linear regression analysis was conducted to assess the relative contribution of teacher stress, years of teaching experience, and the amount of behavior management training to the probability rating teachers gave for each of the seven strategies for each vignette, for research questions 2 and 3. A logit transformation was conducted on the dependent variables before the regression analysis was performed, due to the fact that the distributions of the dependent variables with raw scores were skewed and that the variables are percentages that are bound by 0 and 100. The 0 and 100 scores were recoded to .50%, and 99.5% to prevent them from being identified as missing data by SPSS.

Age, gender, and grade level taught were not included in the analysis, for several reasons. Age was not included because it was highly correlated with both years of experience and amount of behavior management training received. Gender was not included because most of the participants were female (72%). In general, studies that examine teachers' strategy selection for dealing with misbehavior do not examine the role of gender, since most of the participants are female (Akin-Little, Little, & Laniti, 2007; Kaplan, 1992; Kher et al., 2000; Lacina-Gifford et al., 2003). Furthermore, in their analysis of the aggregate data on the Teacher Stress Inventory, Fimian and Fastenau (1990) found that the scores of males and females were very close to each other on the TSI. Grade level taught was also excluded from analysis, since there is no evidence in the literature that grade level taught impacts teachers' decisions at the elementary level.

Logistic regression analysis was conducted to examine the relative contribution of teacher stress, years of teaching experience, and amount of behavior management training received on whether or not participants picked the effective strategy for each of the vignettes. To conduct the logistic regression analysis, a dichotomous dependent variable was created using the probability ratings participants gave for using the strategy that has been identified as the most effective in dealing with the specific misbehavior described in each vignette. If participants provided a probability rating above 50% for the strategy that has been identified as effective for that vignette, their response was labeled 1, meaning they selected the effective strategy. If they provided a probability rating at or below 50%, then their response was labeled 0. The 50% cut-off point was selected after reviewing the probability ratings the participants gave, both for the effective strategy and the six ineffective strategies. The researcher made sure that using this cut-off point eliminated the chance that an effective strategy that has received the maximum probability rating would be classified as ineffective. The logistic regression analysis was conducted only for the probability ratings of strategies that were identified as effective for each vignette.

For Vignette 1, the effective strategy was "moving closer to the student and cueing appropriate behavior" ($M = 79.08$, $SD = 24.58$), with 15.5% of the participants giving a rating of 50% or less, and 88.5% of the participants giving a rating of more than 50% for the probability of using the strategy, indicating that most teachers picked the effective strategy for dealing with an inattention problem exhibited by a student. For Vignettes 2 and 3, "praising others who are exhibiting appropriate behavior" was the effective strategy ($M = 70.42$, $SD = 31.57$ for Vignette 2, and $M = 71.96$, $SD = 30.70$

for Vignette 3). For Vignette 2, 26.2% of the participants gave a probability rating of 50% or less for using the "praise" strategy, and 73.8% of the participants gave a probability rating of more than 50%. For Vignette 3, 25% of the participants gave a probability rating of 50% or less, while 75% of the participants gave a probability rating of more than 50% for using the "praise" strategy.

One-way ANOVAs were also conducted to follow up on the findings of the repeated measures ANOVA to determine whether the participants' probability ratings for each strategy change based on the type of behavior problem exhibited. A correlational analysis was conducted to examine the relationship between stress levels and the types of strategies selected (those that have been identified as effective and ineffective in the literature for each of the three vignettes). Finally, for research question 4, a correlational analysis was conducted to examine the relationship between stress and the types of information that teachers use to pick a strategy, since only 70 participants responded to this question, which is below the sample size required to conduct a multiple regression analysis, as indicated above.

RESULTS

Research Question 1: *Do levels of reported teacher stress and years of teaching experience influence teachers' strategy (ignore, pass problem to parent, to principal, punish, move closer, praise, isolate) selection?*

It was hypothesized that reported teacher stress would lead to ineffective strategy selection, while teacher experience would lead to more effective strategy selection. The findings of the linear regression analysis for each of the vignettes are summarized in Tables 4.2, 4.3, and 4.4. Only those strategies that were significantly predicted by at least one of the independent variables are included in the tables. It is also important to note here that teacher stress and years of experience were not significantly correlated, but the direction of the relationship between the two variables was negative ($r = -0.20$).

For Vignette 1, the correct response was "moving closer," and for Vignettes 2 and 3, the correct response was "praise." For Vignette 1, regression analysis results with logit transformations revealed that teacher stress was a significant predictor of the use of "passing problem to parents" ($\beta = .31$, $p < .01$), indicating that that stress led to more use of the ineffective strategy, "passing problem to parent." This finding supported the hypothesis that stress would lead to selection of ineffective strategies. However, none of the variables significantly predicted the use of the effective strategy for Vignette 1. In addition, years of experience was not a significant predictor

TABLE 4.4   Regression Analysis for Vignette 1

Variable	Parents Strategy (Ineffective)			Principal Strategy (Ineffective)			Closer Strategy (Effective)		
	B	SEB	β	B	SEB	β	B	SEB	β
Years of Experience	−.01	.03	−.04	−.01	.02	−.04	−.04	.03	−.14
Teacher Stress	1.24	.44	.31**	.30	.36	.09	−.76	.45	−.19
Behavior Management Training	.11	.13	.09	.22	.11	.22*	.08	.14	.07

*$p < .05$; **$p < .01$

for the use of any of the strategies; however, the direction of its relationship to the ineffective strategies was negative, as predicted (see Table 4.4). Stress and years of experience did not have a significant impact on the ineffective strategies of ignoring, isolation, punishment, and praise.

For Vignette 2, regression analysis results with logit transformations revealed that stress was a significant predictor of "passing problem to parents" ($\beta = .26$, $p < .05$) (see Table 4.5), indicating that stress led to the selection of an ineffective strategy, as predicted. Years of teaching experience significantly and negatively predicted the use of "praise" ($\beta = -.26$, $p < .05$), and the use of "moving closer" ($\beta = -.32$, $p < .01$) (see Table 4.3). In line with this finding, years of teaching experience was significantly and negatively correlated with the "moving closer" strategy. These findings indicate that more experience led to less use of the effective strategy "praise" and less use of the ineffective strategy "moving closer" for Vignette 2. This was contrary to the prediction that more experience would lead to selection of effective strategies. None of the independent variables significantly predicted the use of ignoring, isolation, punishment, and passing problem to principal strategies, all of which are ineffective.

For Vignette 3, regression analysis with logit transformations also revealed that stress was a significant predictor of the use of "passing problem to parent" ($\beta = .21$, $p < .05$), as predicted, indicating that as stress level in-

TABLE 4.5   Regression Analysis for Vignette 2

Variable	Parent Strategy (Ineffective)			Closer Strategy (Ineffective)			Praise Strategy (Effective)		
	B	SEB	β	B	SEB	β	B	SEB	β
Years of Experience	−.03	.03	−.12	−.08	.03	−.32**	−.08	.04	−.26*
Teacher Stress	1.18	.48	.26*	.34	.42	.09	−.78	.54	−.16
Behavior Management Training	.35	.15	.25	.05	.13	.04	.18	.17	.12

*$p < .05$; **$p < .01$

creased the use of "passing problem to parent" increased as well. Years of experience significantly and negatively predicted the use of the "passing problem to principal" ($\beta = -.24$, $p < .01$) strategy (see Table 4.6), indicating that as years of experience increased the use of "passing problem to principal" strategy decreased as predicted. However, none of the variables significantly predicted the use of the effective strategy, which was unexpected, given that experience should lead to effective decision making. The findings also indicated that stress and years of experience did not influence the probability ratings given for the use of isolation, punishment, praise, and ignoring strategies.

To better understand the role the three predictor variables played in whether effective strategies were more likely to be selected for each of the three vignettes, logistic regression analyses were also conducted for each of the vignettes (see Table 4.7). As explained in the data analysis section, in these analyses only the probability rating participants gave for the effective strategy was examined, and the dependent variable was converted to a dichotomous variable, which was coded as either 1 or 0. A score of 1 indicated that a probability rating higher than 50% was given for the strategy. Results indicated that for Vignette 1, where the effective strategy is "moving closer," teacher stress alone significantly impacts the probability of using the effective strategy for the problem described in the vignette ($\beta = .64$, $p < .01$, *Cox & Snell* $R^2 = .40$; see Table 4.7), indicating that as stress levels increased the odds of selecting the effective strategy increased. This was an unexpected finding, since stress has been shown to lead to ineffective decision making and not selecting the effective strategy.

For Vignette 2, the results were slightly different in that both teacher stress and years of teaching experience were identified as significantly contributing to the probability of using the effective strategy, which was "praise." The results indicated that it took two steps to enter the variables that significantly improved the logistic regression model. The chi-squares for both the model in Step 1 and the model in Step 2 were significant ($\chi^2 = 18.24$, $p < .01$ for the Step 1, and $\chi^2 = 22.86$, $p < .01$ for the Step 2). This indicates that the first variable added to the model, which was again teacher stress, significantly impacts the dependent variable (Step 1); that adding a second variable, which in this case is years of experience, significantly improves the model; and that the model including two variables is significant. The -2 Log likelihood (indicates how well the model fits the data) was 98.20 for Step 1, and 93.59 for Step 2. In Step 1, 73.8% of the cases were predicted correctly. The *Cox & Snell* $R^2 = .19$ indicates that teacher stress accounted for 19% of the variance in strategy use. When years of experience was added to the model, the two variables together accounted for 24% of the variance in strategy use (*Cox & Snell* $R^2 = .24$), and the percentage of cases predicted correctly increased to 77.4%. In Step 1, for each unit of increase in teacher stress, the

TABLE 4.6 Regression Analysis for Vignette 3

Variable	Parents Strategy (Ineffective)			Principal Strategy (Ineffective)			Isolation Strategy (Ineffective)			Praise Strategy (Effective)		
	B	SEB	β	B	SEB	β	B	SEB	β	B	SEB	β
Years of experience	-.04	.03	-.12	-.05	.02	-.24*	-.02	.03	-.05	-.05	.04	-.17
Teacher Stress	1.05	.52	.21*	.39	.35	.11	.71	.51	.15	-.48	.54	-.10
Behavior Management Training	.42	.16	.28*	.40	.11	.36**	.39	.16	.27*	.17	.17	.11

$^*p < .05$; $^{**}p < .01$

TABLE 4.7   Logistic Regression Predicting Use of Effective Strategy "Moving Closer" for Vignette 1

Variable	B	SE	Odds Ratio	Wald Statistics
Teacher stress	.64	.118	1.90	29.88**

** $p < .01$

odds of selecting the effective strategy increased from 1 to 1.453. In Step 2, for each unit of increase in years of experience, the odds of selecting the effective strategy decreased from 1 to .950. Overall, the results indicated that teacher stress had a positive and significant effect on selecting the effective strategy ($\beta = .37$, $p < .01$), and years of experience had a significant and negative effect on selecting the effective strategy ($\beta = -.05$, $p < .05$). The two variables together had a significant and positive effect on the use of the effective strategy for Vignette 2 ($\beta = .57$, $p < .01$; see Table 4.8) indicating that as stress level increased, the odds of selecting the effective strategy increased. These findings are contrary to the hypothesis that stress is related to ineffective decision making, and years of experience is related to effective decision making, since they support exactly the opposite relationships.

Finally, for Vignette 3, for which "praise" is the effective strategy, teacher stress emerged as the only variable that significantly impacted the probability of using the effective strategy for the behavior problem described in the vignette ($\beta = .40$, $p < .01$, *Cox & Snell* $R^2 = .22$; see Table 4.9). This finding indicated that as stress level increases, the odds of selecting the effective

TABLE 4.8   Logistic Regression Predicting the Use of the Effective Strategy "Praise" for Vignette 2

Variable	B	SE	Odds Ratio	Wald Statistics
Step 1: Teacher stress	.37	.09	1.45	15.87**
Step 2: Experience	−.05	.02	.95	4.40*
Teacher Stress	.57	.14	1.78	16.75**

* $p < .05$; ** $p < .01$

TABLE 4.9   Logistic Regression Predicting the Use of the Effective Strategy "Praise" for Vignette 3

Variable	B	SE	Odds Ratio	Wald Statistics
Teacher stress	.40	.10	1.49	17.62**

** $p < .01$

strategy increases and as such, did not support the prediction that stress leads to the selection of ineffective strategies.

Research Question 2: *Do the different behavior problems described in the vignettes influence the probability ratings of using each of the seven strategies?*

A repeated measures ANOVA with logit transformations was conducted to address this question. As predicted, the results indicated that there was a main effect of vignettes [$F(2, 166) = 6.42$, $p = .002$, $\eta^2 = .07$], which showed that participants provided higher probabilities for all strategies for some vignettes compared to other vignettes. There was also a main effect of strategy [$F(4.94, 410.15) = 130.50$, $p = .000$, $\eta^2 = .61$], which indicates that all participants had a preference for some strategies over others. Finally, there was a vignette and strategy interaction [$F(9.29, 770.91) = 5.87$, $p = .000$, $\eta^2 = .07$], which indicates that teachers respond with different strategies to different types of misbehavior (see Table 4.10). These findings were also confirmed by one-way ANOVAs, which demonstrated that the vignette type impacts selection of each strategy. Overall, the findings demonstrate that teachers know that different strategies have to be used for different behavior problems, and that a strategy that works in one situation is not as effective in another situation.

Research Question 3: *Does reported teacher stress influence the kind of information teachers use to choose a strategy to deal with the disruptive behavior?*

Only correlational analysis was conducted to examine the impact of stress on the kind of information used to choose a strategy. Since reduction in cognitive performance due to stress can manifest itself by restricted use of relevant cues (Bar-Tal, Raviv, & Spitzer, 1999), it was predicted that stress would be correlated with the use of irrelevant information. As predicted, the results showed that teacher stress was significantly and positively corre-

TABLE 4.10   Analysis of Variance for Vignette and Strategy Variables

Source	df	SS	MS	η^2	p	F
Vignette	2	40.71	20.35	0.07	.002	6.42**
Error	166	526.16	(3.17)			
Strategy	4.94	7087.34	1434.23	0.61	.000	130.50**
Error	410.15	4507.68	(10.99)			
Vignette × Strategy	9.29	166.48	17.92	0.07	.000	5.87**
Error	770.91	2355.62	(3.06)			

** $p < .001$

lated with the use of information that was identified as irrelevant ($r = .256$, $p < .05$), indicating that as stress level increased, the use of irrelevant information in making a decision increased.

Research Question 4: *Does the amount of behavior management training influence the types of strategies teachers choose?*

Amount of behavior management training received significantly predicted the use of the "passing problem to principal" strategy for Vignette 1 ($\beta = .22$, $p < .05$; see Table 4.4), indicating that more behavior management led to an increase in passing problem to principal. It was also a significant predictor for the incorrect strategies of "passing problem to parents" ($\beta = .28$, $p < .05$), "passing problem to principal" ($\beta = .36$, $p < .01$), and " isolation" for Vignette 3 ($\beta = .27$, $p < .05$; see Table 4.6), which was unexpected as it indicates that more behavior management training let to an increase in using ineffective strategies for Vignette 3. Also unexpected was the finding that behavior management training did not significantly predict the use of the effective strategies for any of the vignettes. Results of the correlational analysis are also in line with these findings; amount of behavior management training received was found to be significantly correlated with the "passing problem to parents" strategy for Vignette 2 ($r = .25$, $p < .05$) and Vignette 3 ($r = .25$, $p < .05$), with the "passing problem to principal" strategy for all three vignettes ($r = .25$, $p < .05$ for Vignette 1; $r = .23$, $p < .05$ for Vignette 2; and $r = .39$, $p < .01$ for Vignette 3), and with the "isolation" strategy for Vignette 3 ($r = .24$, $p < .05$), indicating that as the amount of behavior management training received increased, the use of some of the ineffective strategies increased for all three vignettes. Results of the logistic regression analysis also confirmed the finding that more behavior management training led to selecting ineffective strategies, which was an unexpected finding, since the goal of behavior management training is to train teachers to make effective behavior management decisions. Findings relevant to each of the three vignettes are summarized in Table 4.11.

DISCUSSION

The results for the first research question show that both teacher stress and years of experience do influence the use of at least some of the seven strategies included in this study. However, some of these relationships are not in the expected direction. For the second research question, as predicted, teachers responded with different strategies to different vignettes. There was a significant main effect of vignettes, indicating that teachers decided what strategy would work best based on the problems described

TABLE 4.11 Summary of Findings

IV	Vignette 1		Vignette 2			Vignette 3		
	Incorrect Strategy/ Parent	Incorrrect Strategy/ Principal	Correct Strategy/ Praise	Incorrect Strategy/ Closer	Incorrect Strategy/ Parents	Incorrect Strategy/ Parents	Incorrect Strategy/ Principal	Incorrect Strategy/ Isolation
Teacher's Stress	Significant	N/A	N/A	N/A	Significant	Significant	N/A	N/A
Experience	N/A	N/A	(−) Significant	(−) Significant	N/A	N/A	(−) Significant	N/A
Behavior Management Training	N/A	Significant	N/A	N/A	N/A	Significant	Significant	Significant

in each vignette. There was also a main effect for strategy, which indicates that teachers favored some strategies over others in general. A further interaction effect shows that teachers picked different strategies for different vignettes. For the third research question, the results show that teacher stress was significantly correlated with the use of information that was irrelevant to the situation at hand. For the fourth research question, the results indicate that amount of behavior management training received did not significantly contribute to the probability of using the effective strategy for any of the vignettes.

Teaching is a highly stressful occupation (Pithers, 1995), and it has been identified as a process of decision making (e.g., Anderson, 2003; Borko et al., 1979). The results of the current study showed that on average teachers reported experiencing moderate levels of stress. Specifically, the mean TSI score for this sample was 2.61, which indicates moderate stress levels, with 25% of the participants scoring above 3.00 (indicating medium strength stress level). This finding has important implications for teaching, and for students, since stress can affect quality of teaching, as well as a teacher's personality, causing them to become cold, insensitive, and possibly more authoritative and rigid, which will lead to ineffective teaching and leaving the profession (Tatar & Horenczyk, 2003; Wiley, 2000). This moderate level of stress was found to be significantly related to the selection of ineffective behavior management strategies and not related to any of the effective strategies in the current study. The results of the logistic regression analysis, however, indicated that as stress level increases, the odds of selecting the effective strategy increases. Perhaps this contradictory finding is due to the possibility that the stress measure used did not tap into the levels of stress the participants were experiencing as they were responding to the vignettes. This finding should be more closely examined using a state stress measure.

Another contradictory finding is the negative relationship between years of experience and the selection of effective strategies that emerged in the logistic regression analysis. One explanation for this finding could be that as teachers gain more experience, they also become more tolerant of overtly bothersome misbehaviors and they become less likely to choose a strategy that has been identified as effective. It is also important to note here that the results do provide partial support for the prediction that as years of experience increase teachers will become less likely to use ineffective strategies and more likely to use effective strategies. Specifically, a significant and negative relationship emerged between years of experience and the use of passing the problem to the principal strategy only for Vignette 3.

The finding that the ineffective strategies of ignoring, isolation and punishment were not significantly predicted by stress and years of experience perhaps indicates that teachers are aware these are ineffective strategies.

This was validated by the results of the repeated measures ANOVA which demonstrated that teachers prefer using some strategies over others. Together these findings show that in general teachers are knowledgeable about what strategies work in dealing with misbehavior. However, this is not always evident in the decisions they make because when teachers are stressed out and anxious, they revert back to using older, more reinforced knowledge that they were exposed to as students, instead of using new knowledge they gained during their training as teachers (Nettle, 1998). Because this older knowledge has been automated, it is less effortful (Feldon, 2007).

Studies that compared the decision-making tendencies of more and less experienced teachers showed that experience served to mediate the impact of stress on decision making (Byra & Sherman, 1993; Copeland et al., 1994; Forlin, 2001). Experience was also found to be associated with lower stress and anxiety levels (Forlin, 2001; Keavney & Sinclair, 1978; Parsons, 1973). Specifically, Forlin (2001) found that greater experience, or greater inclusion and participation in formal training, are associated with less stress. This, coupled with the finding that teacher stress is a significant predictor of the use of ineffective strategies, highlights the importance of providing teachers, particularly teacher trainees, with opportunities to gain more experience in the use of effective behavior management strategies and to learn to deal with stress effectively through courses and workshops.

However, a related finding from the current study warrants caution with respect to providing behavior management training through courses and workshops. The amount of behavior management training received was significantly and positively associated with three strategies that have been identified as ineffective strategies in addressing the misbehaviors described in the vignettes. This indicates that there is a need to reexamine how behavior management training is provided in these workshops. Perhaps incorporating more hands-on experiences during behavior management would be more beneficial to teachers, as well as teacher trainees.

The finding that stress positively correlated with the use of an ineffective behavior management strategy also has important implications for teaching. For example, Lacina-Gifford et al. (2003) found that when strategies used were threatening or punitive, it led to undesirable responses from students, such as fear and resistance, which could impact student performance negatively. Use of ineffective management strategies to deal with a particular misbehavior could also increase the occurrence of that behavior and disrupt the flow of the lesson, which could lead to increased teacher stress. The finding that stress was correlated with the use of irrelevant information could have important implications for students as well, as this indicates that when under stress, teachers might be more likely to base their decisions regarding students on irrelevant factors like a student's gender, race, ethnicity, or attractiveness, instead of the student's actual performance (Bessenoff & Sherman, 2000; Rosenthall, 2002). This highlights the importance of providing teachers with decision-making training as part of their teacher education programs.

While this study found no significant impact of years of experience on teacher stress, and years of experience was negatively related to the use of effective strategies (indicating that experience does not necessarily lead to effective strategy use), examination of the same variables with a substantially larger sample might prove otherwise. However, it is also possible that there may not be a relationship between years of experience and teacher stress, because as times change, possible sources of stress might also change, so the coping strategies that worked 30 years ago may not be effective today. In addition, the negative relationship between years of experience and effective strategies might be due to the fact that what was considered an effective strategy when these teachers first started teaching may subsequently have changed. Also, dichotomizing the 1–100 scale might have led to losing some nuances in the findings.

Finally, this study only included elementary school teachers. A more comprehensive study that allows room to compare student teachers with those who have been teaching for at least five years, on all of the predictor variables as well as the dependent variable, would also provide a better assessment of the role experience plays in the stress/decision making relationship. With a large enough sample size, a comparison between those who have reported low, moderate, and high levels of stress could be conducted to examine differences in strategy selection among these groups.

The field of teacher decision making could also benefit from studies that reexamine older models of decision making by Shavelson and Stern (1981) and by Snow (1972) to test the extent to which they can provide insight about teachers' decision making as it relates to behavior management issues. The knowledge gained from such an examination could then be used to assess the extent to which the conflict stress model of Janis (1993) and the cognitive load theory of Sweller (1988, 1994) are applicable.

Although years of experience, amount of behavior management received, and teacher stress have been identified as factors that impact teachers' interactive decisions, studies that have examined how they contribute to the prediction of what strategies teachers use to deal with different types of behavior problems have been rare. This study demonstrated that indeed these three factors, especially teacher stress and years of experience, play an important role in teachers' strategy selection to deal with misbehavior. This affirms the importance of examining teacher stress–decision making relationship in terms of comprehensive decision making models.

REFERENCES

Akin-Little, K. A., Little, S. G., & Laniti, M. (2007). Teachers' use of classroom management procedures in the United States and Greece. *School Psychology International, 28,* 53–62.

Anderson, L. W. (2003). *Classroom assessment: Enhancing the quality of teacher decision making.* Mahwah, NJ: Lawrence Erlbaum Associates.

Bar-Tal, Y., Raviv, A., & Spitzer, A. (1999). The need and ability to achieve cognitive structuring: Individual differences that moderate the effect of stress on information processing. *Journal of Personality and Social Psychology, 77,* 33–51.

Baradell, J. G., & Klein, K. (1993). Relationship of life stress and body consciousness to hyper vigilant decision making. *Journal of Personality and Social Psychology, 64,* 267–273.

Bessenoff, G. R., & Sherman, J. W. (2000). Automatic and controlled components of prejudice toward fat people: Evaluation versus stereotype activation. *Social Cognition, 18,* 329–353.

Blessing, S. B., & Anderson, J. R. (1996). How people learn to skip steps. *Journal of Experimental Psychology: Learning, Memory, and Cognition, 22,* 576–598.

Borko, H., Cone, R., Russo, N., Shavelson, R. J. (1979). Teachers' decision making. In P. L. Peterson & H. J. Walberg (Eds.), *Research on teaching* (pp. 136–160). Berkeley, CA: McCutchan.

Brophy, J., & McCaslin, M. (1992). Teacher's reports of how they perceive and cope with problem students. *The Elementary School Journal, 93,* 3–68.

Brown, S., & Nagel, L. (2004). Preparing future teachers to respond to stress: Sources and solutions. *Action in Teacher Education, 26,* 34–42.

Byra, M., & Sherman, M. A. (1993). Preactive and interactive decision-making tendencies of less and more experienced preservice teachers. *Research Quarterly for Exercise and Sports, 64,* 46–55.

Chan, D. W. (2003). Hardiness and its role in the stress-burnout relationship among prospective Chinese teachers in Hong Kong. *Teaching and Teacher Education, 19,* 381–395.

Chinn, C. A., & Brewer, W. F. (1993). The role of anomalous data in knowledge acquisition: A theoretical framework and implications for science instruction. *Review of Educational Research, 63,* 1–49.

Clark, C. M. (1988). Asking the right questions about teacher preparation: Contributions of research on teacher thinking. *Educational Researcher, 17,* 5–12.

Copeland, W. D., Birmingham, C., DeMeulle, L., D'Emilio-Caston, M., & Natal, D. (1994). Making meaning in classrooms: An investigation of cognitive processes in aspiring teachers, experienced teachers, and their peers. *American Educational Research Journal, 31,* 166–196.

Feldon, D. F. (2007). Cognitive load and classroom teaching: Double-edged sword of automaticity. *Educational Psychologist, 42,* 123–137.

Fimian, M. J. (1984). The development of an instrument to measure occupational stress in teachers: The teacher stress inventory. *The British Journal of Educational Psychology, 57,* 277–293.

Fimian, M. J., & Fastenau, P. S. (1990). The validity and reliability of the teacher stress inventory: A re-analysis of aggregate data. *Journal of Organizational Behavior, 11,* 151–157.

Fimian M. J. (2008). *The teacher stress inventory info site.* Retrieved from http://www.instructionaltech.net/TSI/index.htm

Folkman, S., & Lazarus, R. S. (1984). If it changes it must be a process: A study of emotion and coping during three stages of a college examination. *Journal of Personality and Social Psychology, 48,* 150–170.

Forlin, C. (2001). Inclusion: identifying potential stressors for regular class teachers. *Educational Research, 43,* 235–245.

Geiger, B. (2000). Discipline in K through 8th grade classrooms. *Education, 121,* 383–393.

Gildea, K. M., Schneider, T. R., & Shebilske, W. L. (2007). Stress appraisal and training performance on a complex laboratory task. *Human Factors, 49,* 745–758.

Grubaugh, S. (1989). Non-verbal language techniques for better classroom management and discipline. *The High School Journal, 73*(1), 34–40.

Houghton, S., Wheldall, K., & Merrett, F. (1988). Classroom behavior problems which secondary school teachers say they find most troublesome. *British Educational Research Journal, 14,* 297–312.

Janis, I. L. (1993). Decision making under stress. In L. Goldberg & S. Breznitz (Eds.), *Handbook of stress* (pp. 56–74). New York, NY: The Free Press.

Kaplan, C. (1992). Teachers' punishment histories and their selection of disciplinary strategies. *Contemporary Educational Psychology, 17,* 258–265.

Keavney, G., & Sinclair, K. E. (1978). Teacher concerns and teacher anxiety: A neglected topic of classroom research. *Review of Educational Research, 48,* 273–290.

Kerlin, T. F. (2002). A comparison of role/task/environment stress experienced by beginning academic and career-technical teachers in southwestern Ohio career-technical schools. *Journal of Vocational Educational Research, 27,* 309–318.

Kher, N., Lacina-Gifford, L. J., & Yandell, S. (2000, April). *Preservice teachers' knowledge of effective classroom management strategies: Defiant behavior.* Paper presented at the Annual Meeting of the American Educational Research Association, New Orleans, LA.

Kishor, N. (1994). Teachers' judgments of students' performance: use of consensus, consistency and distinctiveness information. *Educational Psychology, 14,* 233–247.

Kyriacou, C. (2001). Teacher stress: directions for future research. *Educational Review, 53,* 27–35.

Lacina-Gifford, L. J., Kher, N., & Besant, K. (2003, April). *Preservice teachers' knowledge of effective classroom management strategies: Underachieving students.* Paper presented at the annual meeting of the American Educational Research Association, Chicago, IL.

Lawrence, J., & Steed, D. (1986). Primary school perception of disruptive behaviour. *Educational Studies, 12,* 147–157.

Mandler, G. (1993). Thought, memory, and learning: Effects of emotional stress. In L. Goldberg & S. Breznitz (Eds.), *Handbook of stress* (pp. 40–55). New York, NY: The Free Press.

Martin, A. J., Linfoot, K., & Stephenson, J. (1999). How teachers respond to concerns about misbehavior in their classroom. *Psychology in the Schools, 36,* 347–358.

Mearns, J., & Cain, J. E. (2003). Relationships between teachers' occupational stress and their burnout and distress: Roles of coping and negative mood regulation expectancies. *Anxiety Stress and Coping: An International Journal, 16*(1), 71–82.

Merrett, F., & Wheldall, K. (1984). Classroom behavior problems which junior schoolteachers find most troublesome. *Educational Studies, 10,* 87–92.

Nettle, E. B. (1998). Stability and change in the beliefs of student teachers during practice teaching. *Teacher and Teacher Education, 14,* 192–204.

Parsons, J. S. (1973). *Assessment of anxiety about teaching using the teaching anxiety scale: Manual and research report.* Austin, TX: Research and Development Center for Teacher Education, University of Texas at Austin.

Pithers, R. T. (1995). Teacher stress research: Problems and progress. *British Journal of Educational Psychology, 65,* 387–392.

Rea-Dickins, P. (2001). Mirror, mirror on the wall: Identifying processes of classroom assessment. *Language Testing, 18,* 429–462.

Ringer, M. M., Doerr, P. F., Hollenshead, J. H., & Wills, G. D. (1993). Behavior problems in the classroom: A national survey of interventions used by classroom teachers. *Psychology in the Schools, 30,* 168–175.

Rosenthal, R. (2002). Covert communication in classrooms, clinics, courtrooms, and cubicles. *American Psychologist, 57,* 839–849.

Shavelson, R. J. (1983). Review of research on teachers' pedagogical judgments, plans, and decisions. *The Elementary School Journal, 83,* 392–413.

Shavelson, R. J., Cadwell, J., & Izu, T. (1977). Teachers' sensitivity to the reliability of information in making pedagogical decisions. *American Educational Research Journal, 14,* 83–97.

Shavelson, R. J., & Stern, P. (1981). Research on teachers' pedagogical thoughts, judgments, decisions, and behavior. *Review of Educational Research, 51,* 455–498.

Shulman, L. S. (1987). Knowledge and teaching: Foundations of the new reform. *Harvard Educational Review, 57,* 1–22.

Snow, R. E. (1972). A model teacher training system: An overview. *Research and Development Memorandum 92.* Stanford, CA: Stanford Center for Research and Development.

Soper, D. S. (2008). The free statistical calculators website. [Online software] Retrieved from http://www.danielsoper.com/statcalc/

Speier, C., Vessey, I., & Valacich, J. S. (2003). The effects of interruptions, task complexity, and information presentation on computer-supported decision-making performance. *Decision Sciences, 34,* 771–797.

Stern, P., & Shavelson, R. J. (1983). Reading teachers' judgments plans and decision making. *Reading Teacher, 37,* 280–286.

Streiner, D. L. (2002). Breaking up is hard to do: The heartbreak of dichotomizing continuous data. *The Candian Journal of psychiatry, 47,* 262–266.

Swanson, H. L., O'Connor, J. E., & Cooney, J. B. (1990). An information processing analysis of expert and novice teachers' problem solving. *American Educational Research Journal, 27,* 533–556.

Sweller, J. (1988). Cognitive load during problem solving: Effects on learning. *Cognitive Science, 12,* 257–285.

Sweller, J. (1994). Cognitive load theory, learning difficulty, and instructional design. *Learning and Instruction, 4,* 295–312.

Tatar, M., & Horenczyk, G. (2003). Diversity-related burnout among teachers. *Teaching and Teacher Education, 19,* 397–408.

Tulley, M., & Chui, L. H. (1995). Student teachers and classroom discipline. *The Journal of Educational Research, 88,* 164–171.

van Merrienboer, J. J. G., & Sweller, J. (2005). Cognitive load theory and complex learning: Recent developments and future directions. *Educational Psychology Review, 17,* 147–177.

Van Voorhis, C. W., & Morgan, B. L. (2001). Statistical rules of thumb: What we don't want to forget about sample sizes. *Psi Chi Journal, 6*(4), 139–141.

Wiley, C. (2000). A synthesis of research on the causes, effects, and reduction strategies of teacher stress. *Journal of Instructional Psychology, 27,* 80–87.

CHAPTER 5

A MIXED METHODS STUDY OF STRESS, COPING, AND BURNOUT AMONG KINDERGARTEN AND ELEMENTARY TEACHERS IN GERMANY

Richard G. Lambert
University of North Carolina at Charlotte

Annette Ullrich
Baden-Württemberg Cooperative State University Stuttgart

Christopher J. McCarthy
University of Texas at Austin

ABSTRACT

Transactional models of stress posit that perceptions of both resources and demands determine the extent to which stress will be experienced. Previous research examining the relationship of teachers' stress levels and coping re-

International Perspectives on Teacher Stress, pages 95–120
Copyright © 2012 by Information Age Publishing
All rights of reproduction in any form reserved.

sources to burnout symptoms in the United States was replicated with kindergarten and elementary teachers in Germany. Participants were 444 elementary teachers in Baden-Württemberg, Germany. Teachers reporting higher stress levels also reported more burnout symptoms than teachers reporting lower stress levels. Teachers reporting low stress prevention and coping skills reported higher levels of some burnout symptoms than did teachers reporting higher stress prevention and coping levels. Qualitative observations and interviews with a subset of teachers with differing patterns of scores on the stress, coping, and burnout measures were conducted. Teachers were classified into four groups: reactive, detached, engaged, and reflective, based on the patterns of interactions with children observed in their classrooms and the attitudes and values about the teaching profession they reported during interviews.

Teacher burnout is an international phenomenon (Lambert & McCarthy, 2006). In order to better understand commonalities and differences in the specific factors that predict teacher stress and burnout across national borders, this study built upon McCarthy, Lambert, O'Donnell, and Melendres' (2009) research on the relationship of United States (U.S.) elementary teachers' experience, stress, and coping resources to burnout symptoms with kindergarten and elementary teachers in Germany. Both McCarthy et al.'s research and the current study were based on Lazarus and Folkman's (1984) transactional model of stress, which hypothesizes that when life demands are encountered, a subjective transaction occurs in which the person weighs perceived demands of the event against perceived capabilities for coping. Perceptions that life demands outweigh coping resources can lead to the stress response, which includes the experience of negative emotions and, in the long term, the potential for burnout symptoms.

OCCUPATIONAL BURNOUT AND TEACHER WELL-BEING FROM A TRANSACTIONAL PERSPECTIVE

Burnout is a term first coined by Freudenberger (1974), who defined it as a loss of idealism and enthusiasm for work. Examining predictors of burnout in teachers was the focus of McCarthy et al.'s (2009) research with U.S. teachers, as well as the current study with German teachers. Teachers represent the largest homogeneous occupational group investigated in burnout research (Schaufeli & Enzmann, 1998) and are widely recognized to be at high risk for excessive stress levels and professional burnout (Dunham & Varma, 1998).

Maslach and Jackson developed the construct of burnout in the 1980s (Maslach & Jackson, 1981; Maslach & Schaufeli, 1993) as well as the Maslach Burnout Inventory (MBI; Maslach, Jackson, & Leiter, 1996) to measure it. The MBI is by far the most common measure found in burnout research and has been used in over 90% of burnout research (Hastings, Horne, & Mitchell, 2004; Schaufeli & Enzmann, 1998). Maslach, Schaufeli, and Leiter (2001) theorized that burnout has three essential components: emotional exhaustion, depersonalization, and personal accomplishment. Emotional exhaustion (EE), which is the most obvious and central aspect of burnout, refers to a depletion of one's emotional resources (Maslach et al., 2001) and feeling exhausted and unable to cope with life demands. Depersonalization (DP) refers to disconnecting oneself from others, and for elementary teachers this may involve the development of negative, unfeeling, callous, and cynical attitudes towards students and the school environment. The third component of burnout is personal accomplishment (PA), which refers to a reduced sense of efficacy and devaluing of one's work with others.

McCarthy et al. (2009) found that individual teacher factors (overall teaching experience as well as experience at their current school, perceived resources and demands, and preventive coping resources) were more strongly associated with burnout symptoms than the school where the teacher worked. McCarthy et al. (2009) measured both classroom demands and classroom resources hypothesized to contribute to elementary teachers' stress using the Classroom Appraisal of Resources and Demands (CARD, school-age version; Lambert, McCarthy, & Abbott-Shim, 2001), which focuses on the demands of the elementary classroom environment as well as specific material resources available to teachers to meet those demands. Transactional models of stress and coping would predict that teachers who rated demands greater than resources would be at risk for experiencing occupational stress.

In addition to examining classroom demands and resources, McCarthy et al. (2009) examined the role of teachers' psychological coping resources as predictors of burnout. The central component of the burnout construct as suggested by Maslach, Jackson, and Schwab (1986), emotional exhaustion, was predicted by a number of variables in McCarthy et al.'s (2009) study of U.S. teachers: years at their current school, classroom demands, stress, and preventive coping resources. These variables accounted for approximately one third of the variance in EE, which is not surprising given that EE is the most obvious manifestation of the burnout syndrome (Maslach et al., 1986).

TEACHING IN U.S. AND GERMAN SCHOOLS

Compared to the education system in the United States, which is based on the idea of educating all students in integrated kindergartens, elementary schools, and comprehensive middle and high schools, Germany has a stratified school system. After the fourth elementary grade, children get separated on the basis of test scores and teacher recommendations (Powell, 2006). In addition, children with special needs in the German system are placed in separate schools, while students in the U.S. are taught in the same schools. While there are notable structural differences in elementary education in the U.S. and Germany, there is evidence that teacher stress and burnout are prevalent in both countries. Both in the United States and in Germany, burnout rates of up to 50% have been reported (Barth, 1997; Byrne, 1999). In the U.S., stress and burnout have been identified as contributors to the shortage and attrition of teachers (Burke, Greenglass, & Schwarzer, 1996), while in Germany, early retirement based on health-related reasons has been a concern for several years (Unterbrink et al., 2007).

There are also differences in educational leadership training. In Germany, principal training is not obligatory, usually it is learning by doing, only 3 out of 16 "Länder" offer a Master of Arts in school administration (Hancock & Müller, 2008). The U.S. has a long history of principal education programs with well defined standards developed by the National Policy Board for Educational Administration. The teacher stress literature has indicated clearly that effective leadership is related to lower teacher stress and burnout (Kyriacou, 2001).

In the United States, high teacher turnover and a national teacher shortage has been an ongoing feature of the education profession (Weisberg & Sagie, 1999). According to Ingersoll and Smith (2004), every second teacher quits after 5 years. In Germany, 74% of all teachers retired early compared to 46% of early retirements in other professions in 2005 (Weber, 2002). For 52% of those who retired early, a psychological or psychiatric diagnosis was given. It is important to identify factors depleting the teaching force in order to best support teachers. Research on teacher stress in German speaking countries has largely been based on a model by Schaarschmidt and Fischer (1996), who conceptualized stress based on personal work-related coping strategies and found four groups: Type B—reduced involvement, high risk for burnout if faced with demands (30%); Type A—overcommitted, at risk for burnout (30%); Type S—under-committed, not at risk (23%); and Type G—characterized by clear, not excessive involvement, not at risk (17%).

The problem with this model is that it does not take preventive coping resources into account. Transactional models take individual coping resources into account and are therefore most suitable in investigating teacher stress and coping. They are based on the assumption that our cognitive appraisal of demands and resources is central to the stress response. According to transactional models, stress results from perceptions of inequality between resources and demands (Lazarus & Folkman, 1984; McCarthy & Lambert, 2006).

PREDICTORS OF STRESS AND BURNOUT

Three groups of variables have been associated with stress and burnout in teachers. They are cultural and societal factors, school-specific factors, and teacher-specific factors. Culture is an environmental variable that impacts individuals' perceptions and behaviors in different ways. Cultural differences include language, geography, political arrangement, historical development, and work values. Hofstede (1980) identified four cultural work value dimensions: individualism versus collectivism, masculinity versus social consciousness, high versus low power distance (more collaboration), and high (many rules) versus low uncertainty avoidance. Cultural differences may impact responses to daily demands and choice of coping strategies. Culture has also an impact on educational systems as well as on epistemological beliefs (see Kokkinos et al., this volume; Chan & Elliott, 2004).

According to Shirom and Mazeh (1988), levels of burnout vary across the career span and cycle from high to low over approximately five-year periods. A higher number of years spent at the same school would then not predict burnout, but a teacher's place in that cycle. Savicki (2002) found that individuals in the low burnout configuration group were significantly older than in the mixed and high burnout configuration groups. The average age in the German teacher sample was higher. This could be a selection bias issue—that is, only teachers with good coping skills continue teaching, which may explain why burnout goes down if the number of years spent at current school increases. It may be related as well to the fact that German teachers are well-respected academic professionals. Most of them are well-paid, tenured civil servants (Ashwill, Foraker, Nerison-Low, Milotich, & Milotich, 1999), which is often a motivational factor to enter a teacher education program (Klinzing, 1990).

School-Specific Factors

Findings for elementary teachers are mixed. Research has shown that in the U.S., middle school and special education teachers have the highest stress levels, which may be attributed to the onset of adolescence. Stress levels have also found to be high for teachers of students with emotional or behavioral disabilities. In Germany, basic secondary and advanced secondary (Hauptschule and Gymnasium) teachers had the highest stress levels, which may be related to the stratified school system and parents trying to prevent their children with special needs from attending a special school because it is perceived as stigmatizing. Students from families with low socioeconomic status or immigration background are overrepresented in basic secondary schools. School-specific factors also include interactions with students and parents. Nowadays, parents advocate more for their children, which may come with an increased tendency to accuse teachers or to complain.

Teacher-Specific Variables

Findings for gender, age, and years of experience are contradictory, but experience has been referred to as an internal coping resource. Buschmann and Gamsjäger (1999) found higher burnout levels in divorced teachers. Personality traits include locus of control with inconsistent findings. But there is support in the literature that self-esteem and the level of regard a person has for him- or herself may result in more effective coping with stress. Plenty of research supports the positive impact of social support on stress and health, which can be from other teachers, from supervisors, or from significant others. Self-efficacy, the belief in one's ability to cope with demands, is also well researched as a predictor of burnout. Self-acceptance, the degree to which one can accept and overcome personal shortcomings, has been identified as a strong predictor of teacher stress, burnout, and health. It can be considered as conceptually central to the construct of preventive coping (Lambert, O'Donnell, Kusherman, & McCarthy, 2006).

Flaws in Previous Research

There is still controversy around the question of whether contextual variables or personality traits contribute more to teacher stress and burnout. Most research uses self-report measures, whereas observations of actual student–teacher interactions and qualitative interviews are more rare and may help to measure situational and other aspects that impact teacher stress levels. The role of values such as respect and responsibility is also under-researched. Respect can be defined as

> the regard due to me and to all other persons on the planet by virtue of our being human. It's not honor or something we have to earn, but precisely that which we don't. Respect forms the restraint side of morality. It's what I restrain myself from doing because it might harm that which I value. (Hanson, 2002, p. 2)

This study sought to extend the current knowledge base beyond the traditional self-report measures of burnout symptoms and perceptions of classroom resources and demands by examining individual differences in teaching style, attitudes toward teaching, and values in the sample of German teachers through direct observation and interviews in classroom.

GOALS OF THE CURRENT STUDY

As a direct follow-up to the studies described earlier (McCarthy et al., 2009; Ullrich et al., in press), the current study was designed to use both quantitative and qualitative evidences to outline a profile of specific subgroups of German teachers based on their perceptions of classroom demands, school-provided classroom resources, and personal coping strategies. The first research question was as follows: (1) Will teachers with varying stress and coping levels, when observed and interviewed in their classrooms, demonstrate differences in teaching approaches, attitudes toward teaching, and values concerning their role as teachers? This question was designed to examine if different patterns of teacher–child interactions would be apparent to outside visitors when teachers with varying levels of occupational stress and stress prevention strategies were observed. An attempt was made to explore and describe individual differences in teacher reactions to stressful situations in teaching. In addition, we were interested in evaluating whether teachers with different response patterns on the closed-ended self-report measures in the study would describe in differing ways their perceptions of the teaching profession and the ethics and values to which they adhere as teachers.

The second and third research questions were designed to examine whether specific individual teacher factors were associated with burnout symptoms. By classifying teachers in subgroups based on their appraisals of classroom demands and resources and coping strategies, we plan to address the following research questions: (2) Is there a difference in reported burnout symptoms between teachers with high and low stress levels? and (3) Is there a difference in reported burnout symptoms between teachers with high and low levels of coping strategies? These research questions were designed to test the theoretical framework developed by Lazarus and Folkman (1984) by evaluating the role of individual teacher perceptions of resources and demands in relation to burnout symptoms. Kindergarten and elementary school teachers are particularly relevant for these research questions as their classroom resources and overall environment is relatively stable throughout the school year, they typically work with the same intact group of students for most of the year, and they tend to have similar demands from day to day. Mixed methods were used to examine why some teachers survive and thrive in specific school environments, while other teachers struggle in the same setting. It is this "individual difference" perspective that was evaluated to help understand why some teachers cope well with the demands of the classroom while others struggle.

METHOD

Participants

Data were collected from German kindergarten and elementary teachers in Baden-Württemberg, the third biggest of the 16 German federal states. The sample consisted of 444 teachers (grades K–4) from schools in four districts (Freiburg, Karlsruhe, Stuttgart, Tübingen).

Procedures

Approval from the Ministry of Education to conduct a survey in the Baden-Württemberg school system was obtained. Principals were approached by email to ask for permission to recruit teachers in their school to participate in the study. Two different alternatives for teacher recruitment were offered: thirteen principals chose the option of allowing the authors to collect data during a staff meeting, and the rest of the participating principals agreed to distribute the questionnaire for the researcher with envelopes to return the surveys confidentially. The questionnaire consisted of three parts: the Classroom Appraisal of Resources and Demands (CARD; Lambert, McCarthy, Abbott-Shim, & Ullrich, 2008), the Preventive Resources Inventory (PRI; McCarthy, Lambert, & Ullrich, 2008), and the Maslach Burnout Inventory (MBI; Enzmann & Kleiber, 1989). Teachers were asked to provide their contact details if they were willing to participate in follow-up observations and qualitative interview.

Measures

Classroom Resources and Demands
The CARD assesses demands of elementary teachers such as classroom environment and material resources available to teachers to meet those demands. It consists of 84 items including demographics and classroom characteristics, classroom demands, and helpfulness of resources to be rated on a 5-point Likert scale. In accordance with Lazarus and Folkman's (1984) theory, a classroom "stress" score can be created for each survey participant by subtracting the total score for the demands section of the CARD from the total score for the resources section of the CARD. Transactional models of stress and coping would predict that teachers who rated demands greater than available resources would be at risk for experiencing occupational stress.

Lambert, McCarthy, O'Donnell, and Melendres (2007) found high sample-specific reliability for both the Demands scale score (Cronbach's alpha = .92) and for the Resources scale score (α = .95). In the current sample, the subscales and the total score for the Resources section yielded sample-specific information with adequate reliability (.828 to .951).

Preventive Coping—Self-Acceptance

Preventive coping resources allow the individual to recognize and deal with life demands so as to avoid the experience of stress (for a further review, see Matheny et al., 1986, and McCarthy, Lambert, Beard, & Dematatis, 2002). McCarthy et al. (2009) used the total score from the Preventive Resources Inventory (McCarthy et al., 2002) to measure overall preventive resources with U.S. elementary teachers. The PRI measures five constructs: perceived control, maintaining perspective, social resourcefulness, scanning, and self-acceptance. Results from a pilot study with the German versions of the CARD and the PRI showed that the survey packet was perceived to be very long, so a modification was made to the research design used by McCarthy et al. (2009) and only the self-acceptance (SAC) scale of the PRI was used. This decision was based on findings from previous research that indicated that SAC was the strongest predictor of stress and health. Therefore, a German translation of one scale, self-acceptance (SAC), was used as a proxy for overall preventive coping resources. McCarthy et al. (2002) defined SAC as "a set of beliefs and behaviors indicating acceptance of self, others, and the world" (p. 25). The self-acceptance scale consists of 16 items and measures how well a respondent is able to accept personal weaknesses and strengths when faced with challenging life situations. Cronbach's alphas of .708/.850 and in the present study of .835. were calculated for self-acceptance (Lambert et al., 2006).

Burnout

The MBI-ES by Maslach et al. (1996) and the German version (MBI-D) by Enzmann and Kleiber (1989) were used to measure teacher burnout. The MBI assesses three dimensions of burnout: (1) emotional exhaustion (EE), (2) depersonalization (DP), and (3) personal accomplishment (PA). It consists of 22 items related to the following three scales: EE is the central quality of the complex syndrome of burnout referring to feelings of being exhausted and overextended emotionally by contact with other people and work, DP refers to the development of a cynical stance toward the individuals one is working for, and PA refers to lowered feelings of competence and personal achievement in one's work (Maslach et al., 2001).

Maslach, Jackson, and Leiter (1997) reported Cronbach's alphas ranging from .88 to .90 for EE, .74 to .76 for DP, and .72 to .76 for PA. The overall Cronbach's alpha for the MBI in a study conducted by Lambert et al. (2009)

was .909 with values of .903, .684, and .750 for the EE, DP, and PA scales. Cronbach's alpha reliability coefficients for the German sample examined in this study were .853 for EE, .619 for DP, and .604 for PA.

Analyses

Following procedures used by McCarthy et al. (2009), the classroom stress score from the CARD was calculated for each respondent by computing the difference between the total score for the demands section of the CARD and the total score for the resources section of the CARD. This was done to test the prediction of transactional models of stress and coping that teachers who rated demands greater than available resources would be at risk for experiencing occupational stress. We used the general form of the reliability of a difference score formula that allows for different variances for each of the component scale scores (Crocker & Algina, 1986) to examine the reliability of the stress score. The reliability of the difference score, using the same method, in previous studies was .945 (McCarthy et al., 2009), .949 (Lambert, 2009) and .950 (Lambert, O'Donnell et al., 2006).

Based on the reliability coefficients of the two CARD scales as well as the difference score, a 95% CI was formed around the difference score of 0 to be sure that teachers who were classified as at risk were really at risk. Cut scores were set and participants were classified in three groups. Only teachers who scored in the Demands greater than Resources (D > R, indicating high stress level) and Resources greater than Demands groups (R > D, indicating low stress level) were retained in the analyses to maximize the differences between the groups with respect to perceived stress. The self-acceptance scale score from the PRI was used to create a high stress prevention and coping group and a low stress prevention and coping group based on the normative data from previous research (Lambert, McCarthy, Gilbert, Sebree, & Steinley-Bumgarner, 2006). Individual teachers were then classified into sub-groups based on the combination of their stress and coping conditions: (1) high self-acceptance/R > D, (2) high self-acceptance/D > R, (3) low self-acceptance/R > D, and (4) low self-acceptance/D > R.

Observation and Interview Procedures

For the purpose of identifying the sample for the qualitative portion of the study, the total sample in each of the four groups was reduced to only those teachers who had volunteered for follow-up interviews and observations during the survey phase of the study. These lists were then randomly ordered. One of the researchers began contacting teachers, starting at the top of each list, to arrange a time to conduct the interviews and observations with the goal of visiting three teachers in each of the four groups for a total of 12 visits. We were able to arrange and conduct eleven visits.

Two members of the research team interviewed each teacher after the classroom visits. One observer had made the initial contact with each teacher and therefore knew the subgroup to which the teacher belonged. The second observer was blinded as to the teacher's group membership. There was a general set of questions to be posed to each teacher. The questions covered the following topics: classroom demands; personal resources to meet classroom demands; classroom and school resources and supports; and relationships with students, parents, and administrators. Each teacher was also asked to help the observers understand whether the day of the visit was a typical one, how stressful the day was, and why. Each interview took on a unique flavor as the teachers were encouraged to extend their conversations on any of the topics they were most interested in discussing. All responses were transcribed and coded for themes using AQUAD (Huber, 2006).

RESULTS

To address the first research question, field notes from the observations and interview transcripts were coded for themes related to interactions with children, approaches to teaching, attitudes toward the profession, and values related to the role of teacher. During the classroom visits, the researchers were able to observe and record field notes about pedagogical strategies, use of instructional time, and interactions with students. In the interviews, teachers revealed their attitudes and guiding principles, which were in essence related to values and ethics. They often defined their ethical responsibilities as a set of values they believed were commonly held by teachers. In addition, they included their perceptions of teachers' responsibilities towards society at large, the teaching profession, and students. Each of the four subgroups of teachers will be described and illustrated with examples from the observations and interviews.

The results of the coding process indicated that teachers who scored low on self-acceptance and perceived demands to be greater than resources could be described as taking a "reactive" approach to teaching. These teachers reported low stress prevention skills and high stress. The main themes regarding their style of interactions with children were high activity levels and low levels of student engagement. These teachers were often following closely to a planned schedule, appeared to be fighting to make it through the material, and seemed to be talking over or past the children. The children responded to this style with a range of off-task behaviors. The central attitudes toward teaching expressed by these teachers were focused on survival. One teacher reported "... I am just trying to get through the day...."

With respect to values, these teachers often referenced activities external to the classroom. For example, a teacher who fell into this category reported that she valued care for the ecosystem and environmental concerns and was willing to put in extra hours to prepare and to collaborate with a close-by University of Applied Sciences on a project related to protection of the environment. She also talked about leading a drama group at the school and how she enjoyed working on their projects. Justice is another value that she mentioned, which is very important in her opinion to preserve relationships with students and families and for everybody to get along with each other. These teachers also shared their values related to student behavior. One remarked, "In order to get along with others the children need to be able to manage themselves first.... I feel responsible for them and I also hold them responsible. They know that they can trust me and come to me if something went wrong."

The results of the coding process indicated that teachers who scored low on self-acceptance and rated resources greater than demands had a more "detached" approach. These teachers reported low stress prevention skills and low classroom stress. These teachers often displayed very consistently flat and unchanging affect in their interactions with the children. They focused on activities the children could do in groups or individually and did not engage in whole group teacher-directed instruction as often as teachers in the other subgroups. One teacher required the children to work at their desks in workbooks during most of the lessons of the day. She also required the students to line up at her desk to have their work checked. Her feedback to the children often consisted of comments about their handwriting, spelling, and ability to follow directions. During each lesson, some advanced children had their work checked very quickly and then played games or talked to other students while other children never completed the tasks. The children reacted to this style with restless behavior, even running around the classroom at times.

These teachers expressed frustrations about their roles as teachers. For example, one teacher remarked, "Everyone is pulling on some part of me.... I would like to have more time to prepare and fewer children in the classroom.... It is always the feeling that you are running out of time. I can't give all of the special attention to some of the children that I know they need." Another remarked, "I am happy I am at the end of my career. I do not want to go down this path any longer. I can't do the lessons with these children that I did with the children just six years ago." These teachers also expressed cynicism about the children and their motivation. For example, one teacher remarked, "Honesty from the children is the part of the job I enjoy the most." Another commented, "These children can't read correctly and can't listen carefully, so what pathway to learning can I take? They have too much exposure to electronic entertainment and are alone so much. I have to be parent and teacher. I have to teach them all of the usual social interactions as well as the academic lessons.... I am afraid for my daughter who is just beginning as a parent."

With respect to values, these teachers often focused on the parents and broader school system policy issues. A teacher in this category reported, "Some parents have lost interest in raising their children or they feel guilty and want to make up for what they know they should be doing but they don't have the time to do." Another added, "The ministry of education is trying to help the current administration win the election so they are pushing through new policies without thinking through things just to please parents." These teachers also focused on their relationships with other educational professionals outside the classroom. One teacher reported that being active in the school leadership team and cooperating with colleagues was very important to her.

The results of the coding process indicated that teachers who scored high on self-acceptance and perceived resources to be greater than demands displayed a "reflective" approach to teaching both in the classroom and in the interview process. These teachers reported high stress prevention skills and low stress. Every activity or lesson observed in the classrooms of these teachers involved interaction with the children, asking them open-ended questions, encouraging their use of oral language, and remaining very attentive to their answers. These teachers displayed a high tolerance for minor distractions and misbehavior. They often were observed coaching children through answers that were not exactly or completely correct. The overall atmosphere in their classrooms was very relaxed, inviting, and positive. Those activities that were teacher-directed whole-group instruction involved a high degree of student participation.

These teachers talked about their ability to transcend the demands of the classroom, not become stressed by daily difficulties, and keep a positive attitude. One teacher commented, "I have good days and bad days, but I don't take it home with me. I accept stress as part of the job. It doesn't affect my overall happiness.... I have never had any stress-related health problems in my career as a teacher and I think it is related to having a positive attitude toward my work."

With respect to values, these teachers often focused on ways they could positively impact the development of children. One teacher in this group reported, "As teachers we are role models every minute and need to be thinking about ways to influence value development and to teach coping skills like impulse control, stress management, and getting along with others." She described how using positive reinforcement with the children pays off and works well with both students and teachers. She reported, "School is not only about learning, it is also about being human. What the students understand is that they like to be respected. So if they like respect in the way other people treat them, they will need to treat others respectfully, too." Another teacher in this group talked about how important perceptions of fairness are to her understanding of the self-esteem of children. She talked about always being careful to make sure that no child is singled out for poor athletic ability during physical education. She asked, "Have you ever looked into the eyes of the last child picked to be on a team?"

The results of the coding process indicated that teachers who scored high on self-acceptance and perceived demands to be greater than resources demonstrated an "engaged" approach to teaching. These teachers reported high stress prevention skills and high stress. These teachers tended to use a variety of instructional strategies such as music and movement, giving classroom duties and responsibilities to children, drawing, reading silently, reading aloud to the class, children reading to the class, whole group and small group activities, traditional lecture and demonstration, and a healthy overall blend of teacher-directed and child-directed activities. These teachers placed a high value on student engagement and intentionally used different strategies to keep the students attentive. One teacher put it this way: "Absolutely it is hard to keep the children engaged at times in meaningful activity. . . . I have learned to use video, CDs, and many of our internal resources that make it easier to prepare."

These teachers placed a high value on reaching each child and strived to find the methods that would be helpful to each child individually. They pushed themselves to use a variety of strategies and to differentiate instruction for each child. One teacher remarked, "I have found that accepting each child along with their strengths and weaknesses, and loving each child, makes it easier . . . this is my coping strategy." These teachers focused more on structural issues and the availability of instructional resources than did teachers in the other groups. One teacher commented, "There are too few workshops, and they are not offered at convenient times, so teachers do not learn to use technology. . . . We spend too little money on equipment, training, and software." Another remarked, "My school does not have enough educational resources . . . and my classes are too large with very different proficiency levels."

With respect to values, these teachers often talked about successful teaching practices and the results of quality instruction. For example, one teacher in this subgroup discussed her views of good teaching quality and the importance of teaching virtues, promoting self-regulation and self-control in order to empower children.

From this point forward, the four sub-groups of teachers will be referred to as the Reactive, Detached, Engaged, and Reflective groups. Table 5.1 includes the percentages of teachers that were classified into each of the groups

TABLE 5.1   Percentage of Teachers in Each Stress Groups by School Type

	Reactive			Engaged	
Kindergarten	Elementary	Total	Kindergarten	Elementary	Total
31.2%	27.8%	28.6%	11.0%	17.0%	15.5%
$n = 34$	$n = 93$	$n = 127$	$n = 12$	$n = 57$	$n = 69$

	Detached			Reflective	
Kindergarten	Elementary	Total	Kindergarten	Elementary	Total
22.0%	17.3%	18.5%	35.8%	37.9%	37.4%
$n = 24$	$n = 58$	$n = 82$	$n = 39$	$n = 127$	$n = 166$

for the kindergarten, elementary, and overall samples. The largest group was the Reflective group with 37.4% of the teachers. The next largest group was the Reactive group with 28.6% of the teachers. The Detached group had 18.5% of teachers. The smallest group was the Engaged group with 15.5% of teachers. We expect the Reactive and Detached groups, the low stress prevention groups, to report higher levels of burnout symptoms than the Engaged and Reflective groups, the high stress prevention groups. Similarly, we expect the high stress groups, the Reactive and Engaged teachers, to report higher levels of burnout symptoms than the low stress groups, the Detached and Reflective groups. Based on the qualitative findings, and from stress and coping theory, we also expect the Reactive group, the interaction between low stress prevention and high stress, to display the most burnout symptoms.

To address research questions two and three, a series of two-way analyses of variance was conducted in which the dependent variables were the scale scores from the MBI, and the independent variables were stress level (high vs. low) and coping skills (high vs. low). Since different versions of the CARD measure were used to form the stress groups for kindergarten and elementary teachers, separate analyses were conducted for these two groups of teachers.

We will examine the kindergarten analyses first (see Table 5.2). For EE, there was a statistically significant main effect for coping skills $(F_{(1,104)} = 12.595, p < .001)$. Teachers with high coping skills reported lower emotional exhaustion than teachers with low coping skills (effect size = −1.041). There was a statistically significant main effect for stress level $(F_{(1,104)} = 18.721, p < .001)$. Teachers with high stress levels reported higher emotional exhaustion than teachers with low stress levels (effect size = 1.033). The EE analyses did not yield a statistically significant interaction between coping skills and stress levels $(F_{(1,104)} = 2.188, p = .142)$.

For DP, there was a statistically significant main effect for coping skills $(F_{(1,104)} = 5.543, p = .020)$. Teachers with high coping skills reported lower

TABLE 5.2 Burnout Scores by Stress Group for Kindergarten Teachers

Outcome measure		Low Coping Low Stress Detached $n = 24$ a	Low Coping High Stress Reactive $n = 34$ b	High Coping Low Stress Reflective $n = 39$ c	High Coping High Stress Engaged $n = 12$ d	Coping main effect	Stress main effect	Int.	Post Hoc Comparison
Emotional exhaustion	Mean	12.04	22.59	8.28	13.46	***	***	ns	
	SD	7.95	10.09	7.00	8.01				
Depersonalization	Mean	3.46	7.29	2.10	4.18	*	**	ns	
	SD	3.93	6.18	2.47	3.84				
Lack of professional accomplishment	Mean	10.42	17.62	8.05	11.55	***	***	ns	
	SD	5.95	5.95	5.56	5.65				
Burnout	Mean	25.17	47.38	18.21	27.25	***	***	*	$b > a, c$
	SD	14.14	19.37	12.09	14.31				

Note: *** $p < .001$; ** $p < .01$; * $p < .05$; ns = not statistically significant

depersonalization than teachers with low coping skills (effect size $= -.713$). There was a statistically significant main effect for stress level ($F_{(1,104)} = 9.715$, $p = .002$). Teachers with high stress levels reported higher depersonalization than teachers with low stress levels (effect size $= .770$). The DP analyses did not yield a statistically significant interaction between coping skills and stress levels ($F_{(1,104)} = .857$, $p = .357$).

For PA, there was a statistically significant main effect for coping skills ($F_{(1,104)} = 11.357$, $p < .001$). Teachers with high coping skills reported lower lack of professional accomplishment scores than teachers with low coping skills (effect size $= -.998$). There was a statistically significant main effect for stress level ($F_{(1,104)} = 18.248$, $p < .001$). Teachers with high stress levels reported higher lack of professional accomplishment than teachers with low stress levels (effect size $= .933$). The DP analyses did not yield a statistically significant interaction between coping skills and stress levels ($F_{(1,104)} = 2.192$, $p = .142$).

For the burnout total score, there was a statistically significant main effect for coping skills ($F_{(1,104)} = 17.280$, $p < .001$). Teachers with high coping skills reported lower average burnout levels than teachers with low coping skills (effect size $= -1.162$). There was a statistically significant main effect for stress level ($F_{(1,104)} = 23.000$, $p < .001$). Teachers with high stress levels reported higher average burnout scores than teachers with low stress levels (effect size $= 1.128$). The BO analyses yielded a statistically significant interaction between coping skills and stress levels ($F_{(1,104)} = 4.080$, $p = .046$). The Tukey HSD procedure was used to conduct post hoc comparisons between cell means, illustrating the source of this interaction effect. The Reactive group scored statistically significantly higher, on average, than both the Detached group (effect size $= 1.259$) and the Reflective group (effect size $= 1.817$). Though not statistically significant, the difference between the Reactive and Engaged groups was also substantial in terms of standardized mean difference effect size (1.085).

Next, we examine the elementary teacher analyses (see Table 5.3). For EE, there was a statistically significant main effect for coping skills ($F_{(1,331)} = 10.820$, $p < .001$). Teachers with high coping skills reported lower emotional exhaustion than teachers with low coping skills (effect size $= -.627$). There was a statistically significant main effect for stress level ($F_{(1,331)} = 44.557$, $p < .001$). Teachers with high stress levels reported higher emotional exhaustion than teachers with low stress levels (effect size $= .898$). The EE analyses did not yield a statistically significant interaction between coping skills and stress levels ($F_{(1,331)} = 1.845$, $p = .175$).

For DP, there was not a statistically significant main effect for coping skills ($F_{(1,331)} = .903$, $p = .343$). However, teachers with high coping skills did report somewhat lower depersonalization than teachers with low coping skills (effect size $= -.254$). There was a statistically significant main effect

TABLE 5.3 Burnout Scores by Stress Group for Elementary Teachers

Outcome measure		Low Coping Low Stress Detached n = 58 a	Low Coping High Stress Reactive n = 93 b	High Coping Low Stress Reflective n = 127 c	High Coping High Stress Engaged n = 57 d	Coping main effect	Stress main effect	Int.
Emotional exhaustion	Mean	20.60	24.75	16.98	23.25	***	***	ns
	SD	6.36	7.22	5.65	8.42			
Depersonalization	Mean	8.14	9.42	7.52	9.30	ns	***	ns
	SD	2.23	4.20	2.90	3.76			
Lack of professional accomplishment	Mean	30.40	31.24	30.33	31.40	ns	ns	ns
	SD	4.51	4.77	5.24	5.38			
Burnout	Mean	57.76	64.98	54.53	63.44	ns	***	ns
	SD	11.94	11.67	10.23	13.62			

Note: *** $p < .001$; ** $p < .01$; * $p < .05$; ns = not statistically significant

for stress level ($F_{(1,331)} = 15.461$, $p = .001$). Teachers with high stress levels reported higher depersonalization than teachers with low stress levels (effect size = .493). The DP analyses did not yield a statistically significant interaction between coping skills and stress levels ($F_{(1,331)} = .408$, $p = .523$).

For PA, there was not a statistically significant main effect for coping skills ($F_{(1,331)} = .008$, $p < .931$). There was not a statistically significant main effect for stress level ($F_{(1,331)} = 2.722$, $p < .100$). The DP analyses did not yield a statistically significant interaction between coping skills and stress levels ($F_{(1,331)} = .040$, $p = .841$).

For the burnout total score, there was not a statistically significant main effect for coping skills ($F_{(1,332)} = 3.210$, $p < .074$). However, teachers with high coping skills did report moderately lower average burnout levels than teachers with low coping skills (effect size = –425). There was a statistically significant main effect for stress level ($F_{(1,332)} = 36.62$, $p < .001$). Teachers with high stress levels reported higher average burnout scores than teachers with low stress levels (effect size = .765). The BO analyses did not yield a statistically significant interaction between coping skills and stress levels ($F_{(1,332)} = .400$, $p = .525$).

DISCUSSION

Distinct patterns of interacting with children, attitudes toward teaching, and values emerged across the four subgroups of teachers. The qualitative evidences demonstrated a pattern of cynicism and frustration for the Detached teachers. The Reactive teachers appeared to be more focused on survival and demonstrated less control over the classroom environment. Reflective teachers showed consistently more interactions with children, more depth in their use of language and open ended questions, and a focus on the development of the whole child. Engaged teachers focused on effectiveness in teaching and student learning outcomes.

The hypotheses regarding different patterns of reported burnout symptoms for the four subgroups were partially supported. The expected patterns of emotional exhaustion emerged for both kindergarten and elementary teachers. The high stress and low coping groups were associated with higher average exhaustion levels, and the magnitude of these effects was large in both groups. The expected main effects for stress and coping emerged across all the components of burnout for the kindergarten group. For the elementary teachers, there was a main effect for stress level with higher stress teachers reporting more symptoms, but only for the EE, DP, and total burnout scales. The expected interaction between stress and coping levels only appeared for the total burnout score with the kindergarten sample. The Reactive teachers, consistent with their focus on survival in

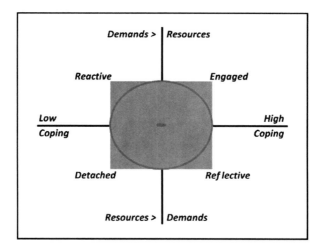

Figure 5.1 Theoretical model of teacher stress and coping.

the work environment, consistently reported the highest levels of burnout symptoms.

Figure 5.1 illustrates graphically the four subgroups of teachers relative to their stress and coping scores. The right side of the graphic shows the two high coping groups, and the left side illustrates the low coping groups. The top half of the graphic contains the demands greater than resources, or high stress group, and the bottom half of the graphic contains the low stress, resources greater than demands groups. The center of the graphic indicates that there are teachers who report scores on both the stress and coping measures that are not far enough away from the overall mean for all teachers to lead to reliable classification into one of the subgroups. These teachers may not fit neatly into one of the four patterns. In Figure 5.2 we have attempted to further illustrate the profiles of the four subgroups by identifying, at the scale and subscale levels, the typical patterns of scores on the stress, coping, and burnout measures.

Policymakers and administrators can use these findings to think strategically about the composition of their staff with respect to membership in the subgroups. Concentrations of teachers in one of the groups may have implications for selecting the content of staff development and for planning the nature of mentoring support for individual teachers. For example, Reactive teachers may become Engaged teachers as they improve their own personal resources in the areas of stress prevention and coping strategies. Similarly, the results of this study suggest that Detached teachers may become more Reflective with increases in stress prevention and coping strategies. Engaged teachers may become more like Reflective teachers as they are able to access more classroom resources and develop healthier appraisals

Reactive		Engaged	
Self-Acceptance	*Low*	Self-Acceptance	*High*
Identity Comfort	*Very Low*	Identity Comfort	*High*
Accepting Limitations	*Low*	Accepting Limitations	*High*
Balance	*Very Low*	Balance	*High*
Stress	*High*	Stress	*High*
Classroom Demands	*High*	Classroom Demands	*High*
Classroom Resources	*Low*	Classroom Resources	*Low*
Burnout	*High*	Burnout	*High*
Emotional Exhaustion	*High*	Emotional Exhaustion	*High*
Depersonalization	*High*	Depersonalization	*High*
Lack of Prof. Accomplishment	*High*	Lack of Prof. Accomplishment	*High*
Detached		Reflective	
Self-Acceptance	*Low*	Self-Acceptance	*High*
Identity Comfort	*Low*	Identity Comfort	*High*
Accepting Limitations	*Low*	Accepting Limitations	*High*
Balance	*Low*	Balance	*High*
Stress	*Low*	Stress	*Low*
Classroom Demands	*Low*	Classroom Demands	*Low*
Classroom Resources	*High*	Classroom Resources	*High*
Burnout	*Low*	Burnout	*Low*
Emotional Exhaustion	*Moderate*	Emotional Exhaustion	*Low*
Depersonalization	*Moderate*	Depersonalization	*Low*
Lack of Prof. Accomplishment	*Low*	Lack of Prof. Accomplishment	*Low*

Figure 5.2 Profiles of the stress groups.

of the balance between classroom demands and resources. Building level administrators may be able to enhance their ability to support teachers by evaluating what Reactive, Engaged, and Detached teachers need in their particular context to become more like Reflective teachers. They may be able to help teachers across the career trajectory become more reflective by enhancing the working environment through offering more supports and resources, helping teachers learn to cope with the stresses of teaching in a more adaptive manner, and helping teachers develop more functional or healthy perceptions of the working environment.

Providing teacher education candidates with the knowledge and skills to become reflective practitioners is also very important. The findings of this study may therefore have implications for teacher education. They may help inform the development of strategies for preparing teachers to capably respond to the increasingly complex demands of teaching, while retaining their initial enthusiasm and motivation to become a teacher. Teacher preparation programs that ensure teacher candidates have access to high-quality role models and reflective practitioners who are continuously developing and refining their teaching and problem solving skills are playing a central role in the development of individual teacher coping and stress prevention strategies, which will in turn help keep the talented and committed in the profession.

Teachers who choose to remain in the profession learn to form cooperative and supportive relationships with colleagues and understand how to interact with children and families in healthy and productive ways. Learning both of these skill sets is a critical induction task for new teachers attempting to adapt successfully to the teaching profession. In addition, they need to acquire the ability to react intuitively to everyday demands (Hargreaves, 2005) and to handle them well. Students expect their teachers to provide them with a sense of optimism, security, and meaning (Branson, 2005). While "getting the job done" may seem to be teachers' main formal responsibility, they are more so than ever required to model appropriate values such as respectful and responsible behaviors. New teachers have to negotiate their way through all of these processes simultaneously, placing them at risk for occupational stress. Teacher stress can be viewed from the perspective of environmental or demand models (Holmes & Rahe, 1967), resource models (Hobfoll, 1989), and transactional models that combine the impact of both resources and demands (Lazarus & Folkman, 1984). Consistent with McCarthy et al.'s (2009) findings for a sample of U.S. elementary teacher sample, this study found that individual teacher perceptions are predictive of burnout symptoms. This study also demonstrated that teacher perceptions of occupational stress and of their personal coping resources are not only related to scores on other self-report measures, but are associated with observed variations in teaching style, attitudes toward the profession, and values. In order to deepen our understanding and interpretation of processes related to the role of values in stress among teachers, more research is needed that examines whether values make a difference in teachers' perceptions of the work environment. Further research is also needed in other regions and other countries to assess the generalizability of the findings.

As Schäfers and Koch (2000) noted, further insights into the relationship between objective and subjective stressors can only be reached by means of classroom observations. While the qualitative interview and observation approach employed in this study yielded valuable insights, an ethnographic approach and the methodological approach of discourse analysis seem to be promising in terms of deepening our understanding and interpretation of processes related to stress among teachers in different cultural contexts. In addition, more research that relates observations of specific teacher activity in the classroom with the survey instruments used in the survey study may allow for further important insights.

AUTHOR NOTE

Partial funding for this study was provided by the Department of Educational Leadership and the Faculty Research Grant Program at UNC Charlotte.

REFERENCES

Ashwill, M. A., Foraker, W., Nerison-Low, R., Milotich, M., & Milotich, U. (1999). *The educational system in Germany. Case Study findings.* Retrieved from http://www2. ed.gov/PDFDocs/GermanCaseStudy.pdf

Barth, A. R. (1997). *Burnout bei Lehrern. Theoretische Aspekte und Ergebnisse einer Untersuchung.* Göttingen: Hogrefe Verlag für Psychologie.

Branson, C. M (2005). Exploring the concept of values-led principalship. *Leadership and Management Journal, 11*(1), 14–31.

Burke, R. J., Greenglass, E. R., & Schwarzer, R. (1996). Predicting teacher burnout over time: Effects of work stress, social support, and self-doubts on burnout and its consequences. *Anxiety, Stress, and Coping, 9*(3), 261–275.

Buschmann, I., & Gamsjäger, E. (1999). Determinanten des Lehrer-burnout. Empirische Arbeit. *Psychologie in Erziehung und Unterricht, 46,* 281–292.

Byrne, B. M. (1999). The nomological network of teacher burnout: A literature review and empirically validated model. In R. Vandenberghe & M. Huberman (Eds.), *Understanding and preventing teacher burnout: A sourcebook of international research and practice* (pp. 15–37). New York, NY: Cambridge University Press.

Chan, K., & Elliott, R. G. (2004). Epistemological beliefs across cultures: Critique and analysis of beliefs structure studies. *Educational Psychology, 24,* 123–142.

Crocker, L., & Algina, J. (1986). *Introduction to classical and modern test theory.* Fort Worth, TX: Harcourt Brace Jovanovich College Publishers.

Dunham, J., & Varma, V. (Eds). (1998). *Stress in teachers: Past, present and future.* London, UK: Whurr Publishers.

Enzmann, D., & Kleiber, D. (1989). *Helfer-Leiden: Streß und Burnout in psychosozialen Berufen* (Helper's distress: Stress and burnout in psychosocial jobs). Heidelberg, Germany: Asanger.

Freudenberger, H. J. (1974). Staff burnout. *Journal of Social Issues, 30,* 159–165.

Hancock, D. R., & Müller, U. (2008). Different system—similar challenges? Factors impacting the motivation of German and U.S. teachers to become school leaders. *International Journal of Educational Research, 48*(5), 299–306.

Hanson, K. (2002). Teaching values in school: An interview with Steve Johnson. *Issues in Ethics, 13*(1). Retrieved from http://www.scu.edu/ethics/publications/iie/v13n1/interview.html

Hargreaves, A. (2005). Educational change takes ages: Life, career and generational factors in teachers' emotional responses to educational change. *Teaching and Teacher Education, 21,* 967–983.

Hastings R. P., Horne S., & Mitchell, G. (2004). Burnout in direct care staff in intellectual disability services: A factor analytic study of the Maslach Burnout Inventory. *Journal of Intellectual Disability Research, 48*(3), 268–273.

Hobfoll, S. E. (1989). Conservation of resources: A new attempt at conceptualizing stress. *American Psychologist, 44*(3), 513–524.

Hofstede, G. (1980). *Culture's consequences: International differences in work related values.* Beverly Hill, CA: Sage.

Holems, T. H., & Rahe, R. H. (1967). The social readjustment scale. *Journal of Psychosomatic Research, 11,* 213–218.

Huber, G. L., & Gürtler, L. (2004). *AQUAD Six. Manual for the analysis of qualitative data.* Tübingen: Ingeborg Huber Verlag.

Klinzing, H-G. (1990). Research on teacher education in West Germany. In R. Tisher & M. Wideen (Eds.), *Research in teacher education: International perspectives* (pp. 89–105). London, UK: Palmer Press.

Kyriacou, C. (2001). Teacher stress: Direction for future research. *Educational Review, 53*(1), 27–35.

Lambert, R. G., & McCarthy, C. J. (2006). *Understanding teacher stress in an age of accountability.* Greenwich, CT: Information Age Publishing.

Lambert, R. G., McCarthy, C. J., & Abbott-Shim, M. (2001). *Classroom appraisal of resources and demands, school-aged version.* Atlanta, GA: Head Start Quality Research Center.

Lambert, R. G., McCarthy, C. J., Abbott-Shim, M, & Ullrich, A. (2008). *Einschätzung von Ressourcen und Anforderungen im Klassenzimmer, Version für die Schule.* (Classroom Appraisal of Resources and Demands, German language version of the school-aged version). Charlotte, NC: The Center for Educational Measurement and Evaluation.

Lambert, R. G., McCarthy, C., Gilbert, T., Sebree, M., & Steinley-Bumgarner, M. (2006). Validity evidence for the use of the Preventive Resources Inventory with college students. *Measurement and Evaluation in Counseling and Development, 39,* 66–83.

Lambert, R. G., McCarthy, C., O'Donnell, M., & Melendres, L. (2007). Teacher stress and classroom structural characteristics in elementary settings. In Gates, G. (Ed.), *Emerging thoughts and research on student, teacher, and administrator stress and coping* (pp. 109–131). Greenwich, CT: Information Age Publishing.

Lambert, R. G., O'Donnell, M., Kusherman, J., & McCarthy, C. J. (2006). Teacher stress and classroom structural characteristics in preschool settings. In R. G. Lambert & C. J. McCarthy (Eds.), *Understanding teacher stress in an age of accountability* (pp. 105–120). Greenwich, CT: Information Age Publishing.

Lazarus, R. S., & Folkman, S. (1984). *Stress, appraisal, and coping.* New York, NY: Springer.

Maslach, C., & Jackson, S. (1981). The measurement of experienced burnout. *Journal of Occupational Behavior, 2,* 99–113.

Maslach, C., Jackson, S. E., & Leiter, M. P. (1996). *Maslach Burnout Inventory (3rd ed.).* Palo Alto, CA: Consulting Psychologists Press.

Maslach, C., Jackson, S. E., & Leiter, M. P. (1997). Maslach Burnout Inventory (3rd ed.). *Evaluating stress: A book of resources.* 1.

Maslach, C., Jackson, S. E., & Schwab, R. L. (1986). *Maslach burnout inventory: Educators survey.* Palo Alto, CA: Consulting Psychologists Press.

Maslach, C., & Schaufeli, W. B. (1993). Historical and conceptual development of burnout. In W. B. Schaufeli, C. Maslach, & T. Marek (Eds), *Professional burn-*

out: Recent developments in theory and research (pp. 1–16). Washington, DC: Taylor & Francis.

Maslach, C., Schaufeli, W. B., & Leiter, M. P. (2001). Job burnout. Annual Review of Psychology, 52, 397–422.

Matheny, K, B., Aycock, D. W., Pugh, J. L., Curlette, W. L., & Canella, K. A. (1986). Stress coping: A qualitative and quantitative synthesis with implications for treatment. The Counseling Psychologist, 14(4), 499–549.

McCarthy, C. J., & Lambert, R. G. (2006). (Eds). Understanding teacher stress in an era of accountability. Greenwich, CT: Information Age.

McCarthy, C.J., Lambert, R. G., Beard, M., & Dematatis, A. (2002). Factor structure of the Preventive Resources Inventory and its relationship to existing measures of stress and coping. In G. S. Gates & M. Wolverton (Eds.), Toward wellness: Prevention, coping, and stress (pp. 3–37). Greenwich, CT: Information Age.

McCarthy, C. J., Lambert, R. G., O'Donnell, M., & Melendres, L. (2009). The relation of elementary teachers' experience, stress, and coping resources to burnout symptoms. The Elementary School Journal, 109(3), 282–300.

McCarthy, C., Lambert, R. G., & Ullrich, A. (2008). Inventar Präventiver Ressourcen (Preventive Resources Inventory, German language version). Charlotte, NC: The Center for Educational Evaluation and Measurement.

Powell, J. (2006). Barriers to inclusion: Special education in the United States and Germany. Boulder, CO: Paradigm.

Savicki, V. (2002). Burnout across thirteen cultures: Stress, and coping in child and youth care workers. Westport, CT: Praeger.

Schaarschmidt, U., & Fischer, A. W. (1996). AVEM. Arbeitsbezogenes Berhaltens-und Erlebensmuster. Manual. (Work-related Patterns of Behavior and Experience.) Frankfurt a. M.: Sweets Test Service.

Schäfers, C., & Koch, S. (2000). Neuere Veröffentlichungen zur Lehrerforschung. Eine Sammelrezension. Zeitschrift für Pädagogik, 46, 601–623.

Schaufeli, W. B., & Enzmann, D. (1998). The burnout companion to study and practice: A critical analysis. London, UK: Taylor & Francis.

Shirom, A., & Mazeh, T. (1988). Periodicity in seniority-job satisfaction relationship. Journal of Vocational Behavior, 33, 38–49.

Smith, T. M., & Ingersoll, R. M. (2004). What Are the effects of induction and mentoring on beginning teacher turnover? American Educational Research Journal, 41(3), 681–714.

Ullrich, A., Lambert, R. G., & McCarthy, C. J. (2010). Comparing stress between elementary teachers in the Unites States and Germany. Technical Report, http://education. uncc.edu/ceme/new_page_reports4.htm.

Unterbrink, T., Hack, A., Pfeifer, R., Buhl-Griesshaber, V., Müller, U., Wesche, H., Frommhold, M., Scheuch, K., Seibt, R., Wirsching, M., & Bauer, J. (2007). Burnout and effort–reward–imbalance in a sample of 949 German teachers. Archives of Occupational and Environmental Health, 80, 433–441.

Weber, A. (2002). Lehrergesundheit-Herausforderung für ein interdisziplinäres Präventionskonzept. (Teachers' health—A challenge for an interdisciplinary prevention concept.) Gesundheitswesen, 64, 120–124.

Weisberg, J., & Sagie, A. (1999). Teachers' physical, mental, and emotional burnout: Impact on intention to quit. *The Journal of Psychology: Interdisciplinary and Applied, 133*(2), 333–339.

CHAPTER 6

EARLY CHILDHOOD TEACHERS' EXPERIENCES WITH CHALLENGING STUDENT BEHAVIOR IN GERMANY

Annette Ullrich
Baden Württemberg Cooperative State University Stuttgart

Richard G. Lambert
University of North Carolina at Charlotte

Christopher J. McCarthy
University of Texas at Austin

Andreas Zimber
Heidelberg University of Applied Sciences

ABSTRACT

Behavior problems are one of the most stressful components in educating young children. In this study, qualitative data from a sample of 186 German

International Perspectives on Teacher Stress, pages 121–138
Copyright © 2012 by Information Age Publishing

kindergarten teachers in Baden-Württemberg, Germany, were analyzed. Using a qualitative approach, teachers' open-ended responses to questions about their perceptions of challenging student behavior and the strategies they employ to handle behavior problems in the classroom were coded in four categories. The behaviors that were mentioned most often were disruptive behaviors, disrespectful behaviors, lack of engagement, and difficulty communicating. Educators perceived them as frustrating because they take away time and energy, because they impede learning processes, and because students who display challenging behaviors oftentimes also suffer from a lack of support from home. Strategies included the use of empathy, consistency, positive behavior support, collaborative efforts, and instructional strategies such as teaching communication or conflict resolution skills. Findings confirm previous research suggesting that more support is needed for early childhood professionals in order to effectively cope with challenging student behaviors.

Due to the growing awareness of the importance of early childhood education, the training of teachers of young children in Germany is currently undergoing a reform. It is an area that is in particular need of improvement (Deutsche Welle, 2005). Until 2007, no university degree was offered for early childhood professionals. A three-year training program was sufficient for early childhood educators to enter the field. This traditional three-year program was said to have many disadvantages, for example, with regard to job mobility, professional recognition, and salaries. However, the new possibility of a bachelor's degree in early childhood education opens new avenues for teachers to work in other countries, which is an advantage in our age of globalization. But it has also effects on the overall early care and education system in Germany and can contribute to teacher stress. For example, the current reform leaves early childhood educators with university degrees unequipped to provide children with grounded experience in early childhood best practices. The reason for this is that teachers at the newly established university programs are often inexperienced with developmentally appropriate practices for young children. It is difficult for experienced early childhood professionals to complete doctoral studies (eligibility for doctoral studies is usually linked to a university degree), which is why they mostly continue to teach in the three-year non-university degree programs.

Results of the Program for International Student Assessment (PISA) Consortium have shown that students with parents who had some level of higher education were four times more likely to be selected to attend an advanced secondary school (Gymnasium) (Deutsches PISA-Konsortium, 2001). Also, in Germany more so than in other countries, a child's access to early education depends on the socioeconomic status of the family. High-achieving countries as measured by PISA as well as in the Third International Math and Science Study (TIMSS) were found to pay particular attention on teacher training and ongoing supports. In order to provide all children with equal opportunities to achieve their full potential, early access to high-quality and best practice education needs to be established and teachers must be provided with ongoing support (OECD, 2004). Ensuring high quality and expanding the number of children who participate in early education at the same time are among the challenges that are currently being tackled in the German early childhood education field (Bertelsmann-Stiftung, 2010).

Among the most stressful demands reported by preschool teachers are challenging student behavior, number of students in the classroom, lack of administrative support, lack of parental support, and lack of instructional resources (Lambert, O'Donnell, Kusherman, & McCarthy, 2006; Moriarty, Edmonds, Blatchford, & Martin, 2001).

TEACHERS' EXPERIENCES WITH CHALLENGING STUDENT BEHAVIORS

Adequate reactions to challenging behaviors of children in preschool settings are among the most important tasks educators need to accomplish in order to establish and maintain a safe learning environment for all children. McCabe and Frede define challenging behavior at the preschool level as "any repeated pattern of behavior that interferes with learning or engagement in social interactions. This includes unresponsiveness to developmentally appropriate guidance and actions such as prolonged tantrums, physical and verbal aggression, disruptive vocal and motor behavior, property destruction, self-injury, noncompliance, and withdrawal" (2007, p. 1). Educators in kindergarten and preschool settings are faced with a wide variety of challenging child behaviors that can be stressful to handle (Abidin, & Robinson, 2002; Dekker, Koot, van-der-Ende, & Verhulst, 2002; Kunz, 2000; Lambert et al., 2006; Male, 2003).

In Germany, increasing concern has been voiced over the number of children in early childhood settings who exhibit challenging behaviors such as not following directions, hitting, biting, temper tantrums, or lack of engagement and social interactions (Sarimsky, 2005).

Challenging behaviors at the preschool age are not only stressors for teachers (Lambert et al., 2006), but they are also predictors of problem behavior in later years, such as antisocial behavior (LaCourse, Côté, Nagin, Vitaro, Brendgen, & Tremblay, 2002). Research has indicated that these behaviors are barriers to the social–emotional development of children and may predict serious conduct disorders such as academic failure and drug abuse (Geiger, 2000; Gresham, Lane, & Lambros, 2000).

Atici (2007) used in-depth interviews with nine student teachers in Turkey prior to and at the end of their student teaching experience and found that teachers used mostly preventive, positive, and less intrusive methods such as nonverbal messages and positive reinforcement. Participants reported an increased sense of efficacy in dealing with problem behaviors over the course of their student teaching experience but also mentioned the need for improvement in instructional strategies. A study in 1999 by the same author found that compared to their Turkish colleagues, British primary school teachers used more systematic behavior management and more preventive approaches like explaining and reminding of classroom rules.

More so than ever and not only in Germany, educators are faced with diverse children. A study by Schreyer and Petermann (2010) examined 188 children from preschools in Bremen and Niedersachsen who were between 44 and 68 months old. Results indicated that children with an immigration background (n=57) displayed more behavior problems than their native peers. Teachers in this study rated hyperactive behaviors higher and pro-social behaviors lower, and parents voiced conflicts with peers more often.

In addition, most teachers have not been trained in how to effectively interact with children with disabilities and developmental delays and to use differentiated strategies to prevent and reduce behavior problems, to increase motivation, and to promote responsible behaviors in children (Baker, 2005; MacDonald, & Speece, 2001; Westling & Theunissen, 2006).

It is clear that handling challenging behaviors can also have an impact on job satisfaction and on perceived levels of stress and strain of early childhood professionals, which includes consequences such as turnover and burnout (Strain & Joseph, 2004) as well as mental health issues (Alkon, Ramler, & MacLennan, 2003).

THE LITERATURE ON STRESS AND COPING

Teaching in general is known as a stressful profession (Kieschke & Schaarschmidt, 2008; Kyriacou, 2001). According to transactional models of stress (Lazarus & Folkman, 1984), occupational and environmental demands can cause stress. If perceived demands outweigh perceived resources for coping, stress responses occur and lead to physiological, behavioral, and psychological stress symptoms (Lazarus & Folkman, 1984; Sapolsky, 1998). Our thoughts about demands impact our perceptions of resources and demands. Kyriacou (2001) distinguishes between stress generated by difficult demands on the teacher (e.g., through disruptive student behavior) and stress related to the individual teacher's self-concept. McCarthy et al. (2002) suggest that preventive coping resources need to be incorporated into the transactional model as identified by Lazarus and Folkman (1984), because such resources allow for control over one's perception of demands as well as the appraisal of one's own capability to cope with those demands.

Challenging student behavior is one of the most frequently reported classroom demands, which potentially produces stress for the teacher. Research has shown a positive relationship between student behavior and teacher burnout (Friedman, 1995; Lambert & McCarthy, 2006), because it prevents teachers from perceiving themselves as effective professionals and from feeling satisfied (Travers & Cooper, 1996).

THE LITERATURE ON BURNOUT

Burnout has been described as a stress-induced phenomenon or reaction (Maslach & Schaufeli, 1993). It can be defined as a specific type of stress or "a response to the chronic emotional strain of dealing extensively with other human beings, particularly when they are troubled or having problems" (Maslach, 1982, p. 3). It is

> a psychological syndrome of emotional exhaustion, depersonalization, and reduced personal accomplishment that can occur among individuals who work with other people in some capacity. Emotional exhaustion refers to feelings of being emotionally overextended and depleted of one's emotional resources. Depersonalization refers to a negative, callous, or excessively detached response to other people, who are usually the recipients of one's services of care. (Maslach, 1993, pp. 20–21)

According to Schaufeli, Maslach, and Marek (1993), reduced personal accomplishment refers to the development of a negative attitude towards one's own work performance, which results in a diminution of mental and physical wellbeing and negatively affects relationships with students and colleagues. Burnout can impact student learning and achievement (Krause, 2003), corrupt the quality of instructional activities, and affect the educational process (Hughes, 2001).

There is also a relationship between challenging student behavior and teacher burnout. Brouwers and Tomic (2000) refer to it as a "self-reinforcing cycle." Children perceive teacher stress and resist efforts to maintain classroom discipline. Also, stressed teachers have less tolerance for challenging behaviors.

SUPPORTING CHILDREN WITH CHALLENGING BEHAVIOR

While teachers can seek professional advice in child development centers (Sozialpädiatrische Zentren), recent research has demonstrated a lack of training and support for teachers of young children with regard to the management of challenging behaviors in Germany (Sarimski, 2005). Preventive strategies include the arrangement of a well-structured and engaging class-room with developmentally appropriate practices, activities, and materials (Alter & Conroy, n.d.; Ratcliff, 2001). Schedules, routines, and rules help children to know what is expected from them. While rules are appropriate for preschool children, younger children benefit more from rituals and routines because they communicate stability and values such as caring or friendship. Rituals can help children during transitions (Ostrosky, Jung, Hemmeter, & Thomas, 2003).

Research has established a link between challenging behavior and low-quality early institutional education (Belsky, 2001; Love et al., 2003). According to Fox, Dunlap, Hemmeter, Joseph, and Strain (2003), high-quality preschool education firstly needs to address the social development of all children as a base tier—for example, through building positive relation-ships (Joseph & Strain, 2004). Second, children at risk for problem be-havior need additional support in social skills and problem-solving skills acquisition. This includes also high-quality adult–child interaction (Dodge & Colker, 2002) and providing children with choices as well as with appeal-ing and well-organized learning centers (Fox et al., 2003). Finally, planned interventions need to be geared towards meeting the needs of children who engage in challenging behaviors (McCabe & Frede, 2007).

POSITIVE BEHAVIOR SUPPORT (PBS)

Dealing with challenging behaviors effectively, in developmentally ap-propriate ways, and using evidence-based practices requires pedagogical knowledge and experience. Establishing a repertoire of behavior support skills is important for teachers because it enables them to provide a frame-work for learning, which supports students in managing themselves and thus reducing teacher stress. Positive behavior support (PBS) is a concept that is effectively used in educational settings and disability services in the United States and Germany (Carr et al., 2002; Clarke, Dunlap, & Stitcher, 2002; Theunissen, 2005).

PBS strategies and interventions are based on research and on human-istic values (Fox et al., 2003). They include environmental arrangement of antecedent stimuli, positive reinforcement, and direct instruction of re-placement behaviors. They are based on person-centered values, scientific principles, and empirical data (Conroy, Dunlap, Clarke, & Alter, 2005). PBS entails reflective practice, a culture of inclusion and respect for the unique-ness of every child and tapping the resources of children, their families, and educators. For example, praising a student who is exhibiting appropri-ate behavior has been identified as an effective positive behavior support strategy for dealing with challenging behavior (see Gokalp, this volume).

The concept of PBS is based on the principles of Applied Behavior Analysis (ABA) (Alberto & Troutman, 2002) and focuses on proactive, positive interventions to prevent challenging behaviors, on individualized support, and on increasing desirable behaviors (Conroy et al., 2005; Safran & Oswald, 2003). Planned PBS interventions begin with a functional analysis of a behavior (FBA) (Hanley, Iwata, & McCord, 2003; Westling & Theunissen, 2006). The antecedents that trigger a certain behavior and consequences to the behavior are assessed by the team as well as parents and family. Based on this assessment, support strategies for teaching new skills (e.g., communication or social skills) are developed (Fox, Dunlap, & Cushing, 2002). In Germany, PBS has only recently received the attention it deserves (Sarimsky, 2005).

Given the growing concern challenging behavior is receiving, early childhood educators are in need of an ongoing support system to help them implement effective behavior support practices (Alkon et al., 2003; Benedict, Horner, & Squires, 2007; Raver, 2002; Strain & Joseph, 2004). There is also a lack of research on young children with challenging behaviors in early childhood settings in Germany (Clarke et al., 2002; OECD, 2004). As Oberhümer (2004) puts it, academic staff at university-level programs for early childhood educators may conduct research in specialist areas; however, professionals with expertise and experience in the field with regard to teaching, supervision, and research are very scarce.

Identifying the nature of challenging behaviors as well as teachers' strategies to handle disruptions in the classroom can contribute to a better understanding of such stress situations. Findings may inform the quality of pre- and in-service programs for professionals in the field of early childhood education. They may also contribute to stronger professional development (Makkonen, 2005; Richin, Banyon, Stein, & Banyon, 2003) and inform teacher pre- and in-service training, which addresses the practical needs of teachers. The purpose of this study is to analyze teacher perceptions of challenging student behavior and the practices teachers implement in their classrooms to minimize disruptions.

METHOD

A survey was administered in person to a sample of 186 early childhood educators from 18 different settings in Baden Württemberg. The surveys were administered at staff meetings by the first author. Participants were given the option to return their survey to the researcher during the meeting or send them to the university. A business reply envelope was provided for this purpose, which ensured anonymity and confidentiality. Data were collected in the fall of 2008.

The questionnaire consists of five parts. The first part includes demographic information, and the second examines incidences and intensity of emotional or behavioral problems. This section asks teachers to indicate the impact the behavior has on them and the atmosphere in their class. When answering these questions, teachers are asked to think of the student with the most challenging behaviors in their class. This part of the questionnaire ends with open-ended questions concerning that specific student. Part three consists of questions related to efficiency in dealing with students, part four looks at interactions with co-workers and administrative support, and part five evaluates teachers' general level of happiness, depression, anxiety, and sleep disturbance over the past weeks. This part of the instrument was developed by Everaert and van der Wolf (2006) at Utrecht University.

The present study focuses on the open-ended questions from part two of the questionnaire concerning a particular student with the most challenging behavior in the classroom. The questions are as follows: (1) Describe the behavior of the student you find most challenging in your class. (2) Why is this behavior the most challenging for you? (3) How, in general, do you handle this student's challenging behavior?

Participants

There were 95.6 % females and 4.4% males. Only 2.7% worked in special education settings. The survey participants had an average of 14.4 years teaching experience and an average of 9.6 years of experience in the current setting. They were between 19 and 59 years old. The average age was 36.5. Group sizes varied from 8 to 39 children with an average number of children of 21.6. Number of children with challenging behaviors varied between 0 and 15 with an average of 3.4 children (see Table 6.1).

TABLE 6.1 Descriptive Statistics for Demographic Information

Variable	%	M	Minimum	Maximum
Gender	Female: 95.6 Male: 4.4			
Age		36.5	19.0	59.0
Years of experience		14.4		
Years of experience in current setting		9.6		
Group size		21.6	8	39
# of children with challenging behaviors		3.4	0	15

Note: n = 186

Data Analysis

Using a software for the analysis of qualitative data (AQUAD), data analysis occurred according to the assumptions of the constant comparative method of grounded theory (Glaser & Strauss, 1967). A total of 689 statements were coded through a process of open coding. Those codes were collapsed through building code catalogs according to the three research questions by grouping related codes.

FINDINGS

1. Teachers' Descriptions of the Most Challenging Student Behaviors

When asked to describe the most challenging behavior they encounter in their class, teachers mentioned a wide range of problem behaviors. Out of 307 coded responses, 165 responses (53.7%) were coded as "disruptive behaviors." Participants reported behaviors like not following directions or rules (45), lack of social skills and/or self-confidence (30), being loud (30), not getting along with others (24), constant attention seeking (20), and seeking adult attention (16) as being the most challenging. Sixty-eight responses (22.1%) were related to "disrespectful behaviors" and comprised physical aggression toward others or materials and argumentative or stubborn behaviors. Forty-eight responses (15.6%) indicated "lack of engagement" behaviors including withdrawal, lack of motivation, and getting distracted easily. Twenty-six responses (8.5%) were coded as "difficulty communicating" and included German language learners (see Table 6.2).

2. Teachers' Reasons for Perceiving Those Behaviors as Challenging or Problematic

Out of a total of 167 coded responses, 52 responses (31.1 9%) described dealing with disruptive behaviors as "frustrating." Concern was reported over having tried many different things but nothing really worked.

TABLE 6.2   Most Challenging Behaviors

Number of Responses[a]	Percentage	Challenging Behavior
165	53.7%	Disruptive behaviors
68	22.1%	Disrespectful behaviors
48	15.6%	Lack of engagement
26	8.5%	Difficulty communicating

[a] $n = 307$

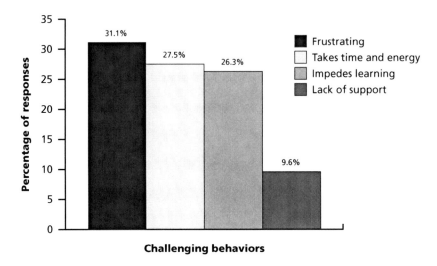

Figure 6.1   Why challenging?

The other two main reasons for concern about problematic student behavior were that having to pay a good amount of attention to just one student takes "time and energy" (46 responses, 27.5%) and that it impedes children's learning (44 responses, 26.3%). Sixteen responses (9.6%) indicated students' family background and a lack of support from home to be problematic (see Figure 6.1).

3. Actions Taken to Handle Challenging Behaviors

A total of 215 codes were given to answers provided to the question about actions that teachers take to handle behavior problems. First, 80 responses (37.2%) described treating children with empathy, patience, respect, and warmth as well as being equally firm and fair as important. This included adopting a positive attitude towards children, establishing relationships with the children, empowering them, and involving them in decisions.

Second, 53 codes (24.7%) referred to consistency with procedures or consequences (e.g., time out, sending the child to the office, or other types of negative reinforcements).

Third, 30 codes (14.0%) included the use of positive behavior support strategies like modeling appropriate behavior, teaching problem solving or conflict resolution skills in social interactions, and positive reinforcement, but also planned ignoring of minor problem behaviors, or proximity control.

Fourth, 28 codes (13.0%) mentioned collaborative strategies, such as communicating with parents or a counseling service, thus seeking support in finding ways to adequately deal with students with challenging behaviors.

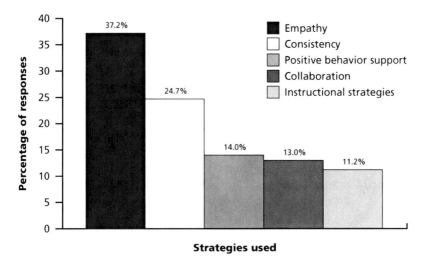

Figure 6.2 Handling challenging behaviors

Fifth, 24 codes (11.2%) referred to the use of instructional strategies such as individualized support (working one on one with a child) to reduce or prevent behavior problems by meeting individual student needs. This included helping a child to explore options, setting goals, considering children's interests, working in small groups, providing choices, and supporting a child's need to express feelings or to communicate (see Figure 6.2).

DISCUSSION

The two main research questions in this study were related to teacher perceptions of type of student behavior and the strategies employed to address them. Consistent with findings from other studies on early childhood educators' perceptions of classroom behavior (Atici, 2007), this study found similar kinds of challenging student behavior. While the types of behavior reported by the teachers in this study may be typical for children in this age group, it is due to their high rate of occurrence that teachers perceive them as stressful and even irritating or at least exhausting. The high occurrence is due to the fact that young children have yet to get used to the expectations related to the role of a student and to being part of a group of children (Geiger, 2000). The two main reasons for teachers' concern about challenging student behavior found in this study were that challenging behaviors interfere with learning and thus with the educators' ability to use their knowledge effectively.

What Teachers Do

Teachers' behavior and the environment they establish are pivotal in promoting learning processes. In order for effective learning processes to occur, educators need to be able to effectively manage challenging child behavior by using preventive strategies (Alter & Conroy, n.d.). In this study, only 11.2% of the responses referred to instructional strategies. Asking for support and collaborative efforts in coping with challenging behaviors were indicated in 13% of the responses. Only 14% of the responses referred to PBS interventions such as environmental arrangement strategies, which are particularly easy to implement in early childhood settings and which are also in line with the emphasis on developmentally appropriate practice in early childhood education (Conroy, Davis, Fox, & Brown, 2002).

Limitations

The early childhood professionals in this study were given the opportunity to comment on three open-ended questions related to problem behavior. Our findings may not accurately reflect their real-world use of strategies used to handle challenging student behaviors. Written responses may not reflect what actually happens in classrooms. Future research should therefore include observational data (Lambert et al., 2006; Teegarden & Burns, 1993). In addition, findings cannot be generalized based on the disadvantages of analyzing singular responses to open-ended questions of a survey instrument. Further research should employ narrative approaches to understanding processes of construction and deconstruction of educators' personal practical knowledge with regard to handling difficult student behavior (Beattie, 1995).

Implications for Future Research

The results of this study provide implications for further research. First, Langfeldt (1992) suggested that the baseline at which a teacher will perceive a certain disruptive behavior in the classroom as problematic varies across cultures. Therefore, it would be interesting to examine teacher perceptions of problem behavior in preschool settings in other countries. Given the social constructivist view of behavior as context-dependent and related to the environmental setting as well as to sociocultural factors, the assumption would be that teachers' perceptions and their management of disruptive student behavior varies.

Second, the impact of personal experiences on teacher beliefs is also an under-researched area that needs further exploration. Assessing teachers' beliefs about the function of problematic student behavior can be important for informing curricular efforts of both pre-service and in-service personnel development programs with regard to effective behavior management strategies (Lovejoy, 1996).

Implications for Practice

A pivotal factor that shapes teachers' beliefs is the quality of pre-service teacher training. Acquiring a repertoire of effective behavior management strategies can help to reduce stress levels in teachers when being confronted with disruptive student behavior. BPS strategies have been proven to be effective with regard to challenging student behavior. Given the support in the literature for the success of positive reinforcement as well as differential reinforcement of alternative behaviors (Alberto & Troutman, 2006), the need for training classroom management strategies is evident if teachers are to cope successfully with challenging student behavior. Better training in this area can potentially reduce stress levels and eventually burnout. It is essential to help teachers to identify causes for difficult student behavior and to assist them in choosing from a variety of possibly useful strategies to use in their classrooms.

Improvement of professional support and in-service training designed to help minimize disruptive influences of problem behaviors on teachers and other students in the classroom is needed. More consultation programs and practice consultants are needed in order to support early childhood teachers to effectively manage challenging behaviors of young children (Alkon et al., 2003; Benedict et al., 2007; OECD, 2004; Raver, 2002).

Given the current reform of the early care and education system in Germany with its lack of personnel and other challenges, the concept of peer-group supervision, a method for the improvement of work-relevant competencies, may be beneficial and a realistic alternative to consultation programs. Implementing peer-group supervision may potentially contribute to stress prevention and health promotion by improving work-related resources such as social support (Zimber & Ullrich, 2011). Most importantly, logistical barriers need to be addressed, especially lack of personnel and sufficient planning time, in order to better support children with challenging behaviors, their families, and early childhood educators.

Experiences from other countries show that teacher quality can be enhanced if experienced professionals provide mentoring and support to beginning teachers to expand their understandings of pedagogy and child development (Kostelnick & Grady, 2009). Finally, systems of self-evaluation can help teachers to increase their skills (Oberhümer, 2004). If teacher satisfaction increases, this may promote higher instructional efficacy, improve student learning, and reduce stress levels in teachers.

REFERENCES

Abidin, R. R., & Robinson, L. L. (2002). Stress, biases, or professionalism: What drives teachers' referral judgments of students with challenging behaviors. *Journal of Emotional and Behavioral Disorders, 10*, 204–212.

Alberto, P. A., & Troutman, A. C. (2006). *Applied behavior analysis for teachers* (7th ed.). Upper Saddle River, NJ: Prentice Hall

Alkon, A., Ramler, M., & MacLennan, K. (2003). Evaluation of mental health consultation in child care centers. *Early Childhood Education Journal, 31*, 91–99.

Alter, P. J., & Conroy, M. A. (n. d.). *Recommended practices.* Preventing challenging behavior in young children: effective practices. Retrieved from http://www.challengingbehavior.org/do/resources/documents/rph_preventing_challenging_behavior.pdf

Atici, M. (2007). A small-scale study on student teachers' perceptions of classroom management and methods for dealing with misbehavior. *Emotional and Behavioral Difficulties, 12*(1), 15–27.

Baker, P. H. (2005). Managing student behavior: How ready are teachers to meet the challenge? *American Secondary Education, 33*(3), 51–64.

Beattie, M. (1995). New prospects for teacher education: Narrative ways of knowing, teaching and teacher learning. *Educational Research, 37*, 53–70.

Belsky, J. (2001). Developmental risks (still) associated with early child care. *Journal of Child Psychology and Psychiatry, 42*, 845–859.

Benedict, E. A., Horner, R. H., & Squires, J. K. (2007). Assessment and implementation of positive behavior support in preschools. *TECSE, 27*(3), 174–192.

Bertelsmann-Stiftung. (2010). *State by State: Monitoring Early Childhood Education.* Retrieved from http://www.bertelsmann-stiftung.de/cps/rde/xchg/SID-4F37F0DE-0840416F/bst_engl/hs.xsl/93540_93551.htm

Brouwers, A., & Tomic, W. (2000). A longitudinal study on teacher burnout and perceived self-efficacy in classroom management. *Teaching and Teacher Education, 16*(2), 239–254.

Carr, E. G., Dunlap, G., Horner, R. H., Koegel, R. L., Turnbull, A. P., Sailor, W., . . . , Fox, L. (2002). Positive behavior support: Evolution of an applied science. *Journal of Positive Behavior Intervention, 4*, 4–16.

Clarke, S., Dunlap, G., & Stitcher, J. P. (2002). Twenty years of intervention research in emotional and behavioral disorders: A descriptive analysis and a comparison with research in developmental disabilities. *Behavior Modification, 25*, 659–683.

Conroy, M. A., Davis, C. A., Fox, J. J., & Brown, W. H. (2002). Functional assessment of behavior and effective supports for young children with challenging behavior. *Assessment for Effective Instruction, 27*, 35–47.

Conroy, M. A., Dunlap, G., Clarke, S., & Alter, P. J. (2005). A descriptive analysis of positive behavioral intervention research with young children with challenging behavior. *Topics in Early Childhood Special Education, 25*(3), 157–166.

Dekker, M. C., Koot, H. M., van-der-Ende., J., & Verhulst, F. C. (2002). Emotional and behavioral problems in children and adolescents with and without intellectual disability. *Journal of Child Psychology and Psychiatry and Allied Disciplines. 43*(8), 1087–1098.

Deutsches PISA-Konsortium (Hrsg.) (2001). *PISA 2000. Basiskompetenzen von Schülerinnen und Schülern im internationalen Vergleich.* (PISA 2000. Basic competencies of students in an international comparison). Opladen: Leske und Budrich.

Deutsche Welle. (2005). *Germany to reform pre-school education.* Retrieved from http://www.dw-world.de/dw/article/0,,1690133,00.html

Dodge, D. T., & Colker, L. (2002). *The creative curriculum.* Washington, DC: Teaching Strategies.

Everaert, H. A., & Wolf, K. C. van der (2006). *Teachers and students. A questionnaire for teachers about students with emotional or behavioral problems.* Utrecht, Netherlands: University of Professional Education Utrecht.

Fox, D. T., Dunlap, G., & Cushing, L. (2002). Early intervention, positive behavior support, and transition to school. *Journal of Emotional and Behavioral Disorders, 10*(3), 149–157.

Fox, L., Dunlap, G., Hemmeter, M. L., Joseph, G. E., & Strain, P. S. (2003). The teaching pyramid. A model for supporting social competence and preventing challenging behavior in young children. *Young Children, 58*(4), 48–52.

Krause, A. (2003). Bedingungsbezogene Analyse psychischer Belastungen von Lehrerinnen und Lehrern. Zur Validität eines neuen Untersuchungskonzepts. *Wirtschaftspsychologie, 5,* 132–134.

Friedman, I. A. (1995). Student behavior patterns contributing to teacher burnout. *The Journal of Educational Research, 88*(5), 281–289.

Geiger, B. (2000). Discipline in K through 8th grade classrooms. *Education, 121,* 383–393.

Glaser, B., & Strauss, A. (1967). *The discovery of grounded theory: Strategies for qualitative research.* Chicago, IL: Aldine.

Gresham, F. M., Lane, K. L, & Lambros, K. M. (2000). Comorbidity of conduct problems and ADHD: Identification of 'fledgling psychopaths.' *Journal of Emotional and Behavioral Disorders, 8,* 83–93.

Hanley, G. P., Iwata, B. A., & McCord, B. E. (2003). Functional analysis of problem behavior: A review. *Journal of Applied Behavior Analysis, 36,* 147–185.

Hughes, R. E. (2001). Deciding to leave but staying: Teacher burnout, precursors and turnover. *International Journal of Human Resource Management, 12*(2), 288–298.

Joseph, G. E., & Strain, P. S. (2004). Building positive relationships with young children. *Young Exceptional Children, 7*(4), 21–29.

Kieschke, U., & Schaarschmidt, U. (2008). Professional commitment and health among teachers in Germany: A typological approach. *Learning and Instruction, 18,* 429–437.

Kostelnick, M. J. & Grady, M. L. (2009). *Getting it right from the start: The principal's guide to early childhood education.* Thousand Oaks, CA: Corwin Press.

Kunz, T. (2000). Wie belastend ist Erziehen? *Theorie und Praxis der Sozialen Arbeit, 39,* 4–6.

Kyriacou, C. (2001). Teacher stress: Directions for future research. *Educational Review, 53*(1), 27–35.

LaCourse, F., Côté, S., Nagin, D. S., Vitaro, F., Brendgen, M., & Tremblay, R. F. (2002). A longitudinal–experimental approach to testing theories of antisocial behavior development. *Development and Psychopathology, 14*(4), 909–924.

Lambert, R. G., & McCarthy, C. J. (2006). *Understanding teacher stress in an age of accountability.* Greenwich, CT: Information Age Publishing.

Lambert, R., O'Donnell, M., Kusherman, J., & McCarthy, C. J. (2006). Teacher stress and classroom structural characteristics in preschool settings. In R. Lambert & C. McCarthy (Eds.), *Understanding teacher stress in an age of accountability* (pp. 105–120). Greenwich, CT: Information Age Publishing.

Langfeldt, H. P. (1992). Teachers' perceptions of problem behaviour: A cross-cultural study between Germany and South Korea. *British Journal of Educational, 62,* 217–224.

Lazarus, R. S., & Folkman, S. (1984). *Stress, appraisal, and coping.* New York, NY: Springer.

Love, J. M., Harrison, L., Sagi-Schwartz, A., van IJzendoorn, M. H., Ross, C., Ungerer, J. A.,..., Chazan-Cohen, R. (2003). Child care quality matters: How conclusions may vary with context. *Child Development, 74*(4), 1021–1033.

Lovejoy, M. C. (1996). Social inferences regarding inattentive, overactive, and aggressive behavior and their effects on teacher reports of discipline. *Journal of Clinical Child Psychology, 25,* 33–42.

MacDonald, V., & Speece, D. L. (2001). Making time: A teacher's report of her first year of teaching children with emotional disorders. *Journal of Special Education, 35,* 84–91.

Makkonen, R. (2005). Taking care of novice teachers. In C. Chauncey (Ed.), *Recruiting, retaining, and supporting highly qualified teachers* (pp. 55–63). Cambridge, MA: Harvard Education Press.

Male, D. (2003). Challenging behavior: The perceptions of teachers of children and young people with severe learning disabilities. *Journal of Research in Special Educational Needs, 3,* 162–171.

Maslach, C. (1982). *Burnout: The cost of caring.* Englewood Cliffs, NJ: Prentice-Hall.

Maslach, C., & Schaufeli, W. B. (1993). Historical and conceptual development of burnout. In W. B. Schaufeli, C. Maslach, & T. Marek (Eds.), *Professional burnout: Recent developments in theory and research* (pp. 1–16). Washington, DC: Taylor & Francis.

McCabe, L. A., & Frede, E. C. (2007). *Challenging behaviors and the role of preschool education.* Retrieved from http://nieer.org/resources/policybriefs/16.pdf

Moriarty, V., Edmonds, S., Blatchford, P., & Martin, C. (2001). Teaching young children: Perceived satisfaction and stress. *Educational Research, 43*(1), 33–46.

Oberhümer, P. (2004). Controversies, chances, and challenges: Reflections on the quality debate in Germany. *Early Years, 24*(1), 9–21,

OECD. (2004). *Early childhood education and care policy in the Federal Republic of Germany.* Retrieved from http://www.oecd.org/dataoecd/42/1/33978768.pdf

Ostrosky, M. M., Jung, E. Y., Hemmeter, M. L., & Thomas, D. (2003). *Helping children understand routines and schedules.* Center on the Social and Emotional Foundations for Early Learning. Retrieved from http://csefel.vanderbilt.edu/kits/wwbtk3.pdf

Ratcliff, N. (2001). Use the environment to prevent discipline problems and support learning. *Young Children, 56/5,* 84–87.

Raver, C. C. (2002). Emotions matter: Making the case for the role of young children's emotional development for early school readiness. *Social Report Policy, 16*(3), 3–18.

Richin, R., Banyon, R., Stein, R., & Banyon, F. (2003). *Induction: Connecting teacher recruitment to retention.* Thousand Oaks, CA: Corwin.

Safran, S. P., & Oswald, K. (2003). Positive behavior support: Can schools reshape disciplinary practices? *Exceptional Children, 69,* 361–373.

Sapolsky, R. M. (1998). *Why zebras don't get ulcers: An updated guide to stress, stressrelated diseases, and coping.* New York: W. H. Freeman.

Sarimsky, K. (2005). Zum Beratungsauftrag der Sozialpädiatrischen Zentren. Fallbeispiele, Chancen und Grenzen der Beratung für Schüler mit geistiger Behinderung und herausforderndem Verhalten. *Geistige Behinderung, 44*(4), 286–308.

Schaufeli, W. B., Maslach, C., & Marek, T. (1993). *Professional burnout. Recent developments in theory and research.* Levittown: Taylor & Francis.

Schreyer, I., & Petermann, U. (2010). Verhaltensauffälligkeiten und Lebensqualität bei Kindern im Vorschulalter und deren Mütter. Ein Vergleich von Kindern mit und ohne Migrationshintergrund. [Behavior problems and quality of life in preschool children and their mothers: Comparing native children and children of immigrant families]. *Zeitschrift für Gesundheitspsychologie, 18*(3), 119–129.

Strain, P. S., & Joseph, G. (2004). Engaged supervision to support recommended practices for young children with challenging behavior. *Topics in Early Childhood Special Education, 24*(1), 39–50.

Teegarden, L. A., & Burns, L. G. (1993). Construct validity of the Sutter-Eyberg Student Behavior Inventory (SESBI): Relation between teacher perception of disruptive behavior and direct observation of problem classroom behavior over a seven-month period. *Child and Family Behavior Therapy, 15,* 43–58.

Theunissen, G. (2005). *Pädagogik bei geistiger Behinderung und Verhaltensauffälligkeiten.* Bad Heilbrunn, Germany: Klinkhardt.

Travers, C. J., & Cooper, C. L. (1996). *Teachers under pressure: Stress in the teaching profession.* London: Routledge.

Westling, D., & Theunissen, G. (2006). Positive Verhaltensunterstützung—Positive behavior support. Ein US-amerikanisches Konzept zum Umgang mit Menschen mit geistiger Behinderung und herausfordernden Verhaltensweisen. *Geistige Behinderung, 45*(4), 296–308.

Zimber, A., & Ullrich, A. (2012). Wie wirkt sich die Teilnahme an kollegialer Beratung auf die Gesundheit aus? Ergebnisse einer Interventionsstudie in der Psychiatriepflege [The impact of peer-group supervision on health outcomes: results of an intervention study in a psychiatric hospital]. *Zeitschrift für Gesundheitspsychologie* [German Journal of Health Psychology], *20*(2), 80–91.

CHAPTER 7

WASHINGTON STATE ELEMENTARY TEACHERS' STRESS

The Importance of Occupational Commitment

Gordon S. Gates and Effie Dean
Washington State University

ABSTRACT

The chapter presents findings from research conducted to partially replicate an earlier study carried out by Jepson and Forrest (2006). Our purpose was to examine perceived stress and the nature of its relationship with variables assessing personality traits and background characteristics using data gathered from a sample of 90 elementary teachers in Washington State. Respondents were teaching in 61 schools from across the state. Our data suggested that elementary teachers in Washington are at risk given elevated stress levels. The teachers who responded to our invitation also reported high levels of commitment and internal locus of control. Both of these personality factors were observed to moderate stress. Further, teachers who are women tended to report higher stress levels than those who are men. Our model explained 30% of these teachers' self-reported stress.

International Perspectives on Teacher Stress, pages 139–153
Copyright © 2012 by Information Age Publishing
139

Teaching is noted as being one of the more stressful professions (Borg, 1990; Kieschke & Schaarschmidt, 2008; Kyriacou, 2001). Stress, as defined by Folkman (1984), is "a relationship between the person and the environment that is appraised by the person as taxing or exceeding his or her resources and as endangering his or her well-being" (p. 840). Studies reveal that high and prolonged levels of stress contribute to poor health and lower work performance (Beehr & Newman, 1978; Cohen, Janicki-Deverts, & Miller, 2007; Furnham, 1992; Ganster & Schaubroeck, 1991; Sethi & Schuler, 1984). Burnout is the syndrome identified as resulting from chronic stress with its associated dimensions of emotional exhaustion, depersonalization, and lack of personal accomplishment (Maslach, 2003). Teacher stress and burnout is found associated with turnover and poor retention of those new to the profession (Norton, 2002; Pei & Guoli, 2007) as well as low job satisfaction and poor performance in the classroom (Klassen, 2010; Klusmann, Kunter, Trautwein, Ludtke, & Baumert, 2008; McCormick, 1997). Teacher turnover has been found to cost districts between \$5,000 and \$18,000 per teacher (Barnes, Crowe, & Schaefer, 2007), not to mention its negative impact on faculty morale and student achievement. Many scholars attribute the elevated stress levels observed for educators as arising from increasing demands and constrained resources evident in the public schools (Bakkar, Hakanen, Demerouti, & Xanthopolou, 2007; Conley & You, 2009; Lambert, McCarthy, O'Donnell, & Wang, 2009).

Demerouti, Bakker, Nachreiner, and Schaufeli (2001) defined the concepts of job demands and job resources and discussed how each contributes to stress. Job demands include those physical, social, or organizational aspects of employment that require sustained physical or mental effort and that incur physiological and psychological costs. Job resources refer to physiological, psychological, social, or organizational aspects that support individuals in carrying out their work. Examples of physical demands in teaching include long hours and heavy workloads (e.g., Conley & You, 2009; McCormick, 1997). Social demands include high expectations, diminished respect, and declining autonomy (e.g., Zurlo, Pes, & Cooper, 2007), particularly evident in recent educational accountability policies (Mabry & Margolis, 2006). Student behavior problems and administrivia have been identified as important sources of stress for teachers too (e.g., Everaert & van de Wolf, 2007; Klassen, 2010; Lambert, McCarthy, O'Donnell, & Melendres, 2007).

Resources form the second part of the stress equation and occupy the role of buffer (Xanthopoulou et al., 2007). Resources or supports for teachers include engaging in physical exercise and relaxation in or out of school (Blair, Collingwood, Reynolds, Smith, Hagan, & Sterling, 1984; Carson, Baumgartner, Matthews, & Tsouloupas, 2010; Hamann & Gordon, 2000). Professional training has also been shown to moderate stress levels of teachers (Zembylas & Papanstasious, 2005). Further, teachers who were empowered to make professional, organizational, and instructional decisions were more satisfied with their jobs than those who worked in schools where such activities were restricted, which suggests that these too are important job resources (Davis & Wilson, 2000; Kahn, Schneider, Jenkins-Henkelman, & Moyle, 2006; Pearson & Hall, 1993).

Lambert et al. (2009) studied 521 elementary teachers and reported the correlation of –.27 between job demands and resources to validate the independence of these constructs. In addition, they found that teachers reported higher stress when they perceived an imbalance in favor of job demands, which was the hypothesized direction. The model of stress advanced in this research gives attention to the interdependence of the two constructs that result in stress and predicts key features of that experience for individuals (Halbesleben & Buckley, 2004). After performing a meta-analysis of findings from 65 studies conducted in various countries from 1998 to 2003, Montgomery and Rupp (2005) concluded "that the subjectively perceived quality of the environment [i.e., demands] and the support structures [i.e., resources] available to individual teachers, both at home and at work, are important for dealing with stressful situations" (p. 479).

The nature of occupational demands and available resources as they contribute to stress has been the focus of research over the past few decades, whereas the relationship between stress and personality has only recently come under scrutiny. Funder (2010) defined personality as being "an individual's characteristic patterns of thought, emotions, and behavior, together with the psychological mechanisms—hidden or not—behind those patterns" (p. 5). Montgomery and Rupp's (2005) meta-analysis examined the personality variables of personal drive, attitude, and Type A behavior. They concluded that "personality mediators were generally relatively highly correlated with other components within the stress cycle" (p. 481). More recently, Alarcon, Eschleman, and Bowling (2009) meta-analyzed 121 studies that measured the following personality variables: self-esteem, self-efficacy, locus of control, emotional stability, extraversion, conscientiousness, agreeableness, positive affectivity, negative affectivity, optimism, proactive personality, and hardiness. Thus, it is not the case of there having been no attention to personality by researchers, it is rather that growth in this field has been exponential as many new constructs and traits have been identified that may better explain differences in how individuals come to perceive and experience stress. What researchers are endeavoring to understand is how individuals can be exposed to many of the same job demands and resources yet not experience similar levels of stress (Parkes, 1994; Travers & Cooper, 1996).

In addition to personality, researchers are interested in background characteristics of individuals as they relate to reported or observed stress.

Background characteristics include variables such as gender, age, ethnicity, and so on. Montgomery and Rupp (2005) found little evidence of differences between the sexes, years of experience, and educational qualifications in their meta-analysis, but many researchers continue to find evidence for such relationships (Klusmann et al., 2008). Klassen (2010) reported that of the 951 teachers in his sample, women scored significantly higher on stress than men (i.e., gender, $\lambda = .98$, $F(5, 943) = 3.54$, $p = .009$). Follow-up analysis revealed differences by gender for both stress from student behavior ($d = .26$) and stress from workload ($d = .27$). Contradictory findings such as these suggest further study remains warranted.

THE STUDY

Environmental factors (i.e., job demands and resources) have been the focus of stress research, leading to calls for increased attention to personality factors and background characteristics for understanding variability in the perception or experience of work-related stress. Individuals interested in teacher stress have responded by undertaking studies that add or focus on personality traits and individual characteristics (Conley & You, 2009; Jepson & Forrest, 2006; Kahn et al., 2006). In light of the new direction taken in teacher stress research and contradictory findings evident in the larger literature on burnout, advice by Shaver and Norton (1980) to educational researchers appears particularly relevant. Shaver and Norton emphasized the importance of replication as a strategy as for assessing the nature of effects, as repeated studies facilitate analysis of "systematic variation of potentially threatening external factors... [and] the conditions under which results will hold" (p. 10).

The present study provides a partial replication of Jepson and Forrest's (2006) nonrandom sample of 95 UK teachers, which explored Type A behavior, achievement striving, occupational commitment, gender, years of experience, school level (primary/secondary), and degree of employment (part-time/full-time) as contributing to stress. Except for school level, their study included no environmental variables. Jepson and Forrest found that occupational commitment possessed the largest percentage of variance explained with a partial standardized coefficient of −59 ($t = -7.4$, $p = .00$), followed by achievement striving with a coefficient of .31 ($t = 3.5$, $p = .00$) and a coefficient of .26 ($t = 3.1$, $p = .00$) for Type A behavior. Many view Type A behavior, achievement striving, and locus of control as overlapping constructs (Bachkirova, 2005; Ward & Eisler, 1987). Alarcon et al. (2009) found locus of control related more consistently than Type A behavior to the three burnout dimensions. The purpose of our study, therefore, was to assess the contribution of personality factors (i.e., locus of control and occupational commitment) and personal characteristics (i.e., gender and years of experience) on perceived stress for a representative sample of elementary teachers in Washington State.

METHODS

In 2008–2009, the year of the study, there were 1,077 regular non-alternative elementary schools in Washington that housed some configuration of pre-kindergarden to 6th grade and included the 4th grade. School data were downloaded from the School Report Card website, which is maintained by the Office of the Superintendent for Public Instruction (OSPI). School level variables reported by OSPI used in the study included district number, building number, grade levels, total student enrollment, percent of students qualified for free and reduced price meals, percent of students per ethnic category (i.e., Asian, Black, Hispanic, and White), percent of students by program (i.e., bilingual and special education), students per classroom teacher, and percent of students passing the 4th grade Washington Assessment of Student Learning (WASL) for the three subjects of reading, mathematics, and writing. The 4th grade student performance on reading was employed to stratify schools into quartiles, and 25 campuses from each quadrant were randomly selected from the population of schools.

Teacher emails from each of the 100 schools selected were gathered and 380 were randomly selected. Four or five teachers were chosen from each campus. Dillman's (2007) Tailored Design Method was followed for surveying teachers. The names and email addresses of the selected teachers were entered into the Skylight Matrix Survey System. Teachers were sent a pre-notification message via email and later a message with the URL for the survey embedded in the body of the text. Two follow-up messages were sent, which thanked those who had responded and repeated the invitation to participate to those who had not. A total of 90 teachers completed the survey, which represented a 24% response rate. Those who responded were found to teach in 61 of the 100 schools sampled. The instruments included in the survey were the Perceived Stress Survey (PSS-10) (Cohen & Janicki-Deverts, in press), the Teacher Occupational Commitment Scale (TOCS) (Jepson & Forrest, 2006), and the Work Locus of Control Scale (WLOCS) (Spector, 1988). The demographic questions of years of experience and gender were asked as final questions.

Cohen and Janicki-Deverts (in press) present data from 26 years of research that used the Perceived Stress Scale (PSS-10) with U.S. samples. The scale was originally developed with 14 items, but has been simplified to become a widely used measure of stress (Cohen, Kamarack, & Mermeistein, 1983). The 10 items employ a Likert scale ranging from 0 = *never*, 1 = *almost never,* 2 = *sometimes,* 3 = *fairly often,* and 4 = *very often.* As examples, questions ask "In the last month, how often have you been upset because of something that happened unexpectedly?" and "In the last month, how often have you felt nervous and 'stressed'?" PSS-10 items also include reversed coded responses to four positively stated items (i.e., items 4, 5, 7, and 8) to protect against and check results for response bias. A cumulative score is generated for the PSS-10. Cohen and Janicki-Deverts (in press) report norms for specific demographic groups for the 2009 data that ranged from 11.1 to 19.1 (*SD* varying from 6.8 to 8.2). The 1,704 White Americans who were surveyed in 2009 possessed a mean of 15.7 (*SD* = 7.5). Respondent scores for this study were examined using Cronbach's alpha and a value of $\alpha = .87$ was calculated, which suggests adequate internal consistency.

Jepson and Forrest (2006) developed the Teacher Occupational Commitment Scale (TOCS). It includes six items that are Likert-type with 1 = *strongly disagree* to 5 = *strongly agree.* An example of one of the items, "I am satisfied in my position as a teacher." UK teachers scored on average 23 (*SD* = 4). Cronbach's alpha was calculated for data gathered for this study, and a value of $\alpha = .86$ was observed.

The final instrument to be discussed is the Work Locus of Control Scale (WLOC), which was created by Spector in 1988. The 16 items employ a Likert scale to assess generalized control beliefs in work settings with a range of 1 = *disagree very much* through 6 = *agree very much.* Items 5, 6, 8, 9, 10, 12, 13, and 16 require reverse scoring. An example of the questions asked on the inventory includes, "On most jobs, people can pretty much accomplish whatever they set out to accomplish." The WLOC has been found to correlate significantly with job satisfaction, intention of quitting, perceived influence at work, role stress and perceptions of supervisory style (Spector, 1988). Previous studies suggest an average score of 38 with a standard deviation of 9.6. Cronbach's alpha was calculated for the scores of the 90 elementary teachers who returned their surveys. The responses were found to be internally consistent (i.e., $\alpha = .83$).

The descriptive analysis began by computing measures of central tendency and variability for each level of state, sample, and respondent campuses using the school level variables of total enrollment, students per teacher, percent of students qualified for free and reduced price meals (LSES), percent of students classified as White, percent of students by program (i.e., bilingual and special education), and percent of students passing the 4th grade WASL in reading, mathematics, and writing. Next, total scores were calculated for the three inventories (i.e., PSS-10, TOCS, and WLOCS) and measures of central tendency and variability for each of the items and total scores were calculated. Gender and years of service were also included in this analysis.

Multilevel modeling could not be performed given the limited size of the sample and lack of nested responses. Therefore, multiple regression procedures were employed to examine the contribution of the variables assessing personality traits and background characteristics on the measure of perceived stress. Specifically, the four independent variables of occupational commitment, locus of control, gender, and years of experience were entered into a regression model to determine the nature of each variables contribution on the dependent variable of perceived stress. The ratio of subjects to independent variables was maintained at 20–1 fulfilling one assumption of regression. The variance inflation factor (VIF) was calculated for each variable in the model to examine the assumption of multicollinearity. Further, scatter plots of the residuals by observed scores on the dependent variable were generated to assess normalcy, linearity, and homogeneity of variance. In both analyses, no violations were apparent.

RESULTS

Sixty-one of the 100 schools sampled employed at least one teacher who responded to the survey. The 90 respondents were examined by their school's student performance quartile, which revealed no discernable pattern. Each quartile was equally represented. The results of the study continue to an examination of the descriptive data for the schools and respondents. The regression analysis follows, which investigated the relationship between the dependent variable of teacher perceived stress and independent variables that assessed environmental factors, personality traits, and background characteristics.

Descriptive Analysis

The school-level data provided by the Office of Superintendent for Public Instruction (OSPI) were analyzed to understand the school contexts of the respondents. Measures of central tendency and variability were calculated on student enrollment and achievement data for the 1,077 regular non-alternative elementary schools in the state, the 100 schools sampled, and the 61 schools that had one or more respondents as shown on Tables 7.1 and 7.2, respectively. If a school had more than one respondent, its scores on the school level data were counted only once. The comparison of student enrollment and achievement data suggest that respondents' were teaching in elementary schools that are fairly representative of those found across the State of Washington. Teachers were working in schools that on average had 450 students. The majority of students in these schools were

TABLE 7.1   School Enrollment

Students	State N = 1,077 μ	Sample n = 100 M	SD	Responded n = 61 M	SD
Total enrollment	418	439	140	454	140
Students per teacher	16	16	2	16	2
Percent LSES	40	42	23	42	23
Percent White	64	67	22	68	24
Percent bilingual	8	11	13	11	13
Percent special education	13	13	4	14	5

TABLE 7.2   School Achievement for the 4th Grade

Percent of students	State N = 1,077 μ	Sample n = 100 M	SD	Responded n = 61 M	SD
Passing reading	73	72	6	72	6
Passing math	52	58	5	51	5
Passing writing	60	61	7	61	7

classified as White (i.e., 68%) and almost half (i.e., 42%) were qualified as low socioeconomic status (LSES). The standard deviations on the variables pertaining to enrollment and achievement suggest the schools of respondents captured the variability present in elementary schools across the state.

Seventy-six of the teachers who responded identified as female and 13 as male. One teacher did not answer the question. Therefore, 84% or a large majority of the study's subjects were female, which reflects the distribution of gender for elementary teachers in the state. The analysis of subject responses to the second demographic question revealed a mean of 16.6 years of teaching ($SD = 10$).

The Perceived Stress Scale (PSS-10) asked respondents to identify the frequency with which they experienced particular emotions during the past month for each item. The items are listed from highest average score to lowest on Table 7.3. The item receiving the highest score pertained to feeling nervous or stressed, which subjects recorded on average as *sometimes*. On this item a mean of 2.4 ($SD = .9$) was observed. The second most frequent indicator of stress was being upset because of an unexpected event, which was also rated *sometimes* and possessed a mean of 1.9 ($SD = .7$). The items that contributed least to their stress scores were those of controlling irritations and feeling confident about handling problems. The average total score of 16.9 ($SD = 5.9$) was calculated for respondents. This mean suggests that as a group the teachers were experiencing elevated stress levels,

TABLE 7.3 PSS Item Analysis (*n* = 90)

In the last month, how often have you . . .	M	SD	Mode
Felt nervous and "stressed"?	2.4	0.9	sometimes
Been upset because of something unexpected?	1.9	0.7	sometimes
Been angered by things outside your control?	1.8	0.8	sometimes
Felt unable to control the important things in your life?	1.8	0.7	sometimes
Felt could not cope with all the things to do?	1.8	0.9	sometimes
Felt that you were on top of things?	1.6	1.1	sometimes
Felt difficulties were piling up not overcome them?	1.6	0.8	sometimes
Felt that things were going your way?	1.6	0.9	sometimes
Been able to control irritations in your life?	1.4	0.7	sometimes
Felt confident to handle your personal problems?	1.3	0.7	very often

which is similar to that observed in previous studies on educators (Jepson & Forrest, 2006; Kahn et al., 2006; Klassen, 2010; Klusmann et al., 2008; Zurlo et al., 2007).

The question on the Teachers Occupational Commitment Scale (TOCS) with the highest mean (4.7) was "I would say that I am a conscientious teacher," while the item with the lowest mean (3.9) was "I often think about leaving the teaching profession." Table 7.4 provides the item analysis for the sample. The average score of 25.7 (*SD* = 4.0) by teachers suggests a high level of occupational commitment. These levels are comparable to those observed in Jepson and Forrest's study (i.e., *M* = 23.3, *SD* = 4.0) for their sample of British educators.

The teacher responses from the WLOCS are shown in Table 7.5. The two items that respondents scored highest were "A job is what you make of it" (*agree very much*) and "In order to get a really good job, you need to have family members or friends in high places" (*disagree moderately*). The least agreed with item was, "Most employees have more influence on their supervisors than they think they do." The scores ranged from 16–96, and the mean was 72.6 (*SD* = 11.2). This average score is more than two stan-

TABLE 7.4 TOCS Item Analysis (*n* = 90)

Question	M	SD	Mode
Conscientious teacher	4.7	0.5	strongly agree
Committed to job	4.5	0.7	strongly agree
Enjoy job	4.4	0.7	strongly agree
Satisfied as a teacher	4.3	0.8	strongly agree
Content with position	4.1	0.9	agree
Think about leaving the profession	3.9	1.1	disagree

TABLE 7.5   WLOCS Item Analysis (*n* = 90)

Question	M	SD	Mode
A job is what you make of it	5.3	0.8	agree very much
Good job family members or friends in high places	5.2	3.9	disagree moderately
Most people are capable of doing their jobs	5.0	0.8	agree moderately
Luck to be an outstanding employee	4.9	1.1	disagree slightly
People can accomplish whatever they set out	4.9	0.7	agree moderately
Luck is the main difference for making money	4.9	1.1	disagree moderately
Who you know is more important than what you know	4.9	1.2	disagree moderately
Promotions are usually a matter of good fortune	4.6	1.0	disagree moderately
You can find a job that gives what you want	4.6	0.9	agree moderately
Getting the job you want is mostly a matter of luck	4.5	1.3	disagree slightly
Making money is primarily a matter of good fortune	4.5	1.0	disagree moderately
Promotions are given to employees who perform well	4.4	0.9	agree slightly
If employees are unhappy they should do something	4.3	0.9	agree very much
To make a lot of money you have to know people	4.3	1.2	disagree moderately
People who perform well generally get rewarded	3.9	1.1	agree slightly
Employees influence supervisors more than thin	3.4	1.1	agree moderately

dard deviations above the mean observed in previous studies. The teacher responses identify a high internal locus of control for this sample.

Regression Analysis

Using data gathered from all teacher respondents, the results of the regression model suggest that three of the four independent variables were statistically significant, as shown on Table 7.6. Table 7.6 presents the observed standardized partial regression coefficients for each personality trait and background characteristic entered into the model, as well as the observed t scores, probabilities, and variance inflation factor (VIF) scores. The value of R = .54 ($F = 8.9$, $p = .000$) was calculated for this model, along with

TABLE 7.6   Predicting Teacher Stress Using Personality and Background Characteristics (*n* = 90)

Independent variables	β	T	p	VIF
Occupational commitment	−.33	−3.1	.00	1.3
Locus of control	−.25	−2.4	.02	1.2
Gender	.22	2.4	.02	1.3
Years of experience	−.05	−0.5	.63	1.0

$R^2 = .30$ and 5.0 as the standard error of the estimate. Thirty percent of the variability in teacher stress was accounted for, with occupational commitment explaining the largest unique effect followed by locus of control and gender. These findings suggest that higher occupational commitment moderated the stress reported by teachers. Individuals who scored higher on locus of control also reported lower stress levels. Women teachers reported higher levels of stress $M = 17.2$ ($SD = 5$) as compared to the men $M = 13.9$ ($SD = 6$). Years of experience teaching was not statistically significant.

The bivariate correlations were examined between years of experience and the other independent variables. None of the relationships evidenced statistical or practical significance. Occupational commitment and locus of control were found to possess 21% shared variance (p= .000), which was the largest bivariate correlation generated through the regression procedures.

LIMITATIONS

The threat to our findings that is most problematic pertains to the possibility of response bias. Three hundred and eighty teachers were included in the sample, which was sent out via internet mail. Ninety teachers responded, or 24% of those contacted. This low response rate may in part be attributable to the use of email, but it is not possible to determine what impact the lack of response had in terms of the generalizability of our results to elementary teachers across the state. What was encouraging, however, was the distribution of teachers who responded across the sampled schools. One hundred schools were randomly selected to create a representative sample of the 1,077 regular non-alternative elementary schools in the state. Teachers who responded were employed one of 61 of these campuses. Examination of the school-level data for the respondents clearly matched the state averages on the observed measures. A further downside of the poor response was the impact it had on the number of responses per campus. We were unable to assess a nested model of stress by teachers within schools, which would better assess the environmental context in which they worked as related to stress.

Supporting our concerns about the representativeness of the sample is the average years of experience observed for the sample. While it is true that teaching is a gray profession, the average of 16 years teaching is higher than would be expected. Our results are probably more applicable to older, more seasoned educators than those who have just entered the profession.

Lastly, the study employed a correlation design for gathering and analyzing data. The cross-sectional sampling inhibits any interpretation of causality. It could be that the observed relationships discussed in the regression model occurred as lower stress levels contributed to higher levels of commitment and enhanced feelings of internal locus of control rather than the other way around. Only for the variable gender is the direction not subject to question. It is not the case, however, that gender causes stress. Gender provides a place-holder for social expectations and other norms and values evident in society that produce the experience of stress. The specification of independent and dependent variables in this study is subject to further study.

CONCLUSION

Although research has substantiated that teaching is a highly stressful occu-pation, not all teachers perceive or experience the imbalance between their job demands and resources as stressful. This study sought to explain the variability in perceived levels of teacher stress for a sample of elementary teachers in Washington State. The results from this investigation suggest that elementary teachers in Washington are at risk given elevated stress lev-els. The teachers who participated in the study also reported being highly committed to the profession and exhibited a high internal locus of control. Both of the assessed personality variables were observed to moderate per-ceived stress. Further, teachers who are women tended to report higher stress levels than those who are men. Our model was able to explain 30% of the self-reported stress for the 90 teachers who responded to the survey.

Given the response rate by teachers, we were unable to assess the school level or environmental variables as contributing to these teachers' percep-tion of stress. We encourage future research to include measures of these variables and compare the contribution of each type of factor (i.e., environ-mental, personality, and characteristics) on stress. Securing an adequate sample size and response rate is necessary.

Our research findings are comparable to those evident in Jepson and Forrest's (2006) study that was conducted in Britain. The low response rate we obtained makes our sample more similar to a convenience sample; how-ever, data on the 61 schools of our respondents suggests that that at least at this level there is some claim to representativeness. Although Jepson and Forrest were able to account for 53% of the variance in teacher stress, both studies found teacher commitment to provide the largest, unique percent-age of explained variance. And for teachers in both samples, commitment moderated stress. Our results suggest that school administrators would do well to attend to ways of maintaining or, if appropriate, fostering teacher commitment. Teacher recognition, professional development, professional learning communities, and so on are identified as programs and practices that with little investment provide critical support for teachers. Halbesle-ben and Buckley (2004) argue from their review of literature that employee commitment can be supported by management through articulating appropriate performance expectations including realistic job descriptions and evaluations. But this should not be interpreted as over developing commitment. Kieschke and Schaarschmidt (2008) discuss several profiles they identified in longitudinal studies of teachers, one of which involved high commitment. Specifically, they found that a large percentage of teachers who exhibited high commitment and lacked coping capacity were burned out. Thus, we recommend professional development that assists educators in understanding the affective component of their work and purposeful engagement in practices that strength resiliency and mindfulness (Gold, Smith, Hopper, Herne, Tansey, & Hulland, 2010; Hargreaves, 2000; Philipp & Schupbach, 2010; Platsidou, 2010).

REFERENCES

Alarcon, G., Eschleman, K., Bowling, N. (2009). Relationships between personality variables and burnout: A meta-analysis. *Work and Stress, 23*(3), 244–263.

Bachkirova, T. (2005). Teacher stress and personal values: An exploratory study. *School Psychology International, 26*(3), 340–352.

Bakkar, A., Hakanen, J., Demerouti, E., & Xanthopolou, D. (2007). Job resources boost work engagement, particularly when job demands are high. *Journal of Educational Psychology, 99*(2), 274–284.

Barnes, G., Crowe, E., & Schaefer, B. (2007). *The cost of teacher turnover in five school districts.* Washington, DC: National Commission on Teaching and America's Future.

Beehr, T., & Newman, J. (1978). Job stress, employee health, and organizational effectiveness: A facet analysis, model, and literature review. *Personnel Psychology, 31*, 655–699.

Blair, S., Collingwood, T., Reynolds, R., Smith, M., Hagan, D., & Sterling, C. (1984). Health promotion for educations: Impact on health behaviors, satisfaction, and general well-being. *American Journal of Public Health, 74*(2), 147–149.

Borg, M. G. (1990). Occupational stress in British educational settings: A review. *Educational Psychology, 10*, 103–126.

Carson, R., Baumgartner, J., Matthews, R., & Tsouloupas, C. (2010). Emotional exhaustion, absenteeism, and turnover intentions in childcare teachers: Examining the impact of physical activity behaviors. *Journal of Health Psychology, 15*, 905–914.

Cohen, S., & Janicki-Deverts, D. (in press). Who's stressed? Distributions of psychological stress in the United States in probability samples from 1983, 2006 and 2009. *Journal of Applied Social Psychology.*

Cohen, S., Janicki-Deverts, D., & Miller, G. (2007). Psychological stress and disease. *JAMA, 298*(14), 1685–1687.

Cohen, S., Kamarack, T., & Mermeistein, R. (1983). A global measure of perceived stress. *Journal of Health and Social Behaviour, 24*, 385–396.

Conley, C., & You, S. (2009). Teacher role stress, satisfaction, commitment, and intentions to leave: A structural model. *Psychological Reports, 105*, 771–786.

Davis, J., & Wilson, S. M. (2000). Principals' efforts to empower teachers: Effects on teacher motivation and job satisfaction and stress. *The Clearing House, 73,* 349–357.

Demerouti, E., Bakker, A. B., Nachreiner, F., & Schaufeli, W. B. (2001). The job demands resources model of burnout. *Journal of Applied Psychology, 86,* 499–512

Dillman, D. (2007). *Mail and internet surveys: The tailored design method update with new internet, visual, and mixed-mode guide.* Hoboken, NJ: Wiley.

Everaert, H., & van de Wolf, J. (2007). Teachers' stress and gender perceptions of challenging student behavior. In G. Gates (Ed.), *Emerging thought and research on student, teacher, and administrator stress and coping: Research on stress and coping in education* (Vol. 5, pp. 93–107). Charlotte, NC: Information Age.

Folkman, S. (1984). Personal control and stress and coping processes: A theoretical analysis. *Journal of Personality and Social Psychology, 46*(4), 839–852.

Funder, D. C. (2010). *The personality puzzle.* New York, NY: W. W. Norton.

Furnham, A. (1992). *Personality at work: The role of individual differences in the workplace.* London, UK: Routledge.

Ganster, D., & Schaubroeck, J. (1991). Work stress and employee health. *Journal of Management, 17,* 235–271

Gold, E., Smith, A., Hopper, I., Herne, D., Tansey, G., & Hulland, C. (2010). Mindfulness-based stress reduction (MBSR) for primary teachers. *Journal of Child and Family Studies, 19,* 184–189.

Halbesleben, J., & Buckley, M. (2004). Burnout in organizational life. *Journal of Management, 30*(6), 859–879.

Hamann, D.L., & Gordon, D. G. (2000). Burnout: An occupational hazard. *Music Educators' Journal, 87*(3), 34–39.

Hargreaves, A. (2000). Mixed emotions: Teachers' perceptions of their interactions with students. *Teaching and Teacher Education, 16,* 811–826.

Jepson, E., & Forrest, S. (2006). Individual contributory factors in teacher stress: The role of achievement . *British Journal of Educational Psychology, 76,* 183–196.

Kahn, J., Schneider, K., Jenkins-Henkelman, T., & Moyle, L. (2006). Emotional social support and job burnout among high-school teachers: Is it all due to dispositional affectivity? *Journal of Organizational Behavior, 27,* 793–807.

Kieschke, U., & Schaarschmidt, U. (2008). Professional commitment and health among teachers in Germany: A typological approach. *Learning and Instruction, 18,* 429–437.

Klassen, R. (2010). Teacher stress: The mediating role of collective efficacy beliefs. *The Journal of Educational Research, 103,* 342–350.

Klusmann, U., Kunter, M., Trautwein, U., Ludtke, O., & Baumert, J. (2008). Teachers' occupational well-being and quality of instruction: The important role of self-regulatory patterns. *Journal of Educational Psychology, 100*(3), 702–715.

Kyriacou, C. (2001). Teacher stress: Directions for future research. *Education Review, 53*(1), 27–35.

Lambert, R., McCarthy, C., O'Donnell, M., & Melendres, L. (2007). Teacher stress and classroom structural characteristics in elementary settings. In G. Gates (Ed.), *Emerging thought and research on student, teacher, and administrator stress and coping: Vol 5 Research on stress and coping in education* (pp.109–130). Charlotte, NC: Information Age Publishing.

Lambert, R., McCarthy, C., O'Donnell, M., & Wang, C. (2009). Measuring elementary teacher stress and coping in the classroom: Validity evidence for the classroom appraisal of resources and demands. *Psychology in the Schools, 46*(10), 937–988.

Maslach, C. (2003). Job burnout: New directions in research and intervention. *Current Directions in Psychological Science, 12* (5), 189–191.

Mabry, L., & Margolis, J. (2006). NCLB: Local implementation and impact in southwest Washington State. *Education Policy Analysis Archives, 14*(23). Retrieved from http://epaa.asu.edu/epaa/v14n23/

McCormick, J. (1997). Occupational stress of teachers: Biographical differences in a large school system. *Journal of Educational Administration, 35*(1), 18–38.

Montgomery, C., & Rupp, A. (2005). A meta-analysis for exploring the diverse causes and effects of stress in teachers. *Canadian Journal of Education, 28*(3), 458–486.

Norton, S. (2002). Let's keep our quality school principals on the job. *The High School Journal, 86,* 50–56.

Parkes, K.R. (1994). Personality and coping as moderators of work stress processes: Models, methods and measures. *Work and Stress, 8*(2), 110–129.

Pearson, L. C., & Hall, B. C. (1993). Initial construct validation of the teaching autonomy scale. *The Journal of Educational Research, 86,* 172–177.

Pei, W., & Guoli, Z. (2007). Survey of occupational stress of secondary and elementary school, teachers and the lessons learned. *Chinese Education and Society, 40*(5), 32–39.

Philipp, A., & Schupbach, H. (2010). Longitudinal effects of emotional labour on emotional exhaustion and dedication of teachers. *Journal of Occupational Health Psychology, 15*(4), 494–504.

Platsidou M. (2010). Trait emotional intelligence of Greek special education teachers in relation to burnout and job satisfaction. *School Psychology International, 31*(1), 60–67.

Sethi, A., & Schuler, R. (1984). *Handbook of organizational stress coping strategies.* Cambridge, MA: Ballinger.

Shaver, J., & Norton, R. (1980). Randomness and replication in ten years of the "American Educational Research Journal." *Educational Researcher, 9*(1), 9–15.

Spector, P. E. (1988). Development of work locus of control scale. *Journal of Occupational Psychology, 61,* 335–340.

Travers, C. J., & Cooper, C. L. (1996). *Teachers under pressure: Stress in the teaching profession.* London, UK: Routledge.

Ward, C., & Eisler, R. (1987). Type A behavior, achievement striving, and a dysfunctional self-evaluation system. *Journal of Personality and Social Psychology, 53*(2), 318–326.

Xanthopoulou, D., Bakker, A., Dollard, M., Demerouti, E., Schaufeli. W., Taris, T., & Schreurs, P. (2007). When do job demands particularly predict burnout? The moderating role of job resources. *Journal of Managerial Psychology, 22*(8), 766–786.

Zembylas, M., & Papanastasiou, E. (2005). Modeling teacher empowerment: The role of job satisfaction. *Educational Research and Evaluation, 11*(5), 433–459.

Zurlo, M., Pes, D., & Cooper, C. (2007). Stress in teaching: A study of occupational stress and its determinants among Italian schoolteachers. *Stress and Health, 23,* 231–241.

CHAPTER 8

ASSESSMENT OF TEACHER DEMANDS AND RESOURCES

Relationship to Stress, Classroom Structural Characteristics, Job Satisfaction, and Turnover

Richard G. Lambert
UNC Charlotte

Christopher J. McCarthy, Colleen McCarthy, and Elizabeth Crowe
University of Texas at Austin

Molly Fisher
University of Kentucky

ABSTRACT

This study used an existing data set to examine how advanced placement (AP) statistics teachers' perceptions of demands and resources in the classroom are related to structural aspects of their classroom as well as their personal

International Perspectives on Teacher Stress, pages 155–174
Copyright © 2012 by Information Age Publishing
All rights of reproduction in any form reserved.

resources for coping with stress, job satisfaction, and intention to leave the profession. Participants were 158 high school teachers who completed measures of classroom demands and resources, personal resources for stress prevention, job satisfaction, and intention to leave the field of teaching. Results indicated that teachers classified as having higher demands differed from teachers classified as having higher resources in terms of classroom size and structural characteristics such as percentages of students with attendance and behavior problems. It was also found that higher resourced teachers reported more job satisfaction, and less of an intention to leave the field. Teachers who indicated specific plans to leave the field also reported higher demands and lower classroom resources. These findings suggest that understanding teacher perceptions of demands and resources in the classroom could be an important component of teacher satisfaction and retention.

While teacher stress is widely acknowledged (Bertoch, Nielsen, Curley, & Borg, 1989), the specific factors that place teachers at risk for stress are not well understood (McCarthy, Lambert, O'Donnell, & Melendres, 2009). Most teachers work in the public sector and are vital to society—they are often recognized along with police and firefighters as public servants society cannot do without. Few would argue about the demanding nature of the work environment of police and firefighters, which have clear sources of stress associated with them (i.e., physical risk, helping people in emergencies). However, the factors associated with teachers' stress may be harder to identify (Lambert & McCarthy, 2006). Teachers usually enter the profession with high ideals but can become quickly disillusioned when confronted with the demands of today's classrooms. For administrators and other school-based professionals to help these teachers, it is essential to identify which teachers are most at risk for stress (McCarthy et al., 2009).

Kyriacou and Sutcliffe (1977) defined teacher stress as a state of negative affect experienced by a teacher as a result of negative perceptions of their work environment. As evidence for the vulnerability of some teachers to excessive stress levels, Ingersoll (2001) noted teacher shortages that result from the "revolving door" of teachers entering then leaving the profession for reasons other than retirement. This very likely includes large numbers of teachers leaving due to excessive occupational stress and burnout. Teachers are the largest homogenous occupational group investigated in burnout research, comprising 22% of all samples used (Schaufeli & Enzmann, 1988). However, job burnout studies over the past 30 years have focused mainly on teachers' workplace conditions (i.e., poor communication, lack of job role specification) as the cause of burnout (Zellars, Hochwarter, & Perrewé, 2004). Zellars et al. (2004) noted that individual teacher factors are often ignored in such research, a point echoed by Wilhelm, Dewhurst-Savellis, and Parker (2000) with respect to teacher stress in general.

Kyriacou and Sutcliffe's (1977) conceptualization of teacher stress as produced by negative perceptions of the work environment is consistent with current stress theory, particularly Lazarus and Folkman (1984)'s transactional model of stress. Hobfoll, Schwarzer, and Chon (1998) described it as the most well-accepted and commonly cited theory in the stress literature. Lazarus and Folkman suggested that stress is the result of subjective, reflexive transactions that occur when life demands are encountered and weighed against one's perceived resources for coping. In the context of teaching, Lazarus and Folkman's theory would suggest that when an educator perceives that classroom demands outweigh available resources for coping with them, stress is the likely outcome.

According to this theory, two teachers might have different perspectives on the relative demands and resources associated with the same classroom. However, very few studies have investigated the central tenet of Lazarus and Folkman's (1984) model, namely that perceptions of both demands and resources need to be considered together when investigating individual perceptions of stress (Moore, 2007). This study builds on data collected from high school teachers by McCarthy, Lambert, Crowe, and McCarthy (2010), who investigated teachers' personal resources for stress prevention, classroom demands and resources, job satisfaction, and intention to leave the field of teaching. Their results indicated that the constructs of teachers' preventive coping resources and job satisfaction were positively related to each other and negatively related to both teachers' perceptions of classroom stress and plans to leave the profession. However, that study did not directly investigate a central tenet of Lazarus and Folkman's (1984) model, namely that teachers could be classified on the basis of their perceptions of demands and resources (Moore, 2007). Further, McCarthy et al. did not analyze structural factors associated with teachers' classrooms such as the types of students they work with and overall class size. The purpose of this study therefore was to reanalyze this existing data set of 158 advanced placement statistics high school teachers in a way that would directly test Folkman and Lazarus' model and that would account for classroom structural factors.

UNDERSTANDING AND ASSESSING TEACHER DEMANDS AND RESOURCES

Resources for teachers can include material assets (such as instructional supplies), other professionals (such as administrators, fellow teachers, school counselors and psychologists), and their own personal resources for coping with, and preventing, stress. Coping resources refer to factors an individual has in place before a stressor is engaged (Matheny, Curlette, Aycock, & Junker, 1993), such as self-confidence and social support. Preventive coping resources are assets useful in preventing, rather than coping with, stressful situations (McCarthy, Lambert, & Brack, 1997). Previous research has suggested that elementary school teachers reporting excessive stress levels also report having lower levels of personal resources for stress prevention (McCarthy, Kissen, Yadley, Wood, & Lambert, 2006). Resources for stress prevention could be particularly relevant for teachers in high-demand classrooms: teachers with higher levels of preventive coping resources may better anticipate and ameliorate classroom situations before they bloom into full-fledged stressors. Put another way, teachers who are good copers may be able to withstand stress, but teachers who are good preventive copers may be able to prevent stress altogether (McCarthy et al., 2009), thus bypassing the negative emotions and stress symptoms that can accompany even a successful encounter with stress (Sapolsky, 2004).

In addition to assessing teachers' personal resources for stress prevention, teacher perceptions of classroom demands and resources were examined using an existing measure of both constructs, Lambert, McCarthy, and Abbott-Shim's (2001) Classroom Appraisal of Resources and Demands (CARD). Originally developed for use with elementary school teachers, the CARD measures teacher perceptions of the demands of the classroom environment as well as specific material resources available to teachers to meet those demands. A revised version of the CARD for use with high school teachers was used in this study to specifically test transactional models of stress and coping, which would predict that teachers who rated demands greater than available resources would be at risk for experiencing occupational stress.

Previous research using the CARD with preschool and elementary teachers has indicated that teachers who perceive themselves as having higher demands in relation to resources are different from other teachers (Lambert, McCarthy, O' Donnell, & Wang, 2009; McCarthy et al., 2009; O'Donnell, Lambert, & McCarthy, 2008). McCarthy et al. (2009) found that they report higher levels of burnout symptoms and work in classrooms that they perceive to be structurally different from those of their peers, including having higher number of students with behavior problems (Lambert, Kusherman et al., 2006) and students with learning disabilities (Lambert, McCarthy, O'Donnell, & Melendres, 2007). Further, Jazaar, Lambert, and O'Donnell (2007) found that elementary teachers reporting an intention to leave their current job for professional reasons, as opposed to personal ones (pregnancy, family move, retirement, etc.), also report higher demands in the classroom, fewer resources provided by schools, and higher levels of occupational stress. A goal of this study was to examine whether such findings could be replicated with teachers at the high school level.

Teachers were classified in this study according to their perceptions of the relative sufficiency of classroom resources and demands. Using procedures developed by Lambert et al. (2007), the demands and resources scales from the CARD were used to create an Appraisal Index, which, in accordance with transactional stress theory, quantifies teachers' appraisals of both self-reported classroom demands and resources. The Appraisal Index was used to classify teachers in this study into three groups: teachers rating themselves as high in classroom resources but low in classroom demands (R > D); those rating classroom demands and resources as equal (R = D), and those rating classroom demands high and resources low (D > R). These teacher classifications will hereafter be referred to as the *resourced, balanced,* and *demand* groups, respectively (McCarthy, Kerne, Calfa, Lambert, & Guzmán, 2010). We then examined whether teachers in each of these three groups differed on reported levels of stress, classroom structural characteristics, job satisfaction, and turnover.

GOALS OF THE PRESENT STUDY

The goals of this study were to address three specific research questions. The first was whether the three groups differed on classroom structural characteristics (total number of students taught and percentages of students who are English language learners or have learning disabilities, poor attendance, and problem behaviors). The second research question examined whether teachers in each group (resourced, balanced, and demand) differed in levels of job satisfaction, preventive coping resources, and plans to leave the field. The third research question examined whether group differences existed for teachers reporting a specific intention to leave the field ("leavers") or intending to stay in the profession ("stayers") on each of the study measures.

METHODS

Participants

The sample for this study consisted of high school teachers who teach an advanced placement (AP) statistics course and were either attending a summer institute to learn more about the process of teaching advanced placement statistics, or were working as readers for Educational Testing Service as part of the annual grading of the AP examination. These teachers were recruited as volunteer participants in a survey about teacher stress. The response rate for the workshop participants was 100.00% (24/24), and the response rate for the grading participants was 50.19% (134/267) for a total response rate of 54.30% (158/291).

When asked about personal background characteristics, the participants reported an average of 17.45 years of teaching experience (SD = 9.52). A total of 3.2% of the teachers indicated that they had less than two years of teaching experience. The participants reported an average of 9.98 years of experience at their current school (SD = 7.56). A total of 13.3% of the teachers reported that they less than two years of experience in their current school. The participants reported the following age categories: 30 years of age or younger (15.2%), 31–40 (21.5%), 41–50 (26.6%), and over 50 years of age (36.7%). The teachers reported the following degrees: bachelor's degree (30.6%), master's degree (63.1%), and doctoral degree (6.4%). The majority of the teachers were female (69.2%). The teachers reported the following ethnicities: Caucasian (89.2%), African American (5.1%), Hispanic (1.9%), Asian (1.9%), and other (1.9%).

The teachers reported that their school used the following schedules: 4 × 4 block (20.3%), AB block (17.1%), hybrid block (10.1%), traditional (41.8%), and other (10.8%). The participants reported an average number of students taught of 111.45 (SD = 38.86). The majority of the teachers reported that they spend their own money on classroom supplies (81.4%). As shown in Table 8.1, the participating teachers reported spending an average of over $200 of their own money on classroom supplies (mean = $236.93, SD = $301.63).

Measures

Classroom Appraisal of Resources and Demands (CARD)
(Lambert et al., 2001)

The CARD is a measure of teacher stress that is grounded in transactional models of stress and coping in that it measures teachers' perceptions of both classroom resources and demands (Lambert et al., 2009). The original version of the CARD was developed for elementary school teachers and consisted of 84 items developed based on a review of literature on teacher stress as well as interviews with teachers and administrators (Lambert, Kusherman et al., 2006).

TABLE 8.1 Teacher Background Characteristics

	Mean	SD	Minimum	Maximum
Total number of students taught	111.45	38.86	19	210
Years of teaching experience	17.45	9.52	1	43
Years of experience in current school	9.98	7.56	1	33
Personal funds spent on supplies	$236.93	$301.63	$0.00	$2,200.00

McCarthy, Lambert, et al. (2010) described the CARD as follows: The classroom demands section of the CARD consists of 35 items that ask teachers to rate the severity of demands based on various aspects of the classroom using a five-point Likert scale ranging from 1, "Not Demanding," to 5, "Extremely Demanding." Items on this scale ask teachers about the following categories of demands: students with problematic behaviors (sample item: disruptive children), other student-related demands (sample item: number of students with poor attendance), administrative demands (sample item: meetings you are required to attend), and lack of instructional resources (sample item: availability of instructional supplies). The Classroom Resources scale contains 29 items that assess the teachers' perceptions of the helpfulness of various school resources. Items on this scale ask teachers to assess the following categories of resources: school support personnel (sample item: administrators at your school), other adults in the classroom (sample item: community volunteers), instructional support (sample item: instructional materials), and specialized resources (sample item: materials for children performing below grade level).

Lambert et al. (2007) found high sample-specific reliability for both the elementary school version of the demands scale score (Cronbach's alpha = .92) and for the resources scale score (α = .95). This study also reported factor analysis results that contribute to confirming the construct validity of the two sections of the CARD (resources and demands). In order for the CARD to assess the relative congruence or incongruence of teachers' perceptions of classroom demands and resources, a central tenet of transactional models of stress which is rarely tested directly, a teacher "stress" score from the CARD can be calculated for each respondent by computing the difference between her/his total score for the demands section of the CARD and the total score for the resources section of the CARD (Lambert, McCarthy et al., 2006). This was done in the current study to test the prediction of transactional models of stress and coping that teachers who rated perceived demands greater than perceived available resources would be at risk for experiencing less job satisfaction and greater intention to leave the field.

Lambert et al.'s (2007, 2009) research has demonstrated sample-specific acceptable levels of both validity and reliability evidence for the information from the Demands, Resources, and Stress scale scores. In this study, items from the elementary school version of the CARD were revised to be appropriate for middle and high school teachers, mostly through wording changes that reflected the fact that such teachers worked with older students. Reliability coefficients for the demands (alpha = .93), resources (alpha = .95), and Stress scales (alpha = .96) were found. These results are consistent with findings from a previous study with high school math teachers (Fisher, 2009), in which the following reliability results were found: demands—alpha = .93, resources—alpha = .91, stress—alpha = .90.

Preventive Resources Inventory (PRI)—Self-Acceptance Scale (SAC)
(McCarthy & Lambert, 2001)

The self-acceptance (SAC) scale from the PRI was used as a brief measure of overall preventive coping resources (McCarthy, Lambert, Crowe, & McCarthy, 2010). The PRI is a self-report measure designed to explore an individual's level of agreement with items assessing their perceived ability to prevent stressful reactions to life circumstances. The PRI contains 82 items and uses a five-point Likert-like scale ranging from "strongly disagree" to "strongly agree." Validity evidence for the PRI has been supportive, and previous research has found hypothesized relationships between theoretically consistent (McCarthy, Lambert, Beard, & Dematatis, 2002) and divergent constructs (Lambert, McCarthy et al., 2006). Since the overall PRI includes five scale scores and 18 subscale scores (Lambert, McCarthy et al., 2006), it was judged to be too lengthy for use in the current study.

The self-acceptance scale of the PRI was chosen for this study, which McCarthy et al. (2002) defined as the degree to which one can accept and overcome personal strengths and weaknesses in demanding life situations. The self-acceptance scale has been suggested as an appropriate proxy for the total score from the full-length version of the PRI in that it has been found to be related to level of perceived stress and burnout in teachers (McCarthy et al., 2006). Items on the SAC address the importance of balance in life as a key to coping and acceptance of life circumstances as important factors in preventing stress. Cronbach's alpha was .91 in this study.

Job Satisfaction
(Koeske, Kirk, Koeske, & Rauktis, 1994)

This 14-item scale was originally developed by Koeske et al. (1994) to assess human service workers' satisfaction with a range of factors. These include working conditions, satisfaction with organizational climate, salary, promotion, and benefits issues. Koeske et al. developed and evaluated the validity of this job satisfaction measure using samples of over 600 individuals gathered over a ten-year time frame with a range of helping professions. Sample-specific alpha reliabilities ranging from .78 to .91 were reported as well as validity evidence through negative correlations of job satisfaction with burnout, depression, and intention to quit one's job. While the original measure asked respondents about their work with "clients," the measure was adapted for McCarthy, Lambert, et al.'s (2010) study and this study by changing "clients" to "students" when appropriate. Otherwise the scale was not altered; Cronbach's alpha reliability for this sample was .88.

Plans to Leave Current Job (PLCJ)
(Fisher, Lambert, & McCarthy, 2009)

The PLCJ is a thirteen-item scale adapted from Fisher (2009) that assesses teachers' job seeking activities and intentions to leave their current positions. The measure includes a series of questions regarding whether the teacher has made specific plans to leave their current position.

McCarthy, Lambert, et al. (2010) used Rasch rating scale model analyses to examine how well the items on the Plans to Leave Current Job (PLCJ) scale measured teachers' intentions and specific steps toward changing jobs. The results of the IRT analyses indicated that the items on the PLCJ scale appear to be working together to measure a single construct. The IRT scaling procedures indicated overall acceptable levels of reliability (alpha = .73) and validity for the measure. Further, it suggested that the items measure a continuum of items that range from relatively easy to pursue by a teacher thinking about leaving the field and commonly reported by teachers, such as merely considering leaving their current job or school, through items that represent relatively more "difficult" tasks, reflecting a stronger commitment to leaving, such as actually applying for another position or making a final decision to leave teaching. The last three items of the PCLJ scale directly ask the respondent whether they intend to return to their current school, current job, and the teaching profession in the following academic year. McCarthy et al. found, using this same sample, 14 teachers (8.86%) reported that they did not intend to return on at least one of these three questions. An additional 8 teachers (5.06%) did not respond to these questions.

Analysis

The following research questions were examined:

1. Are there differences in reported classroom structural characteristics between high school mathematics teachers based on whether teachers were classified in the demand group (D > R), the balanced group (D = R), and the resourced group (D < R)?
2. Are there differences in job satisfaction, stress prevention, and reported plans to leave their current job between high school mathematics teachers based on whether teachers were classified in the demand group (D > R), the balanced group (D = R), and the resourced group (D < R)?
3. Are there differences in job satisfaction, stress prevention, and stress levels between high school mathematics teachers based on their reported intentions to leave their current job?

In order to clarify how the first and second research questions were operationalized, note that scale scores were formed using the two scales of the CARD: demands and resources. Following Lambert et al.'s (2007) procedures, subtracting standardized versions of the scales scores, demands minus resources, created a difference score, hereafter referred to as an appraisal index. The reliability of a difference score formula (Crocker & Algina, 1986) was used to examine the reliability of the stress score. This difference score was used to classify teachers into three stress level groupings: demands greater than, equal to, or less than available resources. Subtracting standardized versions of the scales scores, demands minus resources, created a difference score that yielded a reliability estimate for this sample of .96. The reliability of a difference score is a function of the reliability of the two scale scores, high for both demands and resources in this sample, and the correlation between the two scores. The CARD scale scores were moderately correlated ($r = -.530$) using data from this sample. Since the difference score approach indicated acceptable reliability, the standard error of measurement for the difference score was calculated using this reliability estimate.

A 95% confidence interval was constructed around a difference score of zero, and the upper and lower bounds of this interval were used to establish the cut scores for classifying teachers. Each teacher was classified into one of three groups: resources greater than demands (R > D) (33.3%), resources equal to demands (R = D) (27.6%), and demands greater than resources (D > R) (39.1%). This last group was hypothesized to be at risk for a stressful experience in the classroom. This method allowed the researchers to be 95% confident that the true score for the difference between resources and demands was not zero in either of the extreme groups. This three-group distinction has proven to be useful in previous research testing transactional models of stress and coping in educational settings (Lambert et al., 2006).

Each participant was then classified on the basis of scores on the appraisal index into one of three groups: resources greater than demands (R > D), resources equal to demands (R = D), and demands greater than resources (D > R). These groups are referred to as the resourced, balanced, and demand groups, respectively.

RESULTS

To address research question one, the three groups formed using the appraisal index were used to form the independent variable for a one way analysis of variance in which the total number of students taught across all sections was the dependent variable. As can be seen in the top row of Table 8.2, there was a statistically significant overall difference between the

TABLE 8.2   Differences Between the Appraisal Groups on Classroom Structural Characteristics

Measure		Appraisal Group			F	Post hoc Comparisons
		Group 1 D < R n = 52	Group 2 D = R n = 43	Group 3 D > R n = 61		
Total Students Taught	Mean	96.69	115.40	122.05	6.67**	1 < 2,3
	SD	40.39	33.58	38.03		

Student Group	% of Students Taught	% of Teachers within Group			χ^2	Post hoc Comparisons
		Group 1 R > D	Group 2 D = R	Group 3 D > R		
English Language Learners	0–5%	66.04%	54.76%	48.28%	4.02	
	6–10%	16.98%	19.05%	20.69%		
	> 10%	16.98%	26.19%	31.03%		
With Learning Disabilities	0–5%	67.92%	71.43%	40.68%	12.81*	
	6–10%	20.75%	16.67%	33.90%		
	> 10%	11.32%	11.90%	25.42%		1,2 < 3
With Poor Attendance	0–5%	71.70%	40.48%	30.00%	21.54***	
	6–10%	13.21%	35.71%	35.00%		
	> 10%	15.09%	23.81%	35.00%		1 < 3
With Problem Behaviors	0–5%	81.13%	61.90%	38.33%	23.90***	
	6–10%	13.21%	23.81%	28.33%		
	> 10%	5.66%	14.29%	33.33%		1,2 < 3

Note: *$p < .05$; **$p < .01$; ***$p < .001$

groups in total student load ($F_{(2,145)} = 6.67$, $p < .01$). Tukey HSD post hoc comparisons indicated that the resourced (R > D) group reported lower teaching loads of students on average (mean = 96.69) than either the balanced (D = R; mean = 115.40) or demand group (D > R; mean = 122.05).

The three-group classification system was also used to form a categorical variable that was cross-tabulated with various classroom structural characteristics within a series of chi square contingency table analyses. As can be seen in Table 8.2, participating teachers reported the percentage of students in their classes who have learning disabilities, poor attendance, behavior problems, or are English language learners. These reported percentages were grouped into the following categories: 0–5%, 6–10%, and greater than 10% of children taught. There was not a statistically significant association between the groups and classroom percentage of English language learners ($\chi^2_{(4)} = 4.02$, $p > .05$). There was a statistically significant association between the groups and classroom percentage of students with learning disabilities ($\chi^2_{(4)} = 12.81$, $p < .05$). Follow-up comparisons of cell percentages indicated that a higher percentage of teachers in the demand group (D > R; 25.42%) reported greater than 10% of their students are English language learners than did teachers in either the balanced (D = R; 11.90%) or the resourced (R > D; 11.32%) groups.

A statistically significant association was found between the groups and classroom percentage of students with poor attendance ($\chi^2_{(4)}$ = 21.54, $p < .001$). Follow-up comparisons of cell percentages indicated that a higher percentage of teachers in the demand group (D > R; 35.00%) reported greater than 10% of their students have poor attendance than did teachers in the resourced (R > D; 15.09%) group. There was also a statistically significant association between the groups and classroom percentage of students with problem behaviors ($\chi^2_{(4)}$ = 23.90, $p < .001$). Follow-up comparisons of cell percentages indicated that a higher percentage of teachers in the demand group (D > R; 33.33%) reported greater than 10% of their students exhibit problem behaviors than did teachers in either the balanced (D = R; 14.29%) or the resourced (R > D; 5.66%) group.

To address research question two, groups of participating teachers with differing levels of perceived occupational stress were again compared. The three-group classification system using the appraisal index was used to form the independent variable for a series of one way analyses of variance in which the job satisfaction, self-acceptance, and plans to leave current job scores served as the dependent variables. As can be seen in Table 8.3, there was a statistically significant overall difference between the groups in Job Satisfaction ($F_{(2,145)}$ = 23.13, $p < .001$). Tukey HSD post hoc comparisons indicated that the resourced group reported higher levels of job satisfaction on average than either the balanced or demand group. The difference between the resourced and demand groups, when expressed as a standard-

TABLE 8.3 Differences Between the Appraisal Groups on Teacher Variables

| Measure | | Appraisal Group | | | F | Post hoc Comparisons |
		Group 1 R > D n = 52	Group 2 D = R n = 43	Group 3 D > R n = 61		
Job Satisfaction	Mean	5.73	5.02	4.74	24.13***	1 > 2,3
	SD	0.70	0.74	0.80		
Self Acceptance	Mean	4.19	4.20	4.06	0.98	
	SD	0.48	0.68	0.58		
Plans to Leave Current Job	Mean	1.98	2.51	3.24	4.08*	3 > 1
	SD	2.07	2.28	2.46		
Reported intention to leave		1.92%	4.88%	20.00%	11.59**	3 > 2,1

Note: $^*p < .05$; $^{**}p < .01$; $^{***}p < .001$

ized mean difference, was 1.40. This would be considered a large effect size and indicates that the demand group is more than a full standard deviation unit lower in job satisfaction than the resourced group.

As shown in Table 8.3, there was not a statistically significant difference between the groups in stress prevention as measured by the self acceptance scale score. There was a statistically significant overall difference between the groups in Plans to Leave Current Job ($F_{(2,145)} = 4.08$, $p < .05$). Tukey HSD post hoc comparisons indicated that the demand group reported having made more plans to leave than the resourced group. This difference, when expressed as a standardized mean difference, was .61. This would be considered a moderate effect size and illustrates that the demand group reported having made, on average, approximately one more specific step toward leaving their current job than those in the resourced group (3.24 vs. 1.98).

The final way in which research question two was addressed was by looking at what percentage of teachers reported an intention to leave their current job in each of the three groups. As was noted in the measures section, three of the items from the Plans to Leave Current Job scale directly address whether the participating teachers intend to return to their current school, current job, and the teaching profession in the following academic year. A total of 14 teachers (8.86%) reported that they did not intend to return on at least one of these three questions. These teachers were identified as "leavers" and the remaining teachers were identified as "stayers." As can be seen in Table 8.2, the demand group was much more likely to be identified as "leavers" (20.00%) than either the balanced group (4.88%) or the resourced group (1.92%), and this difference was statistically significant ($\chi^2_{(2)} = 11.59$, $p < .01$).

To address research question three, as seen in Table 8.4, a series of independent t-tests was conducted to compare these groups across various indicators of occupational stress. The leavers reported higher classroom demands on the CARD than the stayers (effect size = .79), and this difference was statistically significant ($t_{(147)} = 2.81$, $p < .01$). The leavers also reported lower classroom resources on the CARD than the stayers (effect size = −.83), and this difference was also statistically significant ($t_{(147)} = 2.91$, $p < .01$). The leavers reported lower levels of job satisfaction on average than the stayers (effect size = −.49); however, this difference was not statistically significant ($t_{(147)} = 1.75$, $p < .10$). The leavers reported making approximately, on average, three more specific plans to leave their current jobs than did the stayers (effect size = 1.61), and this difference was statistically significant ($t_{(147)} = 5.56$, $p < .001$). The leavers reported higher average scores on self-acceptance scale score, than the stayers (effect size = .32); however, this difference was not statistically significant ($t_{(147)} = 1.16$, $p > .10$). Finally, the leavers reported much higher stress than the stayers, as measured by the

TABLE 8.4 Differences Between Leavers and Stayers on Teacher Self-Report Variables

Measure		Intend to Stay $n = 135$	Intend to Leave $n = 14$	Effect Size	t
Demands	Mean	48.90	56.56	0.79	2.81**
	SD	9.66	10.12		
Resources	Mean	50.70	42.67	–0.83	2.91**
	SD	9.64	11.65		
Job Satisfaction	Mean	5.21	4.79	–0.49	1.75
	SD	0.85	0.86		
Plans to Leave Current Job	Mean	2.26	5.57	1.61	5.56***
	SD	2.07	2.62		
Self Acceptance	Mean	4.13	4.31	0.32	1.16
	SD	0.59	0.37		

Note: $^*p < .05$; $^{**}p < .01$; $^{***}p < .001$

CARD appraisal index (effect size = .93), and this difference was statistically significant ($t_{(147)} = 3.25$, $p < .001$).

The consistent pattern of differences, across both structural classroom characteristics and occupational stress related measures, between the demand group of teachers (D > R) and other teachers, suggested an additional exploratory research question. Can the foundational variables in this study, membership in the appraisal index groups and making concrete plans to leave one's current job, be used to predict which teachers have a higher probability of making the decision to leave their current jobs? To address this question, a logistic regression model was used. The dependent variable in the model was a teacher's membership in the leaver group, and the independent variables were a teacher's membership in the CARD demand group and the Plans to Leave Current Job scale score.

For ease of interpretation in the univariate comparisons used to address the primary research questions of this study, the Plans to Leave Current Job scale score was formed by simply taking a sum of all of the questions endorsed. In this way, the resulting variable could be directly interpreted as the number of specific plans a teacher reported having made. This scale score approach has shown promise as a measure of reported teacher job seeking behaviors (Fisher, 2009). In a previous study using this same sample (McCarthy, Lambert, et al., 2010) the researchers found that the items in this scale were not all of the same item difficulty. Furthermore, the items were found to reasonably measure a single unidimensional construct when the Rasch rating scale model, a special case of the one parameter Item Response Theory (IRT) model, was used to examine the construct validity and item information characteristics for the Plans to Leave Current Job scale. This analytic approach yields a series of diagnostic statistics about the measurement properties of the items and scale and widely accepted criteria for acceptable measurement properties were met using the data from this sample (McCarthy, Lambert, et al., 2010). The resulting ability estimate was used in the logistic regression model as it not only considered item difficulty in the formation of the scale scores, but was considered a more robust measure of the underlying construct for use in the multivariate model.

In the logistic regression model, membership in the CARD demand group (D > R) was found to be highly predictive of leaving one's current job. Teachers in this group were 5.72 times more likely to report their intentions to leave their current jobs than other teachers and this odds ratio was statistically significant ($\beta = 1.744$, $p < .02$). The Rasch ability estimate for the Plans to Leave Current Job scale, when controlling for appraisal group membership, was also predictive of being in the leaver group. For every increase of one standard deviation unit in this score, teachers were 2.687 times more likely to report their intentions to leave their current jobs than other teachers. This odds ratio was statistically significant ($\beta = .989$, $p < .001$).

DISCUSSION

Teachers are unlikely to be effective when they have a negative perception of their work environment (Kyriacou & Sutcliffe, 1977). Transactional models of stress suggest that both teachers' perceptions of demands and resources need to be considered together in identifying which are most vulnerable to stress (Lazarus & Folkman, 1984), but few studies have investigated this central proposition directly (Moore, 2007). This study built on a previous analysis of data collected from high school teachers by McCarthy, Lambert, et al. (2010), who investigated teachers' personal resources for stress prevention, classroom demands and resources, job satisfaction, and intention to leave the field. McCarthy, Lambert, et al. (2010) found the expected relationships among these variables, but did not directly account for individual teacher perceptions of the relative sufficiency of their demands and resources, nor were classroom structural factors taken into account. This study addressed both limitations by examining classroom structural factors and using Lambert et al.'s (2007) procedures to classify teachers into one of three groups: demand, resourced, and balanced.

The results for the first research question provide compelling evidence for structural differences in the classrooms of teachers classified in the demand group. They reported higher numbers of students instructed, and with respect to the percentages of students listed in Table 8.2, teachers in the demand group reported higher percentages of students with learning disabilities, poor attendance, and problem behaviors. It is important to note that these results do not necessarily suggest that students in these categories are inherently stressful or problematic. However, professionals working in the schools, such as principals and other administrators, may want to consider how structural aspects of the classroom can impact teacher stress and consider assigning more resources to teachers who perceive themselves to be in high demand situations.

In addition to analyzing group differences in the structural factors of teachers' classrooms, research question two was designed to assess group differences in teachers' preventive coping resources, job satisfaction, and intention to remain in the profession. In a previous study using this data set, McCarthy, Lambert, et al. (2010) found that each of these variables was interrelated as theoretically predicted: teachers with higher preventive coping resources reported lower classroom demands, greater job satisfaction, and fewer intentions to leave field. This study sought to address whether these findings were replicated when teachers are classified according to the theoretical principles of transactional models of stress. The results for research question two suggested mixed support: resourced teachers reported the most job satisfaction and higher demand teachers reported the strongest intention to leave the field, as predicted. Group differences were not found, however, for teachers' self-reported levels of preventive coping resources. This last finding contradicts stress theory (Matheny et al., 1993), which suggests that teachers' personal coping resources for preventing stress should impact their perceptions of classroom demands and resources. Given that McCarthy, Lambert, et al. (2010) did find a weak correlation between preventive coping resources and classroom demands in this sample, it is possible that collapsing teacher demands into three groups, as was done in this study, obscured this weak relationship. Further research is needed to better understand what types of resources best protect teachers from stress.

One of the most problematic aspects of teacher stress is that it may contribute to teacher turnover. Ingersoll (2001) noted that teacher shortages in the United States result from the revolving door of teachers entering the field then choosing to leave for reasons other than retirement. Research question three was designed to examine whether teachers in this sample who had made the decision to leave the field of teaching ($n = 14$, 8.86% of sample), labeled "leavers," differed from the rest of the sample on each of the study variables. In previous data analyses using this sample, McCarthy, Lambert, et al. (2010) examined the relationship between overall scores on the PLCJ and the PRI, CARD, and job satisfaction, but did not examine whether there were group differences between "leavers" and "stayers." The finding that leavers reported higher classroom demands and lower classroom resources is consistent with stress theory (see Table 8.4), although the lack of significance found for self-acceptance was once again contrary to theoretical predictions. However, the lack of a significant difference on job satisfaction was surprising, particularly given McCarthy, Lambert, et al.'s (2010) finding of a robust relationship between scores on job satisfaction and PCLJ for the overall sample. The logistic regression conducted as part of research question three demonstrated that when scores on the PCLJ and membership in the demand group (D > R) are both used to predict membership in the leaver group, statistical significance was achieved, and teachers in the demand group were 5.72 times more likely to also identify themselves as belonging to the "leaver" group.

The results of this study suggest the potential utility of transactional models in understanding the perceptions that teacher have of the classroom environment. Teachers' perceptions of structural characteristics of their classrooms are also reflected in their overall perceptions of how demanding their classrooms are. Professionals in schools seeking to reduce teacher stress and turnover may want to pay careful attention to the perceptions of each teacher in their school, which may provide important information about which are most vulnerable to stress and possibly those who are considering leaving the field. Transactional theories of stress can also be useful in understanding that is mainly necessary to equalize demands and resources as much as possible to reduce stress. Resources do not have to vastly exceed demands for individuals to feel challenged and energized by life demands (Lazarus & Folkman, 1984). The overall pattern of results in this study did not suggest systematic differences between balanced and resourced teachers—rather, it was the demand teachers in particular who reported structural differences in their classrooms and who seemed most inclined the leave the profession. As a first step in efforts at intervention, therefore, measures such as the CARD may provide evidence about which teachers are perceiving their work environments as negative, the hallmark of teacher stress (Kyriacou & Sutcliffe, 1977).

Limitations and Suggestions for Future Research

While the analyses used in this study extended the results of McCarthy, Lambert, et al. (2010), it will be important to replicate these findings with other samples to verify that these results are not capitalizing on chance associations in this particular sample. Further, the sample for this study consisted of experienced mathematics teachers volunteering for summer training and ETS services, and these teachers are obviously not representative of all high school teachers. It is also important to note that the classroom structural characteristics included in the analyses were based on teacher self-report and not school records or observations in the classroom. Future research may benefit from a source of more precise information regarding student characteristics. The type of schedule used in each teacher's school was not included in the analyses of classroom structural characteristics. It is possible that schedule type is related to some of the classroom structural characteristics used in these analyses, and future research with larger sample sizes of each schedule type could examine this possibility.

REFERENCES

Bertoch, M. R., Nielsen, E. C., Curley, J. R., & Borg, W. R. (1989). Reducing teacher stress. *Journal of Experimental Education, 57,* 117–128.

Crocker, L., & Algina, J. (1986). *Introduction to classical and modern test theory.* Orlando, FL: Holt, Rinehart and Winston.

Fisher, M. (2009). *Should I stay or should I go? Stress, coping, and retention among novice teachers.* Unpublished doctoral dissertation, The University of North Carolina at Charlotte.

Fisher, M., Lambert, R., & McCarthy, C. (2009). *Plans to leave current job.* Charlotte, NC: The Center for Educational Measurement and Evaluation.

Hobfoll, S. E., Schwarzer, R., & Chon, K. K. (1998). Disentangling the stress labyrinth: Interpreting the meaning of the stress as it is studied in the health context. *Anxiety, Stress, and Coping, 11,* 181–212.

Ingersoll, R. M. (2001). Teacher turnover and teacher shortages: An organizational analysis. *American Educational Research Journal, 38,* 499–534.

Jazaar, M., Lambert, R. G., & O'Donnell, M. (2007). An investigation of elementary teacher stress to guide educational administrators in curbing the early career departure of elementary school teachers. In L. K. Lemasters & R. Papa (Eds.), *At the tipping point: Navigating the course for the preparation of educational administrators* (pp. 59–72). Lancaster, PA: DEStech Publications.

Koeske, G.F., Kirk, S.A., Koeske, R.D., & Rauktis, M.B. (1994). Measuring the Monday blues: Validation of a job satisfaction scale for the human services. *Social Work Research, 18*(1), 27–35.

Kyriacou, C., & Sutcliffe, J. (1977). Teacher stress: A review. *Educational Review, 29,* 299–306.

Lambert, R. G., Kusherman, J., O'Donnell, M., & McCarthy, C. J. (2006). Teacher stress and classroom structural characteristics in preschool settings. In R. G. Lambert, & C. J. McCarthy (Eds.), *Understanding teacher stress in an era of accountability* (Vol. III, pp. 105–120). Greenwich, CT: Information Age.

Lambert, R. G., & McCarthy, C. J. (Eds.). (2006). *Understanding teacher stress in an era of accountability.* (Vol. III). Greenwich, CT: Information Age.

Lambert, R. G., McCarthy, C. J. & Abbott-Shim, M. (2001). *Classroom appraisal of resources and demands, school-age version.* Atlanta, GA: Head Start Quality Research Center.

Lambert, R. G., McCarthy, C. J., Gilbert, T., Sebree, M., & Steinley-Bumgarner, M. (2006). Validity evidence for the use of the Preventive Resources Inventory with college students *Measurement and Evaluation in Counseling and Development, 39,* 66–83.

Lambert, R. G., McCarthy, C. J., O'Donnell, M., & Melendres, L. (2007). Teacher stress and classroom structural characteristics in elementary settings. In G. Gates, M. Wolverton, & W. Gmelch, (Eds.), *Emerging thought and research on student, teacher, and administrator stress and coping* (pp. 109–131). Charlotte, NC: Information Age Publishing.

Lambert, R. G., McCarthy, C. J., O' Donnell, M., & Wang, C. (2009). Measuring elementary teacher stress and coping in the classroom: Validity evidence for the classroom appraisal of resources and demands. *Psychology in the Schools, 46,* 973–988.

Lazarus, R. S., & Folkman, S. (1984). *Stress, appraisal, and coping.* New York, NY: Springer.

Matheny, K. B., Aycock, D. W., Curlette, W. L., & Junker, G. N. (1993). The coping resources inventory for stress: A measure of perceived resourcefulness. *Journal of Clinical Psychology, 49*(6), 815–830.

McCarthy, C. J., Kerne, V. H., Calfa, N., Lambert, R. G., & Guzmán, M. (2010). An exploration of school counselors' demands and resources: Relationship to stress, biographic, and caseload characteristics. *Professional School Counselor, 13,* 146–158.

McCarthy, C. J., Kissen, D, Yadley, L., Wood, T., & Lambert, R. G. (2006). Relationship of teachers' preventive coping resources to burnout symptoms. In R. G. Lambert & C. J. McCarthy (Eds.), *Understanding teacher stress in an era of accountability* (Vol. III, pp. 179–196). Greenwich, CT: Information Age.

McCarthy, C. J., & Lambert, R. G. (2001). *Preventive resources inventory.* Austin, TX: University of Texas Department of Educational Psychology.

McCarthy, C. J., Lambert, R. G., Beard, L. M., & Dematatis, A. P. (2002). Factor structure of the Preventive Resources Inventory and its relationship to existing measures of stress and coping. In G. S. Gates, M. Wolverton, & W. H. Gmelch (Eds.), *Research on stress and coping in education* (pp. 3–37). Greenwich, CT: Information Age Publishing.

McCarthy, C. J., Lambert, R., & Brack, G. (1997). Structural model of coping, appraisals, and emotions after relationship breakup. *Journal of Counseling and Development, 76*(1), 53–64.

McCarthy, C.J., Lambert, R.G., Crowe, R. W., & McCarthy, C.J. (2010). Coping, stress, and job satisfaction as predictors of advanced placement statistics teachers' intention to leave the field. *NASSP Bulletin, 94,* 306–326.

McCarthy, C. J., Lambert, R. G., O'Donnell, M. & Melendres, L. (2009). Relationship of elementary teachers' experience, perceived demands, and coping resources to burnout symptoms. *Elementary School Journal, 109,* 1–19.

Moore, K. (2007). Foreword. In G. Gates, M. Wolverton, & W. Gmelch (Eds.), *Emerging thought and research on student, teacher, and administrator stress and coping* (pp. vii–x). Charlotte, NC: Information Age.

O'Donnell, M., Lambert, R., & McCarthy, C. (2008). School poverty status, time of year, and elementary teachers' perceptions of stress. *Journal of Educational Research, 102,* 152–160.

Sapolsky, R. M. (2004). *Why zebras don't get ulcers: An updated guide to stress, stress-related diseases, and coping.* New York, NY: W. H. Freeman.

Schaufeli, W. B., & Enzmann, D. (1998). *The burnout companion to study and practice: A critical analysis.* London, UK: Taylor & Francis.

Wilhelm, K. Dewhurst-Savellis, J., & Parker, G. (2000). Teacher stress? An analysis of why teachers leave and why they stay. *Teachers and Teaching: Theory and Practice, 6,* 291–304.

Zellars, K., Hochwarter, W., & Perrewé, P. (2004). Experiencing job burnout: The roles of positive and negative traits and states. *Journal of Applied and Social Psychology, 34,* 887–911.

CHAPTER 9

ASSESSING MULTICULTURAL COMPETENCE AND STRESS WITH TEACHERS

Chris McCarthy, Sonia Hart, Colleen McCarthy
Betsy Crowe, and Michele Guzmán
University of Texas at Austin

Rich Lambert
University of North Carolina at Charlotte

Jenson Reiser
University of Texas at Austin

ABSTRACT

This study (1) examined the effectiveness of a workshop on multicultural competence for teachers, and (2) replicated a study examining how teachers' perceptions of demands and resources in the classroom are related to their personal resources for coping with stress, job satisfaction, and intention to leave the profession. Participants were 77 elementary, middle, and high school teachers in a central Texas school district. Approximately one-third attended a workshop on dismantling stereotypes, and the remaining participants served as controls. All participants were given a vignette to assess multicultural competence and

International Perspectives on Teacher Stress, pages 175–194
Copyright © 2012 by Information Age Publishing
175

the Diversity Experiences Questionnaire (DEQ), which assessed stress experienced in dealing with students, parents, and administrators around diversity issues in school settings. At six-week follow-up, participants were contacted by e-mail to complete these measures again through an online survey system, as well as the following additional measure: the Preventive Resources Inventory—Self Acceptance Scale (PRI-Self-Acceptance), the Classroom Appraisal of Demands and Resources (CARD), a job satisfaction measure, and a measure of their Plans to Leave Current Job (PCLJ).

Results showed no significant time or intervention effect for vignette responses or teachers' responses on the DEQ—Stress or Frequency scales for students, teachers, or administrators. However, participants who reported utilizing workshop materials and ideas did report statistically significantly higher scores on the preparedness scale of the DEQ for working with students and parents at time two. In order to analyze how classroom resources and demands were associated with stress, job satisfaction, and intention to leave the profession, we classified teachers into the following three groups based on their CARD scores: demands < resources, demands = resources, and demands > resources, and compared the three groups on a series of stress-related outcomes. There were statistically significant differences between the groups on job satisfaction, stress associated with classroom diversity (DEQ), and intention to leave the field. Post hoc comparisons revealed that the demands > resources group reported lower job satisfaction, higher stress, and more likelihood to leave the profession.

While not significantly different for workshop attendees, the results of this study suggested the potential utility of using vignettes to assess multicultural competence. Vignettes offer the opportunity to evaluate responses that approximate actual behaviors, and are not time intensive to complete. Further, the results suggested that teachers perceiving high demand levels in relationship to classroom resources experience lower levels of job satisfaction and may be more likely to leave teaching. Such teachers may also find it more demanding to address the needs of diverse classrooms.

Teaching is clearly a stressful profession, and numerous chapters in this volume have investigated the phenomenon of stress in different countries. However, while research across national borders suggests the universality of stress, countries have their own unique histories with respect to race and broader diversity issues. The United States has a particular legacy of segregation, and later desegregation, with respect to education. Given this aspect of U.S. history, it seems plausible therefore that working with diverse classrooms could be a significant source of stress for teachers.

Teacher stress associated with classroom diversity is an inherently complex issue. This study had several objectives aimed at better understanding this phenomenon: first, we evaluated the effectiveness of a workshop designed to help teachers dismantle stereotypes in classroom interactions. In this part of the study, we were interested in examining whether such interventions helped teachers work with diversity in the classroom. The second part of the study replicates research conducted by Lambert, McCarthy, McCarthy, Crowe, and Fisher (this volume) using the Classroom Appraisal of Resources and Demands (CARD) with a sample of advanced placement statistics teachers in the United States. Because that study used only AP statistics teachers who may not be representative of other teachers, and because teachers' perceptions of diversity in the classroom were not addressed, in this study we replicated Lambert et al.'s procedures with educators across all levels of teaching and included a measure of teachers' experiences with diversity. The final objective stemmed from the need to use appropriate instruments to measure teacher stress associated with diversity: (1) we developed a shortened version of the Classroom Appraisal of Demands and Resources (S-CARD) so it could be given to teachers multiple times without excessive time burdens; (2) we developed a new measure designed to evaluate teachers' experience with diversity in the classroom, the Diversity Experiences Questionnaire (DEQ); and (3) we developed a vignette and coding system for evaluating teachers' capacities for dismantling stereotypes in the classroom. The analyses used to address the first two research objectives gave us information about the reliability and validity of these new measures.

EXAMINING TEACHER MULTICULTURAL COMPETENCE (MCC)

Multicultural competence (MCC) has been conceptualized as the awareness, knowledge, and skills that practitioners need to be able to work effectively with human diversity. Existing research, mainly in the area of multicultural counseling competence, relies on individual self-report rather than assessing demonstrated competencies. This can be problematic, as self-reports have several limitations, including a response bias related to social desirability as well as little empirical evidence that the responses correlate to actual behavior (Ponterotto, Mendelsohn, & Belizaire, 2003).

We examined teachers' multicultural competence (MCC) in this study using diversity-related vignettes to assess demonstrated competence before and after a workshop on how to address stereotyping behaviors. The workshop topic was "dismantling stereotypes," which was an hour-long discussion-based seminar led by one of the researchers. During this session, teachers increased their awareness of the stereotypes they subscribe to through an experiential exercise, learned about how and why people stereotype, and learned techniques for effectively addressing stereotyping in the classroom.

We were interested in whether teachers would demonstrate increased multicultural competence in handling student situations involving stereotyping after workshop participation. Den Brok, van Eerde, and Hajer (2010) posited that multiple methods of measurement are needed to show the full picture of interpersonal competence of teachers in diverse classrooms, but Worthington, Soth-McNett, and Moreno (2007) noted the dearth of studies in the literature that go beyond exploring *self-reported* MCC. We also found few studies in our literature review that attempted to examine concrete and demonstrated indicators of competence. Given that, our study aimed to show demonstrated, as opposed to self-reported, multicultural competence.

One approach to measuring demonstrated MCC is to evaluate responses to hypothetical multicultural situations. Studies by Brabeck, Rogers, Sirin, Henderson, Benvenuto, Weaver, and Ting (2000) and Sirin, Brabeck, Satiani, and Rogers-Serin (2003) pioneered research in this area by developing the Racial Ethical Sensitivity Test (REST), which consisted of five videotaped scenarios followed by an interactive interview in order to measure teachers' ethical sensitivity to racial and gender intolerance in schools. Such procedures were impractical for this study, but Guzmán, Calfa, Kern, and McCarthy (2011) used multiple written scenarios about multicultural situations presented to school counselors using an online survey tool. Participants were asked to write about how they would respond to these situations, and the responses were coded by raters as to the level of MCC demonstrated in the response. Guzmán et al. (2011) found that raters demonstrated adequate levels of reliability and that school counselor self-ratings of MCC did not predict vignette ratings of demonstrated MCC. However, it was found that younger school counselors with less experience had higher ratings on some vignettes, possibly due to more recent graduate school training emphasizing multicultural competence (Guzmán et al., 2011). This study built on that research by utilizing a pre/post design to assess whether teachers attending a professional development workshop on dismantling stereotypes exhibited differences in their responses to a vignette about students demonstrating stereotyping behavior.

EXAMINING TEACHER DEMANDS AND RESOURCES

As was noted by Lambert et al. (this volume), very few studies have investigated the central tenet of Lazarus and Folkman's (1984) model, namely that both perceptions of demands and resources need to be considered together when investigating individual perceptions of stress (Moore, 2007). Our second study objective therefore was addressed by replicating Lambert et al.'s classification of teachers using the CARD. Lambert et al. (this volume) described the importance of investigating both teacher perceptions of demands and resources in the classroom in order to be consistent with transactional theories of stress. Lazarus and Folkman (1984) maintain that stress is the result of subjective, reflexive transactions that occur when life demands are encountered and weighed against one's perceived resources for coping. In the context of teaching, Lazarus and Folkman's theory would suggest that when an educator perceives that classroom demands outweigh available resources for coping with them, stress is the likely outcome.

The demands and resources scales from a shortened version of the CARD (S-CARD) were used to create an appraisal index (for a description of this procedure, see Lambert et al., this volume) for participants in this study. This index was used to classify teachers into three groups: teachers rating themselves as high in classroom resources but low in classroom demands $(R > D)$; those rating classroom demands and resources as equal $(R = D)$, and those rating classroom demands high and resources low $(D > R)$. Lambert et al. named these teacher classifications as *resourced, balanced,* and *demand* groups, respectively.

Lambert et al. (this volume) found that resourced AP statistics teachers reported more job satisfaction and less intention to leave the field. They noted that understanding teacher perceptions of demands and resources in the classroom could be an important component of teacher satisfaction and retention. In order to test the replicability of these findings, the same variables were analyzed in this study using a broader range of teachers, including elementary, middle, and high school teachers teaching various subjects in a school district in central Texas. Specifically, we examined whether the CARD classification system revealed group differences on the following variables: teachers' personal resources for preventing stress, job satisfaction, and intention to leave the profession. As was noted above, because teachers' perceptions of diversity in the classroom were fundamental to this study and were not addressed in Lambert et al.'s study, we also included a measure of teachers' experiences with diversity in these analyses.

SUMMARY OF STUDY OBJECTIVES

There were three objectives of this study: first, to evaluate the effectiveness of a stereotype dismantling workshop using diversity-related vignettes. The second objective of this study replicates analyses by Lambert et al., and extends this research by replicating it with teachers across all levels (K–12) and by examining teachers' perceptions of stress caused by diversity-related issues with students, parents, and administrators. The final objective centered upon the development of several study measures: (1) we developed a short version of the Classroom Appraisal of Demands and Resources (S-CARD), (2) developed a new measure designed to evaluate teachers' experience with diversity in the classroom, the Diversity Experiences Questionnaire (DEQ), and (3) developed a vignette and coding system for evaluating teachers' capacities for dismantling stereotypes in the classroom.

The analyses used to address research objectives one and two also gave us information about the reliability and validity of these new measures in order to address this last research objective.

METHODS

Participants and Procedure

Participants were teachers from a central Texas school district who voluntarily signed up for the study at an annual diversity conference or participated as part of required professional development. The school district is located in a city of nearly 50,000 residents. Due to its close proximity to a large city, it has experienced rapid growth in the past few decades. The majority of residents are of White, European descent (approximately 65%), while a majority of the remainder identify as Hispanic/Latino (24%) or African American (14%).

There were 79 participants in this study; 89.5% were female and 76.3% were White/European Americans, 17.1% Latino/a, and 3.9% African American. A total of 48.6% currently taught at the elementary school level, 41.9% at the middle school level, and 9.5% at the high school level. On average, participants had taught for 4.77 years ($SD = 4$) at their current grade level. Participants also reported that 30.3% of them had worked at the elementary school level for 1–5 years, 9.2% for 6–10 years, 17.1% for 11–22 years, and 6.6% for 24–28 years. At the middle school level, 28.9% taught for 1–5 years, 10.6% for 6–10 years, and 21.8% for 11–22 years, and at the high school level, 13.2% taught for 1–5 years and 7.9% taught for 7–14 years. The average class size was 20.79 ($SD = 8.8$).

In terms of multicultural training, 20.8% said they had no multicultural training, and 79.2% had multicultural training. Fifty percent of teachers reported that their multicultural training was considered mandatory, and 57.1% reported that they had received multicultural training from outside of their school district. When asked to rate the quality of their multicultural training, 7.8% rated "fair," 16.9% "satisfactory," 44.2% "good," and 31.2% "excellent." When asked how much multicultural competency training was integrated into their classroom, 2.6% reported it was "not at all" integrated, 14.3% "limited," 37.7% "somewhat," 32.5% "a good amount," and 13% reported it was "well integrated." Participants in the intervention condition were asked if they utilized workshop information at follow-up, and reported the following: 21.4% "not at all," 14.3% "very little," 42.9% "somewhat," 21.4% "a good amount."

When asked of their plans to leave the teaching profession, 45.95% reported that they had considered leaving the teaching profession in the past five years, and 33.33% considered leaving in the past year; 16.22% of participants had applied for a job outside the teaching profession within the past five years, and 8.67% within the past year. When asked of their plans for transferring to a different school or district, 53.38% reported that they had considered transferring in the past five years, and 32.67% in the past year; 26.85% of participants had applied for a job in a different school or district within the past five years, and 12.00% within the past year, while 9.46% reported that they had applied for a different job in their current school in the past five years, and 4.00% in the past year. Nearly all—92.62% of participants—intended to remain teaching at their current school for the next school year and 98.00% intended to remain teaching for the next year.

Participants in the intervention group (36.4% of the total sample) attended a workshop on stereotyping and completed pre- and post-surveys, while control group participants (63.6%) answered only the pre- and post-questionnaires. One of the authors conducted the workshops with a blend of elementary, middle, and high school teachers entitled "Dismantling Stereotypes: Fostering Deeper Diversity Awareness." Each workshop had 30 or more participants who attended for 75 minutes. The workshop had participants explore diversity situations within an educational setting by presenting information on stereotypes, taking part in a self-reflective activity, and engaging in small- and large-group discussions regarding stereotypes and their potential impact. All participants in the control and intervention conditions were asked to fill out a diversity vignette before beginning the workshop, and then again six weeks after participation, in addition to measures on diversity experiences, perceived classroom demands and resources, job satisfaction, and intent to stay in the profession (see description of instruments below).

Instruments

Diversity Experiences Questionnaire (DEQ)

This survey was constructed by the study authors. The DEQ assessed the frequency, stressfulness, and preparation the participants experienced in regard to diversity issues in school settings. Based on the methods used by Matheny and Cupp (1983) to adapt a measure of stressful life experiences, this measure consisted of (1) ten questions about frequency of, stressfulness of, and preparation for issues of diversity with students; (2) five questions measuring the same three variables for issues with parents of students; and (3) six questions for issues with administrators. Items were pilot tested with school counselors to develop item content and clarity before being used in the study.

Diversity Vignette

The diversity vignette exercise was modeled from vignette prompts developed for a study of school counselor stress (Guzmán et al., 2011). The prompt asks how participants would respond to or intervene in a group of African American students making fun of a Latino student as presented in the following scenario:

> Before the bell rings, a group of African American students are sitting together in the classroom talking and laughing. The group is "ripping" on one of their peers about his overgrown lawn. "The weeds are so high that I need a GPS system to get from the sidewalk to your house." The student being picked on turns to a Latino student, "Hey Jose, how much would I have to pay you to mow my lawn?" How might you respond or intervene?

Participants read the scenario independently and were instructed to write their response to this situation. The vignette was coded by members of the research team on a four-point ranking scale (0, 1, 2, and 3). The coding rubric was modeled after Guzmán et al.'s (2011) study with school counselors and measured the teachers' demonstrated ability to respond to the situation in a multiculturally competent way. For example, a three-point response could address the issue of stereotyping groups by reflecting on how African Americans have also been stereotyped. In addition, a three-point response would also bring up how stereotyping affects people. An example of a three-point response from a participant was:

> I would continue to listen in and let Jose answer this question. If he didn't answer the other student's question then I would interject and ask the student, "Why did you ask Jose how much he would charge?" I would give him some to reflect and see how he answers. Then I would ask, "Why didn't you ask me? I'm Mexican. I was born in the U.S. but my family is of Mexican descent. Just because someone is Mexican doesn't give you the right to stereotype and pick on someone like that and make derogatory comments. Making them feel less than because of their ethnicity."

A two-point response made reference to or addressed explicitly the fact that the situation involved stereotyping or prejudice but did not go any further in helping the students learn to dismantle stereotypes. A two-point response simply included some language that reflected awareness of stereotyping but indicated no further intervention:

> I would let them know that the comment was rude and it offended me just to hear it. I would also explain that stereotyping is not okay and asks the "how would you feel if you were asked..." or stereotyped.

A one-point response exhibited a "universal" intervention, which addressed the inappropriateness of the comment but not the issue of stereotyping directly. Instead, the participant would identify the situation as mean, not nice, or insensitive but did not include any language demonstrating awareness of or reference to stereotyping and its effects in a meaningful way. An example of a one-point response stated:

> I always talk with my students that they need to talk with and about each other the way they want to be treated. I then ask them better ways they could have handled the situation.

A zero-point response was given to teachers who wrote that they would ignore the situation and instead redirect the class to other activities without addressing the situation in any corrective manner. For example, a zero-point response said:

> I would casually joke about how tough it is to keep the grass cut and how I could use some help myself. I would redirect the conversation and turn students' attention to our class topics for the day.

Four of the authors coded the vignettes. Scoring criteria were developed and the coders first rated vignettes independently and then worked as a group to resolve differences in codes assigned to each vignette. This process was iterative, in that a set of vignettes were coded, differences in coding were discussed and resolved, and then the scoring criteria were adjusted to refine criteria that caused inconsistency or confusion for the coders. Overall, the four coders reached an initial inter-rater reliability of 42% at Time 1 and 43% at Time 2 when coding independently. After continued discussion among the raters, they reached 100% consensus, and these ratings were used in the study analyses.

Measures of Stress, Coping, and Classroom Demands and Resources

The following measures replicated research conducted by Lambert et al. (this volume). Brief descriptions of each measure follow, and reliabilities for these measures and the DEQ are presented in Table 9.1. More lengthy information for each study measure can be found in the chapter titled, "Assessment of Teacher Demands and Resources: Relationship to Stress, Classroom Structural Characteristics, Job Satisfaction, and Turnover" (Lambert et al., this volume).

Preventive Resources Inventory-Self-Acceptance

The PRI is a self-report measure designed to explore an individual's level of agreement with items assessing their perceived ability to prevent stressful reactions to life circumstances. The self-acceptance scale (PRI-

TABLE 9.1 Correlations Between Scale Scores

	Self Acceptance	Job Satisfaction	Plans to Leave	Classroom Demands	Classroom Resources	Stress	Student Stress	Parent Stress	Administrative Stress
Self Acceptance	0.915								
Job Satisfaction	0.345	0.882							
Plans to Leave	0.004	−0.381	0.839						
Classroom Demands	0.077	−0.053	0.155	0.834					
Classroom Resources	0.040	0.430	−0.225	−0.071	0.927				
Stress	0.025	−0.330	0.260	0.732	−0.732	0.888			
Student Stress	−0.415	−0.391	0.081	0.428	−0.217	0.443	0.883		
Parent Stress	−0.291	−0.226	0.211	0.465	−0.028	0.339	0.604	0.896	
Administrative Stress	−0.326	−0.235	0.174	0.401	−0.174	0.395	6.659	0.706	0.922

Note: Cronbach's alpha reliabilities are reported in italics on the main diagonal of the matrix.

Self-Acceptance; McCarthy, Lambert, Beard, & Dematatis, 2002) is a 15-item scale used to assess overall preventive coping resources, and uses a five-point Likert scale ranging from "strongly disagree" to "strongly agree." Specifically, this subscale assesses the degree to which one can accept and overcome personal strengths and weaknesses in demanding life situations (McCarthy et al., 2002). The self-acceptance scale has been suggested as an appropriate proxy for the total score from the full-length version of the PRI in that it has been found to be related to level of perceived stress and burnout in teachers (McCarthy, Kissen, Yadley, Wood, & Lambert, 2006).

Classroom Appraisal of Resources and Demands-Short Version (S-CARD)

This study used a shortened version of the Classroom Appraisal of Resources and Demands (S-CARD). The CARD measures teacher stress and is grounded in the transactional model of stress and coping (Lambert, McCarthy, & Abbott-Shim, 2001). The measure asks teachers to rate the severity of demands and helpfulness of resources in the classroom using a five-point Likert scale ranging from 1, "not demanding," to 5, "extremely demanding." Scores on a 12-point demand scale and 12-item resource scale can be combined to form an overall teacher stress scale score.

The S-CARD, used in this study, yields a classroom demand score (mean = 50.003, SD = 10.005), a classroom resource score (mean = 50.003, SD = 10.002), and a stress score based on the differences between the two scale scores (mean = –.001, SD = 14.642). T-score scaling (mean = 50, SD = 10) is used for the demands and resources scale. Therefore, this sample of teachers reported, on average, typical levels of classroom demands and resources. Compared to the national norm for the stress score (mean = 0, SD = 15), this sample of teachers, on average, reported expected stress levels. The Cronbach's alpha reliability coefficients, using this sample and the short form of the CARD, were as follows: demands = .834, resources = .927, and stress = .888. For additional details regarding the scoring, subscales, and validity evidence for the CARD measure, the reader is referred to Lambert, McCarthy, O'Donnell, and Wang (2009).

Job Satisfaction
(Koeske, Kirk, Koeske, & Rauktis, 1994)

This measure contains fourteen items and was adapted from Koeske et al. (1994) to assess teacher-reported satisfaction with working conditions, organizational climate, salary, promotion, and benefits issues. Koeske et al. reported developing and evaluating the validity of this measure using with over 600 individuals. These studies occurred over a ten-year timeframe with a range of helping professions. Sample-specific alpha reliabilities ranging from .78 to .91 were reported by Koeske et al. as well as validity evidence through negative correlations of job satisfaction with burnout, depression, and intention to quit one's job. Cronbach's alpha reliability for this sample was .88.

Plans to Leave Current Job (PCLJ)
(Fisher, Lambert, & McCarthy, 2009)

The Plans to Leave Current Job is a 13-item scale adapted from Fisher et al. (2009). The PCLJ assesses teacher's job-seeking activities and intentions to leave their current positions. Items on the measure ask respondents a series of questions regarding whether they had made specific plans to leave their current position. Cronbach's alpha reliability for this study was .84. Additional information about this measure is included in the preceding chapter by Lambert et al. (this volume).

Procedures

The first phase of data collection was from teachers in a central Texas school district attending a diversity conference sponsored by the district. The second phase of data collection occurred when the study workshop was given to teachers on one middle school campus. All participants in the intervention condition attended the Dismantling Stereotypes workshop, which occurred at the diversity conference and was given again for teachers at one middle school campus. Control group participants were recruited from the diversity conference among teachers not attending the workshop. Since all participants in the second phase of data collection participated in the workshop, they were all included in the intervention condition.

The Dismantling Stereotypes workshop was offered in two independent sessions during the conference and again at a middle school campus later in the semester. Before beginning the workshop, participants were told that they could volunteer to participate in a study. Copies of the study cover letter and part one of the questionnaire were handed out to everyone so that those who were not interested in participating did not feel singled out. In phase one, all participants completed a short demographics inventory, the Diversity Experiences Questionnaire (DEQ), and stereotype vignette. Participants also provided their name and e-mail in order to be contacted six weeks after the conference to complete the second phase of the study. Participants then completed the Dismantling Stereotypes workshop.

At time two of the data collection six weeks later, all participants were sent an internet link to a survey with the study measures, which included the DEQ, stereotype vignette measure, PRI-self acceptance scale, the Classroom Appraisal of Demands and Resources-Short Version, the job satisfaction measure, and the PCLJ. Reminder emails were sent to participants who did not respond to the first email one week later, and a second, final reminder was sent two weeks after the initial email. In order to protect confidentiality, no identifying information was associated with any of the data collected from the participants. Participants were informed that by completing the second, online phase of the study, they would receive a $10 Target gift certificate sent through PISD inter-campus mail. The same procedures were followed for participants recruited for the study later in the semester at a middle school campus.

As was noted, participants for the control group were recruited during the lunch session of the diversity conference. Signs were posted in the school library where teachers were allowed to sit for lunch and researchers made an announcement about the study and circulated the cover letter and surveys. The same procedure as described above was repeated for these participants with the exception that they did not attend the workshop after completing the questionnaire packet.

RESULTS

Study Objective One—Workshop Effectiveness

There was no significant improvement in teachers' vignette responses before and after the Dismantling Stereotypes workshop. Those who attended the workshop did not perform better on the vignettes than those who did not. However, nonwhite teachers were found to score significantly higher on the vignettes than White teachers at the second data collection point ($\chi^2 = 6.285$, $p = .012$). Workshop attendance also was not related to teachers' responses on the DEQ-Stress or Preparedness scales for students, teachers, or administrators. Exploratory analyses were conducted to see if teachers' responses for the entire sample differed on the DEQ from Time 1 to Time 2. Interestingly, teachers' reports about the stressfulness and frequency of these events showed a statistically significant decline from Time 1 to Time 2. However, participants also reported a statistically significant decrease in how prepared they felt in handling diversity in the classroom with respect to students and administrators, but not parents.

Participants who participated in the intervention were asked if they utilized what they learned, and those who reported utilizing workshop materials or ideas did report statistically significantly higher scores on the DEQ preparedness scale for dealing with students ($R^2 = .231$, $p = .033$) and parents ($R^2 = .258$, $p = .012$). In other words, it was found that attendance at the workshop alone was not sufficient to increase self-reports of preparedness: Teachers needed to implement the material learned.

Research Question Two—Examination of Teacher Stress

Table 9.1 contains the correlations between the scale scores from by the various measures in the study. The CARD scale scores can be used to classify teachers into three groups: resources greater than demands (R > D, 28.9%), demands equal to resources (D = R, 47.4%), and demands greater than resources (D > R, 23.7%). The D > R group is considered to be at risk for occupational stress. One-way ANOVA was used to investigate differences between teachers in these three groups for the following dependent variables: self-acceptance, job satisfaction, plans to leave education, student stress, parent stress, and administrative stress. These analyses were designed to examine whether the teachers in the D > R group also reported lower stress prevention skills, lower job satisfaction, more plans to leave the profession, and higher stress levels than did the other groups. Prior to conducting these analyses, we first demonstrated that there were no differences in class size between the groups ($F_{(2,73)}$ = .245, p = .784).

We decided to analyze only DEQ scores at Time 1 for research objective two. The rationale for choosing Time 1 is that at this point all of the participants were responding to the measure without the diversity training offered to participants, and therefore were not likely to be differentially responding based on ideas provided by the researchers. This seemed a reasonable precaution even though the pattern of results above showed only a difference between DEQ scores at Time 1 and Time 2 due to time, and not workshop participation.

There were statistically significant differences between the three groups for the following dependent variables: job satisfaction ($F_{(2,73)}$ = 4.253, p = .018), and on the DEQ, student stress ($F_{(2,73)}$ = 11.863, p < .001), parent stress ($F_{(2,73)}$ = 4.620, p = .013), and administrative stress ($F_{(2,73)}$ = 7.287, p < .001). Tukey HSD post hoc comparisons indicated that the D > R group had statistically significantly lower average job satisfaction and higher stress than teachers in the other two groups. There were not statistically significant differences between the groups for the self-acceptance ($F_{(2,73)}$ = 2.183, p = .120) and plans to leave education ($F_{(2,73)}$ = 2.505, p < .089) scale scores.

As shown in Table 9.2, standardized mean difference effect sizes were calculated to represent the difference between the D > R group and the other two groups for each dependent variable. There were moderately large differences in job satisfaction between the D > R group and teachers in both the D = R (d = .643) and R > D (d = .678) groups. There were very large differences in student stress between the D > R group and teachers in both the D = R (d = −1.347) and R > D (d = −1.381) groups. There were large differences in parent stress between the D > R group and teachers in both the D = R (d = −.677) and R > D (d = −.893) groups. There were also large differ-

TABLE 9.2   Differences Between the Stress Groups

Measure		Group 1 D < R (n = 22)	Group 2 D = R (n = 36)	Group 3 D > R (n = 18)	Post Hoc	Effect Sizes 1 vs. 3	Effect Sizes 2 vs. 3
Self Acceptance	Mean	4.006	4.265	4.011		−0.010	0.492
	SD	0.742	0.369	0.516			
Job Satisfaction	Mean	5.325	5.289	4.619	1,2 > 3	0.678	0.643
	SD	0.826	0.801	1.042			
Plans to Leave	Mean	3.909	5.444	6.778		−0.628	−0.292
	SD	3.963	3.850	4.570			
Student Stress	Mean	1.742	1.757	2.362	1,2 < 3	−1.381	−1.347
	SD	0.498	0.450	0.449			
Parent Stress	Mean	1.971	2.169	2.789	1,2 < 3	−0.893	−0.677
	SD	0.908	0.835	0.916			
Administrative Stress	Mean	1.687	1.894	2.434	1,2 < 3	−1.032	−0.746
	SD	0.603	0.594	0.724			

ences in administrative stress between the D > R group and teachers in both the D = R ($d = -1.032$) and R > D ($d = -.746$) groups.

As shown in Table 9.3, there were also statistically significant differences between the groups with respect to the percentage of teachers reporting that they had made the decision to pursue a different job ($\chi^2_{(2)} = 6.066$, $p = .048$). For the D > R group, 55.6% reported having made the decision to leave as compared to 38.9% for the D = R group and 18.2% for the R > D group. We also conducted a logistic regression analysis (see Table 9.4) to examine the likelihood that teachers would report an intention to leave the profession. The independent variables in this analysis were membership in the D > R group and job satisfaction scores. In the first step in the model, only membership in the D > R group was included, and these teachers had almost three times more likelihood of reporting an intention to leave (odds ratio = 2.986) than teachers in the other two groups. When job satisfaction was entered into the model, membership in the D > R group was no longer a statistically significant predictor. The model results indicated that for every increase of one point on the job satisfaction measure teachers would be more than two times less likely to report an intention to leave (odds ratio = .295). Since research objective three relies on an evaluation of the performance of the newly developed measures utilized in this study, consideration of this objective will be used to begin the discussion section.

TABLE 9.3   Intention to Leave Current Job by Stress Group

		Group		
		D < R (n = 22)	D = R (n = 36)	D > R (n = 18)
Intend to stay	%	81.8%	61.1%	44.4%
	n	18	22	8
Intend to leave	%	18.2%	38.9%	55.6%
	n	4	14	10

TABLE 9.4   Intention to Leave Current Job by Stress Group

Step	Predictor	β	Exp(β)	p
I	D > R group	1.094	2.986	0.047
II	D > R group	0.408	1.504	0.523
	Job satisfaction	−1.220	0.295	0.001

DISCUSSION

Research objective three of this study examined the psychometric properties of the three exploratory measures used in this study. The first was the short-ened version of the CARD. Several of the coefficients presented in Table 9.1 demonstrate validity evidence for the short form of the CARD by illustrating how it yields scale scores that are related both to each other and other mea-sures of similar constructs with expected magnitude and direction. For exam-ple, the Demands and Resources scales appear to be measuring separate con-structs and were not correlated with each other ($r = -.071$). The CARD short form demands score was moderately correlated with the measures of student stress ($r = .428$), parent stress ($r = .465$), and administrative stress ($r = .401$). Similarly, the CARD short form stress score was moderately correlated with the same measures of student stress ($r = .443$), parent stress ($r = .339$), and admin-istrative stress ($r = .395$). The measure of job satisfaction was moderately posi-tively correlated with the CARD short form resources score ($r = .430$), moder-ately negatively correlated with the CARD short form stress score ($r = -.330$), but not correlated with the CARD short form demands score ($r = -.053$). It is also interesting to note that the self-acceptance score was moderately nega-tively correlated with the measures of student stress ($r = -.415$), parent stress ($r = -.291$), and administrative stress ($r = -.326$).

The DEQ was also found to be a reliable measure, and while teacher scores did not differ before and after the workshop, the measure demonstrated robust correlations with other study instruments, suggesting it may be useful for further research in this area. Additionally, differences were observed in CARD classification groups for analyses in which the DEQ was the dependent measure. These results indicated that teachers who perceived classroom demands as high were also likely to perceive higher demands associated with diversity in the classroom. One surprising finding was the change in teacher scores from Time 1 to Time 2 in this study, which indicated that teachers found diversity situations less frequent and less stressful as the semester progressed. This was contrary to our expectations and necessitates future research. It is possible that such trends could simply represent measurement error from teachers not recalling their responses from the first time they took the DEQ. It is also possible that teachers became accustomed to situations involving diversity in the classroom over time due to increased experience and familiarity with the situations.

Turning to research objective one, the results suggested the potential utility of using vignettes to assess MCC. We were able to code the vignettes in a reliable manner, and they seemed to yield useful information about teachers' capacities for responding to diversity scenarios.

The results for the vignette scores, as developed and coded for this study, suggest the need for further research on the best ways to understand and assess MCC. While teachers' responses on the vignettes were not found to differ before and after a stereotype-dismantling workshop, differences were found for teachers who reported using the workshop information. We found the challenges of utilizing scenarios and vignettes to assess competencies were varied: It was labor-intensive for investigators as compared to self-report measures. We also found many challenges associated with being consistent in scoring vignettes based on the limited information provided in the vignette responses (i.e., most teachers answered the vignettes with only a few sentences).

Research objective two replicated findings by Lambert et al. (this volume), who found that teachers who perceived classroom demands as high relative to their resources experienced less job satisfaction and reported more plans to leave the profession. Imbedded in the second question of this study, as an extension of Lambert et al.'s research, was an examination of whether high-demand teachers also experienced more stress associated with diversity in the classroom. We were able to replicate Lambert et al.'s findings that teachers in the demand group reported lower levels of satisfaction and no difference in teachers' preventive coping resources, but we failed to replicate Lambert et al.'s finding that overall scores on the PLCJ were higher for teachers in the demand group. This may be due to the lower sample size and statistical power in this study and the lower reliability of the S-CARD, which contained fewer items than the full length CARD. The finding in this study that teachers in the demand group also reported higher levels of stress on the DEQ may suggest an important link between teachers perceptions of stress in general and those due to working with diverse classrooms.

A consistent pattern of results from the CARD classification was observed with respect to items from the PCLJ indicating which teachers had made the decision to leave the field. As can be seen in Table 9.3, over half of the teachers reporting intentions to leave the profession were in the demand group. The logistic regression analysis (see Table 9.4) used to examine the likelihood that teachers would report an intention to leave the profession as a function of membership in the demand group indicated that when job satisfaction was entered into the model, membership in the demand group was no longer a statistically significant predictor. These results are consistent with McCarthy, Lambert, Crowe, and McCarthy's (2010) finding that the relationship of teacher appraisals of classroom demands and resources and intention to leave the field is mediated by job satisfaction. In other words, perception of an imbalance of classroom demands and resources was found to be associated with low job satisfaction, which in turn was associated with intention to leave the field.

Limitations and Suggestions for Future Research

A number of limitations should be noted in interpreting the results of this study. First, the sample for the study was relatively small, and we gathered proportionally more follow-up data from control group participants. Second, the lack of results for the intervention group may suggest the need for longer and more sustained interventions. A third notable limitation is the use of exploratory measures developed specifically for this study, which need further research as to their reliability and validity.

We hope that this study will generate future research about how to best promote and measure teacher MCC. Specifically, how can we take the multicultural competencies that have been developed over the last 30 years and utilize them to formulate a standardized and consistent rating system for responses to situations highlighting multicultural competence in teachers? Finally, the possible link found in this study between classroom stress and stress associated classroom diversity will be important to address in future research. While this study found that teachers classified as high in demands also reported multicultural situations as stressful, we were not able to ascertain if there was a causal relationship between these constructs or if both were influenced by other variables not assessed in this study. Given that classrooms in the United States are diverse, understanding the interrelationship between teacher stress and MCC seems to be a critical area for future research.

ACKNOWLEDGEMENTS

The authors wish to acknowledge the Pflugerville Texas School District for their participation in this study and the Division of Diversity and Community Engagement at the University of Texas at Austin for providing funding for gift cards used to recruit participants.

REFERENCES

Brabeck, M. M., Rogers, L. A., Sirin, S., Henderson, J., Benvenuto, M., Weaver, M., & Ting, K. (2000). Increasing ethical sensitivity to racial and gender intolerance in schools: Development of the racial ethical sensitivity test. *Ethics & Behavior, 10,* 119-137.

den Brok, P., van Eerde, D., & Hajer, M. (2010). Classroom interaction studies as a source for teacher competencies: The use of case studies with multiple instruments for studying teacher competencies in multicultural classes. *Teachers And Teaching: Theory And Practice, 16*(6), 717–733.

Fisher, M., Lambert, R., & McCarthy, C. (2009). *Plans to leave current job.* Charlotte, NC: The Center for Educational Measurement and Evaluation.

Guzmán, M. G., Calfa, N. A., Kern, V., & McCarthy, C. J. (2011). *Examination of multicultural competencies in school counselors.* Unpublished manuscript.

Koeske, G.F., Kirk, S.A., Koeske, R.D., & Rauktis, M.B. (1994). Measuring the Monday blues: Validation of a job satisfaction scale for the human services. *Social Work Research, 18*(1), 27–35.

Lambert, R. G., McCarthy, C. J., & Abbott-Shim, M. (2001). *Classroom appraisal of resources and demands, school-age version.* Atlanta, GA: Head Start Quality Research Center.

Lambert, R. G., McCarthy, C. J., O' Donnell, M., & Wang, C. (2009). Measuring elementary teacher stress and coping in the classroom: Validity evidence for the classroom appraisal of resources and demands. *Psychology in the Schools, 46,* 973–988.

Lazarus, R. S., & Folkman, S. (1984). *Stress, appraisal, and coping.* New York, NY: Springer.

Matheny, K. B., & Cupp, P. (1983). Control, desirability, and anticipation as moderating variables between life change and illness. *Journal of Human Stress, 9*(2), 14–23.

McCarthy, C. J., Kissen, D., Yadley, L., Wood, T., & Lambert, R. G. (2006). Relationship of teachers' preventive coping resources to burnout symptoms. In R. G. Lambert & C. J. McCarthy (Eds.), *Understanding teacher stress in an era of accountability* (Vol. III, pp. 179–196). Greenwich, CT: Information Age.

McCarthy, C. J., Lambert, R. G., Beard, L. M., & Dematatis, A. P. (2002). Factor structure of the Preventive Resources Inventory and its relationship to existing measures of stress and coping. In G. S. Gates, M. Wolverton, & W. H. Gmelch (Eds.), *Research on Stress and Coping in Education* (pp. 3–37). Greenwich, CT: Information Age.

Moore, K. (2007). Foreword. In G. Gates, M. Wolverton, & W. Gmelch, (Eds.), *Emerging thought and research on student, teacher, and administrator stress and coping* (pp. vii–x). Charlotte, NC: Information Age Publishing.

Ponterotto, J. G., Mendelsohn, J., & Belizaire, L. (2003). Assessing teacher multicultural competence: Self-reporting instruments, observer report evaluations, and a portfolio assessment. In D. B. Pope-Davis, H. K. Coleman, W. Liu, R. L. Toporek, D. B. Pope-Davis, H. K. Coleman, ... R. L. Toporek (Eds.), *Handbook of multicultural competencies: In counseling & psychology* (pp. 191–210). Thousand Oaks, CA: Sage.

Sirin, S. R., Brabeck, M. M., Satiani, A., & Rogers-Serin, L. (2003). Validation of a measure of ethical sensitivity and examination of the effects of a previous multicultural and ethics courses on ethical sensitivity. *Ethics and Behavior, 13*(3), 221–235.

Worthington, R. L., Soth-McNett, A. M., & Moreno, M. V. (2007). Multicultural counseling competencies research: A 20-year content analysis. *Journal of Counseling Psychology, 54*, 351–361.

CHAPTER 10

BURNOUT AND COPING STRATEGIES ACROSS PRIMARY AND SECONDARY PUBLIC SCHOOLTEACHERS

Russell L. Carson
Louisiana State University

Costas N. Tsouloupas
University of Nicosia

Larissa K. Barber
Northern Illinois University

ABSTRACT

Using Lazarus and Folkman's (1984) transactional model of coping and Hobfoll's (1989, 2001) Conservation of Resources (COR) theory, this study set out to determine the role, if any, that teaching level plays in teacher burnout, coping strategies, and the effectiveness of coping strategies in predicting teacher burnout. Participants were 646 full-time primary ($n = 302$) and secondary ($n = 344$) public schoolteachers from five school districts across the Southeastern and Midwestern regions of the U.S. Data were collected via self-report online surveys. Initial results indicated that classroom demands (class size, positive

International Perspectives on Teacher Stress, pages 195–218
Copyright © 2012 by Information Age Publishing
All rights of reproduction in any form reserved.

and negative student interactions), one teacher resource (years of experience), and one facet of burnout (emotional exhaustion) significantly differed across primary teachers, but not the use of specific coping strategies. Exploratory factor analyses also indicated that specific coping strategies were best categorized into active (instrumental support, planning, emotional support, positive reframing) and defensive (venting, behavioral disengagement, self-blame), in line with COR theory. Hierarchical regression across all teachers (controlling for demands and resources) indicated that active strategies were a significant predictor of depersonalization and personal accomplishment, whereas defensive strategies predicted depersonalization and emotional exhaustion. More interestingly, significant interactions indicated that the association between defensive strategies and two dimensions of burnout (depersonalization, reduced personal accomplishment) was stronger in secondary teachers than primary teachers, with no reduced personal accomplishment–depersonalization association in primary teachers. The association between active strategies and reduced personal accomplishment was also marginally stronger in secondary teachers. These findings suggest that (1) coping–burnout relationship can vary across teaching levels, and (2) a dichotomous (active *vs.* passive) coping classification might be more appropriate for future teacher coping studies.

Burnout, conceptualized as consisting of three dimensions: *emotional exhaustion* (i.e., feeling emotionally drained by the intense contact with others), *depersonalization* (i.e., negative, detached attitudes towards others), and *reduced personal accomplishment* (i.e., reduced sense of competence and achievement at work) (Maslach, Leiter, & Schaufeli, 2008), continues to be a significant and international phenomenon among teachers. When compared with other human service professions, teachers have been repeatedly found to exhibit higher levels of burnout (Maslach, Jackson, & Leiter, 1996; Schaufeli & Enzmann, 1998). Of particular concern have been primary (Malik, Mueller, & Meinke, 1991) or secondary (Byrne, 1999) schoolteachers with neurotic, introverted, or negative affective personalities (Carson, Plemmons, Templin, & Weiss, 2011; Kokkinos, 2007; Teven, 2007). Adverse outcomes have been shown to be related to teachers' ill health, withdrawal behaviors, reduced efficacy beliefs, and turnover intentions (Cropanzano, Rupp, & Byrne, 2003; Dormann & Kaiser, 2002; Tsouloupas, Carson, Matthews, Grawitch, & Barber, 2010). However, little research has directly examined differences in coping strategies and burnout in primary versus secondary school teachers, and how these differences may be due to variation in classroom demands and teacher resources.

TRANSACTIONAL THEORY OF COPING

A critical and growing concern among educational researchers across the globe has been to understand the coping processes associated with teachers' burnout feelings via Lazarus and Folkman's (1984) transactional model. This model portrays stress as a derivative of the conscious evaluation between one's perceived *demands* of any given situation and one's perceived *resources* to handle that situation. In this reflexive transaction, if the situation is perceived to present a demand that threatens, harms, or challenges one's capabilities and resources to meet that demand, it triggers both a stress reaction and the motivation to engage in specific coping strategies to address this perceived stress reaction. Burnout, then, would be the byproduct of unsuccessful attempts to cope with the stress reaction (Chang, 2009; McCarthy, Lambert, O'Donnell, & Melendres, 2009). Important implications from the transactional theory of coping are twofold: (1) stress and burnout stem from a collective blend of demands and resources found externally (environment) or internally (capabilities), and (2) the motivation to cope with a stressful situation is largely dependent upon an individual's *cognitive* appraisal of the situation (Aldwin, 2009; Chang, 2009).

The coping strategies one chooses in response to stress have been proposed to fall within two broad categories: problem-focused and emotion-focused coping (Folkman & Lazarus, 1980). These categorizations are largely based on the function served (i.e., addressing the situation or one's reaction to the situation) and whether the related conditions are believed to be changeable or not. *Problem-focused coping* includes strategies that are directed towards solving the problem that is causing the stressful situation because the related conditions are seen as changeable. Examples include planning in order to avoid a similar situation in the future and seeking instrumental support (i.e., advice) from others on how to manage the situation (Carver, Scheier, & Weintraub, 1989). It can be argued then that a teacher's stress might be relieved or lessened by problem-focused strategies just by the fact that the teacher's main focus and efforts are attuned to deal with the problem. Thus, by utilizing such strategies can help a teacher maintain calmness and composure while dealing with the stressor and disallowing unwanted thoughts or emotions to interfere with his/her efforts.

Emotion-focused coping includes strategies that focus on managing what is believed to be the only changeable element—the emotional discomfort associated with the stressful situation. Examples include expressing one's thoughts and emotions to others in order to "let it out" (i.e., catharsis), seeking emotional support (i.e., listening and empathy) from others in an attempt to improve one's mood, reframing the stressful situation in a more positive way (i.e., an opportunity to learn from the experience), and diffusing the stressful situation through humor (Carver et al., 1989). Problem-focused strategies are considered active-oriented because they attempt to eliminate the sources of stress, while the emotion-focused strategies are considered passive-oriented because cognitive or physical palliative techniques are employed to lessen the negative feelings of stress. Carver et al. (1989) proposed a third broad category, *avoidant-focused coping*, which consists of both cognitive and behavioral strategies aimed at escaping from (i.e., mentally distracting oneself) or conceding to (i.e., blaming self or giving up) the stressful situation.

A Conservation of Resources Approach to Teacher Coping and Burnout

Teacher burnout research relative to Lazarus and Folkman's (1984) transactional theory of coping has produced mixed results that are often difficult to decipher due to differences in the categorization of coping strategies. Studies comparing avoidant coping strategies to either a combination of both problem-focused and emotion-focused strategies (termed as "active coping," "adaptive coping," or "control coping"), or problem- or emotion-focused strategies separately have generally found that negative outcomes of job stress or burnout dimensions were more prevalent with the use of avoidant coping strategies. This relationship has been consistently shown among teachers (Chan & Hui, 1995; Hastings & Brown, 2002; Holt, Fine, & Tollefson, 1987; Laugaa, Rascle, & Bruchon-Schweitzer, 2008; Montgomery & Rupp, 2005) and non-teaching occupational groups (Evans, Bryant, Owens, & Koukos, 2004; Koeske, Kirk, & Koeske, 1993). Teacher burnout investigations have also contrasted problem-focused and emotion-focused coping strategies only. Consistent with human service professional scholarship (Jenaro, Flores, & Arias, 2007), research has shown that problem-focused coping strategies are much more effective in minimizing teachers' burnout or work pressure feelings than emotion-focused coping strategies (Kieffer, 1994; Parker & Martin, 2009; Wong & Cheuk, 1998).

Perhaps these findings indicate that another theoretical framework guiding the classification of strategies is warranted. Specifically, conservation of resources (COR) theory (Hobfoll, 2001) suggests that coping strategies may lie on a continuum from "defensive" to "active" strategies based on the amount of cognitive, emotional, and/or physical control one has to exert to engage in a certain type of coping. *Defensive strategies* require little to no effort, with the least being avoidant strategies such as *behavioral disengagement* (i.e., lowering efforts or giving up), *self-distraction* (i.e., ignoring a stressor by focusing on other activities), or *self-blame* (i.e., criticizing or finding oneself at fault). Some emotion-focused strategies would also be classified as defensive (e.g., *venting*), because the individual is merely tolerating the emotional discomfort with little purposive self-monitoring. Alternatively, more *active strategies* require significant self-regulatory effort, such as problem-focused strategies of *instrumental support* (i.e., seeking constructive feedback to change one's behavior) and *planning* (i.e., investing resources in order to change behaviors in the future). Under this theoretical classification, *positive reframing* (i.e., giving a positive spin for something that happened), *emotional support* (i.e., getting comfort and understanding from someone"), and *humor* (i.e., using laughter, a funny comment, or a joke to relief stress) would be classified as a more active strategy because they require a significant amount of cognitive effort. Thus, these emotion-focused, active strategies would logically be related to less burnout, similar to the other problem-focused, active strategies.

An "active" vs. "defensive" (also referred to as "passive") theoretical classification of coping strategies have received some support from educational researchers. Montgomery and Rupp (2005) proposed a theoretical-empirical model of teacher stress, whereby active coping or passive coping strategies were proposed as the two core mechanisms that teachers might apply when faced with a stressful situation. They operationalized active coping as consisting of high effort cognitive (i.e., changing perspective), behavioral (i.e., seeking advice or understanding), or emotional strategies (i.e., thinking positively) to deal with the stressful situation, whereas passive coping was operationalized as low-effort cognitive or behavioral strategies that actually seek to avoid dealing with the stressful situation (i.e., avoidance, disengagement). Average absolute correlation sizes from their meta-analysis indicated that the application of active coping strategies ($r = .27$) were more effective mediators for influencing burnout than passive coping strategies ($r = .09$). Similarly, Holt et al. (1987) divided high-stress female elementary teachers into high burnout and low burnout groups and found that the low burnout group engaged in more active coping strategies (i.e., positive reframing), while the high burnout group engaged in more passive coping strategies (i.e., get angry). Thus, it is possible that the active versus defensive classification may be a better approach than problem-focused versus emotion-focused (and avoidance) groupings, especially given the inconsistent relationships of specific emotion-focused strategies with burnout. For example, while many studies show that emotion-focused strategies are more maladaptive than problem-focused strategies (Kieffer, 1994; Parker & Martin, 2009; Wong & Cheuk, 1998), emotional support has been linked with lower levels of burnout (Chan & Hui, 1995). This makes sense in the context of the active versus defensive categorization, because emotional support (seeking comfort and understanding) takes more interpersonal self-monitoring and control than simply venting (complaining about one's problems and expressing strong negative emotions).

Coping Resources and Demands Related to Teacher Burnout

Consistent with both Lazarus and Folkman's (1984) transactional theory and COR theory (Hobfoll, 1989, 2001), the employment of coping strategies to mitigate teacher burnout is often dependent on the presence of certain demands and resources. Classroom demands are those environmental circumstances that, when unsuccessfully met by the available resources, can elicit a stress response. One classroom demand related to teacher burnout and the associated coping strategies has been the perception of work overload relative to the amount and type of teacher contact with students. More specifically, educational researchers have found that teachers report higher levels of emotional exhaustion when teaching larger classes (Byrne, 1999; Cano-García, Padilla-Muñoz, & Carrasco-Ortiz, 2005; Russell, Altmaier, & Van Velzen, 1987) or classes with high amounts of student misbehavior (Carson et al., 2011; Kokkinos, 2007; Tsouloupas et al., 2010). Teachers have reported the highest levels of emotional exhaustion when high exposure to challenging student behavior is combined with the frequent usage of avoidant coping strategies (Hastings & Brown, 2002). Furthermore, the management of positive interactions with students, especially when the expressed feelings are not genuine, can also exacerbate higher reports of teacher burnout dimensions (Barber, Grawitch, Carson, & Tsouloupas, 2011; Zhang & Zhu, 2008).

Teacher resources, on the other hand, are an accumulation of both individual and environmental circumstances available to a teacher relative to personal qualities (i.e., sex, ethnicity), skill attributes (i.e., years of experience), and characteristics of the school setting (i.e., school district). COR theory provides a thorough overview of types of resources, including those that are overlooked by other approaches, or casually referred to as "demographic characteristics" without providing a theoretical rationale to their connection to stress outcomes. Beyond intuitive resources such as *energies* (that help individual acquire things of value; e.g., time, energy, money, or knowledge) or *object resources* (physical things of value; e.g., an office, car, or house), *conditions* and *personal characteristics* are strong predictors of stress-related outcomes.

Conditions such as seniority or tenure in the workplace are important predictors of stress resiliency (and subsequently burnout) because they are valued by society and carry both tangible and intangible benefits (e.g., higher pay, prestige, or power). *Personal characteristics* can also influence one's experience of stress because they entail an individual's orientation towards events and others. These orientations (or perceptions) may affect how one interacts with the physical and social environment (and likewise, how they are treated by others in various social contexts). Common demographic variables such as age, sex, and ethnicity can fall under this category, as well as personality traits (e.g., neuroticism or optimism) or attitudes (e.g., work-related attitudes such as job involvement and organizational commitment).

Not surprisingly, teacher resources have been shown to be associated with teachers' coping strategies and burnout dimensions in relatively unique and at times conflicting ways. For instance, the influence of teachers' sex and years of experience on burnout levels and coping strategies has been inconsistent over the years (Burke & Greenglass, 1989a; Chan & Hui, 1995; Pierce & Molloy, 1990; Russell et al., 1987). Montgomery and Rupp's (2005) meta-analysis of 65 independent studies on teacher stress and burnout revealed that differences in background information, such as sex and years of experience, was the strongest indicator for teachers' use of avoidant-like strategies. Conversely, González-Morales, Rodríguez, and Peiró (2010) recently found that only in male primary and secondary teachers did problem-focused coping strategies reduce emotional exhaustion, while social support-seeking strategies increased emotional exhaustion. The work-related attitude of job involvement has been a personal characteristic linked to burnout and other negative outcomes such as turnover intentions (Blasé, 1982; Weiqi, 2007). Job involvement is defined as a "psychological identification with a job" (Kanungo, 1982, p. 97), which describes individuals who derive a large portion of their self-esteem and identity from their work role. Lastly, accessible and ample school-level resources (i.e., job enhancement opportunities, human and material support) have been shown to prevent teacher burnout across all kinds of school districts and teaching levels (Betoret, 2006; Cano-García et al., 2005; Goddard, O'Brien, & Goddard, 2006; Grayson & Alvarez, 2008), but only reduced job stress among primary and not secondary teachers (Betoret, 2009).

A STUDY ACROSS TEACHING LEVELS

The reviewed research is lacking in several ways. First, burnout studies that have simultaneously examined all three coping categories have been limited to non-teacher samples (Evans et al., 2004). Second, the teacher studies that are available have yet to identify a coherent classification of strategies using *specific* coping strategies of most relevance to mitigating burnout (e.g., Hastings & Brown, 2002; Kieffer, 1994; Wong & Cheuk, 1998) beyond some support for the problem-focused strategies of planning and social support (Chan & Hui, 1995; Parker & Martin, 2009). Third, teacher burnout and coping literature has emerged from a scattered sample of either primary (Holt et al., 1987; Kieffer, 1994; Laugaa et al., 2008; McCarthy et al., 2009) or secondary (Betoret, 2006; Chan & Hui, 1995; Wong & Cheuk, 1998) teachers across various countries (i.e., United States, China, Australia, and France), without making direct comparisons among teaching levels. In fact, the sole burnout and coping-related studies that included both primary and secondary teachers was either performed with a specific U.S. teacher population of special educators (Hastings & Brown, 2002) or in Spain with a focus more on school coping resources than strategies (Betoret, 2009).

As a result, recommendations emanating from the teacher burnout and coping research may not be contextually appropriate to the classroom demands and resources of primary and secondary teachers (Sorenson, 2007). We argue that comparing teachers' coping strategies and their associations to affiliated burnout dimensions across school levels may help identify the most effective coping tactics for teachers specific to their setting. The purpose of this study was threefold. First, we examined whether the use of specific coping strategies and overall levels of burnout differed based on teaching level (primary vs. secondary) among U.S. public school teachers. Second, we sought to identify an appropriate classification of specific strategies based on the varied theoretical approaches to coping strategy categories (e.g., problem-focused vs. emotion-focused vs. avoidance; active vs. defensive). Finally, we explored whether coping strategy categories predicted each burnout dimension beyond factors related to classroom demands and teacher resources, and if this effect differed by teaching level.

METHODS

Participants

Participants were 646 full-time primary ($n = 302$) and secondary ($n = 344$) public school teachers (female = 561, male = 85; 91% Caucasian American, 9% African American) from five school districts across the Midwestern (4% in district 1) and Southeastern (13% in district 2, 17% in district 3, 25% in district 4, 42% in district 5) regions of the U.S. In the U.S., primary schools consist of students aged 5–11 years, and secondary schools consist of students aged 12–18 years. Most primary teachers (87%) taught every subject area to the same set of pupils, while the majority of the secondary teachers (75%) mainly taught one of the "core" subject areas (e.g., math, science, English, social studies) to a number of different sets of pupils. Enrichment teachers (e.g., art, physical education, music, and family and consumer science) were included in both the primary (13%) and secondary (25%) teacher samples.

Measures

Teacher Burnout

Teacher burnout was assessed using Byrne's (1994) 12-item version of the Maslach Burnout Inventory–Educators Survey (MBI-ES; Maslach, Jackson, & Schwab, 1996). Byrne found that the full MBI-ES was inadequately variant across secondary teachers. The subscales of emotional exhaustion (e.g., "I feel emotionally drained from my work"), depersonalization (e.g., "I feel I treat some students as if they were impersonal objects"), and reduced personal accomplishment (e.g., "I feel I'm positively influencing other people's lives through my work") contained four items each. Teachers were asked to indicate how often they experienced each item at their job on a 7-point scale ranging from 0 (never) to 6 (every day).

Coping Strategies

Nine coping strategies were assessed using the brief Coping Orientations to Problem Experienced, or COPE (Carver, 1997). Two coping strategies were problem-focused: instrumental support (3 items; e.g., "I get help and advice from other people") and planning (3 items; e.g., "I think hard about what steps to take"). Four coping strategies were emotion-focused: positive reframing (3 items; e.g., "I look for something good in what happened"), emotional support (3 items; e.g., "I get comfort and understanding from someone"), venting (3 items; e.g., "I express my negative feelings"), and humor (2 items; e.g., "I make jokes about it"). Three coping strategies were avoidant-focused: self-distraction (2 items; e.g., "I turn to other work activities to take my mind off things"), behavioral disengagement (3 items; e.g., "I give up trying to deal with it"), and self-blame (2 items; e.g., "I criticize myself"). The coping classifications were based on human service professional studies (Evans et al., 2004; Jenaro et al., 2007) and each item was assessed using a 4-point Likert scale that ranged from 1 (I haven't been doing this at all) to 4 (I've been doing this a lot).

Classroom Demands and Teacher Resources

Classroom demands were assessed via several school setting circumstances including school district, average class size, and frequency of positive or negative interactions experienced with students. Student interaction frequency was rated as a perception on a scale of 1 (almost never occurs) to 5 (occurs very frequently). Items pertaining to teachers' sex, years of experience, and job involvement were used to assess teacher resources. Job involvement was assessed using Kanungo's (1982) 5-item questionnaire (a = .72), with response options ranging from 1 (strongly disagree) to 7 (strongly agree). An example is, "I am very much involved personally in my job."

Procedure

After approval was granted from the affiliated Institutional Review Board and the central administration of each school district, data were collected using the online survey software—SurveyMonkey (Finley, 1999). The administrative assistants from each school district distributed a cumulative total of 2,484 e-mail teacher invitations with the survey link enclosed in the e-mail. The e-mail invitations also served as a consent form, and the teachers were informed that clicking the survey link meant they consented to partici-pate in the study. Teachers were given two weeks to submit a completed sur-vey before a reminder e-mail was sent by the administrative assistants to the initial teacher sample. Seven hundred and four teachers submitted online surveys (28% response rate). Removal of incomplete surveys and exclusion of teachers who indicated having class sizes of fewer than eight students resulted in a final teacher sample of 646 (total response rate of 26%). The current response rate is consistent with reported research and meta-data that showed the expected response rates for online surveys ranged between 25 to 30% for public service and customer service employees in the U.S. (Ipathia, 2009; Kaplowitz, Hadlock, & Levine, 2004). Statistical significance for all data analyses was set at $p \leq .05$.

RESULTS

Preliminary Analyses

Pearson chi-square (χ^2) tests were conducted to assess the level of in-dependence between primary and secondary teachers with all categorical demands and resources variables. A greater proportion of female teachers (53%) taught in the primary schools, and male teachers (92%) taught in the secondary schools, $(\chi^2 = 58.32, p < .01)$. However, the teacher–gender ratio of our sample reflected in approximation the national teacher–gen-der ratio statistics of K–12 teachers in the United States (78.3% females and 21.3% males). Moreover, chi-square analyses indicated that there were no significant differences in the proportions of teacher ethnicities and school districts represented across the primary and secondary teaching levels. In terms of core versus enrichment courses, a significantly greater proportion of teachers at the secondary level taught enrichment courses (24.7%) than primary level teachers (12.6%; $\chi^2 = 15.34, p < .01$).

Zero-order correlation for all study variables within the primary and secondary teacher groups are presented in Table 10.1. It is important to note that all Cronbach's α coefficients met the .70 criterion (Nunnally & Bernstein, 1994) except for the burnout dimension of depersonaliza-tion ($\alpha = .65$) and the avoidant-focused coping strategy of self-distraction ($\alpha = .45$). As a result, self-distraction was removed from further analyses, while depersonalization was kept given its marginally acceptable coefficient and centrality to the study. Depersonalization results should be read with some caution.

TABLE 10.1   Bivariate Correlations for Primary (n = 302) and Secondary (n = 344) Teachers

Variable	1	2	3	4	5	6	7	8	9	10	11	12	13	14	15	16	17
1. Average Class Size	—	.03	.10	-.03	.04	.07	.16**	.03	-.03	-.02	-.08	-.03	.00	.04	-.10	-.02	-.02
2. Pos. Student Interactions	-.05	—	-.22**	-.12*	.21**	-.26**	-.24**	-.42**	.05	.15**	.25**	.07	-.16**	.07	.09	-.25**	-.16**
3. Neg. Student Interactions	.14**	-.42**	—	-.23**	-.14*	.36**	.31**	.32**	-.03	-.06	-.11	.01	.23**	.08	.05	.18**	.19**
4. Years of Teaching Experience	-.02	.02	-.06	—	.07	-.16**	-.14*	-.20**	-.11	.02	-.01	-.08	-.18**	-.17**	.01	-.08	-.09
5. Job Involvement	-.05	.26**	-.11	.13*	(.72)	-.19**	-.16**	-.33**	.10	.22**	.19**	.02	-.09	.04	-.03	-.13*	.01
6. Em. Exhaustion	.04	-.27**	.44**	-.12*	-.16**	(.89)	.56**	.27**	.01	-.08	-.17**	.01	.37**	.18**	.07	.28**	.34**
7. Depersonalization	.08	-.36**	.41**	-.10	-.23**	.57**	(.65)	.38**	-.07	-.13*	-.17**	-.11*	.27**	.17**	-.02	.30**	.29**
8. Red. Personal Accomplishment	.10	-.44**	.34**	-.05	-.35**	.33**	.41**	(.81)	-.10	-.18**	-.23**	-.10	.16**	-.10	-.12*	.17**	.14**
9. Instrumental Support	-.04	.08	.06	-.06	.14*	.03	-.05	-.17**	(.86)	.42**	.42**	.80**	.36**	.16**	.12*	-.02	.12*
10. Planning	-.10	.13*	-.06	-.01	.23**	-.12*	-.22**	-.26**	.52**	(.78)	.64**	.27**	-.01	.04	.17**	-.14*	.01
11. Pos. Reframing	-.11*	-.26**	-.19**	-.01	.14*	-.22**	-.25**	-.36**	.41**	.56**	(.75)	.28**	.00	.14*	.19**	-.12*	.00
12. Emotional Support	-.03	.06	.01	-.05	.14*	.07	-.06	-.14*	.78**	.42**	.33**	(.88)	.31**	.16*	.12*	.00	.11
13. Venting	.03	-.16**	.25**	-.11	-.04	.43**	.35**	.20**	.13*	.13*	-.05	.34**	(.74)	.30**	.16**	.41**	.45**
14. Humor	.03	-.04	.08	-.09	-.05	.16**	.20**	-.01	.11*	.05	.23**	.09	.23**	(.79)	.17**	.24**	.25**
15. Self-Distraction	-.09	-.04	.00	-.04	.04	.20**	.12*	-.05	.17**	.17**	.18**	.23**	.33**	.26**	(.45)	.13*	.20**
16. Behavioral Disengagement	-.02	-.20**	.16**	.03	-.02	.27**	.38**	.27**	-.16**	-.16**	-.14*	-.05	.36**	.25**	.22**	(.76)	.50**
17. Self-Blame	-.06	-.10	.09	-.11*	.18**	.27**	.28**	.14*	.08	.03	.02	.13*	.34**	.17**	.25**	.35**	(.76)

Note: Pos. = Positive; Neg. = Negative; ; Em. = Emotion; Red. = Reduced. Cronbach's a coefficients for multi-item variables are on the diagonal (in parentheses). Pearson correlations for the Primary teacher data are above the diagonal and Secondary teacher correlations are below the diagonal.

*p < .05. **p < .01.

Main Analyses

Differences in Demands, Resources, Coping Strategies, and Burnout by Teaching Level

Multivariate analysis of variance tests (MANOVAS) were conducted with the remaining continuous variables to detect differences across primary and secondary teachers with respect to demands and resources, as well as coping strategies and burnout differences. As displayed in Table 10.2, classroom demands (Wilks's $\lambda = .95$, $F_{(3, 636)} = 11.30$, $p < .01$), teacher resources (Wilks's $\lambda = .98$, $F_{(2,622)} = 4.96$, $p < .01$), and burnout (Wilks's $\lambda = .96$, $F_{(3,642)} = 8.14$, $p < .01$) differed significantly across teaching levels, but not coping strategies (Wilks's $\lambda = .98$, $F_{(8, 637)} = 1.63$, ns). Primary teachers reported more frequent positive (4.52 vs. 4.41; $F_{(1,638)} = 5.16$, $p < .05$) and negative interactions with students (3.03 vs. 2.84, $F_{(1,638)} = 5.26$, $p < .05$) than secondary teachers, whereas secondary teachers reported more years of

TABLE 10.2   Means and Standard Deviations for Primary ($n = 302$) and Secondary ($n = 344$) Teachers

Variable	Primary Teachers		Secondary Teachers		Wilks's λ	Univariate F
	M	SD	M	SD		
Classroom Demands					0.95**	
Average Class Size	19.99	5.49	23.99	16.92		15.35**
Positive Student Interactions	4.52	0.58	4.41	0.68		5.16*
Negative Student Interactions	3.03	0.92	2.84	1.00		5.26*
Teacher Resources					0.98**	
Years of Teaching Experience	13.53	9.27	15.68	10.47		6.96**
Job Involvement	4.09	1.10	3.96	1.12		2.13
Burnout Dimensions					0.96**	
Emotional Exhaustion	3.38	1.60	3.05	1.63		6.90**
Depersonalization	1.18	1.11	1.35	1.21		3.43
Reduced Personal Accomplishment	1.16	1.05	1.27	1.18		1.72
Specific Coping Strategies					0.98	
Instrumental Support	2.10	0.73	1.99	0.78		3.70
Planning	2.08	0.67	2.13	0.69		0.98
Positive Reframing	1.99	0.70	1.96	0.65		0.26
Emotional Support	2.10	0.83	1.95	0.87		5.05*
Venting	1.21	0.75	1.15	0.71		1.13
Humor	1.40	0.93	1.40	0.91		0.01
Behavioral Disengagement	0.53	0.63	0.46	0.61		1.83
Self-Blame	1.13	0.87	1.13	0.82		0.01

$^*p < .05$; $^{**}p < .01$

full-time teaching experience (15.67 vs. 13.53; $F_{(1,623)} = 6.96$, $p < .01$) and larger average class sizes (23.99 vs. 19.99; $F_{(1,638)} = 15.34$ $p < .01$) than primary teachers. Primary teachers also reported higher levels of emotional exhaustion (3.38 vs. 3.05; $F_{(1,644)} = 6.90$, $p < .01$) than secondary teachers.

Coping Categorization

To determine the best categorization of coping strategies (e.g., active vs. defensive, problem-focused vs. emotion-focused, avoidance, etc.), an exploratory factor analysis (EFA) was conducted with the seven remaining coping strategies (i.e., with the exclusion of self-distraction). The Varimax rotated factor matrix using principal axis factoring yielded a two-factor solution (cumulative percent of variance explained = 44.78%). The first factor accounted for 26.09% of the item variance (Eigenvalue = 2.09), and consisted of instrumental support (0.86), emotional support (0.71), planning (0.64), and positive reframing (0.59). The second factor accounted for 18.70% of the item variance (Eigenvalue = 1.50), and consisted of venting (0.69), behavioral disengagement (0.65), self-blame (0.58), and humor (0.34). Given that humor fell below the 0.40 threshold for acceptable rotated factor loadings in social sciences research (see Ford, MacCallum, & Tait, 1986), this item was dropped and another factor analysis was conducted. The results improved, with the new two-factor solution accounting for a cumulative 49.32% of variance (Factor 1 = 30.11%; Factor 2 = 19.21%), with all items loading on the same factors as the first solution. These factors closely approximated the COR theory categorizations of active (instrumental support, emotional support, planning, positive reframing) versus defensive (behavioral disengagement, venting, self-blame) coping strategies. Internal consistency estimates for the new active coping strategies variable for primary (0.78) and secondary (0.89) teachers were acceptable (0.79 across the entire sample). Estimates for the defensive coping strategies variables were acceptable for primary (0.71) teachers, but only marginally acceptable for secondary teachers (0.61; 0.66 across the entire sample). Table 10.3 shows the correlations for the newly created coping variables with classroom demands, teacher resources, and burnout dimensions.

Correlational results for the two-factor coping strategy approach were consistent across teaching levels. Average class size (a classroom demand) and years of teaching experience (a teacher resource) were the only variables that were not significantly associated with active or defensive coping strategies. Active strategies were also unrelated to emotional exhaustion, while defensive strategies showed no association with job involvement. In both teaching groups, active strategies were positively associated with job involvement and positive student interactions and negatively associated with depersonalization and personal accomplishment. Defensive strategies were

TABLE 10.3 Bivariate Correlations with Active and Defensive Categorizations among Primary (n = 302) and Secondary (n = 344) Teachers

	Primary Teachers		Secondary Teachers	
Variable	Active[a]	Defensive[b]	Active[a]	Defensive[b]
Average Class Size	−0.05	0.00	−0.08	−0.03
Positive Student Interactions	0.16**	−0.23**	0.16**	−0.18**
Negative Student Interactions	−0.03	0.25**	−0.04	0.22**
Years of Teaching Experience	−0.04	−0.09	−0.06	−0.03
Job Involvement	0.15**	−0.08	0.20**	0.06
Emotional Exhaustion	−0.06	0.42**	−0.06	0.43**
Depersonalization	−0.14*	0.35**	−0.17**	0.43**
Reduced Personal Accomplishment	−0.17**	0.19**	−0.28**	0.26**

[a] Instrumental support, emotional support, planning, and positive reframing
[b] Venting, self-blame, and behavioral disengagement
$^*p < .05$; $^{**}p < .01$

negatively associated with positive student interactions and positively associated with negative student interactions and all three burnout dimensions.

Main Effect Predictors of Burnout and Coping Interactions with Teaching Level

A hierarchical multiple regression analysis was conducted to examine the usefulness of coping strategies in predicting each burnout dimension among primary and secondary teachers, respectively. Classroom demands (i.e., average class size, frequency of positive and negative interactions with students, and core vs. enrichment subjects) were entered in the first step, along with teaching level (primary = 0; secondary = 1), whereas the second step consisted of teacher resource variables (sex, years of teaching experience, job involvement). Previous research reported classroom demands (e.g., class size, frequency of positive and negative interactions with students) and teacher resources (e.g., teaching experience) to highly relate with teacher burnout (Burke & Greenglass, 1989b; Chan, 2007; Tsouloupas et al., 2010). Additionally, the present study showed correlations between the student interaction variables and the burnout measures to be some of the highest found for this sample. For the above reasons, these variables were controlled to account for some true between teacher level variance in burnout that was not related to the classroom demands or teacher resources. Active and defensive strategies were entered in the third step (these continuous variables were mean-centered before calculating interaction terms and entering them into the model to alleviate multicollinearity issues; Aiken & West, 1991), with the two coping strategies by teaching level interaction terms entered in the fourth step. The results of the hierarchical regression across all teachers can be found in Table 10.4.

TABLE 10.4 Hierarchical Regression Results for All Teachers (*N* = 633)

	EE Model		DP Model		RPA Model	
	ΔR²	β	ΔR²	β	ΔR²	β
Step 1: School demands	0.18**		0.18**		0.22**	
Teaching Level		–0.04		0.07		0.03
Freq. Positive Interactions		–0.07		–0.11**		–0.35**
Freq. Negative Interactions		0.27**		0.22**		0.16**
Avg. Class Size		0.01		0.06		0.04
Subject Taught		–0.01		0.01		–0.03
Step 2: Teacher resources	0.02**		0.02**		0.07**	
Sex		0.08*		–0.05		–0.02
Years of Experience		–0.01		–0.03		–0.06
Job Involvement		–0.12*		–0.13*		–0.24**
Step 3: Coping strategies	0.11**		0.11**		0.04**	
Active[a]		–0.07		–0.13**		–0.11*
Defensive[b]		0.31**		0.25**		0.07
Step 4: Interactions	0.01		0.01*		0.01*	
Active × Teaching Level		0.00		0.00		–0.09†
Defensive × Teaching Level		0.05		0.12*		0.11*
Total R²	0.30**		0.31**		0.34**	

Note: EE = emotional exhaustion; DP = depersonalization; RPA = reduced personal accomplishment; for teaching level, 0 = primary and 1 = secondary; for subject taught, core = 0 and 1 = enrichment; for sex, 0 = male and 1 = female.
[a] Instrumental support, emotional support, planning, and positive reframing
[b] Venting, self-blame, and behavioral disengagement
* $p < .05$; ** $p < .01$; † $p < .10$

In terms of classroom demands, teaching level was unrelated to each of the three burnout dimensions, as well as average class size and type of subject taught (core vs. enrichment). Increased frequency of positive interactions predicted lower reports of depersonalization ($\beta = -.11$, $p < .01$) and reduced personal accomplishment $\beta = -.35$, $p < .01$), whereas frequency of positive interactions predicted higher levels of all three burnout dimensions ($\beta = .27$, $p < .01$ for emotional exhaustion; $\beta = .22$, $p < .01$ for depersonalization; $\beta = .16$, $p < .01$ for reduced personal accomplishment). With respect to teacher resources, years of experience was not predictive of burnout, but women reported higher levels of emotional exhaustion ($\beta = .08$, $p < .05$). Job involvement was the strongest predictor in this step and was significantly associated with lower reports of emotional exhaustion ($\beta = -.12$, $p < .05$), depersonalization ($\beta = -.13$, $p < .05$), and reduced personal accomplishment ($\beta = -.24$, $p < .01$).

Coping strategies were found to predict a significant amount of variance beyond classroom demands and teacher resources for emotional exhaustion ($\Delta F_{(2,623)}$ = 49.83, $p < .01$, ΔR^2 = .11), depersonalization ($\Delta F_{(2,623)}$ = 47.45, $p < .01$, ΔR^2 = .11), and reduced personal accomplishment ($\Delta F_{(2,623)}$ = 19.10, $p < .01$, ΔR^2 = .04). Specifically, active strategies were negatively associated with depersonalization (β = −.13, $p < .05$), and reduced personal accomplishment (β = −.11, $p < .05$), while defensive strategies were positively associated with depersonalization (β = .25, $p < .01$) and emotional exhaustion (β = .31, $p < .01$).

Finally, teaching level by coping strategy interactions did not account for additional variance in the depersonalization ($\Delta F_{(2, 621)}$ = 3.61, $p < .05$, ΔR^2 = .01) and reduced personal accomplishment ($\Delta F_{(2, 621)}$ = 4.09, $p < .05$, ΔR^2 = .01) models, but not for emotional exhaustion ($\Delta F_{(2, 621)}$ = 0.66, ns, ΔR^2 = .00). The effect of defensive strategies on depersonalization differed by teaching level (β = .12, $p < .05$), with post-hoc analyses indicating a stronger effect in secondary teachers (β = .38, $p < .05$) in comparison to primary teachers (β = .29, $p < .05$). The effect of defensive strategies on reduced personal accomplishment also differed by teaching level (β = .11, $p < .05$), with post-hoc analyses indicating a stronger effect in secondary teachers (β = .22, $p < .01$) than primary teachers (β = .06, ns). Although the active strategies by teaching level interaction was only marginally significant for predicting reduced personal accomplishment (β = .09, $p < .10$), it is worth noting a similar trend between teaching groups: the active coping predictor was stronger in secondary teachers (β = −.22, $p < .01$) compared to primary teachers (β = −.11, $p < .05$).

SUMMARY AND DISCUSSION

The study set out to determine the role, if any, that teaching level plays in teacher burnout, coping strategies, and the effectiveness of coping strategies in predicting teacher burnout. Based on Lazarus and Folkman's (1984) transactional theory of coping, we expected that because of the unique classroom demands and teacher resources encountered at each teaching level, primary and secondary public school teachers would differ in (1) their feelings of burnout, (2) their use of specific coping strategies, and (3) how well specific coping strategies predicted teacher burnout. In general, our expectations were partially supported. The relative importance of teaching level did not always hold true as outlined below.

Study findings indicated that despite the many classroom demands (e.g., average class size, frequency of positive and negative interactions with students) and teachers' resources (e.g., sex, years of teaching experience) that significantly varied across primary and secondary teachers, burnout dimensions or the use of specific coping strategies did not, with the exception of emotional exhaustion and emotional support. Even though previous research had produced competing results regarding the stress (Malik et al., 1991) or burnout (Byrne, 1999) levels of primary and secondary teachers, teacher burnout and coping researchers typically ignore the potential effect of teaching level by studying primary (Holt et al., 1987; Kieffer, 1994; Laugaa et al., 2008; McCarthy et al., 2009) and secondary (Betoret, 2006; Chan & Hui, 1995; Wong & Cheuk, 1998) schoolteachers separately. The available research in conjunction with findings from this study demonstrates the need for additional burnout and coping investigations with both primary and secondary schoolteachers (e.g., Betoret, 2009; Hastings & Brown, 2002). There is clearly not enough consistent evidence to suggest that teacher burnout or certain coping strategies are more pervasive to schoolteachers at one teaching level over the other.

The need to consider teaching level differences was further underscored with the notable differences that surfaced relative to the utility of specific coping strategies in the prediction of teacher burnout. Specifically, the use of defensive strategies (i.e., venting, behavioral disengagement, and self-blame) had a stronger positive effect on depersonalization and reduced personal accomplishment in secondary teachers as compared to primary teachers. In fact, post-hoc analyses indicated that the association between defensive strategies and reduced personal accomplishment was statistically significant only among secondary teachers, whereas the defensive strategies–depersonalization link was significant in both samples (but differed in levels of intensity). Thus, the nonsignificant defensive strategy main effect in the full sample might be due to attenuation. These findings are consistent with research indicating that, regardless of the socioeconomic status of the school, secondary teachers tend to accumulate more negative work-related feelings and outcomes (i.e., burnout, lower job involvement) than primary teachers (Blasé 1982; Day, Simmons, Stobart, Kingston, & Gu, 2007). On the other hand, the beneficial effect of active coping strategies (i.e., instrumental support, emotional support, planning, and positive reframing) on depersonalization and reduced personal accomplishment appeared to remain stable across both samples, including its lack of association with emotional exhaustion. It is interesting to note that, although the effect only approached significance, there was a trend toward active coping strategies being more strongly linked to reduced personal accomplishment in the secondary teachers as well. In the simplest sense, these findings confirm the use of planning strategies and seeking out supportive individuals as means for teachers to cope with job stressors (Chan & Hui, 1995; Parker & Martin, 2009).

These findings also add meaning to previous work by suggesting that the effectiveness of both coping strategies in lessening teacher burnout feelings may be due, in part, to a distinction of teaching level. That is, when our data are combined with Chan and Hui's (1995) findings, it appears that defensive strategies (similar to their avoidant coping strategies) have a stronger relationship with burnout in secondary teachers than primary teachers and may not have a discernable effect on personal accomplishment among primary teachers. We speculate that these collective findings reflect an imbalance that occurs between work demands and employee resources, as suggested by Lazarus and Folkman (1984) and Hobfoll (1989). Specifically, some classroom demands and teacher resources may vary across teaching levels, beyond those related to teacher–student relations as shown in this study, and contribute to the coping–burnout relationship are teachers' perceived influence of the adult populations in and around the school setting. Past research suggests that teachers who favorably viewed the involvement and support of administrators, parents, or community members were less likely to report burnout (Betoret, 2006, 2009; Carson et al., 2011; Grayson & Alvarez, 2008). Betoret (2009) compared teaching levels and found that tangible school resources, such as abundant school equipment or personnel support, were only effective in curbing job stress among primary teachers. Clearly, the present study and Betoret's (2009) study provide a helpful guide for follow-up research to contrast the coping–burnout relationship across teaching levels.

Another possible teacher resource difference across teaching levels that could explain the varied coping–burnout relationships may stem from actual individual differences of primary and secondary teachers. In fact, McCarthy et al. (2009) found that individual differences between and within teachers accounted for a greater variability of burnout than differences between schools. Although their study was performed solely with elementary teachers, it is possible that differences in the qualities or attributes of teachers (beyond features of sex or years of teaching experience) who work at primary or secondary levels may be just as helpful (if not more) in explaining the use of specific coping strategies and their prediction of burnout than unique differences in the school demands or teacher resources available at each teaching level. The most consistent individual variables found to be related to teacher burnout have been neurotic or introverted personality traits (Cano-García et al., 2005; Kokkinos, 2007; Teven, 2007), negative dispositional affect (Carson et al., 2011), and stress-promoting habits and susceptibilities (McCarthy et al., 2009). Teachers may use certain types of coping strategies because of similar individual variables and others, such as teachers' flexibility in the perceived controllability of stressful situations and resultant coping patterns (Cheng, 2001). Researchers should examine if, indeed, teaching level differences in the coping–burnout relationship can be simply credited to the individuals differences of those who are attracted to teach at the primary or secondary level.

THEORETICAL CONSIDERATIONS

From a broader perspective, study findings did reveal inconsistencies regarding relationships between the three broad categorizations (i.e., problem-focused, emotion-focused, and avoidant-focused) of coping strategies and burnout in teachers. As previously found with both non-teacher (Evans et al., 2004; Koeske et al., 1993) and teacher samples (Chan & Hui, 1995; Hastings & Brown, 2002; Holt et al., 1987; Laugaa et al., 2008), it was no surprise that defensive coping strategies (venting, self-blame, behavioral disengagement) were related to increased burnout and active coping strategies (instrumental support, planning, emotional support, positive reframing) were related to less burnout. However, what was a bit surprising based on prior teacher coping–burnout patterns (Kieffer, 1994; Parker & Martin, 2009; Wong & Cheuk, 1998) was that only one emotion-focused coping strategy (venting) was found to be best classified as a defensive strategy, while positive reframing and emotional support were negatively associated with burnout. These findings indicated that viewing emotion-focused coping strategies as being maladaptive may be unwarranted given that specific strategies were differentially categorized as active or defensive strategies and related to burnout (Hastings & Brown, 2002). Taken together with past research (Holt et al., 1987; Montgomery & Rupp, 2005, future teacher stress and burnout researchers should consider the adoption of an active vs. defensive (or passive) theoretical classification when examining coping strategies.

PRACTICAL SIGNIFICANCE OF THE STUDY

The results of the present study provide clear implications for practitioners and teacher educators in the field. Regardless of teaching level, it would seem beneficial for both pre-service and in-service teachers to learn how to positively reframe a stressful situation rather than blaming oneself for its occurrence of simply "venting" to others. Reevaluating the emotional meanings attached to a particular situation, mainly referred to in the literature as cognitive reappraisal (Gross, 1998) or deep acting (Hochschild, 2003), is known to be an effective means to down-regulate negative emotions and up-regulate positive emotions (Gross, Richards, & John, 2006). These goals can be met in a variety of ways, and depending on when they are employed in relation to when the emotion is evoked, Sutton (2004, 2005) found they might look differently with teachers: preventative (i.e., identifying stressful situations, defuse through humor, self talk); at the emotional cue (i.e., think of a serene place, remind self of a teacher's purpose, deep breathing); or responsive (i.e., talk to others, learn from the stressful incident). In many ways, these cognitive change/reframing strategies add further credence to the use of active coping strategies as several reflect both the problem-focused and emotion-focused strategies examined in this study. If Rowe's (1999) longitudinal study with healthcare professionals is any indication, equipping teachers with such strategies is possible and will reduce burnout over time. Carson et al. (2011) found some initial evidence for the burnout-reducing potential of cognitive change strategies, even among the most negatively oriented teachers.

CONCLUDING REMARKS

Using Lazarus and Folkman's (1984) transactional model of coping and Hobfoll's conservation of resources theory (1989, 2001), this study highlights the importance of how one classifies coping strategies, as well as considering teaching level differences relative to the coping–burnout relationship in teachers. Results give researchers and professionals in the field some initial information regarding helpful coping strategies for diminishing teacher burnout across both teaching levels, as well as with only primary or secondary teachers. Although the results are most applicable to American public schoolteachers, there is some evidence that the organizational nature of primary and secondary schools can also vary across cultures (Gaziel, 1993) and nations (Tatar & Horenczyk, 2003); that is, the educational system and norms, citizens' attitudes toward education and learning, community interests, and working conditions can certainly create unique contextual demands and resources that are influential to the coping behaviors and burnout levels of teachers. In line with the international perspective of this edited book, we encourage future researchers to discern if teaching level differences in the coping–burnout relationship between coping strategies and burnout exist among intercultural and cross-national teacher samples.

AUTHOR NOTE

Russell L. Carson is an Assistant Professor in the Department of Kinesiology at Louisiana State University, USA. Costas N. Tsouloupas is a Lecturer in the Department of Life and Health Sciences at the University of Nicosia, Cyprus. Larissa K. Barber is an Assistant Professor in the Department of Psychology at Northern Illinois University, USA.

This chapter was presented at the 2010 annual meeting of the American Educational Research Association in Denver, Colorado. Publication of related reports of the emotional exhaustion data appearing in this chapter can be found in Barber et al. (2011) and Tsouloupas et al. (2010). A special thanks to Matthew J. Grawitch for his ongoing editorial assistance with this work. Correspondence concerning this article should be addressed to Russell L. Carson, Department of Kinesiology, Louisiana State University, Baton Rouge, Louisiana, 70803-7101; rlcarson@lsu.edu.

REFERENCES

Aiken, L. S., & West, S. G. (1991), *Multiple regression: Testing and interpreting interactions*. Newbury Park, CA: Sage Publications.

Aldwin, C. M. (2009). *Stress, coping and development: An integrative perspective* (2nd ed.). New York, NY: Guilford Press.

Barber, L. K., Grawitch, M. J., Carson, R. L., & Tsouloupas, C. N. (2011). Costs and benefits of supportive versus disciplinary emotion regulation in teachers. *Stress and Health, 27*(3), e173–e187.

Betoret, F. D. (2006). Stressors, self-efficacy, coping resources, and burnout among secondary school teachers in Spain. *Educational Psychology, 26*(4), 519–539.

Betoret, F. D. (2009). Self-efficacy, school resources, job stressors and burnout among Spanish primary and secondary school teachers: A structural equation approach. *Educational Psychology, 29*(1), 45–68.

Blasé , J. J. (1982). A Social-psychological grounded theory of teacher stress and burnout. *Educational Administration Quarterly, 18*(4), 93–113.

Burke, R. J., & Greenglass, E. R. (1989a). Psychological burnout among men and women in teaching: An examination of the Cherniss model. *Human Relations, 42*(3), 261–273.

Burke R. J., & Greenglass, E. R. (1989b). The clients' role in psychological burnout in teachers and administrators. *Psychological Reports, 64*, 1299-1306.

Byrne, B. M. (1994). Burnout: testing for the validity, replication, and invariance of causal structure across elementary, intermediate, and secondary teachers. *American Educational Research Journal, 31*(3), 645–673.

Byrne, B. M. (1999). The nomological network of teacher burnout: A literature review and empirically validated model. In R. Vandenberghe & A. M. Huberman (Eds.), *Understanding and preventing teacher burnout* (pp. 15–37). New York, NY: Cambridge University Press.

Cano-García, F. J., Padilla-Muñoz, E. M., & Carrasco-Ortiz, M. Á. (2005). Personality and contextual variables in teacher burnout. *Personality and Individual Differences, 38*(4), 929–940.

Carson, R. L., Plemmons, S., Templin, T. J., & Weiss, H. M. (2011). "You are who you are": A mixed-method study of affectivity and emotional regulation in curbing teacher burnout. In G. M. Reevy & E. Frydenberg (Vol. Eds.), *Research on stress and coping in education: Vol. 6. Personality, stress and coping: Implications for education* (pp. 239–265). Charlotte, NC: Information Age.

Carver, C. S. (1997). You want to measure coping but your protocol's too long: Consider the Brief COPE. *International Journal of Behavioral Medicine, 4*, 92–100.

Carver, C. S., Scheier, M. F., & Weintraub, J. K. (1989). Assessing coping strategies: A theoretically based approach. *Journal of Personality and Social Psychology, 56,* 267–283.

Chan, D. W. (2007). Burnout, self-efficacy, and successful intelligence among Chinese prospective and in-service school teachers in Hong Kong. *Educational Psychology, 27,* 33–49.

Chan, D. W., & Hui, E. K. P. (1995). Burnout and coping among Chinese secondary school teachers in Hong Kong. *British Journal of Educational Psychology, 65*(1), 15–25.

Chang, M.-L. (2009). An appraisal perspective of teacher burnout: Examining the emotional work of teachers. *Educational Psychology Review, 21*(3), 193–218.

Cheng, C. (2001). Assessing coping flexibility in real-life and laboratory settings: A multimethod approach. *Journal of Personality and Social Psychology, 80,* 814–833.

Cropanzano, R., Rupp, D. E., & Byrne, Z. S. (2003). The relationship of emotional exhaustion to work attitudes, job performance, and organizational citizenship behaviors. *Journal of Applied Psychology, 88,* 160–169.

Day, C., Sammons, P., Stobart, G., Kingston, A., & Gu, Q. (2007). *Teachers matter: Connecting lives, work and effectiveness.* Maidenhead: Open University Press.

Dormann, C., & Kaiser, D. M. (2002). Job conditions and customer satisfaction. *European Journal of Work and Organizational Psychology, 11*(3), 257–283.

Evans, G. D., Bryant, N. E., Owens, J. S., & Koukos, K. (2004). Ethnic differences in burnout, coping, and intervention acceptability among childcare professionals. *Child & Youth Care Forum, 33*(5), 349–371.

Finley, R. (1999). SurveyMonkey [Online survey software]. Palo Alto, CA: SurveyMonkey.com, LCC.

Folkman, S., & Lazarus, R. S. (1980). An analysis of coping in a middle-aged community sample. *Journal of Health and Social Behavior, 21,* 219–239.

Ford, J. K., MacCallum, R. C., & Tait, M. (1986). The application of exploratory factor analysis in applied psychology: A critical review and analysis. *Personnel Psychology, 39,* 291–314.

Gaziel, H. M. (1993). Coping with occupational stress among teachers: A cross-cultural study. *Comparative Education, 29*(1), 67–79.

Goddard, R., O'Brien, P., & Goddard, M. (2006). Work environment predictors of beginning teacher burnout. *British Educational Research Journal, 32*(6), 857–874.

González-Morales, M. G., Rodríguez, I., & Peiró, J. M. (2010). A longitudinal study of coping and gender in a female-dominated occupation: Predicting teachers' burnout. *Journal of Occupational Health Psychology, 15*(1), 29–44.

Grayson, J. L., & Alvarez, H. K. (2008). School climate factors relating to teacher burnout: A mediator model. *Teaching & Teacher Education, 24*(5), 1349–1363.

Gross, J. J. (1998). The emerging field of emotion regulation: An integrative review. *Review of General Psychology, 2,* 271–299.

Gross, J. J., Richards, J. M., & John, O. P. (2006). Emotion regulation in everyday life. In D. K. Snyder, J. A. Simpson, & J. N. Hughes (Eds.), *Emotion regulation in families: Pathways to dysfunction and health* (pp. 13–35). Washington, DC: American Psychological Association.

Hastings, R. P., & Brown, T. (2002). Coping strategies and the impact of challenging behaviors on special educators' burnout. *Mental Retardation, 40*(2), 148–156.

Hobfoll, S. E. (1989). Conservation of resources: A new attempt at conceptualizing stress. *American Psychologist, 44*, 513–524.

Hobfoll, S. E. (2001). The influence of culture, community, and the nested self in the stress process: *Advancing Conservation of Resources Theory, 50*, 337–421.

Hochschild, A. R. (2003). *The managed heart: Commercialization of human feeling* (2nd ed.). Berkeley, CA: University of California Press.

Holt, P., Fine, M. J., & Tollefson, N. (1987). Mediating stress: Survival of the hardy. *Psychology in the Schools, 24*(1), 51–58.

Ipathia, Inc. (2009). *Online survey response rates and times: Background and guidance for industry.* Retrieved from http://www.supersurvey.com/papers/supersurvey_white_paper_response_rates.pdf

Jenaro, C., Flores, N., & Arias, B. (2007). Burnout and coping in human service practitioners. *Professional Psychology: Research & Practice, 38*(1), 80–87.

Kanungo, R. N. (1982). Measurement of job and work involvement. *Journal of Applied Psychology, 67*(3), 341–349.

Kaplowitz, M. D., Hadlock, T. D., & Levine, R. (2004). A comparison of web and mail survey response rates. *Public Opinion Quarterly, 68*, 94–101.

Kieffer, J. C. (1994). Using a problem-focused coping strategy on teacher stress and burnout. *Teaching and Change, 1*(2), 190–206.

Koeske, G. F., Kirk, S. A., & Koeske, R. D. (1993). Coping with job stress: Which strategies work best? *Journal of Occupational and Organizational Psychology, 66*(4), 319–335.

Kokkinos, C. M. (2007). Job stressors, personality and burnout in primary school teachers. *British Journal of Educational Psychology, 77*(1), 229–243.

Laugaa, D., Rascle, N., & Bruchon-Schweitzer, M. (2008). Stress and burnout among French elementary school teachers: A transactional approach. *European Review of Applied Psychology, 58*(4), 241–251.

Lazarus, R. S., & Folkman, S. (1984). *Stress, appraisal, and coping.* New York, NY: Springer.

Malik, J. L., Mueller, R. O., & Meinke, D. L. (1991). The effects of teaching experience and grade level taught on teacher stress: A LISREL analysis. *Teaching and Teacher Education, 7*(1), 57–62.

Maslach, C., Jackson, S. E., & Leiter, M. P. (1996). *Maslach Burnout Inventory manual* (3rd ed.). Palo Alto, CA: CPP.

Maslach, C., Jackson, S. E., & Schwab, R. L. (1996). Maslach burnout inventory-educators survey (MBI-ES). In C. Maslach, S. E. Jackson & M. P. Leiter (Eds.), *MBI manual* (3rd ed., pp. 27–32). Palo Alto, CA: CPP.

Maslach, C., Leiter, M. P., & Schaufeli, W. (2008). Measuring burnout. In C. L. Cooper & S. Cartwright (Eds.), *The Oxford handbook of organizational well-being* (pp. 86–108). Oxford, UK: Oxford University.

McCarthy, C. J., Lambert, R. G., O'Donnell, M., & Melendres, L. T. (2009). The relation of elementary teachers' experience, stress, and coping resources to burnout symptoms. *Elementary School Journal, 109*(3), 282–300.

Montgomery, C., & Rupp, A. A. (2005). A meta-analysis for exploring the diverse causes and effects of stress in teachers. *Canadian Journal of Education, 28*(3), 458–486.

Nunnally, J. C., & Bernstein, I. H. (1994). *Psychometric theory* (3rd ed.). New York, NY: McGraw Hill.

Parker, P. D., & Martin, A. J. (2009). Coping and buoyancy in the workplace: Understanding their effects on teachers' work-related well-being and engagement. *Teaching and Teacher Education: An International Journal of Research and Studies, 25*(1), 68–75.

Pierce, C. M. B., & Molloy, G. N. (1990). Psychological and biographical differences between secondary school teachers experiencing high and low levels of burnout. *British Journal of Educational Psychology, 60,* 37–51.

Rowe, M. M. (1999). Teaching health-care providers coping: Results of a two-year study. *Journal of Behavioral Medicine, 22*(5), 511–527.

Russell, D. W., Altmaier, E., & Van Velzen, D. (1987). Job-related stress, social support, and burnout among classroom teachers. *Journal of Applied Psychology, 72*(2), 269–274.

Schaufeli, W. B., & Enzmann, D. (1998). *The burnout companion to study and practice: A critical analysis.* Washington, DC: Taylor & Francis.

Sorenson, R. D. (2007). Stress management in education: Warning signs and coping mechanisms. *Management in Education, 21*(3), 10–13.

Sutton, R. E. (2004). Emotional regulation goals and strategies of teachers. *Social Psychology of Education, 7,* 379–398.

Sutton, R. E. (2005). Teachers' emotions and classroom effectiveness: Implications from recent research. *Clearing House: A Journal of Educational Strategies, Issues and Ideas, 78*(5), 229–234.

Tatar, M., & Horenczyk, G. (2003). Diversity-related burnout among teachers. *Teaching and Teacher Education, 19,* 397–408.

Teven, J. J. (2007). Teacher temperament: Correlates with teacher caring, burnout, and organizational outcomes. *Communication Education, 56*(3), 382–400.

Tsouloupas, C. N., Carson, R. L., Matthews, R., Grawitch, M. J., & Barber, L. K. (2010). Exploring the association between teachers' perceived student misbehaviour and emotional exhaustion: The importance of teacher efficacy beliefs and emotion regulation. *Educational Psychology, 30*(2), 173–189.

Weiqi, C. (2007). The structure of secondary school teacher job satisfaction and its relationship with attrition and work enthusiasm. *Chinese Education and Society, 40*(5), 17–31.

Wong, K.-S., & Cheuk, W.-H. (1998). Beginning teachers' experience of being spurned, coping style, stress preparation, and burnout. *Chinese University Education Journal, 26*(1), 117–129.

Zhang, Q., & Zhu, W. (2008). Exploring emotion in teaching: Emotional labor, burnout, and satisfaction in Chinese higher education. *Communication Education, 57*(1), 105–122.

CHAPTER 11

EFFECTS OF COLLABORATIVE PROBLEM SOLVING ON STRESS, BURNOUT, AND COPING RESOURCES IN EARLY CHILDHOOD SPECIAL EDUCATORS

Jennifer Singleton, Pamela Shue, and JaneDiane Smith

ABSTRACT

While many studies have addressed the increasing teacher turnover rates, reasons for teacher burnout, and generic solutions for decreasing burnout, few studies have implemented proactive strategies to decrease teacher stress and burnout. An intervention used in a previous study (collaborative problem solving sessions) was implemented among three early childhood special educators in a public separate school for children with severe disabilities. A mixed-methods research design was used in order to gain quantitative information about participants' levels of stress, burnout, and coping resources before and after the intervention. Qualitative information was also gained regarding current stressors and coping resources among the participants. Results showed the collaborative problem solving sessions were effective in

International Perspectives on Teacher Stress, pages 219–242
Copyright © 2012 by Information Age Publishing

decreasing all participants' levels of stress and burnout within a six-week intervention period. Stress-related themes were found, including a lack of social support, administrative issues, and workload-related factors. Increases in coping resources were also found among one of the participants with coping-related themes including positive personal relationships. Findings indicate a need for increased collaboration among special educators during team planning meetings in which problems can be solved systematically. Building a sense of trust and empathy among special educators may also be an important buffer against stress in the workplace.

Work-related stress affects individuals in every type of occupation. Whether the occupation entails working with young children or heading a multi-million dollar company, at some point in time, every person will experience some level of stress on the job. Stress may evolve from working late hours, having an overload of tasks to complete, or just being dissatisfied with the job in general. These are all issues often faced by early childhood special educators. A small amount of stress is to be expected in the workplace, but stress can turn into a more serious issue. Exposure to stress over an extended amount of time, paired with contrasting views of job expectations, may lead to the psychological state of job burnout (Maslach, 2003).

Although the effects of job burnout have likely been experienced for many decades, the conceptualization of the term did not appear in research until the 1970's (Maslach, Schaufeli, & Leiter, 2001). Job burnout has its roots in the human services field where individuals work directly with clients and tend to be more emotionally involved in their jobs (Maslach et al., 2001). Educators have been a recent focus of job-related burnout because they are emotionally tied to their students, take on large workloads, and work collaboratively with other adults (Maslach et al., 2001). Examining job-related burnout among special educators extends this concept further. Maslach et al. (2001) suggest the higher the level of need (e.g., physical, emotional, educational) of the children, the more likely the educator is to experience job burnout.

Special educators, especially those working with children with severe disabilities, may be at the highest risk of experiencing job burnout. Expending an exorbitant amount of emotional support for these children can add to the stress of unending paperwork and adaptation of curriculum that is required of all special educators. The recent economic state compounds this issue for many educators in the form of stagnant salaries or loss of additional benefits (e.g., loss of insurance coverage, reduction of bonuses).

The increasing burnout among special educators has led to an increase in turnover rates. A study conducted by Boe, Cook, and Sunderland (2008) revealed that total teacher turnover in the 2000–2001 school year was 90,000 as compared to 54,000 in the 1991–1992 school year. With this increase in turnover comes an increase in substitute teachers or other provisionally licensed teachers who have little experience working with students with disabilities. These steadily increasing rates of turnover are a detriment to the education of children with disabilities, as these students need qualified teachers who can successfully adapt the curriculum to best meet their needs.

There is a multitude of research in publication relating to the various reasons for teacher burnout and attrition and generic solutions for reducing teacher burnout and attrition. Very few empirical studies have been conducted on programs to combat teacher burnout. This is a problem for the field of education because teachers are becoming increasingly burned out, causing them to leave their teaching positions. Without knowledge of how to reduce teacher burnout, the problem will continue to grow, leaving millions of children with disabilities without trained professionals to provide a proper education.

FACTORS LEADING TO BURNOUT

There are several broad reasons teachers give for experiencing burnout. These reasons include personal factors, administrative issues, and workload-related factors.

Personal factors such as health, raising a family, and retirement were all listed as reasons for turnover in two studies (Boe et al., 2008; Kaff, 2004). However, childrearing is a common reason for leaving the workforce for many young women, regardless of their line of work. Another personal factor affecting teacher burnout is the person's ability to cope with stressors (O'Donnell, Lambert, & McCarthy, 2008). According to O'Donnell et al. (2008), the fewer coping resources (e.g., maintaining perspective, scanning the environment) an individual possesses, the more likely he or she will be to experience stress. Prolonged exposure to these stressors may ultimately lead to burnout.

Administrative issues can also add to job-related stress and burnout. This can include receiving a low salary, having a lack of supplies or assistance, or just an overall perceived lack of support from colleagues and administration (Billingsley, 2004b; Boe et al., 2008; Gersten, Keating, Yovanoff, & Harniss, 2001; Nance & Calabrese, 2009; U.S. Department of Education, 2005). In a qualitative study conducted by Kaff (2004), one teacher reported that "special education is treated like the 'stepchild'" (p. 12). Without proper administrative support, teachers are left to fend for themselves when they need assistance with overwhelming job-related tasks.

Special educators face heavy workloads on a daily basis. Lesson planning, developing each child's individualized education plan (IEP), and behavior modification plans all require teachers to spend a significant amount of time outside of the classroom. The amount of paperwork and lack of time to complete paperwork and plan lessons was noted by teachers in several studies (Billingsley, 2004b; Kaff, 2004; Nance & Calabrese, 2009; U.S. Department of Education, 2005; Zabel & Zabel, 2001). Personal factors, administrative issues, and workload-related factors all play a significant role in teacher burnout and turnover rates; however, few teachers have the necessary tools to decrease stress before it leads to burnout.

PROPOSED STRESS AND BURNOUT REDUCTION STRATEGIES

Although the causes of burnout have been studied extensively, the strategies to reduce burnout in the research have been merely a generic overview of ideas for improvement. Many studies list ideas such as teacher retention programs and mentors, increasing administrative support, reducing paperwork, increasing professional development, and fostering collegial relationships (Billingsley, 2002, 2004a; Brownell, Hirsch, & Seo, 2004; Fore, Martin, & Bender, 2002; Leko & Smith, 2010). However, none of these studies include any specific strategies on how to reduce stress and burnout. O'Donnell et al. (2008) suggest teaching coping mechanisms in order to help teachers manage their stress; however, they do not include any information on specific coping strategies that lead to a reduction in stress. In order to decrease teacher burnout and turnover, school systems need specific research on how to implement positive practices within the schools.

After an extensive review of the literature, only one study was found that tested a proactive solution to combat special education teacher stress and burnout. This study, the Teacher Support Program, was developed in western North Carolina in order to provide resources for educators such as collegial support and problem solving, current research, and peer mentoring programs (Westling, Herzog, Cooper-Duffy, Prohn, & Ray, 2006). The core component of the program was the Collaborative Problem Solving/Mutual Teacher Support (CPS/MTS) sessions. These sessions were held at central locations (not within schools), after school hours, where teachers met to collaboratively work out problems they were experiencing in the classroom with other educators and a facilitator (Westling et al., 2006). Teachers who participated in CPS/MTS sessions rated them highly with regard to providing collegial support, addressing their personal problems, increasing their empathy for others, and establishing a sense of competence in their teaching; however, teachers did find attending the sessions outside the regular school hours sometimes created additional stress (Westling et al., 2006). Another study found the use of planning (i.e., reflecting and strategizing) in solving problems to be a predictive factor in achieving lower scores on the lack of personal accomplishment section of the Maslach Burnout Inventory (i.e., a measure used to indicate burnout levels) (Dorz, Novara, Sica, & Sanavio, 2003).

STRESS AND BURNOUT MODELS

Lazarus and Folkman's transactional model of stress helps clarify how stress is manifested (1984). They describe stress as a product of an environmental stressor and a person's reaction to that stressor; the relationship between the stressor and the person is reciprocal (Lazarus & Folkman, 1984). Job stress can be ultimately defined by Robert Karasek's theory that stress is a product of job demands and decision latitude (i.e., control over demands) (Karasek, Triantis, & Chaudhry, 1982). Karasek's theory postulated that experiencing a higher level of job demands paired with low decision latitude leads to an increase in exhaustion, depression, job dissatisfaction, and overall life dissatisfaction (Karasek, 1979). If stress is not managed, it can ultimately lead to job burnout. Several studies concluded, however, that social support from coworkers can reduce the effects of stress before it turns into burnout (Johnson & Hall, 1988; Karasek et al., 1982).

Studies involving job burnout are based upon the model for job-related burnout developed by Maslach and Freudenberger (Maslach et al., 2001). There are three main identifiers which must be present in order to qualify as job burnout: emotional exhaustion or "feelings of being overextended and depleted of one's emotional and physical resources," sense of detachment or "negative, callous, or excessively detached response to various aspects of the job," and lack of accomplishment or "feelings of incompetence and a lack of achievement and productivity at work" (Maslach et al., 2001, p. 399). Maslach et al. (2001) also suggest burnout can be "caught" by others working closely with a burned-out individual. This can lead to an overall negative work environment.

The research suggests that social support, especially from colleagues, is crucial to lowering rates of burnout among working professionals (Maslach et al., 2001). This is evident in the development of Maslach et al.'s (2001) six key areas employees need to minimize burnout: workload, control, reward, community, fairness, and values. The most important of these may be developing a sense of community and building trusting relationships among those who work closely together. McCarthy, Lambert, and Brack (1997) also discuss the use of *combative coping strategies* and their ability to decrease negative emotions involved with stress over time. These strategies include things such as being part of a social support network and using problem-solving skills (McCarthy et al., 1997). In order to facilitate burnout reduction programs, it is beneficial to focus not only on the individual who is experiencing burnout, but the environment in which he or she works (Maslach et al., 2001).

The purpose of this study was to examine the effect of an intervention on teacher stress and burnout by implementing collaborative problem-solving sessions (similar to the CPS/MTS sessions from the Teacher Support Program) among early childhood special educators in a public separate school for children with severe disabilities.

In conducting this program within a school setting, it was crucial to start with the preschool team. Elementary school-based preschool classrooms are often separated from the rest of the school. Bennett and LeCompte (1990) summarized the isolation felt by early elementary teachers due to the fact that they stay with their students all day within the classroom, rarely interacting with other coworkers (as cited in McCarthy, Lambert, O'Donnell, & Melendres, 2009). It is hypothesized that preschool teachers may be at risk of isolation as well since they work with the same children all day and rarely leave the room. The majority of the research available on stress and burnout in early childhood special education relates to interventionists working within the home setting; therefore, further research is needed to identify the needs of school-based early childhood special educators.

In conducting this study, there were two major research questions that needed to be answered. What effects will the collaborative problem-solving sessions have on teacher stress and burnout? What effects will the collaborative problem-solving sessions have on teachers' coping resources? In this study, *coping resources* are defined as "one's capacities for dealing with potentially demanding events" (McCarthy et al., 1997, p. 54). By researching these questions, the field of early childhood special education will potentially be better prepared to proactively combat increasing attrition rates by reducing levels of teacher burnout and stress and increasing teacher coping resources.

METHOD

A mixed-methods case study was conducted using three stress and burnout scales as well as two researcher-developed questionnaires in order to obtain detailed results on the benefits and limitations of the intervention. Transcription data from each collaborative problem-solving session was also used to obtain qualitative information to support the quantitative findings.

Participants/Setting

Three preschool special education teachers in a public separate school for children with severe disabilities were invited to participate in the study.

The school was located in a large urban area in a southeastern state. All three teachers were Caucasian females and ranged in age from 32 to 39. The participants had all been employed in their current position for two years. Prior special education teaching experience of the participants ranged from 10 to 16 years.

Measures

The Classroom Appraisal of Resources and Demands (CARD) (pre-school version; Lambert, Abbott-Shim, & McCarthy, 2005) was used in order to identify teacher stress levels as shown through the differences between perceived classroom resources and classroom demands. The CARD contains 65 items divided into two sections (classroom demands and classroom resources), on which teachers were asked to rate items on a five-point Likert scale according to how demanding or helpful the items were (1 = not demanding/helpful, 5 = very demanding/helpful) (McCarthy et al., 2009). McCarthy et al. (2009) summarize the scale's high construct and criterion validity as well as reliability in a variety of studies.

The Preventative Resources Inventory (PRI) (McCarthy & Lambert, 2004) was used to assess the teachers' coping resources. This measure contains 82 items in which teachers were asked to rate statements related to various coping strategies on a five-point Likert scale based on their level of agreement with each statement (1 = strongly disagree, 5 = strongly agree) (McCarthy et al., 2009). McCarthy et al. (2009) summarize this measure's high construct and concurrent validity based on several studies.

The Maslach Burnout Inventory–Educators Survey (MBI-ES) was used to measure the teachers' burnout levels. This measure consists of 22 items on which participants were asked to rate statements on how frequently they occur based on a seven-point scale (0 = never, 6 = every day) (McCarthy et al., 2009). McCarthy et al. (2009) summarize the MBI-ES's strong reliability and validity evidence based on several studies.

Two questionnaires developed by the researcher were created based on previous studies (Kaff, 2004; Maslach et al., 2001) in order to gain additional qualitative information. The pre-intervention questionnaire contained five open-ended questions addressing the participants' years of experience in various special education settings, their personal definition of burnout, factors that led to their perceived burnout, and expected outcomes of the intervention. Two items used a five-point scale to rate each participant's perceived level of burnout (1 = not at all burned out, 5 = significantly burned out) and perceived coworker levels of burnout (1 = significantly less burned out, 5 = significantly more burned out). The post-intervention questionnaire contained two open-ended questions addressing the positive and negative aspects of the intervention. Four 5-point scales were used to assess participants' perceived level of personal burnout and co-worker burnout (as measured in the pre-intervention questionnaire) as well as the effectiveness of the intervention (1 = not at all effective, 5 = significantly effective) and the perceived change in burnout level (1 = significantly decreased, 5 = significantly increased). The final question used a checklist to address whether or not participants would recommend the intervention for use across the school (1 = not recommended, 2 = recommended with changes, 3 = recommended as is).

Procedure

Institutional Review Board (IRB) approval was gained from the participating university as well as the school district prior to implementation. Two pilot collaborative problem-solving sessions were held among other grade level teams in order to make sure the sessions ran smoothly and the researcher was able to effectively facilitate each session. Pilot sessions received positive reactions from participants and resulted in only one change in the order of the steps on the collaborative problem-solving form.

The complete intervention lasted eight weeks and took place during prearranged team planning times during the school day. During the first session, each participant was asked to complete the CARD, PRI, and the MBI-ES. They also completed a short, researcher-developed questionnaire about their perceptions of burnout among themselves and their colleagues as well as their expected outcomes from participating in the collaborative problem-solving sessions. After participants completed the measures, the researcher introduced the collaborative problem-solving sessions to the participants by giving an outline of how each session would run. Participants were asked to begin brainstorming problems they were facing at that time. After the first session, all future sessions were audio taped in order to provide more accurate qualitative data.

Starting the second week, collaborative problem-solving sessions were implemented once a week for approximately one hour. The sessions lasted for six weeks and were facilitated by the researcher who was not a part of the preschool team. The facilitator was also in charge of bringing in any needed specialists (e.g., behavior management specialist, psychologist, counselor) to address specific classroom issues. Participants were encouraged to notify the facilitator ahead of time if they felt an additional specialist would be a beneficial member to the problem-solving team for that particular week. No specialists were requested throughout the duration of the study due to the fact that the topics discussed did not warrant a specialist's input.

For each session, participants were asked to come with problems they were facing in their classroom. All of the participants had to choose a problem and work together to complete a Collaborative Problem-Solving Form, created by the researcher based on Amauta International, LLC's article, "Facilitating Collaborative Decision-Making in Six Steps" (Weinberg & Brandon, 1999). The form used an eight-step approach to help participants solve their problems collectively. These steps included clearly defining the problem, listing the possible causes of the problem, deciding the ultimate goal of the problem at hand (vision statement), creating a decision map of steps needed to accomplish the goal (breaking down the ultimate goal into small achievable steps), describing the evaluation method (deciding what kind of data to collect and how to collect it), creating an implementation plan (set specific dates of when steps must be complete), collecting data, and evaluating the outcomes. The group focused on one problem at a time, rotating among participants to ensure all problems were addressed. A single problem was discussed over several meetings when necessary. The facilitator's role in the process was to guide the participants in filling out the form correctly, as well as to push the participants to think systematically about each problem instead of only reacting emotionally. Ultimately, the role of the facilitator faded as the weeks progressed; however, it was imperative to have someone model and encourage the process during the first few sessions. After each session, audio recordings were electronically transcribed by the researcher.

During the eighth and final session, participants were asked to complete the CARD, PRI, and the MBI-ES a second time. They also completed a researcher-developed questionnaire about their current levels of burnout and provided feedback on the benefits and limitations of the collaborative problem-solving sessions. The researcher asked clarifying questions as needed after completion of the questionnaire.

Analyses

After completion of the intervention, all measures were scored in order to see if stress and burnout rates as well as coping resources were affected by the implementation of collaborative problem-solving sessions. Data from the CARD and MBI-ES scales were collected and scored from the pre- and post-tests. The CARD was scored by obtaining the mean score for all items related to classroom demands and the mean score for all items related to classroom resources. The means were derived from the responses on the 5-point Likert scale based on how demanding or helpful the content on each item was perceived to be. Scores ranged from one to five in each area. The overall stress score was obtained by comparing perceived classroom resources and perceived classroom demands; high teacher stress was a product of classroom demands outweighing classroom resources, average teacher stress was a product of equivalent classroom resources and classroom demands, and low teacher stress was a product of classroom resources outweighing classroom demands.

The MBI-ES was scored by totaling the ratings for each subsection as well as the total score for the entire scale. Subscores for Emotional Exhaustion (EE), which addressed how emotionally drained a teacher felt, ranged from 0–54. Subscore ratings for EE were categorized as follows: 0–17 low EE, 18–35 moderate EE, 36–54 high EE. Subscores for Depersonalization (DP), which addressed negative attitudes, ranged from 0–30. Subscore ratings for DP were categorized as follows: 0–9 low DP, 10–19 moderate DP, 20–30 high DP. Subscores for Lack of Personal Accomplishment (LPA), which addressed feelings of incompetence, ranged from 0–48. Subscore ratings for LPA were categorized as follows: 0–16 low LPA, 17–32 moderate LPA, 33–48 high LPA. Since possible burnout scores on the MBI-ES ranged from 48–84, overall burnout rates were categorized as follows: 48–59 low burnout, 60–72 moderate burnout, and 73–84 high burnout.

The PRI was used to evaluate the participants' ability to prevent stress. Data from the PRI were collected and scored from the pre- and post-tests. The changes in scores from pre- to post-test were summarized according to participant. The PRI was scored by obtaining the mean score for all items overall and also looked at several different coping skills including self-acceptance, "the degree to which one can accept and overcome shortcomings, imperfections, and limitations in dealing with demanding life situations"; scanning, "one's perceived ability to recognize, anticipate, and plan for demands or potential stressors"; social resourcefulness, "the ability to draw a social network of caring others who can act as a buffer against life demands"; perceived control, "the belief that one can cope successfully with life demands and manage situations that could potentially become stressful"; maintaining perspective, "attitudes and beliefs consistent with preventing stressful situations and keeping stress-produced emotions at manageable levels"; and overall ability to prevent stress (McCarthy et al., 2009, p. 289).

Transcriptions of the collaborative problem-solving sessions were individually coded by the three researchers according to each individual participant by identifying main ideas in the transcription of each collaborative problem-solving session. The team then met together to examine and identify the main ideas and sort them into dominant themes. The themes were collapsed into four overall themes (lack of social support, administrative issues, workload-related factors, and coping resources) for each participant, which was supported by previous research on causes of teacher stress and coping skills. Dominant themes identified in the coding process were consistent among all researchers; the only exception was that two of the researchers noted a lack of equality (i.e., higher number of students on caseloads, lack of planning time in preschool, lack of substitutes for preschool), which was not identified by the third researcher.

RESULTS

The following cases describe the impact of the intervention on each individual participant. All participants' names have been changed to ensure confidentiality. Each case outlines the effect of the intervention on the participant's stress, burnout, and coping resources.

Brittany

Brittany, a preschool teacher with 11 years of experience working in a self-contained special education setting with children ages three to eleven and two years' experience working in an inclusive preschool program, began the study showing high levels of stress with her perceived classroom demands outweighing her perceived classroom resources based on her CARD scores (see Table 11.1). Her burnout level on the MBI-ES was also in the highest category. According to a self-assessment, Brittany defined burnout as "being so physically, emotionally, [and] mentally tired that you just can't function anymore," and by that definition, felt she was moderately burned out. She presumed her colleagues were experiencing similar levels of burnout. She believed that the "go, go, go" atmosphere, high numbers of significant physical/medical need children, lack of planning time, and administrative demands all contributed to her moderate levels of burnout. Brittany hoped to gain more help in the classroom, a longer planning period, and positive ideas to help lower her stress by participating in the collaborative problem-solving sessions.

During the six-week intervention, Brittany expressed several issues she was facing in the classroom. Qualitative data showed Brittany faced significant stress related to the heavy workload she contended with each day. This stemmed from the high level of students' physical, medical, and educational needs. The sheer number of students on her caseload proved to be an arduous task as she described: "We can't even, right now, take a walk to the park or around the building or anything like that, because we don't have enough arms to do something like that," referring to the fact that there are only three adults in the room having to push eight or nine wheelchairs. She also noted challenges with medically fragile students taking a toll on her emotions when she faced her "second episode, where in my opinion 911

TABLE 11.1 Changes in Stress, Burnout, and Coping Scores

Scale	Participant 1		Participant 2		Participant 3	
	Pre-Test	Post-Test	Pre-Test	Post-Test	Pre-Test	Post-Test
CARD						
Classroom Demands	3.18	2.84	3.31	2.28	1.90	2.27
Classroom Resources	2.57	3.52	3.10	3.72	3.45	4.14
Overall Stress	D > R	D > R	D > R	D = R	D = R	R > D
MBI						
Emotional Exhaustion	27	30	25	23	40	45
Depersonalization	11	2	7	6	0	0
Lack of Personal Accomplishment	36	36	35	34	37	27
Overall Burnout	74	68	67	63	77	72
PRI						
Self-Acceptance	3.66	3.86	4.33	4.53	2.86	2.80
Scanning	3.00	3.66	4.16	4.05	2.83	3.05
Social Resourcefulness	3.71	3.85	4.14	4.07	3.92	3.78
Perceived Control	3.47	3.80	4.00	4.28	3.09	3.00
Maintaining Perspective	3.06	3.66	4.20	4.40	3.53	3.33
Overall Coping Resources	3.31	3.74	4.15	4.25	3.30	3.21

Note: Changes in CARD and PRI scales that were ± 0.4 were considered meaningful. Changes in MBI scores that were ± 4 were considered meaningful. D refers to perceived classroom demands. R refers to perceived classroom resources.

should have absolutely been called [since the child was facing a medical emergency]"; however, the parent requested the situation be dealt with by the child's personal nurse instead. With state-mandated caseload sizes, IEP requirements, and increased educational expectations for children with disabilities, Brittany realized she had little time to deal with all the extra work that goes along with teaching children with special needs.

Brittany perceived a lack of resources, communication, and administrative support within her school, which made her feel as if the heavy workload was impossible to bear. Brittany expressed that having no planning time contributed to this stress. She felt as if the master schedule was created by administration with little input from the teachers, giving her a planning time that was virtually useless. According to her, "originally what we were doing was we were coming back from lunch and we were going right into our literacy time … it was just disastrous." This lack of perceived support left a lasting effect on Brittany, leading her to believe that there was nothing she could do to change the lack of planning time. After working with her teammates for the first three weeks of the intervention using the collaborative problem-solving form, Brittany finally felt like she had some of her stress under control. She noted, "At least I feel like I am getting something done every day."

In dealing with an increased workload and administrative issues, Brittany also faced a lack of social support within her school. While she had a positive working relationship with her teaching assistants, Brittany found it was often difficult working with related service personnel and special area teachers. She presumed much of the staff at her school did not value preschool and often treated them unfairly. While this caused some minor frustration, Brittany struggled the most with dealing with parents of her students. In the fourth problem solving-session, Brittany discussed an issue she was facing with one of her students' mothers about his current educational placement. She expressed her desire for suggestions on how to handle difficult parents during IEP meetings. Comments from parents such as, "You know, Brittany, it's just preschool" made her feel as if her work was not valued. While noting her aggravation with this particular family, she also shared a source of support throughout that time. An outside central office representative had been supportive throughout the whole process and "[hadn't] shied away from the meetings and [had] absolutely told me, I will absolutely be at every single meeting with you." After talking to the her colleagues about her problem, she was able to complete the collaborative problem-solving form with their help in order to devise a plan of action for working with this family. Brittany was grateful for the suggestions and seemed to have a sense of calm upon leaving the collaborative problem-solving session. In the fifth and sixth weeks of the intervention, Brittany shared her satisfaction with simply talking about her frustrations with her colleagues and not filling out a collaborative problem-solving form for any specific issue.

Although Brittany showed frustration with her increased workload, administrative issues, and lack of social support; throughout the six-week intervention, Brittany also showed her ability to use a variety of coping resources to deal with these stressors. Brittany showed great social resourcefulness in her ability to draw on others for support. She looked to her teaching assistants, other teachers, parents, administration, and other outside resources (i.e., central office staff, program specialists) to help her deal with problems she was facing. She also showed her ability to scan her environment for possible stressors and look for ways to alleviate them. She showed great flexibility in scheduling activities in her classroom and was able to use a variety of data to make informed decisions and be prepared to meet challenges. Finally, she showed she could maintain perspective by keeping a positive attitude throughout the entire process and using active listening strategies to show her colleagues support.

Upon completion of the study, Brittany's CARD scores showed she perceived her classroom demands to decrease and her classroom resources to increase, which shows a decrease in overall stress; however, her classroom demands still outweighed her classroom resources, keeping her in the highest category of stress. Her overall MBI-ES burnout score dropped into the moderate burnout category. Within the MBI-ES, a drop from moderate DP to low DP should be noted, showing a large decrease in her negative experiences with colleagues. Brittany was the only participant to show significant changes in her PRI coping resources scores from pre- to post-test. She showed gains in her ability to maintain perspective, scanning, and overall stress prevention.

In a post-test self-assessment, Brittany felt her burnout level decreased to only slightly burned out, which she felt was right on par with the rest of her colleagues. She rated the collaborative problem-solving process as highly effective at solving her problems and suggested it for use among all grade levels throughout the school year. She described several positive aspects of the program, including being able to talk about her problems and being heard by her peers, seeing that she was not the only one experiencing problems in her classroom, and getting ideas from several people on how to solve her problems.

Donna

Donna, a preschool teacher with 14 years of experience in a self-contained special education setting working with children ages three to seven, and two years' experience working in an inclusive setting with children ages five to six, began the study showing high levels of stress with her perceived classroom demands outweighing her perceived classroom resources based on her CARD scores (see Table 11.1). Her burnout scores on the MBI-ES were in the moderate category. According to a self-assessment, Donna defined burnout as "physically, emotionally, and mentally exhausted," and by that definition, felt she was moderately burned out. She presumed her colleagues were experiencing slightly lower levels of burnout. She believed that the "high class size and never-ending paperwork" contributed to her moderate levels of burnout. Donna felt a smaller caseload and duty-free planning could be possible with some sort of intervention. She wanted to see her preschool team work together to solve problems and support each other after participating in the collaborative problem-solving sessions.

During the six-week intervention, Donna expressed several issues she was facing in the classroom. Qualitative data showed that she was facing a heavy workload, which was causing her stress. This emerged from her discussions of the high level of physical, medical, and emotional needs of the students on her caseload, the state-mandated caseload limits and IEP requirements, and the amount of school activities she attended with her class. She found it hard to juggle the amount of work she faced without an efficient amount of time to plan each day.

Administrative issues, such as a lack of communication throughout the school, intensified the effects of her heavy workload. She felt as if the master schedule was created with little input from the teachers, which led to a planning time that was not conducive to her classroom needs. When faced with the reality of teaching assistants taking over the classroom while she took her planning time, Donna shared her feelings, saying, "I would just feel guilty about asking them to do something that I know that I should be doing." The large number of children caused her to question the plausibility of leaving the room for planning time: "We have problems transitioning because we have so many kids...we have eight...changing eight kids or you know [tube feeding]...it's a lot for two people to handle. Really it needs to be three people working together to get that done." After working together to complete the collaborative problem-solving process and going through a trial period of having duty-free planning time, Donna noted, "I tried it on Monday just to see if I could get most of it done by 12:00, you know, and it's fine."

For Donna, a lack of social support appeared to be the most dominant stressor in her day-to-day routine. Donna struggled to deal with a teaching assistant who often had a negative attitude and failed to perform her duties in an effective manner. The two did not communicate effectively, resulting in increased tension in the classroom. Donna also noted a lack of social support among related service personnel and other teachers within the school.

Throughout the intervention, Donna revealed her ability to use several coping resources to deal with the stressors she was facing. Her social resourcefulness was evident in her use of teaching assistants, nurses, parents, and outside staff to help overcome problems. Donna showed her appreciation for being able to talk with her colleagues during the sessions noting, "We never get a chance to really talk, talk about stuff." In the fourth week of the intervention, she offered support to a colleague in dealing with a parent issue and did so without the support of the facilitator, showing an increase in initiation. Donna also showed success in scanning her environment to locate and prevent possible stressors by being flexible with her schedule, using data to make decisions, and planning ahead. In the fifth week of the intervention, Donna was injured and unable to attend work for the last three weeks of the study, therefore only receiving four weeks of the intervention.

Donna completed the scales and questionnaire from home during the eighth week of the study based on her participation during the first five weeks of the study. Upon completion, Donna's CARD scores showed that she perceived her classroom demands to decrease and her classroom resources to increase, making her classroom resources equal to her classroom demands. This showed a reduction in her overall stress, putting her in the average stress category. Her MBI-ES burnout score decreased slightly, staying in the moderate burnout category. She did not have a strong negative or positive perception of how she coped with stress and showed minor changes on the PRI from pre- to post-test.

In a post-test self-assessment, Donna felt that her burnout level slightly decreased but that she was still moderately burned out, and she felt her burnout was slightly higher than the rest of her colleagues. She rated the collaborative problem-solving process as highly effective at solving her problems and suggested it for use across the entire school, not only within team planning meetings. She described the positive aspects of the collaborative problem-solving sessions being the fact that they were very helpful, useful, and easy to do.

Natalie

Natalie, a preschool teacher with three years' experience working in a self-contained preschool special education setting and seven years' experience working in an inclusive preschool setting, began the study showing average levels of stress with her perceived classroom resources equal to her perceived classroom demands based on her CARD scores (see Table 11.1). Her MBI-ES burnout scores, however, were in the highest category. According to a self-assessment, Natalie defined burnout as "stressed out; tired of doing what you are currently doing," and by that definition felt she was moderately burned out. She presumed her colleagues were experiencing similar levels of burnout. She believed that the "number of students, level of student needs, pay, colleagues, and high academic expectations" contributed to her moderate levels of burnout. Natalie was not sure what to expect from participating in the collaborative problem-solving sessions.

Throughout the collaborative problem-solving sessions, Natalie expressed some stress relating to the heavy workload involved in special education. The increase in educational demands for students with disabilities, IEP requirements, and large caseload size at times could be frustrating. However, Natalie had nearly ten years' experience working with children with severe disabilities and had become accustomed to these aspects of the job.

Natalie experienced most of her stress in dealing with administrative issues such as a lack of resources, communication, and support. Natalie struggled with not having an appropriate planning time during the school day due to the lack of administration communication in creating the master schedule. When discussing possible options on how to rearrange the schedule to include a planning time, Natalie was hesitant when asked how she felt about leaving the room for planning. She noted, "I'll be honest, I just worry about our assistants." She constantly discussed having to worry about her assistants getting upset with her, and how it caused her a great amount of stress. When it came time to implement changes in the master schedule, Natalie showed high levels of frustration and hopelessness, "I just say let's forget it…it just ain't happening." Dealing with the lack of planning time throughout the school year made it easy for her to just give up on the possibility of change. Eventually, Natalie did take her planning time each day and was grateful for the opportunity to make the change in the schedule.

A major change took place during week four of the intervention for Natalie; one of her teaching assistants went on maternity leave, leaving her with only one assistant for the last few weeks of the study. The high level of students' physical and medical needs paired with the lack of help led to an increased amount of stress for Natalie. She described the physical pain of the job: "I don't mind changing [diapers], but it wears on your body." Without the help of two assistants, these types of tasks increased in frequency, adding to her physical and emotional exhaustion.

For Natalie, the lack of substitutes available at her school was astounding. According to her, taking care of nine children with severe disabilities was nearly impossible without a substitute teacher to assist in the room. She voiced her frustration with her assistant being on maternity leave and the lack of substitute teachers to fill her position, stating, "At this point, I'll take Joe off the street! I don't care!" Without help from a substitute, it was all she could do to keep the physical needs of the children met, leaving educational needs second.

Natalie also discussed during the intervention how she felt a lack of social support among the rest of the school staff, as they did not seem to understand the importance of preschool. She felt "like [preschool is] not taken serious. That's how I feel." She expressed her desire for others in the school to learn more about what the preschool teachers do and not view them as simply "babysitters." She also felt on occasion that she lacked social support from her teaching assistants, related service personnel, and other teachers within the school.

While the stress of working with a large caseload and one less assistant seemed to be increasing for Natalie, she still was able to exhibit several coping resources throughout the intervention. She showed a great amount of social resourcefulness by turning to a variety of people to assist her in difficult situations. She sought the support of her teaching assistants, other teachers within the school, parents, related service personnel, and administration. She was also able to effectively scan her environment to identify and eliminate stressors by being flexible in her scheduling, using data to make decisions and plan ahead, and using the resources provided to her to the best of her ability. During the hard times, she showed her ability to maintain perspective by staying positive, and offering support to other colleagues through active listening and sharing positive stories. Natalie offered advice to a colleague on a difficult parent situation, stating, "I think regardless of [what school the child is placed in], I think as long as you go in [to the IEP meeting] and you say what you feel [about the best placement for him] and say what you know is right, then nothing else matters." She also demonstrated self-acceptance by understanding her roles as the teacher. In the last two weeks of the intervention, Natalie was able to talk freely with her colleagues, sharing her general frustrations, but not filling out any collaborative problem-solving forms.

In the eighth week of the study, after completing post-test scales, Natalie perceived her classroom demands to increase but also perceived her classroom resources to increase according to her CARD scores. This led to the perception that classroom resources outweighed classroom demands, moving her into the lowest stress category. Her MBI-ES burnout score dropped to the moderate burnout category. Within the MBI-ES, an increase in EE should be noted, showing an increase in fatigue and frustration, and a decrease in LPA, showing an increase in productivity at work. She did not have a strong negative or positive perception of how she dealt with stress and showed minor changes from pre- to post-test on the PRI.

In a post-test self-assessment, Natalie felt there was no change in her burnout level and that she was still moderately burned out. She perceived her burnout level to be similar to the rest of her colleagues. She rated the collaborative problem solving process as moderately effective at solving her problems and suggested it for use across the entire school. Natalie noted the positive aspects of the collaborative problem-solving process as being able to share her feelings with others, as well as being able to work together to create a planning time during the school day.

DISCUSSION

Two major research questions were addressed through this study. The first question concentrated on what effects the collaborative problem-solving sessions had on participants' stress and burnout. The results of the pre- and post-tests showed that the collaborative problem-solving sessions were effective for all three participants in reducing their overall levels of stress and burnout, regardless of any new external stressors faced during the intervention period. These results are consistent with the findings of Westling et al. (2006) and Dorz et al. (2003) in that collaborative problem solving may lead to an overall decrease in stress and increase in ability to cope with stressors. While quantitative data provided important information about participants' levels of stress and burnout, qualitative data gained through transcriptions of each collaborative problem-solving session helped identify specific stressors experienced by the participants, providing further insight into why special educators face high levels of stress.

Several factors noted in the previous research as possible causes of burnout were consistent with the themes identified during each of the collaborative problem-solving sessions. The data showed that these themes were a lack of social support, administrative issues, and workload-related factors.

A lack of social support in the workplace was found to be a source of stress for these three special educators. This included relationships with other teachers, teaching assistants, related service personnel, administrators, and even parents. This was found to be a common stressor for all three participants. Parent relationships were found to be a major stressor for these special educators. Dealing with difficult parents who disagree with the teacher's teaching style or student expectations can be mentally draining. Having a lack of parental support made Brittany feel as if her work was not valued. Maslach et al. (2001) found thatstrong research showing a lack of social support in the workplace is linked to burnout. This was likely true among the preschool special educators in this study who faced strains in relationships with both colleagues and parents. While personal relationships played a huge role in the stress level of the participants, administrative issues were equally stressful in the school setting.

Consistent with previous findings (Billingsley, 2004b; Boe et al., 2008; Gersten et al., 2001; Nance & Calabrese, 2009; U.S. Department of Education, 2005), the participants found administrative issues such as budget concerns and a perceived lack of support to be tremendous stressors in their work. With the current economic state, many schools are facing a major budget crisis causing stagnant teacher salaries and limited school resources. Research has shown receiving a low salary may lead to burnout and ultimately attrition (Maslach et al., 2001; Provasnik & Dorfman, 2005). Participants in the study noted the low salary as a constant source of stress, but felt they had no control over this issue.

The perceived lack of support and communication with administrators and other colleagues was also discussed as a source of stress for the participants. This is consistent with the findings of Westling et al. (2206), Billingsley (2004b), and Kaff (2004) that a lack of perceived support may cause an increase in teacher stress levels. The participants felt their lack of participation in creating the master schedule was a source of frustration due to the fact that their scheduled planning time did not meet the needs of their students. Karasek's (1979) job strain model reflects this perspective in that job strain results from a lack of decision making over work-related demands. While administrative issues caused some level of stress for the participants, the workload-related factors may have been the most overwhelming.

The workload special educators face is tremendous, with the biggest areas of concern stemming from the level of students' physical, medical, and educational needs and the amount of paperwork required. Consistent with previous research, the participants in this study found that the range of student disabilities and needs in the classroom was a huge source of stress (Billingsley, 2004; Kaff, 2004; Westling et al., 2006). The class size alone was stressful enough, but the physical and medical needs of the children led to physical and mental exhaustion for the participants. Dealing with the needs of the children was often overwhelming, but adding in the tremendous amount of paperwork required for special education added to the ever-increasing stress levels of these teachers.

The participants' number one concern was the lack of planning time allotted to complete the overwhelming amount of paperwork for lesson planning, IEPs, and transition plans. Several researchers agreed that heavy workloads coupled with a lack of planning time can lead to burnout and ultimately attrition (Maslach et al., 2001; Provasnik & Dorfman, 2005; Westling et al., 2006). While a wide variety of stressors were present for the participants in this study leading to high levels of burnout, there were also some positive aspects noted throughout the sessions.

The second research question this study addressed was the effects the collaborative problem-solving sessions had on participants' coping resources. The results of the pre- and post-tests showed that the collaborative problem-solving sessions were effective for Brittany in increasing her coping resources. Most of the participants showed average to high coping resources in the beginning of the study, possibly accounting for the relatively small changes over the eight-week study. While quantitative data provided important information about participants' coping resources, qualitative data gained through transcriptions of each collaborative problem-solving session helped identify specific coping resources experienced by the participants, providing further insight into how special educators deal with high levels of stress.

All three teachers showed their social resourcefulness by creating relationships with other teachers and staff. Pugach, Blanton, Correa, McLesky, and Langley (2009) found that peer relationships were more important to beginning teachers than formal mentors and that teacher retention may be increased through professional collaboration. Having a positive relationship with colleagues may help relieve much of the stress that is experienced by special educators. A study conducted by Schlichte, Yssel, and Merbler (2005) validates these feelings in summarizing the stress felt by a special educator facing social isolation in her school: "[I]f she only had a good relationship with other staff members and administrators, the job would be, in her words, 'do-able'" (p. 37).

Increasing positive personal relationships was an important benefit of participating in the study according to the participants. This supports Greenglass et al.'s (1996) study showing that emotional support from colleagues may lead to a decrease in depersonalization and emotional exhaustion, leading to an overall decrease in burnout among participants. Having someone to turn to in times of need may have been the most important factor for participants in this study.

LIMITATIONS

There are a few limitations to note when looking at the results of this study. The small sample size was one of convenience and therefore may not generalize to all other populations. The set of problems faced by these early childhood special educators may differ from other early childhood special educators based on school, student population, and region. The intervention only lasted eight weeks, therefore limiting the potential changes in stress, burnout, and coping resources. Results may improve with a longer study. Finally, Donna only received four weeks of the intervention due to an injury; therefore, her changes in stress and burnout may also be attributed to the time away from work.

IMPLICATIONS FOR FURTHER RESEARCH

It may be beneficial to extend the current study to involve a larger number of participants over a longer period of time in order to see the extended benefits of collaborative problem solving. Administrators are encouraged to identify potential stressors faced by early childhood special educators and work proactively to reduce those stressors. Several researchers agree on the importance of creating sufficient planning time within the school day in which teachers can collaborate and problem solve in order to decrease their stress and become empowered to set and reach their goals (Gersten et al., 2001; Kaff, 2004; Nichols & Sosnowsky, 2002; Thorton, 2010). This study shows the effectiveness of collaborative problem solving among early childhood educators through the decrease in stress and burnout for all three participants in an eight-week period. Administrators and teachers need to be aware of how to use this process in order to combat the ever-increasing issue of teacher stress and burnout to possibly stop the increase in teacher attrition.

CONCLUSIONS

It is crucial for the field of special education to look at positive interventions to help fight the increasing stress and burnout levels faced by teachers each and every day. By implementing collaborative problem-solving sessions within team planning times, teachers will be able to talk about their problems with their peers and work together to build solutions. In the long run, this will not only benefit the well-being of the teachers by decreasing their stress and burnout, but will increase student achievement by allowing trained professionals to stay in the field longer, doing the work they were meant to do.

REFERENCES

Bennett, K. P. & LeCompte, M. D. (1990). *The way schools work: A sociological analysis of education.* New York, NY: Longman.

Billingsley, B. S. (2002). Improving special education teacher retention: Implications from a decade of research. *Journal of Special Education Leadership, 15,* 20–26.

Billingsley, B. S. (2004a). Promoting teacher quality and retention in special education. *Journal of Learning Disabilities, 37,* 370–376.

Billingsley, B. S. (2004b). Special education teacher retention and attrition: A critical analysis of the research literature. *The Journal of Special Education, 38,* 39–55.

Boe, E. E., Cook, L. H., & Sunderland, R. J. (2008). Teacher turnover: Examining exit attrition, teaching area transfer, and school migration. *Exceptional Children, 75,* 7–31.

Brownell, M. T., Hirsch, E., & Seo, S. (2004). Meeting the demand for highly qualified special education teachers during severe shortages: What should policymakers consider? *Journal of Special Education, 38,* 56–61.

Dorz, S., Novara, C., Sica, C., & Sanavio, E. (2003). Predicting burnout among HIV/AIDS and oncology health care workers. *Psychology and Health, 18,* 677–684.

Fore, C., III, Martin, C., & Bender, W. N. (2002). Teacher burnout in special education: The causes and the recommended solutions. *The High School Journal, 86,* 36–44.

Gersten, R., Keating, T., Yovanoff, P., & Harniss, M. K. (2001). Working in special education: Factors that enhance special educators' intent to stay. *Exceptional Children, 67,* 549–567.

Greenglass, E., Fiksenbaum, L., & Burke, R. J. (1996). Components of social support, buffering effects and burnout: Implications for psychological functioning. *Anxiety, Stress & Coping: An International Journal, 9*(3), 185–197.

Johnson, J. V., & Hall, E. M. (1988). Job strain, work place social support, and cardiovascular disease: A cross-sectional study of a random sample of the Swedish working population. *American Journal of Public Health, 78,* 1336–1342.

Kaff, M. S. (2004). Multitasking is multitaxing: Why special educators are leaving the field. *Preventing School Failure, 48*(2), 10–17.

Karasek, R. A. (1979). Job demands, job decision latitude, and mental strain: Implications for job redesign. *Administrative Science Quarterly, 24*(2), 285–308.

Karasek, R. A., Triantis, K. P., & Chaudhry, S. S. (1982). Coworker and supervisor support as moderators of associations between task characteristics and mental strain. *Journal of Occupational Behaviour, 3,* 181–200.

Lambert, R. G., Abbott-Shim, M., & McCarthy, C. J. (2005). *Classroom appraisal of resources and demands, preschool version.* Charlotte, NC: The Center for Educational Evaluation and Measurement.

Lambert, R. G., McCarthy, C. J., & Abbott-Shim, M. (2005). *Classroom appraisal of resources and demands, preschool version.* Charlotte, NC: The Center for Educational Evaluation and Measurement.

Lazarus, R. S., & Folkman, S. (1984). *Stress, appraisal, and coping.* New York, NY: Springer.

Leko, M. M., & Smith, S. W. (2010). Retaining beginning special educators: What should administrators know and do? *Intervention in School and Clinic, 45,* 321–325.

Maslach, C. (2003). Job burnout: New directions in research and intervention. *Current Directions in Psychological Science, 12,* 189–192.

Maslach, C., Jackson, S. E., & Leiter, M. P. (1997). *Maslach Burnout Inventory (3rd ed.). Evaluating stress: A book of resources. 1,* 191–218.

Maslach, C., Schaufeli, W. B., & Leiter, M. P. (2001). Job burnout. *Annual Review of Psychology, 52,* 397–422.

McCarthy, C.J., & Lambert, R.G. (2004). *Preventive Resources Inventory.* Austin, TX: University of Texas, Department of Educational Psychology.

McCarthy, C. J., Lambert, R. G., & Brack, G. (1997). Structural model of coping, appraisals, and emotions after relationship breakup. *Journal of Counseling and Development, 76,* 53–64.

McCarthy, C. J., Lambert, R. G., O'Donnell, M., & Melendres, L. T. (2009). The relation of elementary teachers' experience, stress, and coping resources to burnout symptoms. *The Elementary School Journal, 109,* 282–300.

Nance, E., & Calabrese, R. L. (2009). Special education teacher retention and attrition: The impact of increased legal requirements. *International Journal of Educational Measurement, 23,* 431–440.

Nichols, A. S., & Sosnowsky, F. L. (2002). Burnout among special education teachers in self-contained cross-categorical classrooms. *Teacher Education and Special Education, 25,* 71–86.

O'Donnell, M., Lambert, R. G., & McCarthy, C. J. (2008). School poverty, time of year, and elementary teachers' perceptions of stress. *Journal of Educational Research, 102,* 152–159.

Provasnik, S., & Dorfman, S. (2005). *Mobility in the teacher workforce: Findings from the condition of education 2005.* National Center for Education Statistics, 1–31. Retrieved from http://www.eric.ed.gov/PDFS/ED485860.pdf

Pugach, M. C., Blanton, L. P., Correa, V. I., McLeskey, J., & Langley, L. K. (2009). *The role of collaboration in supporting the induction and retention of new special education teachers.* (NCIPP Doc. No. RS-2ES). University of Florida, National Center to Inform Policy and Practice in Special Education Professional Development Website. Retrieved from: http://www.ncipp.org/reports/rs_2es.pdf

Schlichte, J., Yssel, N., & Merbler, J. (2005). Pathways to burnout: Case studies in teacher isolation and alienation. *Preventing School Failure, 50,* 35–40.

Thorton, H. J. (2010). Excellent teachers leading the way: How to cultivate teacher leadership. *Middle School Journal,* 36–43.

U.S. Department of Education, National Center for Education Statistics, Institute of Education Sciences. (2005). *Mobility in the teacher workforce.* Retrieved from http://nces.ed.gov/pubs2005/2005114.pdf

Weinberg, S., & Brandon, M. (1999). *Facilitating collaborative decision-making in six steps.* Retrieved from http://amauta-international.com/iaf99/Thread4/weinberg.html

Westling, D. L., Herzog, M. J., Cooper-Duffy, K., Prohn, K., & Ray, M. (2006). The teacher support program: A proposed resource for the special education profession and an initial validation. *Remedial and Special Education, 27,* 136–147.

Zabel, R. H., & Zabel, M. K. (2001). Revisiting burnout among special education teachers: Do age, experience, and preparation still matter? *Teacher Education and Special Education, 24,* 128–139.

CHAPTER 12

UNDERSTANDING TEACHER STRESS IN AN AGE OF GLOBALIZATION

Richard G. Lambert
University of North Carolina at Charlotte

Annette Ullrich
Baden-Württemberg Cooperative State University Stuttgart

What aspects of teacher stress, coping, and stress prevention are associated with the school and classroom context? What aspects of teacher stress, coping, and stress prevention are associated with stable personality traits? What aspects of teacher stress, coping, and stress prevention are malleable, teachable skills, and therefore responsive to psycho-educational processes? The answers to these questions are likely to emerge only through the interaction between the development of richer theoretical models and more complex research designs. Much of the current teacher stress research is conducted with convenience samples, in well-researched settings, using a narrow range of self-report measures. While such studies capitalize on the centrality of perceptions in our current understanding of the processes that lead to the subjective experience of occupational stress for teachers, the field will be

International Perspectives on Teacher Stress, pages 243–246
Copyright © 2012 by Information Age Publishing
All rights of reproduction in any form reserved.

advanced by more particularized theoretical definitions of the specific coping strategies that are most useful in a variety of classroom settings and situations. As our research designs include more classroom observations and purposeful sampling from teachers in varying contexts and with varying degrees of healthy, functional appraisals of the demands and resources involved in the teaching process, a more particularized understanding of both the emotion- and problem-focused coping strategies that are effective with particular subgroups of students can emerge.

Under what conditions is social support among teachers maximally effective in reducing occupational stress levels? What can we learn about social support as a coping mechanism for teachers from the current focus on professional learning communities? Educational systems around the world differ greatly in the nature of the working conditions they offer to teachers, the preparation they provide and require for entry into the profession, and the ongoing supports they offer to those in the field.

As globalization accelerates the movement of labor and capital around the world, teachers in many countries are serving more culturally diverse classrooms than they have faced in their careers. Many teachers are experiencing new forms of role strain as they reach the limits of their multicultural competence. There is even increasing evidence of a global marketplace for teachers as teaching professionals themselves move across borders to meet the demands of multinational corporations and their global labor force, serve the children of expatriates, and fill shortages of language instructors. The second section of this volume presents a set of studies from a consortium of international researchers. By examining teacher stress and coping issues in varying cultural contexts, they help address questions regarding coping strategies for teachers that are context-free and therefore universal, as well as those that are more context dependent. These studies can thereby make a contribution to the emerging theoretical complexity that will be required to understand teacher stress in an age of globalization.

The second section of the book has five chapters. These chapters report the results of a large, multinational study of teacher stress that used common measures and research design features across different cultural contexts. These studies reveal the advantages of planning such a large collaborative study with a consortium of productive researchers from many countries and academic disciplines. They also illustrate the diversity of methods and findings that can emerge from the combination of collective use of core measures and local freedom to supplement the research protocol with context-specific data sources. Such a large-scale research endeavor was not without its challenges. These studies bring to light the complexities of translation, structural differences in educational systems, and the limitations that emerge when attempting to sample teachers across such diverse settings.

Huub Everaert's study, titled, "Measuring the Perceived Incidence of Challenging Student Behavior: The Development of the Utrecht Challenging Student Questionnaire for Teachers (UCSQT)," focuses on teacher perceptions of student behavior using the UCSQT, which measures two dimensions of challenging student behavior, namely externalizing and internalizing behaviors. It also provides an overview of the development of the UCSQT (three studies) as well as results from a fourth study on the internal consistency of the UCSQT.

The second chapter, "A Quali–Quantitative Analysis of Two Open Questions from Italian Data," by Castelli, Pepe, and Addimando discusses research on the construct validity of the UCSQT. Using a mixed-methods design, the authors collected data from a sample of 518 teachers. They found that teachers' qualitative responses accurately reflected and corroborated their statistical results, thus providing evidence for the overall validity of the underlying theoretical constructs of the UCSQT. Their study employed novel methods that helped reveal patterns in the qualitative data that both illustrate what is being measured by the UCSQT and help the reader more fully understand the subjective experience of teachers who serve children with challenging behaviors.

Volochkov and Popov's study entitled "Stress in Teacher–Student Interactions and Teacher Activeness as a Positive Coping Resource" explores the relationship of teacher stress regarding challenging student behaviors and a construct identified as "teacher activeness." This construct was measured by the Teacher Professional Activeness Questionnaire (TAQ). They conceptualized "teacher activeness" as a coping resource related to how teachers respond intentionally to stressful classroom situations. The authors found that levels of stress decreased as "teacher activeness" increased, illustrating the potentially important role of this construct in the stress equation. They recommend the inclusion of "teacher activeness" in educational professional development in order to help teachers become more effective in promoting student learning outcomes and more socially and emotionally balanced professionals.

The fourth chapter by Pang and Tao is titled, "Teacher Stress in Working with Behavioral Problems of Students in Hong Kong." They report the results of a study of 1,210 elementary teachers in Hong Kong and compare their results to findings from seven other countries (Italy, the Netherlands, Russia, South Africa, Surinam, and the United States). Similar to the results from the studies in Russia and the Netherlands, Chinese teachers rated behaviors coded as "Full of Activity/Easily Distractible" as among the most challenging student behaviors. Their results illustrate that teacher beliefs, sense of self-efficacy, negative affect, and self-critical attitude moderate the effects of challenging student behaviors on teacher stress. Teacher beliefs were more strongly associated with teacher stress than were school characteristics, confirming the centrality of teacher appraisals in the occupational stress process.

The fifth and last chapter, entitled "Predictors of Elementary Teachers' Burnout Symptoms: The Role of Teachers' Personal Resources, Perceptions of Classroom Stress, and Disruption of Teaching," is authored by McCarthy, Lambert, O'Donnell, Villarreal, and Melendres. In an effort to better understand teacher perceptions of classroom stress, they tested disruption of teaching and classroom demands as possible mediators between preventive resources and burnout symptom using structural equation modeling. Though the hypotheses were not completely confirmed, all independent variables were associated with burnout symptoms in the predicted direction. A rival model with good fit was proposed that helps illustrate and inform our understanding of the complex and multifaceted aetiology of teacher burnout.

This volume demonstrates the complexity of the constructs of teacher stress and coping, especially with regard to cultural differences. It helps deepen our understanding of individual differences in appraisals of job-related demands and resources, the resulting individual differences in stress levels, and the relationship of these processes to a variety of other variables (teacher coping strategies, child behavior, parental expectations, teacher workload, class size, etc.). When taken as a body of work, this research indicates that individual differences in teacher experiences can only be interpreted within an in-depth understanding of cultural context and knowledge of the structure of educational systems. The value of this volume lies in its insights regarding strategies to support teachers individually, corporately, and structurally. In the end, the development of educational policy that reduces teacher stress is a worthy goal in itself, and it can impact the retention of quality practitioners. Furthermore, such policies are pathways to a healthier teacher corps, one capable of modeling social–emotional problem solving for children, enhancing the social climate of schools, and enriching the classroom learning environment.

PART II

UNDERSTANDING INTERNATIONAL TEACHER STRESS USING A MONO-METHOD, MULTI-CONTEXT APPROACH

CHAPTER 13

MEASURING THE PERCEIVED INCIDENCE OF CHALLENGING STUDENT BEHAVIOR

The Development of the Utrecht Challenging Student Questionnaire for Teachers (UCSQT)

Huub A. Everaert
HU University of Applied Sciences Utrecht

ABSTRACT

Over the years 2001–2006 we developed the Utrecht Challenging Student Questionnaire for Teachers (UCSQT) to assess the incidence of teachers' daily interaction with the most challenging student and the perceived stress that this becomes for them. The UCSQT measures two dimensions of challenging student behavior, termed externalizing and internalizing behavior. Externalizing behavior focuses on three factors: (1) against the grain, (2) full of activity/easily distractible, and (3) aggressive/hostile. Internalizing factors are: (1) needs a lot of attention/weak student, (2) easily upset, and (3) failure syndrome/excessively perfectionist. In this article we report the results of two

International Perspectives on Teacher Stress, pages 249–266
Copyright © 2012 by Information Age Publishing
All rights of reproduction in any form reserved.

Principal Axis Factoring (PAF) studies and one Confirmatory Factor Analysis (CFA). Over the independent samples, a replicable and interpretable factor structure was found.

It has been over three decades since Pratt's (1978) review of literature drew attention to the demanding nature of teachers' work with young children who exhibit problem behaviors. Managing student behavior is the most consistently mentioned concern teachers identify when asked about stress-related aspects of their work (Borg, 1990). Teachers frequently report feeling hurt by and angry with disruptive students (Durivage, 1989). Successive confrontation with students over inappropriate behavior can lead to a negative attitude and harmful classroom atmosphere (Lamude & Scudder, 1992; Lamude, Scudder, & Furno-Lamude, 1992). Furthermore, the influx of students with behavior management issues into regular classrooms, as a result of inclusion and integration-oriented policies, has incurred new and additional duties for teachers who have either limited or no formal training for working with such students (Brophy, 1996; Wilson, Gutkin, Hagen, & Oats, 1998). Unsurprisingly, progress for these students tends to be minimal, which adds more stress for teachers (Coladarci, 1992). In sum, negative student–teacher interactions and work overload place considerable strain on the coping resources of teachers (Borg, 1990; Boyle, Borg, Falzon, & Baglioni, 1995). Continual exposure to challenging demands can seriously deplete a teacher's emotional and physical resources, leading to loss of satisfaction with teaching, as well as impulsivity, rigidity, or feelings of anger, guilt, and self-doubt (Coie & Koeppl, 1990; Van der Wolf & Defares, 1994). Student behavior figures high as a cause of demotivation for teachers (Kiziltepe, 2006). Indeed, recent studies across multiple contexts show that the number of children in a classroom with problem behavior is the most predictive indicator of stress for teachers (Lambert, McCarthy, O'Donnell, & Melendres, 2007; Lambert, O'Donnell, Kusherman, & McCarthy, 2006).

Given that the concentration (i.e., percentage of the total class enrollment) of challenging children is predictive of stress levels, some researchers have, for example, advised administrators "to assess the classroom social environment early in the academic year and consider transferring some children with problem behaviors to different classrooms to establish a more positive balance between classrooms" (Lambert et al., 2006, p. 116) as a strategy for diminishing the gap between teaching demands and coping abilities. On the surface, such a recommendation would seem appropriate, but the effectiveness of such action can be undermined by large differences in what teachers perceive to be problematic behavior. The mere counting of undifferentiated problem behaviors in classrooms and subsequent adjusting of students leaves unaddressed the facility that some teachers demonstrate in coping with difficult-to-handle students. There are various factors that explain such differences, including, for example, the compatibility of teacher and student personalities, teacher tolerance for ambiguity or chaos, and what a teacher defines as appropriate student behavior. A more nuanced way for teachers to communicate how they perceive and reflect on their dealings with specific kinds of challenging behavior was the task we accepted. In this way, our research continues in the tradition of the transactional school of thought and the goodness-of-fit theory set forth by Thomas and Chess (1977, 1984). Student–teacher relations can be conceptualized as a product of mutual appraisal and the combined characteristics of student and teacher.

This chapter provides an overview of the development of the Utrecht Challenging Student Questionnaire for Teachers (UCSQT), which is an instrument we designed for gathering information about teachers' subjective perceptions of such behavior and the resultant stress they experience. This approach contrasts with the well-known, objective use of DSM-IV-RT criteria set by psychiatrists and trained psychologists. Our purpose was not about disregarding the DSM-IV-RT criteria or diagnoses, but given the daily, normal activities of teachers and students in classrooms, we were looking for a non-clinical approach to map these interactions from the perspective of teachers themselves. Coping with challenging students is considered an integral part of teachers' everyday work. We wanted to find out more about the kinds of students that teachers find most challenging and also most stressful.

REWRITING ITEMS EVALUATING
PROBLEMATIC BEHAVIOR

Our efforts began by drawing on the work of Greene, Abidin, and Kmetz (1997). We adopted their approach by asking respondents to focus on a specific student in their classroom who displayed challenging behavior. But whereas Greene et al. (1997) concentrated on the levels of stress associated with problematic student behavior, we requested teachers to simultaneously evaluate the incidence and resulting hindrance of such behavior. Our approach to measuring the incidence and hindrance of problematic behavior was based on the work of Brophy (1996). In his work, Brophy identified 12 types of difficult students based on behavioral traits that teachers often encountered in their classrooms. These were: (1) low-achieving students, (2) failure syndrome students, (3) overly perfectionistic students, (4) underachieving students, (5) hostile-aggressive students, (6) passive-aggressive students, (7) defiant students, (8) hyperactive students, (9) distractible students, (10) immature students, (11) students rejected by their peers, and (12) shy/withdrawn students. Using these 12 types we generated a pool of items concerned with student behaviors. We discussed, reviewed, and elaborated at length, in various settings, and with teachers to subsequently arrive at a list of 22 problem behaviors. The questionnaire asked teachers to rate each behavior twice, the first time with respect to how often it occurred and the second time to indicate the degree to which the specific behaviors interfere with or hinder the teacher's goals and effectiveness in instruction (Everaert, 2003; Everaert & Van der Wolf, 2006).

STUDY 1

In order to follow up on suggestions put forward by teachers to measure both the incidence of problematic behavior and its related stress, we conducted Study 1 in the autumn of 2003 with 284 elementary and special education teachers. After data cleaning, our respondents were 70% female who had an average of 14.5 years of teaching experience. As expected, the majority of the most challenging students they identified were boys (83%) who were on average 9.0 years old ($SD = 3.1$). Principal axis factoring (PAF) with varimax rotation was performed on the responses that used Likert scales from 1 (doesn't happen at all) to 5 (happens a lot) to assess their incidence. Our procedures conformed to those used in exploratory factor analysis (EFA), which is essentially a data-driven technique that attempts to arrive at a minimum number of interpretable factors to explain the correlations among a set of items. The factorability of the correlation matrix judged by Keyser-Meyer-Olkin test (KMO = .80) and Bartlett's test of sphericity (χ^2 (231) = 2345.06, $p < .0000$) were positive. The MSA statistics varied from .71 to .87. These are above .70 and, phrased in the words of Kaiser himself, such statistics vary from "middling" to "meritorious" (as cited in Pett, Lackey, & Sullivan, 2003, p. 78). Six factors were extracted. Loadings of variables on factors, communalities, and percentages of variance and covariance are shown in Table 13.1. The numbering of the extracted factors is based on an earlier conducted PAF using a much larger item pool. The item numbers reflect the randomized order in the questionnaire used in a later study conducted in 2006 (see Study 3).

With the exception of the fifth factor (F5—failure syndrome/excessively perfectionist), every factor in Table 13.1 has at least two items that load greater than .60, facilitating the naming of the factors. Given the content of the items and their factor loadings, the interpretation of the factors was conceptually sensible and the labeling of the factors turned out to be rather straightforward. The resultant factors were F1—against the grain (i), F2—full of activity/easily distractible (i), F3—needs a lot of attention/weak student (i), F4—easily upset (i), F5—failure syndrome/excessively perfectionist (i), and F6—aggressive/hostile (i). Our factor analysis of the 22 in-

TABLE 13.1 Factor Loadings, Communalities, Percents of Variances and Covariance for Principal Axis Factoring (PAF) Rotation on Incidence of Behavioral Challenging Items (N = 284, Autumn, 2003)

Item	F_1[a]	F_3	F_2	F_4	F_6	F_5	Communalities[b] 6 Factors
F1 P2BQ23i ... breaks rules on purpose.	.86						.81
F1 P2BQ19i ... deliberately seeks conflict with adults	.76						.61
F1 P2BQ07i ... undermines the rules	.68		.30				.62
F1 P2BQ17i ... is belligerent towards me.	.56						.42
F3 P2BQ12i ... always finds the work difficult		.77					.62
F3 P2BQ03i ... needs everything to be spelled out for him/her		.76					.62
F3 P2BQ11i ... has trouble following instructions		.71					.51
F3 P2BQ22i ... has obvious learning difficulties		.63					.42
F2 P2BQ21i ... is much more active than the other students.			.75				.61
F2 P2BQ02i ... is unable to sit still			.73				.54
F2 P2BQ01i ... distracts the other students			.61				.46
F2 P2BQ20i ... leaves his/her seat more often than other students			.57				.40
F4 P2BQ18i ... is hard to reassure whenever he/she is upset.				.74			.60
F4 P2BQ05i ... makes more of a fuss than others /P2BQ13i ... cries more often. [combined]				.59			.40
F4 P2BQ14i ... is overly sensitive to moods.				.59			.43
F4 P2BQ15i ... shows a strong reaction when something happens			.32	.55			.43
F6 P2BQ06i ... is destructive					.79		.71
F6 P2BQ09i ... damages other people's property					.65		.54
F6 P2BQ10i ... is very aggressive; hits, kicks, bites.	.32			.28	.61		.56
F5 P2BQ08i ... hands in work giving remarks such as: 'it will be wrong anyway'	.27					.74	.63
F5 P2BQ16i ... is not quite satisfied with end results.				.30		.57	.42
F5 P2BQ04i ... ascribes success to good luck.						.52	.32
Eigenvalue	2.44	2.24	2.13	1.86	1.71	1.30	
Percent of variance	11.10	10.17	9.67	8.44	7.79	5.93	
Cumulative percent of variance	11.10	21.27	30.95	39.38	47.17	53.10	
Percent of covariance	20.89	19.18	18.24	15.92	14.64	11.13	

Note. Items with a cut-off loading value of .25 are not shown in the table. Numbering of items is based upon the random order in the questionnaire to be administered Spring, 2006.

[a]F1 Against the grain (i), F2 Full of activity/Easily distractible (i), F3 Needs a lot of attention/Weak student (i), F4 Easily upset (i), F5 Failure syndrome/Excessively perfectionist (i), and F6 Aggressive/Hostile (i)

cidences and stress items resulted in an identical factor structure for each of the two constructs.[1]

STUDY 2

Study 2 was designed to re-examine the factor structure identified earlier using a more favorable cases-to-item ratio in a new sample of teachers. The ideal ratio of cases to factors is a much-debated topic. A guiding principle is to have at least ten cases for each item (Garson, 2011), although the subject-to-variables ratio devised by Gorsuch (1983) advises 200 or more cases. Bearing this in mind, we tested the questionnaire in the field once more during the autumn of 2004. In this study, 725 teachers answered all 22 items with respect to the most challenging student they could think of in their classroom. Following the advice of some of the teachers involved, the anchors of the items in this study were rescaled from 1–5 to 0–4.

In terms of the sample, the teachers in Study 2 were 78% female and reported an average class size of 20 students. Their average teaching experience was 14 years. Participants were mainly recruited in the Dutch provinces of Noord-Holland, Zuid-Holland, Zeeland, Utrecht, Gelderland, and Noord-Brabant. The challenging students that teachers had in mind were mostly boys (85%) who were on average 8.3 years old ($SD = 2.5$). Because of the psychometric nature of the present studies, only cases where all 22 UCSQT items were completed were included in the analyses.

The factor analysis procedures explained for the earlier study were repeated on the data gathered for this second study. Factor analyses are essentially exploratory procedures and given the role of the sampling error their results should be interpreted cautiously. Cross-validation using independent data sets such as that described here is highly recommended (Brown, 2006). Both a Kaiser-Meyer-Olkin measure of sampling adequacy of .86, and Bartlett's test of sphericity (χ^2 (231) = 6339.00, $p < .0000$) indicated excellent factorability of the correlation matrix for this larger data set gathered for this second study. MSA statistics varied from .81 to .93 and supported this conclusion. The same PAF criteria were applied as before, that is, eigenvalues > 1, an orthogonal solution followed by varimax rotation. Results of the additional PAF on the new data set are shown in Table 13.2.

The similarity between both PAFs for Study 1 (see Table 13.1) and Study 2 (see Table 13.2) is striking. Study 2 resulted in the very same factor structure explaining 54% of variance. Factors that emerged again were labeled, as were F1—against the grain (i), F2—full of activity/easily distractible (i), F3—needs a lot of attention/weak student (i), F4—easily upset (i), F5—failure syndrome/excessively perfectionist (i), and F6—aggressive/hostile (i). All items but one (F4 P2BQ15i) loaded on their original factor. The proportions of item variance explained by the factor structure (h^2) oscillated between .71 and .31. To sum up, given the relatively low number of items per factor and the more or less balanced values of the communalities within their congeneric factors, the PAF solutions were judged as favorable. Over two independent samples, a replicable and interpretable factor structure was extracted from data gathered by the UCSQT. Reconsidering our theoretical approach, we began to discuss the possibility of two dimensions of challenging student behavior that we named as externalizing (including F1, F2, and F6) and internalizing (including F3, F4, and F5). There seemed, however, to be some overlap in factors F2 and F4 that needed further clarification.

TABLE 13.2 Factor Loadings, Communalities, Percents of Variances and Covariance for Principal Axis Factoring (PAF) Rotation on Incidence of Behavioral Challenging Items (N = 725, Autumn, 2004)

Item	F_2ᵃ	F_1	F_3	F_6	F_4	F_5	Communalitiesᵇ 6 Factors
F2 P2BQ02i ... is unable to sit still.	82						71
F2 P2BQ20i ... leaves his/her seat more often than other students.	69						55
F2 P2BQ01i ... distracts the other students.	65	35					56
F2 P2BQ21i ... is much more active than the other students.	64						43
F4 P2BQ15i ... shows a strong reaction when something happens.	46						31
F1 P2BQ23i ... breaks rules on purpose.		77					65
F1 P2BQ07i ... undermines the rules.	32	72					65
F1 P2BQ19i ... deliberately seeks conflict with adults.		67					50
F1 P2BQ17i ... is belligerent towards me.		51					35
F3 P2BQ03i ... needs everything to be spelled out for him/her.			77				67
F3 P2BQ12i ... always finds the work difficult.			71			29	62
F3 P2BQ11i ... has trouble following instructions.			70				57
F3 P2BQ22i ... has obvious learning difficulties.			56			28	40
F6 P2BQ06i ... is destructive.				83			80
F6 P2BQ09i ... damages other people's property.				74			65
F6 P2BQ10i ... is very aggressive; hits, kicks, bites.		33		52			44
F4 P2BQ18i ... is hard to reassure whenever he/she is upset.					70		60
F4 P2BQ05i ... makes more of a fuss than others /P2BQ13i ... cries more often. [combined]					60		41
F4 P2BQ14i ... is overly sensitive to moods.	26				58		53
F5 P2BQ08i ... hands in work giving remarks such as, 'it will be wrong anyway'.			26			79	72
F5 P2BQ16i ... is not quite satisfied with end results.						54	39
F5 P2BQ04i ... ascribes success to good luck.			31			51	42
Eigenvalue	2.55	2.33	2.28	1.77	1.50	1.49	
Percent of variance	11.59	10.61	10.38	8.05	6.82	6.77	
Cumulative percent of variance	11.59	22.20	32.58	40.63	47.45	54.22	
Percent of covariance	21.39	19.55	19.13	14.85	12.58	12.50	

Note. Items with a cut-off loading value of .25 are not shown in the table. Numbering of items is based upon the random order in the questionnaire to be administered Spring, 2006.
ᵃF1 Against the grain (i), F2 Full of activity/Easily distractible (i), F3 Needs a lot of attention/Weak student (i), F4 Easily upset (i), F5 Failure syndrome/Excessively perfectionist (i), and F6 Aggressive/Hostile (i).

STUDY 3

The results of these earlier studies boosted our confidence that we were on the right track with the UCSQT as an instrument for mapping teachers' views on their most challenging students. In Study 3, we set out to perform the next step in improving the questionnaire, further test the replication of its factors, and begin examining other issues relevant to validity. For example, to gauge the validity of the incidence of challenging behavior, we included in the packet that was given to teachers in the spring of 2006 the General Health Questionnaire (GHQ-12) as a measure of teacher stress (Koeter & Ormel, 1991). In addition, we modified the UCSQT by asking teachers to respond to 23 rather than 22 items on the incidence of challenging student behavior. We split a previous item: "makes more of a fuss than others and cries more often" into two separate items. This was the only substantive change we made as a final improvement on the item pool. Anchor items ranged from 0–4.

The packet containing the UCSQT and GHQ-12 was delivered to 359 primary school teachers in The Netherlands. Of this group, 323 subjects completed all incidence items and were included in the analyses. Almost 79% percent of these subjects were female. Their teaching experience averaged 17.4 years (SD = 11.3). More boys (79%) than girls (21%) were selected as their most challenging pupils. The average age of the children selected by the teachers was just under 9 years (M = 8.7, SD = 2.1). The reported class size averaged about 21 students. As in the previous studies, several students of the HU University of Applied Research Utrecht collected the data. Questionnaires were left in teachers' rooms or handed out at staff meetings. An introductory letter stated the purpose and the importance of the research. Participants were given the option of returning the questionnaire in a prepaid envelope to the university. In several cases, surveys were sealed in an envelope and collected by the school itself. As in the previous studies, anonymity was guaranteed. No differences in results could be traced to the fieldworkers who collected the data.

Based on our previous studies, we had a clear sense of the number of factors and items that were assessed by the UCSQT. Rather than using the procedures of exploratory factor analysis (EFA) we employed those of confirmatory factor analysis (CFA). EFA is essentially data-driven, and the objective of exploratory factor analysis is to evaluate the minimum number of interpretable factors to explain the correlations among a set of items. In CFA, the number of factors and the patterns of item-factor loadings are specified a priori. A fundamental strength of CFA approaches is the ability to deal explicitly with measurement error (Brown, 2006). CFA is typically conducted after one or more EFAs to foster the development and refinement of the measurement model. CFA provides answers that help establish the convergent and discriminate validity of the theoretical constructs. A last advantage of CFA over EFA is the availability of several explicit goodness-of-fit criteria. In CFA, the specified factor solution is evaluated in terms of how well the sample correlation or covariance matrix of the measured items is reproduced.

Several CFA models of the revised pool of 23 items were fit using EQS 6.1 (Bentler, 2005). All analyses were based on the raw data matrices, a necessary requirement in the robust analysis of categorical data. Although imputation of missing values based upon the EM algorithm may be considered standard by now in *SEM* (Enders, 2006, 2007), given the psychometric purpose of the study, only the data of subjects who filled out all 23 incidence items were included. In order to correct for data characteristics that did not perfectly meet assumptions underlying normal theory estimators, the Satorra-Bentler scaled χ^2 and derived statistics were employed. This strategy is often recommended in case of non-normality and ordered categorical data (Finney & DiStefano, 2006). The evaluation of model fit was based on multiple criteria that reflected statistical, theoretical, and practical consideration. Five different robust fit indices will be reported: the S-B χ^2 statistic, the comparative fit index (CFI), the normed fit index (NFI), the non-normed fit index (NNFI), and the root mean-square error of approximation (RMSEA) with the 90%-confidence interval. In general, the target values for the selected fit indices CFI, NFI and NNFI should be ≥ .95, while a RSMEA ≤ .05 also indicates good model fit. In evaluating correlation residuals (also labeled standardized residuals in EQS output), figures >|1.0| indicate a big difference between observed and predicted covariances (Kline, 2005).

The initial CFA model hypothesized a priori that: (a) responses to the incidence of challenging student behavior could be explained by six factors; (b) each of the 23 items would have a non-zero loading on the factor it was designed to measure, and zero-loadings on all other factors; (c) the 6 factors would be correlated; and (d) error/uniqueness terms for the item would be uncorrelated. That is, factor F4 Easily upset was set to load with five items and factors F1—against the grain (i), F2—full of activity/easily distractible (i), and F3—needs a lot of attention/weak student (i), were each loaded using four items. Factors F5—failure syndrome/excessively perfectionist (i), and F6—aggressive/hostile (i) were specified to load with three items.

At first glance and by generally applied standards, the fit of the initial CFA model should be considered as unsatisfactory ($S\text{-}B\,\chi^2$ (215) = 660.841, $p < .0000$, CFI = .869, NFI = .812, NNFI = .846, RMSEA = .075 with 90% CI between .067 and .082, and about 84% of the standardized residuals are between –0.1 and 1.0). However, given specification differences by definition between PAF and CFA models in general, the model fit may be judged as surprisingly good, especially when taking into account that, when PAF is used as a precursor to CFA, oblique solutions are more likely to generalize to CFA than orthogonal solutions (Brown, 2006).[2] In the end, about 85% of covariance in the data set is explained by the oblique model, as indicated by the CFI.

In order to detect strain in the initial oblique model solution, the largest standardized residuals were studied further. Of the ten largest standardized residuals, item F4 P2BQ18i showed up six times. Disconcertingly, the initial model did not explain the correlation between F4 P2BQ18i and F4 P2BQ05i (r = .341) and between F4 P2BQ18i and F4 P2BQ14i (r = .425), and it seemed fair to conclude that factor loadings of F4 P2BQ05i (b = .452), F4 P2BQ14i (b = .554) and F4 P2BQ18i (b = .418) are underestimated in the model (see Table 13.3). Also, R-square of F4 P2BQ18i is with a score of .18, well below the minimum standard criteria of .20 as given by Brown (2006). These results suggested that there must be some misspecification in factor F4. In addition, these analyses revealed that item F1 P2BQ07i ("undermines the rules") needed reworking. We judged the item as probably worded too vaguely, a deduction that was supported in the closer inspec-

TABLE 13.3 Maximum Likelihood Robust Parameter Estimates for Initial CFA Model (N = 323, Spring 2006)

Parameter	Unstanderdized	SE	Standerdized
	Factor loadings		
F1 → P2BQ07i	1.000[*]	--	.715
F1 → P2BQ17i	.815	.089	.568
F1 → P2BQ19i	1,183	.096	.758
F1 → P2BQ23i	1,253	.093	.809
F2 → P2BQ01i	1.000[*]	--	.627
F2 → P2BQ02i	1,394	.120	.765
F2 → P2BQ20i	1,753	.167	.870
F2 → P2BQ21i	1,592	.156	.799
F3 → P2BQ03i	1.000[*]	--	.768
F3 → P2BQ11i	.954	.068	.741
F3 → P2BQ12i	.949	.066	.772
F3 → P2BQ22i	.961	.070	.681
F4 → P2BQ05i	1.000[*]	--	.452
F4 → P2BQ13i	1,771	.205	.783
F4 → P2BQ14i	1,164	.163	.554
F4 → P2BQ15i	1,485	.166	.758
F4 → P2BQ18i	.875	.130	.418
F5 → P2BQ04i	1.000[*]	--	.515
F5 → P2BQ08i	1,525	.200	.814
F5 → P2BQ16i	1,266	.167	.682
F6 → P2BQ06i	1.000[*]	--	.722
F6 → P2BQ09i	.967	.091	.742
F6 → P2BQ10i	.961	.089	.696
	Measurement error variances		
$E_{P2BQ01i}$	.785	.069	.607
$E_{P2BQ02i}$	.700	.071	.415
$E_{P2BQ03i}$	.783	.114	.411
$E_{P2BQ04i}$	1,119	.100	.735
$E_{P2BQ05i}$	1,617	.106	.796
$E_{P2BQ06i}$	.864	.121	.479
$E_{P2BQ07i}$	.770	.078	.489
$E_{P2BQ08i}$	.478	.098	.337
$E_{P2BQ09i}$	.717	.091	.449
$E_{P2BQ10i}$	.922	.100	.515
$E_{P2BQ11i}$	.839	.087	.450
$E_{P2BQ12i}$	.686	.100	.404
$E_{P2BQ13i}$	.820	.087	.387
$E_{P2BQ14i}$	1,268	.102	.693
$E_{P2BQ15i}$	.677	.081	.426
$E_{P2BQ16i}$	.743	.116	.535
$E_{P2BQ17i}$	1,122	.108	.677
$E_{P2BQ18i}$	1,497	.107	.825
$E_{P2BQ19i}$	.831	.091	.425
$E_{P2BQ20i}$	.498	.074	.242
$E_{P2BQ21i}$	.730	.080	.362
$E_{P2BQ22i}$	1,204	.118	.537
$E_{P2BQ23i}$	.667	.091	.346

Variances and covariances of factors[?]

	F1	F2	F3	F4	F5	F6
	.804 (.108)	.507 (.100)	1.124 (.130)	.414 (.095)	.403 (.093)	.940 (.133)
F1 Against the grain (i)	--					
F2 Full of activity/Easily distractible (i)	.319 (.066)	--				
F3 Needs a lot of attention/Weak student (i)	.196 (.065)	.241 (.059)	--			
F4 Easily upset (i)	.357 (.063)	.343 (.066)	.248 (.055)	--		
F5 Failure syndrome/Excessively perfection:	.197 (.047)	.081 (.032)	.334 (.059)	.173 (.043)	--	
F6 Aggressive/Hostile (i)	.507 (.074)	.305 (.063)	.268 (.073)	.286 (.059)	.177 (.050)	--

Standerdized variances of factors

	F1	F2	F3	F4	F5	F6
F1 Against the grain (i)	1.000					
F2 Full of activity/Easily distractible (i)	.500	1.000				
F3 Needs a lot of attention/Weak student (i)	.206	.319	1.000			
F4 Easily upset (i)	.619	.748	.364	1.000		
F5 Failure syndrome/Excessively perfection:	.345	.179	.496	.424	1.000	
F6 Aggressive/Hostile (i)	.583	.442	.261	.459	.287	1.000

[*]Not tested for statistical significance; p < .05 for all other unstanderized estimates [b]Robust standard errors between ()

tion of the input correlation matrix prior to all statistical reasoning. A total of 12 out of 22 possible F4 P2BQ07i item correlations are above .30. Item F4 P2BQ07i seems to indicate a student is challenging in general, without specifying what kind of behavior the student exhibits according to the teacher. Summing up, in future studies we determined to rephrase or even drop items F1 P2BQ07i and F4 P2BQ18i.

At this point in our analysis, we faced the question of whether there was sufficient structure within the data to justify proceeding with our original idea of specifying six latent factors divided into internalizing and externalizing challenging student behaviors. To answer this question, we determined that we should examine the discriminate validity of the UCSQT using the collected data. Table 13.4 presents the correlations between factor scores and Cronbach's alphas for each of the studies.

In all the studies, there is a moderate to fairly strong correlation between F1—against the grain (i), F2—full of activity/easily distractible (i), and F6—aggressive/hostile (i). The correlation between F1 and F6 was strong throughout ($r = .51$ in Study 1, $r = .50$ in Study 2, and $r = .47$ in Study 3). The correlations between F1 and F2 (and concomitantly between F6 and F2) are also in line with the theoretical underpinnings ($r = .33$ in Study 1, $r = .34$ in Study 2, and $r = .43$ in Study 3) of three factors delineating externalizing student behavior. With regard to internalizing challenging student behavior, the correlations between internalizing factors are not so clear. In all studies, the correlations between F3—needs a lot of attention/weak student (i) and F5—failure syndrome/excessively perfectionist (i) are in accordance with our main view ($r = .29$ in Study 1, $r = .51$ in Study 2, and $r = .40$ in Study 3). The same is more or less true for correlations between F4—easily upset (i) and F5—failure syndrome/excessively perfectionist (i). It seems justifiable to conclude that there are indeed two clusters of different types of challenging student behavior: internalizing versus externalizing. However, the correlations between F4 and various externalizing factors (e.g., $r = .33$ with F6 in Study 1, $r = .39$ with F1 in Study 2, and $r = .48$ and $r = .55$ with F1 and F6 respectively in Study 3) are less convincing. As can be seen in Table 13.4, the homogeneity of scales expressed by Cronbach's alphas is in general above the criterion of $> .70$ set by Nunnally (1978).

Now that we have shared and discussed the various properties of the data from these three studies, it is appropriate to examine the relationship between incidence and hindrance that the UCSQT purports to evaluate. Similar to incidence, the anchor scales covering the hindrance of specific behavior ranged from 0 (not stressful at all) to 4 (very stressful). In general, the correlation between the collateral counterparts incidence and hindrance on each scale is high. More specifically, the correlations are stronger for scales capturing external rather than internal behavior and range from .66 (F5—failure syndrome/excessively perfectionist) to .84 (F1—against the grain).

TABLE 13.4   Factor Correlations and Internal Consistency of Factors in Study 1, 2, and 3

Study 1 (N = 284)	F1	F2	F3	F4	F5	F6	Cronbach's alpha
F1 Against the grain (i)	--						.841
F2 Full of activity/Easily distractible (i)	.332	--					.772
F3 Needs a lot of attention/Weak student (i)	-.080	-.016	--				.816
F4 Easily upset (i)	.254	.210	.082	--			.734
F5 Failure syndrome/Excessively perfectionist (i)	.139	.015	.288	.286	--		.667
F6 Aggressive/Hostile (i)	.509	.347	-.004	.334	.083	--	.804
M	3.173	3.795	3.183	3.467	2.397	2.614	
SD	1.061	0.925	1.009	0.910	0.894	1.140	
Study 2 (N = 725)							
F1 Against the grain (i)	--						.800
F2 Full of activity/Easily distractible (i)	.335	--					.807
F3 Needs a lot of attention/Weak student (i)	.128	.253	--				.819
F4 Easily upset (i)	.390	.350	.368	--			.699
F5 Failure syndrome/Excessively perfectionist (i)	.183	.159	.512	.400	--		.728
F6 Aggressive/Hostile (i)	.496	.309	.245	.361	.194	--	.805
M	1.910	2.724	1.666	2.239	1.191	1.171	
SD	1.030	0.956	1.074	0.925	0.955	1.074	
Study 3 (N = 323)							
F1 Against the grain (i)	--						.801
F2 Full of activity/Easily distractible (i)	.434	--					.849
F3 Needs a lot of attention/Weak student (i)	.182	.272	--				.828
F4 Easily upset (i)	.477	.549	.271	--			.743
F5 Failure syndrome/Excessively perfectionist (i)	.263	.152	.396	.415	--		.696
F6 Aggressive/Hostile (i)	.470	.365	.211	.393	.208	--	.761
M	1.797	2.490	1.726	2.330	1.154	1.458	
SD	1.055	1.101	1.127	0.962	0.947	1.082	

Note. Correlations among factors of Studies 1, 2, and 3 are based upon summing scores of items 'by hand,' an approach advocated by Pedhazur and Schmelkin (1991), instead on factor scores automatically genereted by the respective EFA analysis. For Study 3, correlations among factors based upon the intial CFA model are also presented in Table 3. In Study 1 Likert-items varied from 1 to 5. In Studies 2 and 3 item anchors varied from 0 to 4.

Furthermore, in assessing the validity of the hindrance scores for these challenging behaviors, we correlated each of our factor scores with the stress score calculated using teacher responses to the General Health Questionnaire (GHQ-12). We observed low to mediocre positive and statistically significant ($p < .05$) correlations between the F1 and GHQ-12 ($r = .13$), F2 and GHQ-12 ($r = .13$) and F4 and GHQ-12 ($r = .15$). Of the different scales dealing with internal behavior, only F4—easily upset (i) is statistically significant.

STUDY 4

In 2006, researchers in six other countries gathered data using the UCSQT. The total sample included 3,527 teachers. Apart from general cultural differences, there were some educational differences between the participating countries that should be acknowledged. Although most participants worked with teachers in primary education, the Russian colleagues in Perm focused on (special) secondary education. About a quarter of the Italian sample (drawn from the area surroundings of Milan) also included teachers employed in (special) primary education as well. Over 20% of the teachers in and around Pretoria from South Africa, the state of North Carolina in the U.S. and The Netherlands had a girl in mind when asked to visualize the most challenging student. About 85% to 90% of teachers from Hong Kong, Italy, Russia, and Surinam were focusing on a boy. The percentage of children diagnosed with a behavioral disorder (i.e., ADHD or autistic behavior) by an expert ranged from 31% (South Africa), 35% (Hong Kong), 37% (Italy), 40% (Russia) to 46% (USA). In this respect, Surinam (7%) and The Netherlands (16%) scored relatively low.

In order to calculate the internal consistency of the scales evaluating challenging students, only teachers who rated all 23 incidence items were included ($N = 3052$). The results are presented in Table 13.5. With the exception of F5—failure syndrome/excessively perfectionist (i), the reported Cronbach's alphas meet the criteria of .70.

CONCLUSION

Theoretical and substantive views put forward by Brophy (1996) and Greene et al. (1997) were incorporated in our studies of teacher perceptions of challenging student behavior and related levels of stress. Our research benefited from their pioneering work. Greene et al. (1997) drew our attention by asking teachers to concentrate on the most challenging student. Inspired by Brophy's categories for assessing different types of difficult students according to their behavior, the items in the USCQT concerning particular student behavior were developed in close cooperation with Dutch teachers. We designed our studies over the years in a search to characterize the challenging student whom teachers perceive as a source of stress that can deplete their emotional and physical resources, leading to loss of satisfaction with teaching, impulsivity, rigidity, or feelings of anger, guilt, and self-doubt. The latent structure of items in all studies was found to be fairly constant over time. That is, over three independent samples within a time span of about three years, a replicable and interpretable factor structure was extracted from the data sets. There is considerable coherence and consistency in the covariance structures of the incidence of challenging student behavior as viewed by teachers. Also, the mean structure was very similar over the years. Nonetheless, in future studies we would have to reconsider the

TABLE 13.5 Internal Consistency for Scales Measuring the Incidence of Challenging Behavior by Country (N = 3052)

	Country							
Scale	Hong Kong (n = 1105)	Italy (n = 443)	Russia (n = 534)	Surinam (n = 149)	South Africa (n = 259)	USA (n = 239)	The Netherlands (n = 323)	
F1 Against the grain (i)	.7796	.7926	.7683	.7721	.7386	.8554	.8007	
F2 Full of activity/easily distractible (i)	.8730	.8213	.7439	.8153	.8154	.8430	.8485	
F3 Needs a lot of attention/weak student (i)	.7109	.8146	.7462	.7688	.7883	.7977	.8278	
F4 Easily upset (i)	.8042	.7336	.6461	.7333	.6819	.7935	.7429	
F5 Failure syndrome/excessively perfection (i)	.6410	.5776	.5377	.5538	.5305	.4569	.6962	
F6 Aggressive/hostile (i)	.8701	.8252	.6388	.7169	.7412	.8177	.7611	

phrasing and exact wording of some of the items in the UCSQT, especially with regard to F4—easily upset.

Having found a more or less clear-cut distinction between externalizing and internalizing student behavior, the UCSQT can be used to categorize different types of challenging student behavior in terms of teachers' subjective perceptions of such behavior and the resultant stress they experience. The correlation between the developed scales and GHQ-12 is positive, but low in general. The distinction between internalizing and externalizing did not help us in differentiating between teachers who are or who are not vulnerable to stress. Also, a distinction between incidence and hindrance did not bring what we expected from it. On theoretical grounds, one might expect that some teachers very often report specific problem behavior, but the extent to which this behavior interferes with the teacher's goals and effectiveness in instruction is not likely to be large. Yet the evidence suggests that this is not the case. If teachers report very specific behavior, they report hindrance as well. If they hardly notice misconduct or learning problems, the associated levels of concomitant distress are equally low. In the perception of teachers, incidence and hindrance as measured by the USCQT seem to change in tandem.

According to Lazarus and Folkman (1984) and strongly advocated in a recent study by Lambert et al. (2006), stress should be explicitly defined as a gap between demands and resources. So far, our analysis has not explicitly taken resources on the student–teacher level into account. Future research and analysis should do so. This brings us to one other limitation for our findings. All the Dutch samples studied are so-called convenience samples. Students of the HU University of Applied Sciences Utrecht contacted colleagues and cooperated in gathering the data. Corrections for possible clustering between respondents would not alter our conclusions nor offer more favorable results. Even results from convenience studies may turn out to be inconvenient.

AUTHOR NOTE

I would like to thank Kees van der Wolf for his close and fruitful collaboration over the years in developing the UCSQT at the HU University of Applied Sciences Utrecht. Also, comments made by Rob Roeser on several drafts of this article were gratefully appreciated. Several students of the HU University of Applied Sciences Utrecht participated in collecting the data: Arjanneke Brandsma, Sabine Bax, Hellen Blom, Annette Dekkers, Menno van Es, Petra den Hollander, Frits van Hout, Gea Hoving, Ingrid Muurman, Gerrit de Peuter, Mimi Poll, Gerda Pool, Ellen Posthumus, Bob van der

Schaaf, Gerbert Sipman, Lindy Slingerland, Albert Sluiter en Wil Vlam. I highly appreciate their efforts in sampling the respondents.

NOTES

1. For the sake of completeness, a principal axis factoring with varimax rotation was also performed on 22 items concerning perceived stress ($N = 272$). This resulted in an identical factor structure, extracting over 60% of the variance. Results are available on request.
2. The orthogonal CFA model was considerably worse (S-B χ^2 (230) = 1057.485, $p < .0000$, CFI = .719, NFI = .669, NNFI = .691, RMSEA = .106 with 90% CI between .099 and .112). The chi-square difference for the orthogonal and oblique 23-item model was highly significant. However, strictly speaking, the Satorra-Bentler correction is not suited for comparing nested models.

REFERENCES

Bentler, P. M. (2005). *EQS 6 structural equations program manual.* Encino, CA: Multivariate Software.

Borg, M. G. (1990). Occupational stress in British educational settings: A review. *Educational Psychology, 10,* 103–126.

Boyle, G. J., Borg, M. G., Falzon, J. M., & Baglioni, A. J. (1995). A structural model of the dimensions of teacher stress. *British Journal of Educational Psychology, 65*(1), 49–67.

Brophy, J. (1996). *Teaching problem students.* New York, NY: Guilford Press.

Brown, T. A. (2006). *Confirmatory factor analysis for applied research.* New York, NY: Guilford Press.

Coie, J. D., & Koeppl, G. K. (1990). Adapting intervention to the problems of aggressive and disruptive children. In S. R. Asher & J.D. Coie (Eds.), *Peer rejection in childhood* (pp. 309–337). New York, NY: Cambridge University Press.

Coladarci, T. (1992). Teachers' sense of efficacy and commitment to teaching. *Journal of Experimental Education, 60,* 323–337.

Durivage, A. (1989). Assaultive behaviour: Before it happens. *Canadian Journal of Psychiatry, 34,* 393–397.

Enders, C. K. (2006). Analyzing structural equation models with missing data. In G. Hancock & R. O. Mueller (Eds.), *Structural equation modeling: A second course* (pp. 313–342). Greenwich, CT: Information Age Publishing.

Enders, C. K. (2007, April 11). *Analysis of missing data.* AERA professional development course. Chicago, IL.

Everaert, H. A. (2003). Het meten van de meester. [Measuring teacher stress]. In K. Van der Wolf (Ed.), *Het hoofd van de meester* (pp. 33–61). Utrecht: Uitgeverij Agiel.

Everaert, H. A., & Van der Wolf, K. C. (2006). Stress in the student–teacher relationship in Dutch schools: A replication study of Greene, Abidin & Kmetz's index of teaching stress (ITS). In R. Lambert & C. McCarthy (Eds.), *Understanding teacher stress in an age of accountability* (pp. 121–143). Greenwich, CT: Information Age Publishing.

Finney, S. J., & DiStefano, C. (2006). Non-normal and categorical data in structural equation. In G. Hancock & R. O. Mueller (Eds.), *Structural equation modeling: A second course* (pp. 269–314). Greenwich, CT: Information Age Publishing.

Garson, G. D. (2011). Factor analysis. *Statnotes: Topics in multivariate analysis.* Retrieved 02/25/2011 from http://www2.chass.ncsu.edu/garson/pa765/statnote.htm

Gorsuch, R. L. (1983). *Factor analysis* (2nd ed.). Hillsdale, NJ: Erlbaum.

Greene, R. W., Abidin, R. R., & Kmetz, C. (1997). The index of teaching stress: A measure of student-teacher compatibility. *Journal of School Psychology, 35*(3), 239–259.

Kiziltepe, Z. (2006). Sources of teacher demotivation. In R. G. Lambert & C. J. McCarthy (Eds.), *Understanding teacher stress in an age of accountability* (Vol. III, pp. 145–162). Greenwich, CT: Information Age Publishing.

Kline, R. B. (2005). *Principles and practice of structural equation modeling* (2nd ed.). New York, NY: Guilford Press.

Koeter, M. W. J., & Ormel, J. (1991). *General health questionnaire: Nederlandse bewerking.* Lisse, The Netherlands: Swets en Zeitinger B.V.

Lambert, R. G., O'Donnell, M., Kusherman, J., & McCarthy, C. J. (2006). Teacher stress and classroom structural characteristics in preschool settings. In R. G. Lambert & C. J. McCarthy (Eds.), *Understanding teacher stress in an age of accountability* (Vol. III, pp. 105–120). Greenwich, CT: Information Age Publishing.

Lambert, R. G., McCarthy, C., O'Donnell, M., & Melendres, L. (2007). Teacher stress and classroom structural characteristics in elementary settings. In G. S. Gates (Ed.), *Emerging thought and research on student, teacher, and administrator stress and coping* (Vol. IV, pp. 109–130). Greenwich, CT: Information Age Publishing.

Lamude, K. G., & Scudder, J. (1992). Resistance in the college classroom: Variations in students' perceived strategies for resistance and teachers' stressors as a function of students' ethnicity. *Perceptual and Motor Skills, 75*(2), 615–626.

Lamude, K. G., Scudder, J., & Furno-Lamude, D. (1992). The relationship of student resistance strategies in the classroom to teacher burnout and teacher type-A behavior. *Journal of Social Behavior and Personality, 7,* 597–610.

Lazarus, R. S., & Folkman, S. (1984). *Stress, appraisal, and coping.* New York, NY: Springer.

Nunnally, J. C. (1978). *Psychometric theory.* New York, NY: McGraw-Hill.

Pett, M. A., Lackey, N. R., & Sullivan, J. J. (2003). *Making sense of factor analysis: The use of factor analysis for instrument development in health care research.* Thousand Oaks, CA: Sage Publications.

Pratt, J. (1978). Perceived stress among teachers: The effects of age and background of the children taught. *Educational Review, 30,* 3–14.

Thomas, A., & Chess, S. (1977). *Temperament and development.* New York, NY: Brunner/Mazel.

Thomas, A., & Chess, S. (1984). Genesis and evolution of behavioral disorders: From infancy to early adult life. *American Journal of Psychiatry, 141*(1), 1–9.

Van der Wolf, K., & Defares P. B. (1994). Stress bij leraren in het basisonderwijs [Stress in primary school teachers]. In N. P. Geelkerken, G. J. J. Goetheer, F. H. J. G. Brekelmans, & F. A. J. van Moorsel (Eds.), *Praktijkboek bedrijfsgezondheidszorg in het onderwijs. Deel C: Instrumenten, hulpmiddelen en methoden* (pp. 45–53). Den Haag, The Netherlands: VUGA.

Wilson, C. P., Gutkin, T. B., Hagen, K. M., & Oats, R. G. (1998). General education teachers' knowledge and self-reported use of classroom interventions for working with difficult-to-teach students: Implications for consultation, preferral intervention and inclusive services. *School Psychology Quarterly, 13*(1), 45–62.

CHAPTER 14

A MIXED METHODS STUDY OF THE RESPONSES TO TWO OPEN-ENDED QUESTIONS REGARDING STRESS IN THE CLASSROOM FROM A SAMPLE OF ITALIAN TEACHERS

**Stefano Castelli, Alessandro Pepe,
and Loredana Addimando**
Università di Milano-Bicocca, Italy

ABSTRACT

In this chapter, we discuss our effort to assess the validity of constructs underlying the Utrecht Challenging Student Questionnaire for Teachers (UC-SQT) (Everaert, this volume) through triangulation of qualitative and quantitative data from a sample of Italian teachers (N = 518). Answers given to open-ended questions P2AQ01 "Describe the behavior of the student you find most challenging in your class" and P2AQ02 "Why is this behavior the

International Perspectives on Teacher Stress, pages 267–288
Copyright © 2012 by Information Age Publishing
All rights of reproduction in any form reserved.

most challenging for you?" were submitted to correspondence analysis of co-occurrences. Results proved to be easily readable and interpretable within the theoretical framework on which the UCSQT is based. Qualitative data also accurately reflected correlations among quantitative data that were peculiar to the Italian sample used in the study. Our findings provide evidence for the overall validity of the theoretical constructs.

A MIXED-METHODS STUDY OF OPEN-ENDED RESPONSES

In this chapter, we discuss our analysis that triangulated qualitative and quantitative data gathered using the Utrecht Challenging Student Questionnaire for Teachers (UCSQT) (Everaert, this volume) for the purpose of assessing the validity of its scales. By comparing data obtained through different methods, the chapter presents our effort to evaluate the accuracy of the phenomena considered by this instrument. Our process can be likened to strategies used by cartographers, in which they take and employ several measurements to create maps of territories. We recognize that this way of using triangulation has been criticized on several counts, but concur with Moran-Ellis et al. (2006), who wrote,

> In this model of triangulation, each method was seen to include unavoidable biases, but these were seen to offset each other (Webb, et al., 1966).... Thus, at the heart of this model of triangulation is the increased confidence in the implied measurement outcomes of the research where there are convergent findings. We call this the 'increased validity' model of triangulation. (p. 47)

As will be discussed later in this chapter, the two methods of questioning (i.e., open-ended and closed-ended) that are used in the UCSQT were found to compensate for errors generated by the other. By using both methods, the UCSQT provides researchers and practitioners different but complementary insights on teacher stress as connected to their perception of problem student behavior.

The procedures and conclusions reached from this study connect with and speak to ongoing discussions on multiple methods and measurement. First, there is reasonable expectation that some overlap exists between teacher responses to closed items on a questionnaire and their answers to comparable open-ended questions. Indeed, the ideas spontaneously[1] expressed by teachers when describing a challenging student reveal to some extent something about "what they have in mind" when they think about problem student (we will deliberately choose not to refer to this as the often-abused concept of social representations—Moscovici, 1961). Additionally, research assistants who administered the UCSQT logged in their field notes the requests they received from teachers to clarify questions, as well as complaints about the length of the instrument. There were, however, no recorded objections regarding its content. Thus, we can infer that the teachers agreed that the questionnaire had at least something to do with teachers' stress and challenging students even as it asked for information from them in two different ways.

Second, it has been argued that questionnaires like the UCSQT encourage subjects to respond in ways that reflect first-hand impressions. According to some, such answers should be considered as naïve, commonsense opinion. However, given the probing nature of several items on the UCSQT and teacher expertise as professionals, we argue that the instrument also gathered something different than simple common opinion. Moreover, in answering the open-ended questions, subjects were recollecting specific experiences from their past, which was very different from the simpler task of recognition that was generally requested by closed-ended questions. The psychological mechanisms involved in these two methods are radically diverse, and the subsequent findings are known to reflect such difference (Lorenzi-Cioldi, 1996; Schuman & Presser, 1981; Schwarz & Hippler, 1991). A famous example is presented by Schuman and Presser (1981) who report data regarding the educational values favored by parents for their children: Within a closed format, 60% of parents chose the item "independent thinking," but only 5% mentioned this theme when asked with an open format.

Finally, open-ended questions are portrayed in the literature as useful when researchers are interested in the salience of a certain theme and when the amount of verbal production, together with the order of recollection, is important. Closed formats, on the other hand, facilitate the evaluation of large numbers of items.

For the purposes of this study, we limited our attention to the comparison of teacher responses to items in the UCSQT concerned with their representation of the challenging student. The first two questions, P2AQ01 "Describe the behavior of the student you find most challenging in your class" and P2AQ02 "Why is this behavior the most challenging for you?", were considered in this study. An in-depth analysis of the other two questions (P2AQ03 "How, in general, do you handle this student's challenging behavior?" and P2AQ04 "Do you have tips for other teachers for handling this kind of behavior?") remain for further inquiry.

METHOD

Sample and Context

Five hundred and eighteen teachers from primary and lower secondary school in the city of Milano and in other urban and suburban areas of Lombardy Region, Italy were given the UCSQT to complete. Most of the respondents ($n = 347$) worked in primary elementary schools (68.3%), whereas 31.7% taught in lower secondary schools ($n = 161$). Furthermore, the distribution of gender in our sample closely resembled the distribution in the population of Italian teachers: In primary schools, 93.9% were women and 6.1% were men (in the population of teachers the percentages are 95.6 and 4.4 respectively), and in lower secondary education 78.6% were women and 21.4% men (in the general teacher population, percentages are 76.5 and 23.5) (Italian Ministry of Education, 2006; fig. 5, p. xxv). The religious background of our participants was as follows: Roman Catholic (92.2%), no religion (6.1%), other (1.7); again, this closely reflected the distribution found in the general Italian teacher population (Wikipedia, 2011). The number of years teaching ranged from 1 to 40 years, with an overall mean of 16.3 ($SD = 10.5$). Mean number of teaching years for the men in our sample was 13.7 ($SD = 9.4$) and for women it was 16.6 ($SD = 10.6$). Italy is an extremely variegated country, however, where averages are seldom of any help. Since our data were collected in the northwestern part of Italy, and on the basis of the availability of school directors, our sample should be considered a convenience sample. We do not claim to have a sample that is representative of the whole population of Italian teachers.

Additionally, in Italy, the system of comprehensive education is comparable with what is found elsewhere in Europe and other developed nations. In contrast to some of these systems, Italian students with disabilities attend "normal" schools, but are helped by special education teachers on a one-to-one basis. There are two main responsibilities for special education teachers: providing direct teaching and interacting with other professionals and parents. Of the 518 teachers we sampled, 440 (84.9%) were general education teachers and a bit less than 15% ($n = 76$) were special education teachers. Since special education teachers have a very particular one-to-one relationship with the students they help—very different from the relationship between a "standard" teachers with her/his class—data from special education teachers were excluded from the present analysis.

Procedures and Analysis

The data analyzed in this study were collected as a part of a larger international comparative research project. The questionnaires were administered to teachers from January, 2006 through June, 2006. Prior to administration, the UCSQT was translated into Italian and piloted. From the pilot we found that the number of missing values was high. We attributed this to the large number of items, as well as the heterogeneity of answer formats and content included in the questionnaire. To overcome such difficulties, we organized plenary meetings in schools where research assistants could supervise and assist teachers in filling out the instrument accurately and completely. Once data were collected, we used several techniques or tools of text analysis.

Phase 1

The simplest method used to analyze data for this study was the frequency count of adjectives. Adjectives were used as they are words that qualify nouns and pronouns to convey more information about the object of a statement. We looked specifically at adjectives that limited or described students. The premise of this analytical procedure rests on the argument that the more frequently an adjective is used, the more salient that concept is in the minds of subjects. Of course, before treating the corpus to statistical analysis, we had to code terms and group each concept with others that were similar. More specifically, we lemmatized the corpus, which is a procedure for reducing all inflected forms or other variants of a certain word to the form in which the word appears in a dictionary (e.g., lacks becomes lack). Following this process, we examined the codes and identified clusters of synonyms. Next, we counted the number of occurrences of each cluster. We recognize that natural linguistic codes are not isomorphic, and for this reason, strictly speaking, for a contemporary linguist synonyms do not exist (Delabastita, 1993). We would also state that our procedures reflect commonly accepted practice in psychological studies.

Phase 2

Meanings can be very diverse from one context to another. For example, the meaning of the word clever is obviously quite different in the two phrases: "the student is very clever in achieving academic results" and "the student is very clever in escaping my control." For this reason, we performed a subsequent series of cluster analyses using as objects for the clustering not the single lexical unit but whole answer.[2] In the second phase, therefore, we employed a more complex procedure. We used word co-occurrence analysis joined by algorithms of factor analysis—a technique named correspondence analysis (Benzécri, 1973; Greenacre, 1984)—in this way, we attempted to understand meaningful units and retain the context in which words were used. Correspondence analysis is a multivariate statistical tool conceptually similar to principal component analysis but appropriate for the treatment of categorical data (rather than continuous data).

The procedure of co-occurrence analysis involves several steps that will be outlined below. These steps were repeated twice, once for P2AQ01 "Describe the behavior of the student you find most challenging in your class" and once for P2AQ02 "Why is this behavior the most challenging for you?"

For the first step, data matrixes are created for the data from each question with each row-vector being one answer. For example, the following six lines each represent one teacher or case with the word(s) that were coded from their responses to the question about the most challenging student:

Case 014 (C014) Hyperkinetic
Case 023 (C023) Aggressive, hyperkinetic
Case 034 (C034) Aggressive, provoking
Case 208 (C208) Hyperkinetic, he lacks attention
Case 280 (C280) Hyperkinetic, aggressive, swearing
Case 401 (C401) Aggressive, ill-mannered

The matrix is formed when these words are entered onto a table, such as that offered on Table 14.1. Once this is accomplished, it is possible to build a data matrix where 1 and 0 stand for presence or absence of a certain word (see Table 14.2).

The data on Table 14.2 were then transformed into a square matrix as shown on Table 14.3, in which rows and columns are words, and each cell contains the number of co-occurrences of w_i and w_j, (i.e., the number of times a certain couple of words are used within a single phrase). Alternatively, we could say that Table 14.3 reveals the number of times that certain words are associated. If Osgood (1959) is right in maintaining that "it seems reasonable to assume that greater-than chance contingencies of items in messages would be indicative of associations in the thinking of the source" (p. 55), then numbers on Table 14.3 reflect the strength of the association of meanings. In the provided example, the association between W_1 (hyperkinetic) and W_2 (aggressive) is stronger than the association between W_3 (provoking) and W_2; as a matter of fact, we have two sentences in the example (C023 and C280) where W_1 and W_2 stand together, and only one sentence (C034) where we find both W_3 and W_2. No association is found between W_1 and W_3 (i.e., in no sentence do the words hyperkinetic and provoking co-occur).

Square matrixes like Table 14.3 were then examined with the usual algorithms for factor analysis and clustering. A hierarchical method of clustering was followed. Specifically, we employed Ward's rule to calculate the distance between clusters using cosine similarity.[4] Each answer was treated as an elementary context (Lancia, 2007) and labeled with four other dichotomous variables, indicating the gender of the teacher (female teacher vs. male teacher), the gender of the student (girl vs. boy), the type of the school (primary school vs. secondary school), and whether the class as a whole could be called challenging or not (challenging class yes vs. challenging class no). Lancia (2007) provides further details about this technique and implications for theories of meaning. Once clusters were identified,

TABLE 14.1 Transformation of Replies to Open-Ended Questions in a Rectangular Matrix (example)

Case number	W_1	W_2	W_3	W_4	W_5	W_6	W_7	...	W_m
C014	hyperkinetic							...	...
C023	hyperkinetic	aggressive						...	...
C034		aggressive	provoking					...	...
C208	hyperkinetic			lack	attention			...	...
C280	hyperkinetic	aggressive					swearing	...	...
C401		aggressive				ill-mannered		...	...
...	...	...	...	...	...		...	...	...
C_n	...	...	...	...	...		...	...	...

TABLE 14.2   Transformation in a Rectangular Co-Occurrences Matrix (example)

Case number	W_1	W_2	W_3	W_4	W_5	W_6	W_7	...	W_m
C014	1	0	0	0	0	0	0	...	...
C023	1	1	0	0	0	0	0	...	...
C034	0	1	1	0	0	0	0		...
C208	1	0	0	1	1	0	0		...
C280	1	1	0	0	0	0	1	...	...
C401	0	1	0	0	0	1	0	...	...
	...	...	...	...	...	...	...	...	
C_n	...	...	...	...	...	...	...	...

TABLE 14.3   Transformation in a Square Co-Occurrences Matrix (example)

	W_1	W_2	W_3	W_4	W_5	W_6	W_7		W_m
W_1	—	2	0	1	1	0	1	...	...
W_2	2	—	1	0	0	1	1	...	...
W_3	0	1	—	0	0	0	0	...	...
W_4	1	0	0	—	1	0	0	...	...
W_5	1	0	0	1	—	0	0		...
W_6	0	1	0	0	0	—	0		...
W_7	1	1	0	0	0	0	—	...	...
	...	...	...	...	...	...	...		
W_m	...	...	...	...	...	...	...		—

the task of the researchers was to assess the factors that form the axes on the output. For the first question, the factors identify how teachers were differentiating challenging students, while for the second question the factors attempted to understand why they found this student's behavior challenging.

Here it will suffice to say that text-based analysis is, as most scientific methods are, a process of deconstruction and reconstruction. As result of deconstruction and subsequent reconstruction processes, something is unavoidably lost:

[t]he deconstruction process carried out by a co-occurrence analysis leaves out three features of word/sentence meaning;

- The reference to the extralinguistic context (or situation), that is the indexicality beloved by the ethnomethodologists.

- The sequential order of the words within the linguistic contexts, that is text cohesiveness and the anaphoric processes.
- The semantic effects of speech acts that is all the relationships between the utterances and their enunciation processes. (Lancia 2007, p. 8)

But, even if such important aspects of natural speech are lost, this approach will prove very powerful to deepen our understanding.

Results

Phase 1. Adjectives Count

From teacher answers to the open-ended question P2AQ01, "Describe the behavior of the student you find most challenging in your class," adjectives were extracted and counted. Several cognitive psychological studies have shown that in spontaneous text productions, positive words are much more diffused than words with a negative connotation (Bolasco & Della Ratta-Rinaldi, 2004). It is the so-called *Pollyanna hypothesis* (Boucher & Osgood, 1969). Positive words are used far more often that negative words among languages and cultures as diverse as Chinese, Finnish, and Turkish. Our data were checked for the prevalence of positive or negative words but, given the negative framing of the question, it was difficult to confirm this Pollyanna hypothesis. As a matter of fact, in the verbal production of our sample there were virtually no positive adjectives.

We thus obtained a list of negative adjectives used by respondents in answering the first open-ended question. The list was composed of a total of 407 adjectives, 257 (63.1%) produced by teachers working in primary schools and 150 (36.9%) by teachers working in lower secondary schools.

The second step of analysis was to put each adjective in one of six categories of problematic behavior postulated by the theory underlying the UCSQT: F1—against the grain, F2—full of activity, F3—weak student, F4—easily upset, F5—failure syndrome, and F6—aggressive/hostile. The list of adjectives was assessed by three independent judges, who put every adjective into a category (inter-rater reliability was very good, Cohen's Kappa > .85). The adjectives on which there was no agreement were dropped from subsequent analysis. We report a few examples of this kind of categorization (see Table 14.4). The results of the count are shown in Table 14.5.

Factors were then sorted, or ranked from highest to lowest, using the percentage of responses. The ranking of the factors from the qualitative data were then compared to those generated from the closed-response or quantitative scaled items concerning the incidence of a certain problem behavior (i.e., how often does it happen). Teachers were asked on the UCSQT to identify the behavior of the student that was most challenging. Table 14.6

TABLE 14.4   Example of Adjectives Categorization

Factor	Label	Adjectives
F1	Against the grain (i)	Intolerant Polemic Provoking
F2	Full of activity/easily distractible (i)	Inattentive Unpredictable Hyperactive
F3	Needs a lot of attention/weak Student (i)	Apathetic Not motivated Dull
F4	Easily upset (i)	Emotional Easily upset Touchy
F5	Failure syndrome/excessively perfectionist (i)	Anxious Self-centered Insecure
F6	Aggressive/hostile (i)	Aggressive Marked by conflict Overbearing

TABLE 14.5   Adjective Count: Results of Categorization

Factor	Scales	Number of Adjectives	
F1	Against the grain (i)	68	(17%)
F2	Full of activity/easily distractible (i)	136	(33%)
F3	Needs a lot of attention/weak Student (i)	87	(21%)
F4	Easily upset (i)	41	(10%)
F5	Failure syndrome/excessively perfectionist (i)	19	(5%)
F6	Aggressive/hostile (i)	56	(14%)
	Total	407	(100%)

shows the results from both procedures to reveal the comparable order for the six factors. Although the procedure and findings are not provided here, we obtained the same results with data from the scales of perceived stress (i.e., the amount of stress perceived by the teacher as a consequence of that behavior).

Phase 2. Correspondence Analysis and Clustering [3]

The original corpus was composed of 431 short texts that were produced as answers to the first open-ended question: P2AQ01 "Describe the behavior of the student you find most challenging in your class." Answers from

TABLE 14.6   Adjective Count: Summary of Qualitative and Quantitative Results

		Qualitative		Quantitative	
	Scales	**%**	**Rank**	**%**	**Rank**
F2	Full of activity/Easily distractible (i)	33	1	42	1
F3	Needs a lot of attention/weak Student (i)	21	2	22	2
F1	Against the grain (i)	17	3	14	3
F6	Aggressive/hostile (i)	14	4	11	4
F4	Easily upset (i)	10	5	7	5
F5	Failure syndrome/excessively perfectionist (i)	5	6	4	6
	Total	100	—	100	—

teachers of primary schools were 282 (i.e., 65.4% of all answers given). Answers from teachers of secondary schools were 149 (i.e., 34.6% of all answers given, 9 missing). The procedure of co-occurrence and cluster analysis as discussed in the methods was followed.

In Figure 14.1 are plotted, on two axes representing two factors, some of the results of correspondence analysis of the texts describing the behavior of the challenging student identified by teachers. In the northern part of the graph, words like leader, disrespectful, overbearing, negative, rude, bullying, and spiteful can be observed. In the southern part of the graph were found words like comprehension, scarce, incapacity, concentration, and sensitive. The western side can be considered rather unpopulated, but going to the east were words like disturb, interrupt, provoke, and leave. The northern or upper part can to be understood simply as the opposite polarity to the southern or lower part of the graph, without any other implication; the same holds for the western or left and for the eastern or right part. In other words, positive or negative values on the axis are just conventional, and emerge as mere artifacts from the algorithms of the calculus.

Following an iterative process, we stopped the cluster analysis when the solution reached five clusters. The five cluster model, after removing outliers, retained 396 of the 431 original texts and produced a distribution that appeared reasonably even (see Table 14.7). Moreover, the solution possessed a variance between clusters that was high ($\sigma^2 b = 1.049$) and a within clusters' variance that was low ($\sigma^2 w = 0.340$), as required by the procedure. Furthermore, the comparison of the two variances was $\sigma^2 b/(\sigma^2 b + \sigma^2 w) = .756$, which is acceptable.

In Figure 14.2 we provide the results of the five cluster analysis, plotted against the same axes found in Figure 14.1. In our experience, it is useful to read these kinds of graphs using the geometric figures that can be drawn between the extreme points of the representation. In the present case, the

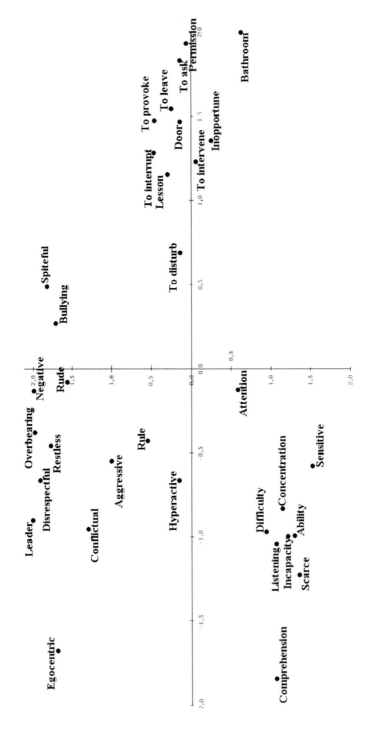

Figure 14.1 Graphical display of correspondence analysis of P2AQ01 "Describe the behavior of the student you find most challenging in your class."

TABLE 14.7   Results of Cluster Analysis (P2AQ01)

Cluster	Number of phrases per cluster	%
1	94	23.74
2	39	9.85
3	110	27.78
4	83	20.96
5	70	17.68
Total	396	100.00

shape is a "triangle" as drawn between Cluster 2 (top-left), Cluster 4 (bottom left) and Cluster 3 (extreme right). Other clusters represent an intermediate position between these extremes.

Given the location of clusters, the following discussion is limited to those three at the extreme of the continuum in order to facilitate identification of the factors forming the triangle observed on the graphs. The most representative[5] sentences for Cluster 2 were: "Frequently conflictual with both teachers and students, insecure, without firm reference points, that's why follows negative leaders in a passive way," "Disrespectful of rules, very egocentric, very anxious and pressing, deaf to all kinds of advice or suggestions," and "Insecure, egocentric, hyperactive, incapable of controlling his emotions and moods." On the other extremity of the axis, Cluster 4 contained sentences like: "Intolerant of every form of school rule, it is difficult for him to stay in the class or in the group, reacts aggressively towards himself and the others," "The student is aggressive towards other students because he finds it difficult to enter relationships and to give others help," and "Absolutely lacks self-esteem, nor does she know her limits, incapable of developing positive relationships with her fellow students, she has very little, if any, interest in participating in class activities."

Identification of a factor given such sentences is something of an art, but we propose these findings indicate the Y axis represents a continuum that ranges from a maximum of students with controllable neuroticism and antisocial attitudes to a minimum represented by very weak students whose self-esteem is impaired and who possess poor communication skills. In other words, we conclude this axis probably reflects how teachers perceived the willfulness of students. Challenging students are those who tend to be too willful or just as problematic without any will at all.

In contrast to the first factor identified on the Y axis with its two clusters, the X axis has one cluster (i.e., Cluster 3) located at the right end. In this cluster we identified the following sentences: "He likes to be the center of

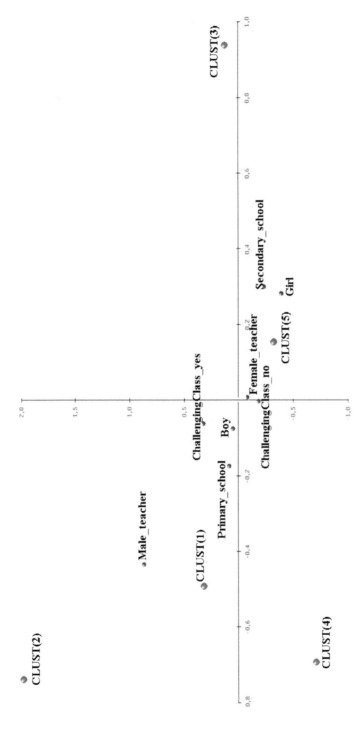

Figure 14.2 Graphical display of cluster analysis of P2AQ01 "Describe the behavior of the student you find most challenging in your class."

attention, he never raises his hand, and he expresses his opinion without much thought, yet he's afraid about how other students are looking at him, many times he does not work because he's angry;" and "He's hyperactive and talks in a loud voice. His comments in class tend to be completely off track. He annoys the other students." This axis obviously refers to the disruption of teaching processes, a concept present also in the quantitative part of the UCSQT (PART2c). No objects appeared in the left part of the graph, which indicated that teacher responses were focused on the disturbance in the teaching process. In none of the answers were students with challenging behavior described as helpful or in positive terms about their contribution in the classroom.

As noted in the methods, we also analyzed the second open-ended question: P2AQ02 "Why is this behavior the most challenging for you?" using correspondence analysis. The results are shown in Figure 14.3 and can be interpreted as demonstrated previously for Figure 14.1.

We found the clustering procedure was impacted by the presence of several highly charged words like unpredictable and unmanageable. After removing the outliers, we obtained a good six-cluster solution (see Table 14.8), which classified 361 answers. The between-cluster variance was high ($\sigma^2 b = 3.793$) and within-cluster variance was low ($\sigma^2 w = 0.304$). The ratio between these two variances was $\sigma^2 b / (\sigma^2 b + \sigma^2 w) = .926$, which is very good. Obviously, given the small relevance of Clusters 3 to 5 and given that they lie on the same axis (see Figure 14.4), we concluded that a three-cluster solution better represented the analysis.

Figure 14.4 graphically displays our findings given the cluster analysis. Starting from the left of the graph with Cluster 6, we observed the following representative answers: "I don't consider him difficult in terms of my relationship with him, but he does disturb and upset other students," "He acts in ways that distract the other students. He can be irreverent toward the teacher, which is disruptive," "He needs a lot of my attention, he takes up precious time, other students could get better results if he wasn't in the class," and "I need to continuously call him back to order. I lose my concentration during lessons and sometimes act irritably," and "He disturbs other students during the lessons and questions my authority in front of the class." Responses in this cluster suggested that teachers attributed their difficulties with challenging students as arising out of the chaos they generated.

On the opposite end of the axis, in Cluster 2, answers included: "[I]t is as if the boy lives in a different reality. Learning is difficult for him since his ability to communicate is impaired, dialogue is impossible. He can't even ask questions," "[I]t is not possible to create a relationship with him he is so impaired," "I find it difficult and his parents are pretty much completely disengaged," "I tried hard to help him, but made little progress with overcoming his fears of connecting with others. He's worsened, closing himself

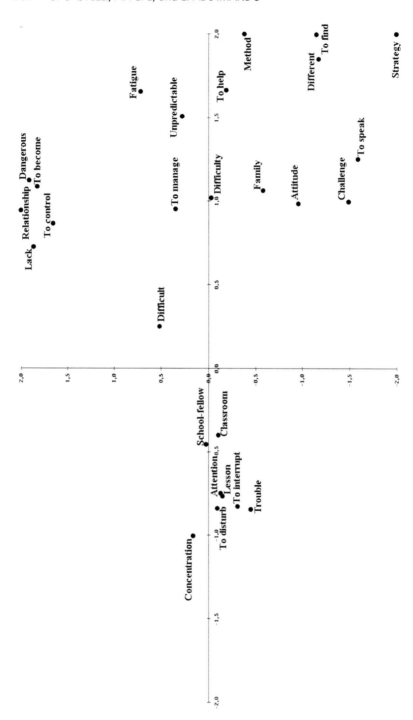

Figure 14.3 Graphical display of correspondence analysis of P2AQ02 "Why is this behavior the most challenging for you?"

TABLE 14.8   Results of Cluster Analysis (P2AQ02)

Cluster	Number of phrases per cluster	%
1	125	34.63
2	110	30.47
3	2	0.55
4	5	1.39
5	7	1.94
6	112	31.02
Total	361	100.00

off," "The child has great intellectual and social potential, but even after three years, even after all appropriate interventions at school and in the family, he remains unable to behave responsibly." What caught our attention about these statements was the weakness of the relationship teachers claimed to have with these students. The cluster exposed the lack of being personally connected to the student, rather than on the work within the classroom, as troubling for teachers.

Cluster 1, which lies between Clusters 6 and 2, exposed language on the part of teachers that was somewhat intermediate the two previously discussed positions. Cluster 1 included statements such as: "I cannot spend all my time calming and keeping under control this student. I have 24 other children in the class," "He frequently finishes the work quickly and calls for my attention. Keeping him occupied prevents me from helping the other children who are not as fast," "He disturbs the class and prevents other children from concentrating. There is just not enough time for individual teaching." Here we find a rather heterogeneous mixture of behaviors that, without necessarily being negative in themselves (for instance, the case of the intelligent child who finishes his work too quickly), nevertheless are viewed as creating problems in the classroom.

DISCUSSION AND CONCLUSION

The various processes of lemmatization and synonymization discussed in this study were purposefully cautious and conservative, in order to preserve as far as possible the original integrity of texts. The results obtained from the first procedure (i.e., count of adjectives in open-ended questions of the UCSTQ) exactly replicated the ranking provided by analyzing the scales that were generated from data gathered through the quantitative section of the questionnaire. In our opinion, this is a good argument in favor of the validity of the quantitative scales themselves. The conclusions from this first

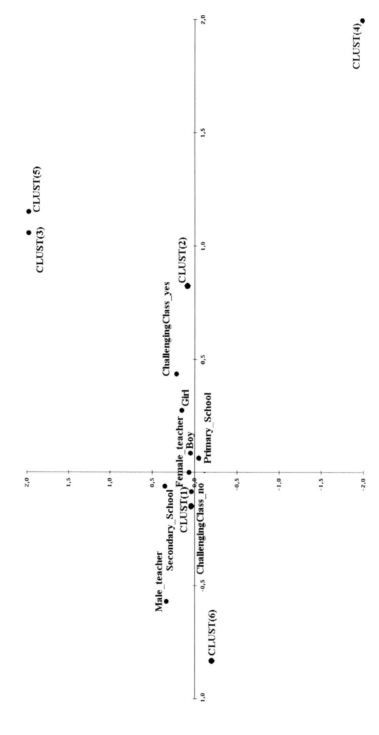

Figure 14.4 Graphical display of cluster analysis of P2AQ02 "Why is this behavior the most challenging for you?"

phase, however, should be recognized as rather limited given that the attempt was to fit the qualitative data into a framework provided by the basic assumptions that guided the construction of the questionnaire.

In contrast, the second phase extracted and examined the structure present in the qualitative data itself. Obviously, we did not expect an exact replica of the conceptual framework of the questionnaire, but rather aimed at obtaining indicators about the teachers' representations of their challenging student. Indeed, in the correspondence analysis carried out on data gathered for question P2AQ01, where the difficult student was described, two main factors appeared. The first is a factor that we labeled as perceived willfulness. It is possible given the polarity of the factor to see that it can be aligned on the one end to the scale F3—needs a lot of attention/ weak student (i). On the other end of the axis, there were other words like hyperactive, restless, aggressive, disrespectful, overbearing, negative, rude, bullying, and spiteful. It is as if teachers were clustering together the three scales of F1—against the grain (i), F2—full of activity/easily distractible (i), and F6—aggressive/hostile (i). Interestingly, this clustering as witnessed from analyzing the qualitative data provides further support for the validity of the questionnaire, since it is coherent with other results where data from the quantitative scales have been analyzed. Specifically, when the incidence scales of stressful behavior generated from the quantitative section of the UCSQT are examined using Pearson's correlation coefficients (see Table 14.9), we found a pattern of covariance that was similar. It appears that Italian teachers in this sample, unlike their peers in other countries, tended to group together these scales.

The above analyses suggest that the qualitative data accurately captured the nuances of what was portrayed by teachers in their responses to the quantitative components of the survey. These findings help in explaining why, in other Italian research studies (Di Pietro & Ramazzo, 2003), the weak student has been found to be the most difficult student for Italian teachers.

TABLE 14.9 Correlations Between Incidence Subscales

Subscale	F1	F2	F3	F4	F5	F6
F1 Against the grain (i)	—	.52**		.20**	.22**	.55**
F2 Full of activity/Easily distractible (i)		—		.10*		.44**
F3 Needs a lot of attention/Weak student (i)			—	.29**	.33**	.21**
F4 Easily upset				—	.33**	.37**
F5 Failure syndrome/Excessively perfectionist (i)					—	.19**
F6 Aggressive/Hostile (i)						—

Note: Sample (N = 439)

All nonsignificant correlations were omitted.

* $p < .05$, two-tailed ** $p < .01$, two tailed

Our findings suggest that teachers in Italy may not be discriminating student behaviors that exhibit aggressiveness, hostility, and hyperactivity, but rather they are interpreting all these behaviors in a similar manner.

The analysis of data concerned with teacher responses to the question of why they are challenged points to outcomes that are in need of further research. We found a monodimensional solution given this correspondence analysis. On the one end of the axis, teacher comments appeared focused on the affective (i.e., the lack of or negative relationship that they possessed with students) to more academic, technical, or classroom management reasons (i.e., the chaos or disturbance introduced in the class by the challenging student). The nature of these findings warrants further investigation. For example, they call for study of teacher stress using personality traits of the teacher (e.g., internal vs. external locus of control). A possible outcome of such work may be improved processes for identifying teachers more prone than others to burnout syndrome and providing them with specific supports that more effectively help them maintain their health and keep them in the profession.

We have one final note that we wish to share. We believe that this work demonstrates that the adoption of a mixed-methods strategy of analysis can give a strong epistemological basis to studies on teachers' stress and commend others to further explore ways such methods can help researchers and practitioners better understand teacher stress and coping.

NOTES

1. The "spontaneity" of an answer to an open-ended question in a questionnaire is debatable.
2. We had to perform some different cluster analyses in order to solve some technical problems, mainly due to a few very peculiar words that appeared together in some very short answers, thus creating very "heavy charged" items which behaved as outliers; they had to be excluded from the analysis in order to obtain a readable result. To give one example, a few very short texts contained the two (very meaningful!) words "aggressive and provocative." These items were the first to segregate from the rest of the corpus, creating such an extreme mini-cluster, very far apart from the other answers, that all the other items collapsed in a small area near to the origin of the coordinates.
3. The following analyses were implemented using the software T-Lab Pro 5.1. More information on this program's package can be found: http://www.tlab.it.
4. Cosine similarity is a vector-based similarity measure very close to Dice's coefficient: In our case, given two lexical units ("1" and "2"), the cosine coefficient was calculated using the following formula: $a/[(a + b)^{1/2} + (a + c)^{1/2}]$, where a is the number of co-occurrences of the two units, b is the number of occurrences of "1" without "2", and c is the number of occurrences of "2" without "1," as summarized in the following table:

	Lexical unit 2		
Lexical unit 1	Present	Absent	Total
Present	a	b	a + b
Absent	c	d	c + d
Total	a + c	b + d	N

5. "Representative" here technically means that a phrase contains the words with the highest value of the associated test measure. This measure, which is borrowed from Lebart, Morineau, and Piron (1995), has three very interesting properties: first, it correlates with absolute contributions (i.e., other measures that quantify the role played by each point of the factor space in accounting for the inertia of each factorial axis) (Greenacre, 1984); second is a sign (+ or −) that can be used to order the points along a factor; and third, a threshold value that we can use to reject the null hypothesis: if the value is smaller than −1.96 or larger than 1.96, we can say that the value is statistically significant ($p \le 0.05$). Throughout this chapter, answers are reported in a sequence following the ranking of their test values.

REFERENCES

Benzécri, J. P. (1973). *L'Analyse des données. Volume II. L'analyse des correspondances [Data analysis. Volume II. Correspondence analysis]*. Paris, France: Dunod.

Bolasco, S., & Della Ratta-Rinaldi, F. (2004). Experiments on semantic categorization of texts: analysis of positive and negative dimension. *Actes des 7es Journées internationales d'Analyse statistique des Données Textuelles [Proceedings of the 7th International Congress on Textual Data Statistical Analysis]*. Louvain-la-Neuve: Presses Universitaires de Louvain, pp. 202–210. Retrieved December 20, 2007 from http://lexicometrica.univ-paris3.fr/jadt/jadt2004/pdf/JADT_018.pdf

Boucher, J., & Osgood C. E. (1969). The Pollyanna hypothesis. *Journal of Verbal Learning and Verbal Behavior, 8*(1), 1–8.

Delabastita, D. (1993). *There's a double tongue. Investigation into the translation of Shakespeare's worldplay, with special reference to "Hamlet"*. Amsterdam, NL: Rodopi.

Di Pietro, M., & Ramazzo, L. (2003). *Lo stress dell'insegnante [Teacher's stress]*. Trento, Italy: Edizioni Erickson.

Greenacre, M. J. (1984). *Theory and applications of correspondence analysis*. New York, NY: Academic Press.

Italian Ministry of Education. (2006). *La scuola statale: sintesi dei dati [State school; some data]*. Retrieved from http://www.pubblica.istruzione.it/mpi/pubblicazioni/2006/dati_06.shtml

Lancia, F. (2007). *Word co-occurrence and similarity in meaning. Some methodological issues*. Retrieved December, 20, 2007 from: http://www.mytlab.com/wctheory.pdf

Lebart, L., Morineau, A., & Piron, M. (1995). *Statistique exploratoire multidimensionnelle*. Paris, France: Dunod.

Lorenzi-Cioldi, F. (1996). *Metodologia per la ricerca psicosociale [Methods in psychosocial research]*. Bologna: Il Mulino.

Moran-Ellis, J., Alexander, V. D., Cronin, A., Dickinson, M., Fielding, J., Sleney, J., & Thomas, H. (2006). Triangulation and integration: processes, claims and implications. *Qualitative Research, 6*(1), 45–59.

Moscovici, S. (1961). *La psychanalyse, son image et son public.* Paris, France: PUF.

Osgood C.R. (1959). The representation model and relevant research methods. In I. De Sola Pool (Ed.), *Trends in content analysis* (pp. 33–88). Urbana: University of Illinois press.

Schuman, H., & Presser, S. (1981). *Questions and answers in attitude surveys. Experiments on question form, wording, and context.* New York, NY: Academic Press.

Schwarz, N., & Hippler, H. J. (1991). Response alternatives: the impact of their choice and presentation order. In P. P. Biemer, R. M. Groves, N. A. Mathiowetz & S. Sudman (Eds.), *Measurement errors in surveys* (pp. 41–56). New York, NY: Wiley.

Webb, E. J., Campbell, D. T., Schwartz, R. D., & Secherst, L. (1966). *Unobtrusive measures: Non-reactive research in the social sciences.* Chicago, IL: Rand McNally.

Wikipedia. (2011). Christianity in Italy. Retrieved from http://en.wikipedia.org/wiki/Christianity_in_Italy.

CHAPTER 15

STRESS IN TEACHER–STUDENT INTERACTIONS AND TEACHER ACTIVENESS AS A POSITIVE COPING RESOURCE

Andrey Volochkov and Alexey Popov
Perm State Pedagogical University, Perm

ABSTRACT

This chapter presents research findings on teacher stress associated with challenging student behavior and teacher activeness and their ability to cope. The Utrecht Challenging Student Questionnaire for Teachers (UCSQT) and Teacher Professional Activeness Questionnaire (TAQ) were administered to a sample of teachers employed in the Perm region of Russia. We compared the effects of school environment against those of teacher activeness on the incidence and stress of the most challenging student behavior in the classroom. The analysis of gathered data convincingly showed that professional activeness of the teacher (as compared with school environment) is an important coping resource.

The research reported in this chapter took place in the Perm region of Russia. The study was conducted as part of a larger cross-cultural research project involving participants from eight countries (i.e., the Netherlands,

International Perspectives on Teacher Stress, pages 289–307
Copyright © 2012 by Information Age Publishing
All rights of reproduction in any form reserved.

the U.S., Italy, Suriname, Hong Kong, South Africa, India, Russia). The Perm region is situated in the Urals at the juncture of Europe and Asia. This region may be called the eastern outpost of Europe, with 99.8% of its territory being in Europe and only 0.2% in Asia. Its size approximates the total area of Austria, Ireland, and the Czech Republic. The population of the region is about 3 million, 76% of whom live in urban settings, with more than a million people living in the city of Perm. Administratively, the region is divided into over 30 districts. The climate is distinguished by a moderate summer (about 25 Celsius in June) and a harsh winter (the usual temperature in February is minus 20).

The Perm region is outstandingly rich in nature resources (i.e., oil, gas, minerals, forests, and large rivers). As a result of such bounty, Perm is one of the most industrialized regions of the Russian Federation, with major industries involved in extracting mineral resources, chemicals, fuel, and timber. It is also a center for metallurgy and engineering. Culturally and scientifically, the Perm region is well-recognized for its ballet, picture gallery collections, antiquities, and universities.

RUSSIAN SYSTEM OF EDUCATION

Public education in Russia is obligatory and free of charge. Children begin their education at the age of 6–7 entering primary school, where they spend four years. As a rule, children in primary school have four or five hours of studies each day with one teacher in classes that are normally between 25–30 students. Students then move on through the "middle stage" (grades 5–9) and onto grades 10 and 11 and graduation. In the middle and higher grades, each subject is taught by a separate teacher. Another aspect of the Russian educational system that is important to note is that students with weakened physical health attend sanatorium-type schools, whereas students with slow mental development study in specialized schools or classes depending on the depth of disorder. There are very few private educational institutions, and public schools serve the majority of the population.

Despite recent efforts to diversify how students are taught, change has been slow and the *traditional approach* or philosophy remains dominant in the region's schools. In most classrooms this means that students are required to assimilate and reproduce "ready knowledge." The function of the teacher in this approach is to explain, control, and transfer knowledge to students. Nonetheless, different models are receiving attention by educators.

Among these relatively new educational ideas, three versions or models of the *developmental approach* are most popular. Each of the three models is based on Vygotsky's (1960) principle known as the *zone of proximal development. School 2100* is the version that is most similar or aligned with the traditional approach. In *School 2100*, teaching is structured to emphasize the combination of ready knowledge assimilation and independent discovery of knowledge. Students' independent knowledge is developed or gained through application of specific problem-solving processes. *Elkonin* is the second version of the developmental approach that is present in Perm schools. In this model, students have to find a previously unknown method of solution by themselves. Rather than focusing on facts or conclusions, most of the attention is concerned with process or the development of theoretical ways of thinking (Davidov, 1996). Third, there is the developmental approach of *Zankov*, which focuses on providing students with optimally challenging tasks that draw on their interests and experiences (Zankov, 1975). Teaching in this model is organized around both sensory-affective and rational modes of cognition. In addition, it requires heterogeneous classes, including students with diverse mental and physical abilities, to facilitate learning.

There has been a long-lasting scientific debate in Russia generally and the Perm region in particular (e.g., traditional versus developmental) on the pros and cons of the various educational models. In this research, we were interested in assessing the incidence of students' challenging behavior and related levels of teaching stress as associated with these different models. Each of the four approaches can be considered a treatment since each provides an environment that influences the nature of teaching. For example, in developmental approaches to education that emphasize autonomy and support rather than control, one might expect less manifestation of problematic behavior and associated teaching stress, as compared to correctional schools or classes where it would be reasonable to expect more problems both as a function of student intake characteristics and highly controlling or punitive methods employed in these settings (Eccles & Roeser, 1999). At the same time, the environment is only one potential influence on the nature of teacher–student interactions and the stress that teachers experience given challenging student behavior (Kiziltepe, 2006). In this respect, we hypothesized the professional activeness of the teacher as an important variable.

TEACHER ACTIVENESS

In Russian psychology, the three concepts of activeness, activity, and behavior are related but have differentiated meanings. For instance, Leontyev (1975, 1979) defined activity as purposeful behavior that is volitional and goal-directed. Activeness, however, is understood as encompassing a larger or more complete process including cognitive appraisal and meaning making, forms involving behavioral norms and related aspects of embodiment, and measures such as assessment of results and affective states following behavior.

It is a perspective that fully appreciates that humans mainly act as subjects (i.e., as bearers of inner, intrinsically determined behavior). The concept of activeness, therefore, can be contrasted, for instance, with the notion of autonomy as studied cross-culturally by self-determination theorists who are focused on differentiating autonomous, self-determined behaviors and their correlates, causes and consequences from those that are heteronomous and other-determined (Chirkov, Ryan, Kim, & Kaplan, 2003).

Petrovskii's (1992) notion of activeness postulated that this quality of the subject's volitional interaction could be best understood as occurring within a *concrete sphere of being*. In holding the activeness of subjects within a concrete sphere of interaction (e.g., teacher role, parent role), Volochkov and Vyatkin (1999) and Volochkov (2003, 2005) identified the following four-part structure: *Activeness potential* reflects the ratio of the need and ability to step towards one's self-determined goals and actions. The *regulative component* is a ratio of unconscious self-regulation and cognitive self-control over behavior. The *dynamic component* is a ratio of performance and creativity in the observed interaction dynamics. Last, the *resulting component* is the outcome of the movement and at the same time commitment to its renewal or cyclic transformation into a new activeness potential. Thus, the structure of activeness of the subject of a concrete sphere of life contains not only components and elements organized in a systemic hierarchy, but also an inner source of this constant dynamic system renewal. Figure 15.1 depicts

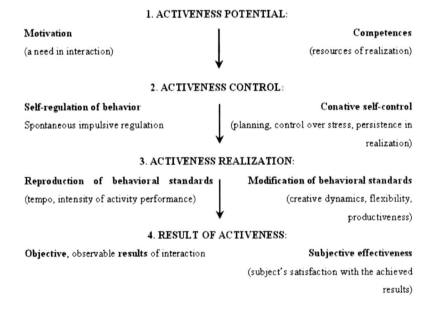

1. ACTIVENESS POTENTIAL:

Motivation   Competences

(a need in interaction)   (resources of realization)

2. ACTIVENESS CONTROL:

Self-regulation of behavior   Conative self-control

Spontaneous impulsive regulation   (planning, control over stress, persistence in realization)

3. ACTIVENESS REALIZATION:

Reproduction of behavioral standards   Modification of behavioral standards

(tempo, intensity of activity performance)   (creative dynamics, flexibility, productiveness)

4. RESULT OF ACTIVENESS:

Objective, observable results of interaction   Subjective effectiveness

(subject's satisfaction with the achieved results)

Figure 15.1 The structure of activeness.

each of these levels and hypothesized direction of flow. We refer readers to literature by Volochkov for a fuller discussion of how we conceptualize the activeness of subjects within a concrete sphere of being.

In this study, we were interested in assessing the various aspects of teacher activeness and examining their relation to the perceived level of student problems and related stress. Specifically, we designed the study to compare the effects of educational method and teacher activeness on the incidence of students' challenging behavior as well as the associated stress as perceived by teachers. We were interested in identifying which of the factors (i.e., educational method or activeness) possessed greater power in predicting the incidence of challenging behavior and related stress.

Thus, the research questions that guided this study were formulated as follows:

1. What types of challenging behaviors do Russian teachers name as most frequent and most stressful, and what do we know about these students who exhibit such behaviors?
2. Are there latent factors that can explain the different types of challenging student behaviors and teacher stress?
3. How are educational environments (as defined by traditional and innovative methods of teaching) in Russian schools related to the challenging student behaviors and teacher stress?
4. How does teacher activeness relate to challenging student behaviors and teacher stress?
5. Which is more important in reducing the incidence of challenging student behaviors and resultant teaching stress: changing the educational environment (e.g., employing a different method of teaching and selecting students prior to enrollment in a class) or adopting an active internal position and "taking up the challenge" (irrespective of the environment where the teacher works)?

METHODS

Participants

The Perm sample of teachers (N = 572) is representative of the territorial and demographic heterogeneity of the 34 administrative units of the Perm region. Sixty-four percent of the teachers worked in primary schools with children aged 7–10 years; the other 36% worked with teenagers aged 11–17 years. As in many nations, women comprise the majority of Russian teachers. Only 13 subjects (2.3%) of the teachers in the sample identified as male. The average number of teaching years was 18 for the sample. Only 21 teachers reported 1 to 3 years of teaching experience. Seventy-eight teachers reported having 5 to 10 years of experience. Most of the teachers (161) have worked in the profession for 15–20 years. One hundred twenty-five teachers possessed 25 years or more experience. Finally, four respondents stated that they had over 40 years of teaching experience. Thus, the teachers in the Perm sample have considerable experience, which reflects today's situation in Russia where young specialists are reluctant to work in educational settings.

Schools

We paid special attention to sampling teachers in ways that represented the demographic and territorial diversity of central and remote, urban and rural areas in the Perm region. In addition, this sample of teachers was representative of the proportions of general, elite, and specialized schools, as well as schools using traditional and innovative educational methods in the Perm region. For instance, 65% of the teachers in the sample worked in schools that employed traditional methods of education; 15% of teachers worked in schools that used the three developmental approaches to education described earlier; and the other 20% of the Perm sample teachers worked in sanatorium-type and correctional schools for students with physical or mental difficulties.

The surveys were distributed among teachers and collected by 37 specialists of local educational committees and governing bodies, each of whom was responsible for administering 10–18 questionnaires. These specialists ("mediators") were employed from all the administrative areas of the Perm region and received several hours of training before administering the survey forms used in this study.

Survey Instruments

Teachers filled out both the Utrecht Challenging Student Questionnaire for Teachers (UCSQT) and the Teacher Professional Activeness Questionnaire (TAQ). The psychometric properties of UCSQT for the sample used in this study are described in detail earlier in this book (see Everaert, this volume). This instrument included a number of scales, including two series of six measuring various types of challenging student behaviors. The scales are F1—against the grain, F2—full of activity/easily distractible, F3—needs a lot of attention/weak student, F4—easily upset, F5—failure syndrome/ excessively perfectionist, F6—aggressive /hostile. Each scale also comes in two variants: the incidence series (measuring how often a specific type of challenging behavior is displayed in the classroom) and the stress series (measuring the level of stress this type of challenging behavior causes in the teacher). Elsewhere in this chapter the incidence and stress series of the challenging behavior scales are marked (i) and (s), as in against the grain (i), or aggressive/hostile (s).

The Teacher Professional Activeness Questionnaire (TAQ) included 45 items that assessed five higher-order scales: (1) professional motivation, (2) self-evaluation of professional competences, (3) self-control over professional actions in a frustrating situation, (4) dynamics of professional activity alteration, and (5) satisfaction with professional activity results (see Figure 15.1). These five subscales comprise the total index "Professional Activeness of a Teacher." Teacher responses to the questionnaire demonstrated high psychometric quality. We paid special attention to evaluating construct validity. Results from an exploratory factor analysis showed that the 45 items were comprised of five orthogonal factors that correspond to the previously identified scales. The reliability of each scale was assessed by using a measure of inner consistency. Cronbach's Alphas for the primary scales ranged between 0.75 (Self-evaluation of professional competences) and 0.86 (Professional motivation). Cronbach's Alpha for the aggregated total scale "Professional Activeness of a Teacher" was 0.92. Average inter-item correlations were also within normal limits (from 0.20 for the questionnaire on the whole to 0.41 for the motivational scale). It should be also noted that the distribution of TAQ sum-scale was close to normal.

Analyses

Several sets of statistical analyses were employed to assess (1) the relation of the incidence of challenging student behaviors on teacher stress and (2) the relative contributions of educational method and teacher activeness on the perceived incidence and level of stress associated with challenging student behaviors. To reveal interrelations between incidence of challenging behavior and associated stress, we employed factor analysis. We used principal component analysis with varimax-normalized and direct oblimin rotation to examine which types of student behaviors and their level of incidence were associated with greater and lesser teacher stress. Next, to explore the relation of educational method and teacher activeness to problem incidence and stress, we used multivariate analysis of covariance (MANCOVA), controlling for the effects of years of teaching experience and place of residence. These were followed by discriminant analyses to study group differences more specifically. We paid special attention to computation of overall effect sizes (η) in order to further compare the effects of educational method and teachers' professional activeness on the incidence of challenging behavior and associated stress.

RESULTS

Incidence of Challenging Behaviors and Teacher Stress

To answer research question 1, we examined the kinds of problems that Russian teachers saw as the most prevalent among their students. Figure 15.2 shows that the most widespread types of challenging behavior reported by these Russian teachers included hyperactivity and an inability to pay attention (F2—full of activity /easily distractible) and weak academic skills (F3—needs a lot of attention /weak student). The least common type of challenging behavior Russian teachers reported involved oppositional behaviors associated with students' academic failure (F6—aggressive/hostile). We were curious if this profile was only characteristic of primary school children, and therefore we made a separate comparison of incidence of challenging behaviors and associated stress between primary grades (children aged 7–10) and teenage grades (11–14-year-olds). We found that both the outline and the proportions did not change. Both in-

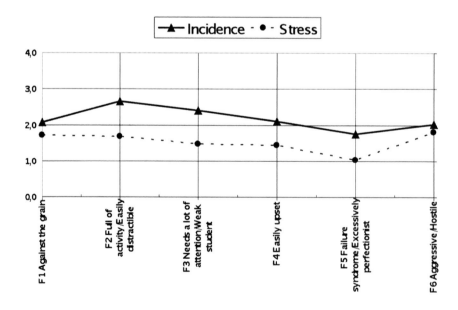

Figure 15.2 Incidence of challenging student behaviors and teacher stress in Perm region, Russia ($n = 572$).

cidence of challenging behavior and stress associated with it turned out to be practically the same for teachers who work with different age groups of students. These profiles, however, do appear to "grow up" a little, with the age of the students. It appears that attention problems and poor academic skills, and not oppositional behavior, represent the most prevalent student problem behaviors as perceived by primary and secondary school teachers in the Perm region of Russia.

We were also interested in the average age and sex of the students that Russian primary and secondary school teachers nominated as displaying the most challenging behaviors. Survey data analysis showed that for 329 teachers who worked in primary grades, the average age of the most challenging student is 9 years, 5 months. This age represents the middle of grade 4. For 198 Perm region teachers who worked with 11–15-year-old teenagers, the average age of such a student is 12.5 years. This age corresponds to grade 7 of Russian school education. Among the 572 challenging students described by teachers in our sample, 10.2% were female and 89.8% were male.

Types of Challenging Student Behaviors and Teacher Stress

While examining data to answer research question 2, we hypothesized that there was a single latent factor lying at the base of various types of challenging behaviors both in terms of their incidence and the level of teacher stress. Principal component analysis with varimax rotation showed that among Russian teachers, the six incidence scales may be combined in two general types of challenging behavior (see Table 15.1).

Thus, the types of challenging behaviors may be split into two groups. The first component combines F1—against the grain (i) and F2—full of

TABLE 15.1 Structure of Interrelations between Incidence of Different Types of Challenging Behaviors in Perm Sample: Principle Component Analysis, Varimax Rotation (N = 572)

Variables	Factor 1	Factor 2
F1 Against the grain (i)	0.73	0.35
F2 Full of activity/Easily distractible (i)	0.82	–0.10
F3 Needs a lot of attention/Weak student (i)	0.05	0.85
F4 Easily upset (i)	0.76	0.17
F5 Failure syndrome/Excessively perfectionist (i)	0.23	0.76
F6 Aggressive/Hostile (i)	0.78	0.28
% of variance	**40.8%**	**25.7%**

activity/easily distractible (i). We labeled this factor as *externalizing* problems (see Everaert, this volume) and interpret it in terms of an aggressive challenge to the professional activeness of the teacher. The second factor is represented by the scales F3—needs a lot of attention/weak student (i) and F5—failure syndrome/excessively perfectionist (i). We labeled this factor *internalizing* problems and interpret it as related to student helplessness resulting from low academic skills and abilities. Probably as in other geographical regions, the two factors, corresponding to externalizing and internalizing difficulties, capture in a broad way the two most general types of challenging students in the Perm sample. Results of the factor analysis using oblique (direct-oblimin) rotation revealed that the correlation between the two problem behavior scales is 0.29. This suggests that the relationship between the two types of behavior is substantial (i.e., challenging students, on average, tend to manifest both externalizing and internalizing problems, partially supporting a single-factor hypothesis).

In our next analysis, we examined the correlations among the stress associated with each of the problem student behaviors. Principal component analysis for the six scales yielded a one-component solution, supporting the hypothesis of a single latent factor. We interpreted these findings to suggest that the scales may be measuring only two general latent constructs: (1) the overall incidence of challenging student behaviors and (2) the overall subjective stress perceived by teachers in relation to those problems. Proceeding from this pattern of interrelations, we determined to explore the multivariate effects of the factors Educational Method and Teacher Activeness on the cumulative and individual measures of the six incidence scales and the cumulative and individual measures of six stress scales separately.

Before proceeding with this analysis, we note that among the many "third variables" that undoubtedly influenced the relationships examined in this study between challenging behaviors, stress, educational approach, and activeness; place of residence (Perm, smaller towns or rural area) and years of teaching experience were seen as particularly important to consider. Teachers and students of the Perm region live and work in different conditions. Undoubtedly, schools of the city of Perm differ significantly from those of small towns and especially villages. Incidence of problematic behavior and associated stress might also depend on the level of teacher experience. This may be explained by less experience in interaction with challenging students. On the other hand, teachers new to the profession are more able to relocate to another school or even leave the profession, which may reduce their stress. With seasoned teachers such possibilities are limited. Too many experienced educators, however, suffer the influence of emotional burnout, which contributes to their being somewhat "deaf" to a number of stressors (Mitina, 1998). Thus, we included place of residence and years of teaching experience as covariates in our analyses of the co-variation in incidence, stress, teaching method, and activeness.

Educational Approach on Incidence of Challenging Behaviors and Teacher Stress

We used two separate series (for incidence scales and stress scales) of multivariate analysis of covariance to address the study's third research question. Educational approach (model of education) served as a factor with five levels: (1) traditional approach ($n = 53$), (2) *School 2100* ($n = 54$), (3) the developmental approach after Elkonin and Davidov ($n = 19$), (4) the developmental approach after Zankov ($n = 32$), and (5) special needs education ($n = 54$). In forming each of the five subsamples, a number of rules were observed in order to insure equal representation of teachers from Perm and the 26 smaller towns of the Perm region. Some equalization was made in the five groups by randomly deleting cases from groups of traditional and special needs teachers. Two variables—place of residence and teaching experience—were included in the model as continuous covariates.

Prior to performing the main analyses, raw data were assessed to insure that they met the main assumptions of multivariate analysis of covariance (e.g., missing data, normality of within-group distributions of variables, normality of covariates, univariate and multivariate outliers). Both incidence and stress variables were moderately skewed; however, the pattern of their distribution was roughly the same for all variables and groups of cases. With $z > 1.96$ criterion, 22 univariate outliers were detected, though none of them were extreme outliers. Because no multivariate outliers were detected on this level, it was decided not to transform any variables.

The ratio of the largest group to the smallest was 2.8 to 1. On the whole, within-group variances were roughly the same. Levene's test indicated homogeneity of variance for all the separate variables. On a $p < .001$ level, Box's test of equality of covariance matrices was insignificant for measures of both stress and incidence. Given these indicators, we viewed the assumptions of homogeneity of variance and covariance matrices as met (Tabachnick & Fidell, 2007). Regression slopes were also homogeneous. The effect of interaction between the two covariates and the factor (educational model) was insignificant in both series (incidence and stress). Multicollinearity and singularity tests were also satisfactory.

Overall Multivariate Effect of the Five-Level Factor
Educational Approach
The overall multivariate effect of the five-level factor Educational Approach on the six scales of incidence of problematic student behaviors

was (after controlling for the effects of teaching experience and place of residence) both statistically significant and quite substantial: Pillai's Trace $F(24, 812) = 1.878$, $p < 0.01$, $\eta = 0.23$. Neither teaching experience nor place of residence was significant in affecting the combined incidence scales. Interestingly, only three out of six follow-up univariate ANOVAs were statistically significant (Bonferroni correction not employed). This indicates that the overall multivariate effect is attributable in part to particular relations between Educational Approach and the incidence of specific kinds of problems. Simple planned contrasts (successive comparisons of each educational model with the traditional), though not orthogonal, showed no differences associated with Educational Approach in aggressive and hostile behaviors (scale F6). In contrast, the developmental approach after Zankov turned out to be most favorable with respect to the remainder of the problem behaviors. Specifically, this approach was associated with teachers who reported fewer students who exhibited problem behaviors represented on the UCSQT .

Next we examined which of the scales contributed most significantly to the overall effect and whether any dimensions of variables could be revealed, within which the five groups differed. Discriminant analysis revealed a single significant variate accounting for 56% of variability. This indicated that there was, in essence, only one dimension of group differences. The second variate was statistically insignificant but still accounted for a large portion (26.9%) of variability. It was evident from examining the structure matrix that the following scales were most important in the first dimension of differences (by order of descending importance in prediction of group membership): F3—needs a lot of attention/weak student (i), F1—against the grain (i), and F6—aggressive/hostile (i). In the second variate, the only variable with a significant weight was F2—full of activity/easily distractible (i) (Table 15.2).

TABLE 15.2 Discriminating Potential of Education Approach for Types of Challenging Behaviors: Incidence Series Rotated Structure Matrix (N = 212)

	Function			
Scale	1	2	3	4
F3 Needs a lot of attention/Weak student (i)	.806*	.189	.172	−.013
F1 Against the grain (i)	.678*	−.035	.149	.261
F6 Aggressive/Hostile (i)	.332*	.087	.212	.172
F2 Full of activity/Easily distractible (i)	.106	.821*	.068	.165
F5 Failure syndrome/Excessively perfectionist (i)	.292	.076	.941*	.135
F4 Easily upset (i)	.198	.212	.140	.908*

Note: Only first function is significant and interpreted in the text. Asterisks denote largest absolute correlation between each variable and any discriminant function.

TABLE 15.3   Variate Centroids for Education Approach (N = 212)

What system (model) of education do you work in?	Function			
	1	2	3	4
Basically traditional	.098	-.036	.054	-.047
"School 2100"	-.158	.346	-.189	-.115
Developing education after Elkonin	-.405	-.053	.168	.007
Developing education after Zankov	-.456	-.296	-.449	.179
Special needs	-.045	.048	.017	.167

Note: Only first function is significant and interpreted in the text.

Examination of group centroids showed that along the first (significant) variate, teachers of Zankov's developmental approach reported the least incidence of challenging behaviors, whereas teachers of the traditional educational approach reported the most (Table 15.3).

These results suggest that a developmental approach that emphasizes students' independence and supports their competence may tend to reduce problem behaviors. Probably, under these conditions, students are likely to feel more competent, which may lead to the lack of necessity to protest against the teaching methods (Eccles & Roeser, 1999).

The multivariate effect of the Educational Approach on the six stress scales was statistically insignificant: Pillai's Trace F (24, 2232) = 1.149, n.s., η = 0.10. The effect size was also small, indicating only 0.012% of explained variance. Teaching experience (treated as a covariate) was a negative and statistically significant predictor of stress associated with students' challenging behavior.

In sum, these analyses revealed that teachers working in schools where traditional educational approaches are employed reported experiencing challenging student behaviors more often. These findings may be explained by the implicit limitations of traditional education, though these data do not allow us to draw such causal conclusions. In addition, there are usually much more challenging students in traditional schools because there is no student selection effect—anyone can and does attend such schools. Such selection effects are characteristic of schools that employ the newer, developmental educational approaches—including in many prestigious schools where not every child is accepted. Therefore it is incorrect to draw conclusions about the advantages of these nontraditional approaches. The discovered effects rather testify to the influence of the environment. As for teacher stress, there seemed to be little difference attributed to the type of educational model. It was seen as affected by the teacher's experience, which is natural because with the course of years teachers normally learn to be "deaf" to some kinds of continuing problematic behaviors.

Apart from this, however, is there any inner resource that helps teachers overcome the stressors? We hypothesized that professional activeness could serve as an important coping factor.

Teacher Activeness on Incidence of Challenging Behavior and Teacher Stress

Teacher Activeness was assessed by the TAQ and subject scores were sorted into one of three levels: high, normative, and low. Each group included 80 cases, among them both urban and rural inhabitants. Post-hoc comparisons showed that these three groups differed significantly with respect to the index of teacher's activeness as measured by the TAQ.

Prior to main analysis, data were examined to see if they met basic MANCOVA assumptions. In this case, the three groups being equal and quite numerous, sufficient statistical power was secured and the analysis proved robust on various measures. The assumptions of homogeneity of variance and covariance matrices were met. Examination of distribution parameters revealed one variable that departed severely from normality (large negative skewness): F5—failure syndrome/excessively perfectionist (s). Square root transformation was applied. Transformation is feasible in this case because Likert scale boundaries are quite conditional. The covariates followed normal distribution. Analysis of univariate outliers was satisfactory; however, one multivariate outlier was evident from Mahalanobis distances at $z > 3.29$. This outlier was excluded from further analysis (case number = 1030). With $p < .001$ as the cutoff point, Box's test of equality of covariance matrices was insignificant both for stress and incidence groups. The data also met the assumptions of homogeneity of regression slopes and absence of singularity/multicollinearity.

Multivariate effect of Teacher Activeness on the six scales of incidence of challenging behavior was statistically insignificant and quite small: Pillai's Trace $F(12, 458) = 1.565$, n.s., $\eta = 0.20$. In follow-up series of univariate ANOVAs, there was only one significant effect out of six, though large even with Bonferroni correction. This is the effect upon F1—against the grain (i) scale ($\eta = 0.2$).

Planned simple contrasts (successive comparison of each group with the group of passive teachers) yielded significant differences between *active* and *passive* teachers along three scales. Active teachers report less challenging student behaviors associated with opposition (F1—against the grain (i)), low abilities (F3—needs a lot of attention/weak student (i)), and failure syndrome (F5—failure syndrome/excessively perfectionist (i)). In follow-up discriminant analysis both the variates were insignificant. Thus, there is no strong association between professional activeness of the teacher and challenging student behaviors. However, it is evident that more active teachers face somewhat less opposing and helpless behaviors. It may be that teacher activeness affects students' academic motivation, which implies more urge to study and less willingness to accuse the teacher of one's own low performance (see Eccles & Roeser, 1999).

Multivariate effect of Teacher Activeness on the six stress scales was unexpectedly large: Pillai's Trace F $(12, 458) = 3.968$, $p < .001$, $\eta = 0.97$. The large effect size was discovered even in spite of the fact that years of teaching experience (the covariate) remained a significant negative predictor of the six scales of stress. All the univariate effects were also statistically significant, effect size varying between 0.36 (F2—full of activity/easily distractible (s)) and 0.58 (F6—aggressive/hostile (s)). In all the cases, the stress reported by teachers who reported normative or high levels of activeness was significantly lower than that reported by teachers who were low on the activeness dimension.

In follow-up discriminant analysis, two variates were singled out, the first one being significant and explaining the overwhelming part (99.3%) of between-group variability. All the six scales loaded onto this dimension of difference considerably high. In order of decreasing importance of the scales in predicting group membership (and vice versa, effect of group membership on the scale), the variables were as follows: F2—full of activity/easily distractible (s), F3—needs a lot of attention/weak student (s), F1—against the grain (s), F4—easily upset (s), F6—aggressive/hostile (s), F5—failure syndrome/excessively perfectionist (s, transformed) (Table 15.4).

Active, normative, and passive group centroids were located at approximately equal distances (Table 15.5). Thus, the dependency, though multivariate, is almost strictly linear. In the group of active teachers, the levels of stress associated with certain types of students' challenging behavior are

TABLE 15.4 Discriminating Potential of Teacher Activeness for Stress Associated with Challenging Student Behaviors: Stress Series Rotated Structure Matrix ($N = 239$)

	Function	
Scale	1	2
F2 Full of activity/Easily distractible (s)	.802*	.395
F3 Needs a lot of attention/Weak student (s)	.784*	−.095
F1 Against the grain (s)	.591*	−.230
F4 Easily upset (s)	.546*	−.186
F6 Aggressive/Hostile (s)	.410*	.160
F5 Failure syndrome/Excessively perfectionist (s)–Transformed	.394*	.355

Note: Only first function is significant and interpreted in the text. Asterisks denote largest absolute correlation between each variable and any discriminant function.

TABLE 15.5 Variate Centroids for Teacher Activeness (_N_ = 239)

Teacher's activeness	Function	
	1	2
Active	−.624	.026
Normative	.053	−.059
Passive	.562	.034

Note: Only first function is significant and interpreted in the text.

TABLE 15.6 Educational Environment and Teacher Activeness: Effect Size Comparison

Factor	Dependent variables	
	Incidence	Stress
Educational environment	0.230	0.10
Professional activeness	0.197	0.97

Note: Partial eta (η) is used as a measure of effect size.

significantly lower than in the groups of normative and passive teachers. Evidently, professional activeness of a teacher is a powerful resource strongly associated with coping.

Finally, the parallel design of the empirical study enabled us to answer research question 5 and compare the effects that "outer" educational environment and "inner" resource of activeness have on the incidence of challenging behaviors and associated teaching stress. The results of this comparison are summarized in Table 15.6.

Thus, the effects of educational approach and teacher's level of activeness on the incidence of students' challenging behavior are approximately the same (and quite low). As far as the level of teaching stress is concerned, however, professional activeness of a teacher, compared to the educational approach used in the school in which she works, is a clear correlate of level of perceived stress, even after controlling for the effects of place of residence and years of teaching experience.

DISCUSSION

Findings presented in the results section can be viewed as consecutive steps undertaken to reach the main goal, that of comparison between internal (Teacher Activeness) and external (Education Approach) factors of dealing with challenging student behaviors and (as a consequence) reducing teaching stress (research question 5). Results expressed in Partial eta (η)

effect sizes clearly show that the effects of internal and external factors on incidence of challenging behaviors are comparable and small to moderate (0.20–0.23), while the effect of activeness (as an internal factor) on teacher stress dramatically outweighs the corresponding effect of educational environment: effect sizes 0.10 and 0.97, correspondingly. Thus, it appears that activeness of teachers is an important phenomenon that is related to how these professionals respond to stressful situations.

Psychology nowadays pays special attention to the problem of "coping behaviors" (Ababkov & Perre, 2004; Bodrov, 2006; Haan, 1965; Krukova, 2005; Lazarus, 1981; Postilyakova, 2005). Coping is a complex mixture of individual and environmental factors (see McCarthy, Lambert, O'Donnell, Villarreal, & Melendres, this volume). Activeness, we propose, indexes a teacher's exercise of autonomous regulation of behavior, including in times of stress and therefore as part of coping responses. However, from our perspective, much of the coping research does not address the underlying mechanism of coping behavior. What mobilizes coping and provides its formation and development? We propose that the intrinsic activeness of the subject within a concrete sphere of being is a source of motivation for positive coping efforts (Chirkov et al., 2003).

From our perspective, activeness provides a framework within which so-called "challenging behaviors" of students are appraised by teachers. In other words, activeness is both a precursor to and an outcome of stressful experiences dealing with a student who is exhibiting problem behavior. Many efforts are underway, in Russia as well as other nations, to help teachers deal more effectively with the increasing prevalence of such challenges. We believe these efforts as well as direct efforts at teaching the dimensions that comprise activeness (see Figure 15.1) can all be fruitful in helping teachers to become more effective, and socially–emotionally balanced, in the classroom (Volochkov, 2003, 2005; Volochkov & Vyatkin, 1999).

What adds to the interesting nature of these findings was that activeness of the teacher had little effect upon the *incidence* of problematic behavior of the most challenging student ($\eta = 0.197$). Thus, it seems that teacher activeness helps a teacher overcome his/her own stress, but not the problematic situation per se. This makes sense if one assumes that problem behavior in children has causes well beyond those of their current teacher. It also suggests the possibility that the activeness of the teacher had an effect on the *estimation of stress associated with the challenging behavior.* Although we cannot make causal attributions given the correlation design employed by the study, these results lend credibility to the argument that with an increase of professional activeness of the teacher the level of stress caused by challenging behavior *decreases.* The sharpness of the stressful challenge that the chief "problem generator" sends to the teacher is successfully "neutralized" by the teacher's professional activeness. Active teachers take up the challenge; passive ones suffer deep stress and may thus "give up." The nature of this interrelationship between teacher activeness and teaching stress in dealing with challenging situations in classroom, either causal or not, has to be further researched.

CONCLUSION

In the research reported in this chapter, we found that the professional activeness of the teacher manifested itself as a mechanism and an inner resource of the most efficient strategies of teacher coping—the strategies of active transformation of, or active adaptation to, stressful situations related to the most challenging student behaviors. It was not student selection, methods of teaching, or other features of the educational environment, but activeness of the teacher that played a major role in the level of stress generated with respect to problem student behaviors. Active teachers accept the challenge of students with special needs and vulnerabilities, often counteracting the potential destructiveness of these problems. As a result, aspects of their professional practice are much better manageable than those of passive or moderately active teachers who suffer more in the presence of occupational stressors. The collected data are useful in the empirical validation of the conception of the "integral activeness of the subject within a concrete sphere of life" developed in the Perm psychological school.

REFERENCES

Ababkov, V. A., & Perre, M. (2004). *Adaptatsiya k dtressu. Osnovi teorii, diagnostiki, terapii* [Adaptation to stress: basics of theory, diagnostics, and therapy]. Saint Petersburg, Russia: Rech.

Bodrov, V. A. (2006). Problema preodoleniya stressa. Chast' 1: "Coping stress" I teoreticheskiye podhodi k ego izucheniyu [The problem of coping with stress. Part 1: "Coping stress" and theoretical approaches to its research]. *Psihologicheskii Zhurnal, 27*(1), 122–133.

Chirkov, V., Ryan, R. M., Kim, Y., & Kaplan, U. (2003). Differentiating autonomy from individualism and independence: A self-determination theory perspective on internalization of cultural orientations and well-being. *Journal of Personality and Social Psychology, 84*, 97–110.

Davidov, V. V. (1996). *Teoriya Razvivayuschego Obucheniya* [The theory of developing education]. Moscow, Russia: INTOR.

Eccles. J. S., & Roeser, R. W. (1999). School and community influences on human development. In M. H. Boorstein & M. E. Lamb (Eds.), *Developmental psychology: An advanced textbook* (4th ed., pp. 503–554). Hillsdale, NJ: Erlbaum.

Haan, N. (1965). Coping and defense mechanism related to personality inventories. *Journal of Consulting Psychology, 29*, 373–378.

Kiziltepe, Z. (2006). Sources of teacher demotivation. In R.Lambert & C. McCarthy (Eds.), *Understanding teacher stress in an age of accountability* (pp. 145–162). Greenwich, CT: Information Age.

Krukova, T.L. (2005). Vozrastniye I krosskulturniye razlichiya v strategiyah sovladayuschego povedeniya [Age-specific and cross-cultural differences in coping behavior strategies]. *Psihologicheskii Zhurnal, 26*(2), 5–15.

Lazarus, R. S. (1981). Stressbezogene transaktionen zwischen person und umwelt [Stress-related interaction between person and environment]. In R. S.Lasarus & R. Launier (Eds.), *Stress: Theorien, untersuchungen, massnahmen* (pp. 213–259). Bern, Switzerland: Huber.

Leontyev, A. N. (1975). *Deyatel'nost'. Soznaniye. Lichnost'* [Activity. Consciousness. personality.]. Moscow, Russia: Politizdat.

Leontyev, A. N. (1979). Kategoriya deyatel'nosti v sovremennoy psihologii [The category of activity in modern psychology]. *Voprosi Psihologii, 3*, 11–15.

Mitina, L. M. (1998). *Psihologiya professional'nogo razvitiya uchitelya* [Psychology of professional development of a teacher]. Moscow, Russia: Flinta.

Petrovskii, V.A. (1992) *Psihologiya neadaptivnoy aktivnosti* [Psychology of non-adaptive activeness]. Moscow, Russia: Konyok-Gorbunok.

Postilyakova, U.V. (2005). Resursi sovladaniya so stressom v raznih vidah professional'noi deyatel'nosti [Resources of coping with stress in different types of professional activity]. *Psihologicheskii Zhurnal, 26*(6), 35–43.

Tabachnick, B. G., Fidell, L. S. (2007) *Using Multivariate Statistics* (5th ed.). Amsterdam, The Netherlands: Pearson International.

Volochkov, A. A. (2003). Aktivnost' subjecta kak faktor psihicheskogo razvitiya (gipotezi, modeli, fakti) [Activeness of the subject as a factor of psychological development (hypotheses, models, facts)]. *Psihologicheskii Zhurnal, 24*(3), 22–31.

Volochkov, A. A. (2005) Problema tselostoi aktivnosti sub'ekta konkretnoi sferi vzaimodeistviya: ponyatie, struktura, diagnostika [Integral activeness of the subject of a concrete sphere of interaction: definition, structure, and diagnostics]. In Z. I. Ryabikina & V. V.Znakov (Eds.), *Lichnost' I bitie: sub'ektnii podhod. Lichnost' kak sub'ekt bitiya: teoretiko-metodologicheskiye osnovaniya analiza: Materiali III Vserossiiskoy nauchno-prakticheskoi konferentsii* [Personality and being: the subject approach. Personality as the subject of being: theoretical and methodological foundations. Proceedings of the III All-Russian scientific conference] (pp. 60–63). Krasnodar, Russia: KubGU.

Volochkov, A. A. & Vyatkin, B. A. (1999). Individualnii stil' uchebnoy aktivnosti v mladshem shkol'nom vozraste [Individual style of academic activeness in primary school age]. *Voprosi Psihologii, 5*, 10–21.

Vygotsky, L.S. (1960). *Razvitiye Visshikh Psihicheskikh Funktsii* [Development of higher psychological functions]. Moscow, Russia: APN RSFSR.

Zankov, L.V. (1975). *Obucheniye I Razvitiye* [Teaching and development]. Moscow, Russia: Pedagogika.

CHAPTER 16

TEACHER STRESS IN WORKING WITH BEHAVIORAL PROBLEMS OF STUDENTS IN HONG KONG

A Comparative Study

I-Wah Pang and Sau-Wai Tao
Hong Kong Institute of Education

ABSTRACT

We surveyed teachers ($N = 1210$) in ordinary primary schools in Hong Kong to explore their perception of the (1) incidence of challenging student behaviors, (2) stress of dealing with challenging student behaviors, (3) beliefs about dealing with challenging student behaviors, (4) areas impacted by challenging student behaviors, and (5) school characteristics. The study compared our data with responses collected from teachers in six countries. Using bivariate correlation, canonical correlation, and one-way ANOVA, we found that teacher stress associated with student challenging behaviors was highly correlated with perceived incidence of challenging behaviors. To a lesser extent, it was significantly correlated with teachers' self-efficacy, negative af-

International Perspectives on Teacher Stress, pages 309–332
Copyright © 2012 by Information Age Publishing

fect, and self-critical attitude, followed by various school characteristics. While various negative impacts on teachers were strongly associated with aggregated teacher stress, stress was more strongly associated with teacher beliefs than with perceived school characteristics. Compared to their counterparts in six other countries, Hong Kong teachers reported the most severe impacts of student behavioral problems and most negative beliefs in working with these students.

Research in a variety of nations has shown that teaching is a highly stressful profession (e.g., Smith, Brice, Collins, Matthews, & McNamara, 2000). High levels of occupational stress over long periods of time are known to lead to burnout and encourage teachers to leave the profession (Golembiewski, Munzenrider, & Carter, 1983). Due to a variety of factors, teachers in Hong Kong are under a great deal of stress. We begin by discussing how broad social and economic changes in Hong Kong contribute to teacher stress. We then focus on one particular source of teacher stress—student behavioral problems. Our analysis focuses on the comparison of teacher stress in Hong Kong with data gathered from teachers in six other countries. We conclude by discussing possible remedies given the fast paced environment in which both macro-level systemic changes and micro-level interactions with difficult students contribute to a challenging work environment for teachers in Hong Kong.

HONG KONG AS CONTEXT

Hong Kong is a Special Administrative Region in China and was a former British colony that was returned to China in 1997. Its current population is about seven million. In the last decade, there has been an influx of immigrants from the Chinese mainland to Hong Kong at an annual rate of 55,000 people.

Economically, Hong Kong is acknowledged as one of Asia's major international financial centers. As China emerges as the "factory of the world," with growing affluence and increasing consumption, there has been a corresponding development in Hong Kong in finance, trade, logistics, and tourism. Owing to the fast economic growth in China, there is increasing competition as well as collaboration between Hong Kong and other parts of China. In short, Hong Kong is at the center of the economic expansion occurring in China and other parts of Asia.

Patterns of work have been changing over the last decade. Ten years ago, the number of hours worked per week ranged from 30 to 49; today it is 50 to 60 hours or more ("Future of Hong Kong's Population," 2007). While working hours of staff at various levels were set between 42 and 45 hours per week, workers were found actually to work 11 to 13 hours extra per week

(Hong Kong Institute of Human Resource Management, 2004). Concerns over the effect of long working hours on the family and the children have been raised: "Working overtime is a common phenomenon across industries, exerting significant psychological pressure on the population. Naturally, this means time spent at home and time appropriated for family matters are sacrificed. Subsequently, this also translates into neglect of children and the elderly" ("Future of Hong Kong's Population," 2007, p. 14).

As in other professions in Hong Kong, teachers are working longer hours per week, and this fact among others has contributed to the considerable stress many teachers are experiencing. Another social phenomenon in Hong Kong that is indirectly affecting levels of stress in the teaching profession is the decreasing fertility rate. In 2005, the number of births per 1,000 women was 966 as compared to 1,342 in 1993 and 1,722 in 1983. This birth rate is significantly lower than those figures in some developed countries in 2005: 1,340 per 1,000 women for Japan, 2,140 for the U.S., and the 1,370 for the UK. Lower birth rates lead to decreasing numbers of students, and as a result, the Hong Kong government has closed down quite a few primary schools in recent years. Fewer schools mean that fewer teachers are necessary. This contributes to a diminished sense of job security.

Educational System

Currently, the government provides twelve years of free and universal basic education for children between the ages of 6–18 years. Noncompulsory kindergarten education starts at age three and can be pursued for three years. Compulsory primary school education begins at six years of age. After a child's completion of six years of compulsory primary education, he or she has six more years of free education in secondary schools.

There are three main types of schools in Hong Kong: government schools, which are operated by the government; aided schools (the majority type), which are fully supported by the government but run by voluntary bodies; and private schools, some of which also receive financial assistance from the government. In addition, there are schools operated by the English Schools Foundations, and also international schools that offer non-local curriculum to non-Chinese-speaking students.

Similar to many developed countries, Hong Kong has undergone a comprehensive series of education reforms in the last decade, including the introduction of a comprehensive curriculum reform, new school-based assessments, inclusive education for those with special needs, comprehensive school reviews, territory-wide system assessments, school-based management, and language competency requirements for teachers. Not only have schools needed to enhance their accountability and transparency, but they have also had to undergo reforms aimed at shifting the predominant modes of teaching and learning in classrooms.

The promotion of inclusive education is believed to be one of the major causes of teacher stress in recent years in Hong Kong. Inclusive education was seen by primary school teachers as the third biggest stressor among twenty policies of education reform (Chan, 2006). In 2003–2004, the government implemented inclusive education on full scale with the backing of the Disability Discrimination Ordinance (1997), its Code of Practice on Education (Equal Opportunities Commission, 2001) and the New Funding Mode of the Learning Support Grant (EDB, 2008), which provides minimal subsidies to schools based on the number of handicapped children they serve. Simultaneously, practical schools and skills opportunity schools were phased out in 2004 and 2005, respectively. These schools used to admit secondary school students with special needs or those who were low-achieving. As a result, an increasing number of students with special needs have been integrated into ordinary schools. Studies of secondary school heads (Caritas Hong Kong Youth and Community Office, 2010) and teachers in primary schools (Tsui & Tse, 2006) suggest that the implementation of inclusive education has increased significantly the workload of teachers and the difficulties in teaching.

In sum, Hong Kong has been engaged in serious education reform. Indeed, Cheng (2007) argued that Hong Kong has been "infected" with the so-called "Education Reform Syndrome." This syndrome is said to be characterized by never-ending reforms, few priorities, and little effectiveness. One consequence of this "syndrome" is the high levels of stress and exhaustion among teachers.

Teacher Stress in Hong Kong

Research has shown that occupational stress among teachers is on the rise in Hong Kong. For instance, a recent study conducted by the Democratic Alliance for Betterment of Hong Kong (DAB) and the Hong Kong Federation of Education Workers (2006) showed that nearly 90% of 800 teachers surveyed said that they were under stress. One out of four teachers said that they had to work up to 71 hours a week, and 56% said that they worked more than 61 hours a week. Another survey (City University of Hong Kong & Professional Teacher Union, 2006) revealed that 97.5% of 443 teachers from 45 primary schools found it hard to handle the extra work that reform, including professional development, entailed. A total of 91.5% of primary school teachers and 87.3% of secondary school teachers reported that they were more stressed than five years ago.

Research has also documented the correlates of teacher stress in Hong Kong. One study reported that 70% of teachers said that their teaching quality was affected because of their levels of occupational stress (DAB, 2002). Another study found that 19.7% of teachers had a certain degree of depression and 13.8% of teachers had general anxiety disorder—rates of depression and anxiety that double the rates for ordinary citizens in Hong Kong (Hong Kong Mood Disorders Center, 2004).

Teachers have begun to take action against what they perceive as an overly stressful workplace environment. In January, 2006, there was a mass teacher demonstration organized by the teacher's union in response to an inappropriate comment of a senior education officer who claimed there was no link between recent reform and the suicide of two teachers. To respond to the concerns of educators, the government has since set aside a total of HK$34 billion (US$ 4.36 billion) to implement measures to reduce teacher stress. The government also set up the Teacher Work Committee to look into the issue, and its conclusions were presented in a report (Education and Manpower Bureau, 2006). The report indicated that the sources of teacher stress were multiple. Besides the additional work introduced when education reforms were implemented, stress was said to have increased given higher expectations and lack of job security described above. In this chapter, we explore how micro-level factors such as problem students in the classroom can contribute to and exacerbate the other considerable job-related stressors that teachers in Hong Kong face today.

Teacher Stress and Students' Behavioral and Emotional Problems

Stress is a response to prolonged and increased pressures that cannot be managed and addressed adequately given an individual's current resources and coping strategies (Kyriacou, 1987). Jarvis (2002) proposed three broad areas of the causal factors in teacher stress, including (1) systemic factors discussed above, including birthrates, demand and support from the government, social support among colleagues, leadership style of the principal, and so on; (2) factors intrinsic to teaching, like workload, role overload, and issues of classroom management and discipline; and (3) cognitive vulnerability of teachers, such as self-defeating beliefs, low efficacy beliefs, and unproductive coping styles. In this section, we explore how student problem behaviors, in conjunction with teacher vulnerability factors, can affect teacher stress.

Previous studies have identified dealing with problem behaviors of students as a major source of teacher stress. In one survey among UK teachers, one of the factors related to teachers' desire to leave the profession was student behavior and discipline problems (Brown, Davis, & Johnson, 2002). Van der Wolf and Everaert (2003) indicated that continual exposure to challenging behavior from students can seriously deplete teachers' emotional and physical resources, leading to self-doubt, loss of satisfaction from teaching, and poorer quality in teaching. Yoon (2002), for instance, found moderate correlations between teacher stress, negative affect, and negative teacher–student relationships. These results give some indication that teacher stress may increase the inappropriate display of negative affect on the part of teachers, which in turn is likely to be perceived by students as adversarial and further exacerbate negative teacher–student interactions in an escalating negative cycle.

In Hong Kong, students' behavioral problems have also been identified as a significant source of teacher stress. Chan (2006) identified six sources of teacher stress, including student misbehavior, parent and community attitudes, workload and nature of work, school management and colleagues, career prospect, and teaching efficacy. Student misbehavior was ranked as the third most stressful aspect of their work by primary school teachers, and the second most stressful aspect by secondary school teachers. In another study of 2,000 teachers, students' emotional–behavioral problem was the fourth biggest stressor among sixteen stressors reported by teachers (Hong Kong Mood Disorders Center, 2004).

THE CURRENT STUDY

The purpose of the current study was to shed further light on students' emotional–behavioral problems as a significant source of teacher stress and to examine individual differences in the ways teachers coped with this particular source of occupational stress. We addressed the following research questions: (1) What are the teacher-reported incidences of various challenging student behaviors in the classrooms in Hong Kong? (2) How stressful are different kinds of behavior problems for teachers? (3) Are the kinds of problems and their related levels of stress different among teachers based on incidences of challenging behavior, their own personal and school characteristics, or their beliefs in working with students with challenging behavior? Besides Hong Kong teachers, data from six other countries with diverse cultural backgrounds were secured for comparison. These data originated from an international study entitled Cross-national Comparisons of Teacher Stress Related to Emotional and Behavioral Problems of Learners, led by Prof. Kees van der Wolf and Dr. Huub Everaert of the Utrecht University of Professional Education, in which Hong Kong (China) was a participating region. The other participating countries include Italy, The Netherlands, Russia, South Africa, Surinam and the United States.

METHODS

Research Procedure

Participants targeted for this study were full-time teachers working in ordinary primary schools in Hong Kong. To achieve a representative sample of this population of teachers, schools were randomly selected based on two criteria: their funding source and their geographical location. Based on funding source, 6 government schools, 25 subsidized schools, 10 private schools, and 8 international schools were selected. In terms of geographical location, 15 schools were selected from those on Hong Kong Island, 17 schools from Kowloon, 7 schools from New Territories East, and 10 schools from New Territories West. A total of 49 schools were selected, representing about 6% of all local ordinary primary schools in 2004–2005. All the teachers in the selected schools were asked to complete a questionnaire. The data obtained were all self-reported by the teachers.

Principals of the selected schools were invited via telephone call and fax to take part in the survey. Questionnaires were delivered in packages to the selected schools from late March to mid April of 2006. A cover letter and an instruction sheet were enclosed. All the full-time teachers in the schools were invited to respond to the questionnaire anonymously within two weeks. Teachers were asked to put their completed questionnaire into a sealed envelope and return it to the school office for collection by the research team. All participants were assured that their data would be kept confidential and used solely for research purposes.

Altogether 1,310 teacher questionnaires were received. This represents a response rate of 69.3%. Among the returned questionnaires, 1,210 were found to be valid. All teacher respondents taught in ordinary primary schools. Among them, 81.7% ($n = 988$) were female and 18.3% ($n = 221$) were male. The teachers worked in different types of schools: that is, 56.0% in aided schools, 15.7% in government schools, 23.7% in private schools, and 4.1% in international schools.

Questionnaire Measures

The English version of the Utrecht Challenging Student Questionnaire for Teachers (UCSQT) designed by Prof. Kees van der Wolf and Dr. Huub Everaert was translated into Chinese. Back translation was undertaken to ensure the accuracy of the translation. Minor amendments were made. For example, in the category of school, so as to fit in the Hong Kong context, different types of schools were included. Both the Chinese and English versions were used in the survey. About 6% of the respondents chose to fill in the English questionnaire, while the majority filled in the Chinese version.

The teacher questionnaire consisted of five sections, and all sections were used in the study. Section one asked for respondents' personal information such as the type of school he/she was working in, gender, age, religion, number of years working as a teacher, and so on. Section two was divided into four parts (A–D), which were focused on the most challenging student in the class the teachers were currently teaching. In section 2A, the respondents were to describe the behaviors of this student, the reason they thought this behavior was challenging, and how they dealt with such behaviors. In section 2B, a list of 23 problematic behaviors were given and teachers were asked, on a five-point Likert scale, how frequent this particular student exhibited each of the behaviors (0 = doesn't happen at all; 4 = happens a lot) and how stressful it was when the student exhibited such behaviors (0 = not stressful at all; 4 = very stressful). Section 2C asked teachers to rate 24 impacts of this student on a five-point scale, ranging from 0 (totally disagree) to 4 (totally agree). The last part of section 2 asked for the personal information of this particularly challenging student including his/her gender, age, having one or both parents, and the situation in the class which this student was in. The third section of the questionnaire contained 13 statements on the beliefs of the teachers in dealing with students' problem behaviors. They belonged to three constructs, namely self-efficacy, negative affect, and self-critical attitude. Respondents were asked to comment on a seven-point Likert scale how much they agreed to the statements (1 = absolutely not true; 7 = absolutely true). Section 4 asked teachers to rate their satisfaction on a five-point scale (1 = I am very displeased about this aspect; 5 = I am very pleased about this aspect) against aspects of their school (school characteristics)—that is, their co-workers, the management, the students' behavior in general, the parents, and their daily routine. In section 5, teachers were asked to rate 12 statements that described their health on a four-point scale (1 = most healthy state; 4 = least healthy state).

In analyzing the Hong Kong data, the six categories of challenging behavior of students were supported by reasonably high Cronbach's alphas, which ranged from 0.64 to 0.88 for perceived incidences of various challenging behaviors and 0.80 to 0.90 for associated level of teacher stress. The six areas of impact of challenging students on teachers were also supported by reasonably high Cronbach's alphas ranging from 0.69 to 0.86. The scales of the self-reported beliefs of teachers, including self-efficacy, negative affect, and self-critical attitude, and the general health of teachers were also supported by acceptable to high Cronbach's alphas ranging from 0.64 to 0.92. Eight other constructs were used to measure the degree of satisfaction of teachers with various aspects of the school they were working in. They again gave rather high Cronbach's alphas, ranging from 0.72 to 0.94, showing good internal consistency among the items within each scale.

Data Analysis

SPSS Release 12.0 was used for data cleaning and analysis. All teacher perceptions were initially examined with descriptive statistics. For the convenience of comparison, aggregated measures of all incidences of challenging behavior and associated stresses were also estimated by averaging the 23 individual measures. It is of special interest in this study to investigate the relationships between teacher perceptions of incidence, stress, impact, and their self-reported beliefs. The statistical techniques of bivariate correlation, one-way ANOVA, and canonical correlation were used. The various perceptions of teachers were compared by local school types, teacher groups, and countries. If there were more than two groups, post-hoc analysis was further carried out to examine if there were significant differences between any two individual groups.

RESULTS

What types of students and behavior problems did the teachers report as the most stressful? It was found that the vast majority (i.e., 88%) of the challenging students that teachers identified were male. The average age of these students was 9.28 years. They were distributed across all grades, with a slightly lower portion studying in lower grades. About one third of the challenging students (i.e., 35%) were diagnosed by a child psychiatrist or psychologist as having ADHD, autism, or other behavioral problems. Most of the challenging students nominated by teachers (i.e., 80%) came from a two-parent family.

Next, we examined whether the perceived incidence or stress level associated with particular problem behaviors differed depending upon the kind of school in which the teacher worked. Results showed that teachers in government schools and subsidized schools reported higher aggregated incidences of challenging behavior ($M = 2.40$ and 2.33, respectively) and higher aggregated teacher stress ($M = 2.13$ and 2.01, respectively) than their counterparts in private schools and international schools. They also suffered from greater impact of the challenging students in the areas of disruption of teaching ($M = 2.14$ and 2.11), frustration working with parents ($M = 1.82$ and 1.82), and loss of job satisfaction ($M = 2.27$ and 2.17) than their counterparts in private and international schools. Teachers from international schools reported least negative impact of the challenging students in all areas. They also scored significantly higher in self-efficacy ($M = 5.40$), lower in negative affect ($M = 0.98$), self-critical attitude ($M = 1.34$), and better general health ($M = 2.03$), when compared to teachers in other types of schools.

Between male and female teachers, there were no significant differences in their perceptions of aggregated incidence of challenging behavior, aggregated stress, and various impacts of the challenging student. There were also no significant differences between them in self-efficacy, negative affect, and general health. However, female teachers scored slightly higher in self-critical attitude ($M = 3.27$, $SD = 1.34$) than male teachers ($M = 3.02$, $SD = 1.22$) ($p < 0.05$).

The perceptions of the more experienced teachers (top 25%) did not vary from those of the less experienced ones (bottom 25%) in terms of aggregated incidence and aggregated stress. However, the former group perceived less self-doubt ($M = 1.52$, $SD = 0.83$) than the latter ($M = 1.74$, $SD = 0.87$) ($p < 0.001$). They also reported higher self-efficacy ($M = 4.77$ vs. 4.52), lower negative affect ($M = 3.32$ vs. 3.69) and lower self-critical attitude ($M = 2.92$ vs. 3.46) than those with less experience ($p < 0.001$). In addition, higher incidence and higher stress were reported by teachers who taught classes with higher proportion of boys ($r = 0.093$, $p < 0.01$; $r = 0.079$, $p < 0.05$). Slightly higher stress was also reported by teachers who taught larger number of classes ($r = 0.059$, $p < 0.05$).

Comparison of the Teacher Perceptions in Hong Kong and Other Countries

One of the main concerns in this study is how Hong Kong teachers differed from their counterparts in the other six countries in their perceptions of the incidence of student challenging behavior, the associated teacher stress, and the impacts of challenging students (see Table 16.1).

It can be seen that the most frequently occurred challenging behavior reported by Hong Kong teachers was full of activity/easily distractible ($M = 2.85$), followed by needs a lot of attention/weak student ($M = 2.36$). Highest level of stress was associated with full of activity/easily distractible behavior ($M = 2.25$), followed by aggressive/hostile behavior ($M = 2.13$). The associated stress of teachers was found to be highly correlated with the incidence of corresponding challenging behavior. The correlation coefficient ranged from $r = 0.69$ to $r = 0.83$, as shown in Table 16.1. Hong Kong teachers ranked second highest in the aggregated incidence of challenging behavior ($M = 2.27$) and third highest in the aggregated teacher stress ($M = 1.95$). A comparison of the perceived impacts of the challenging students on teachers is shown in Table 16.2.

TABLE 16.1 International Comparison of Incidences of Challenging Behaviors and Associated Teacher Stresses

Student challenging behaviors	Perceived Incidence (i)		Perceived Stress (s)		Correlation between Incidence and Stress (Hong Kong), r
	Hong Kong Mean (SD)	Other Countries Range of Mean (SD)	Hong Kong Mean (SD)	Other Countries Range of Mean (SD)	
Against the grain	2.22 (0.89)	1.84 (1.07)–2.48 (1.04)	2.03 (1.00)	1.52 (1.09)–2.50 (1.13)	0.79***
Full of activity/easily distractible	2.85 (0.96)	2.53 (1.10)–3.14 (0.97)	2.25 (0.99)	1.54 (0.89)–2.84 (1.07)	0.70***
Needs a lot of attention/weak student	2.36 (0.88)	1.80 (1.15)–2.83 (1.02)	1.90 (0.93)	1.07 (0.96)–2.44 (1.11)	0.71***
Easily upset	2.28 (0.89)	1.79 (0.94)–2.38 (0.97)	2.02 (0.95)	1.31 (0.81)–2.04 (1.20)	0.78***
Failure syndrome/excessively perfectionistic	1.50 (0.89)	1.18 (1.00)–2.08 (1.04)	1.21 (0.92)	0.65 (0.78)–1.94 (1.12)	0.69***
Aggressive/hostile	2.15 (1.16)	1.44 (1.22)–2.47 (1.18)	2.13 (1.20)	1.31 (1.12)–2.47 (1.24)	0.83***
Aggregated	2.27 (0.70)	1.94 (0.73)–2.55 (0.70)	1.95 (0.82)	1.34 (0.72)–2.37 (0.88)	0.77***

*** $p < 0.001$

TABLE 16.2   A Comparison of the Impacts of Challenging Students

Area of Impact	Hong Kong Mean (SD)	Other Countries Range of Mean (SD)
Disruption of teaching	2.03 (0.96)	1.26 (0.97)–2.26 (1.02)
Frustration working with parents	1.71 (0.97)	0.97 (1.02)–1.75 (1.17)
Loss of job satisfaction	2.07 (1.06)	0.84 (0.97)–2.02 (1.25)
Self-doubt	1.62 (0.85)	1.08 (0.81)–1.63 (1.17)
Social distance from student	1.66 (0.91)	0.80 (0.90)–1.52 (1.17)
Motivates and inspires teacher	2.45 (0.60)	2.32 (0.70)–2.64 (0.84)

Hong Kong teachers reported that they received very high or the highest negative impact from the challenging student in all five areas, when compared to their counterparts in other countries. However, comparable impact was found with the positive impact of Motivates and Inspires Teachers for teachers in Hong Kong.

Teachers' Beliefs and General Health

The self-reported beliefs/general health of teachers in working with challenging students are shown in Table 16.3. Among teachers of all the surveyed countries, Hong Kong teachers reported highest self-critical attitude ($M = 3.22$), very high negative affect ($M = 3.54$) and very low self-efficacy ($M = 4.64$). They also reported the highest score for general health ($M = 2.27$), suggesting they had the worst self-perceived general health.

Further, it can be seen that the aggregated incidence of challenging behavior and aggregated teacher stress were significantly correlated with the three teacher beliefs in working with challenging students and perceived general health at a level of $p < 0.001$, with *Pearson r* ranging from –0.186 to 0.430 (see Table 16.4). While negative affect and self-critical attitude were positively correlated with perceived aggregated incidence and aggregated

TABLE 16.3   A Comparison of Teacher Beliefs and General Health

Teacher Beliefs/General Health	Hong Kong Mean (SD)	Other Countries Range of Mean (SD)
Self-efficacy	4.64 (0.90)	4.70 (1.03)–5.42 (0.96)
Negative affect	3.54 (1.17)	3.01 (1.20)–3.65 (1.62)
Self-critical attitude	3.22 (1.33)	2.31 (1.34)–3.03 (1.73)
General health	2.27 (0.54)	1.75 (0.43)–2.09 (0.57)

TABLE 16.4 Correlations between Aggregated Incidence/Stress and Teacher Beliefs, their General Health & School Characteristics

Teacher Beliefs, General Health and School Characteristics	Aggregated Incidence	Aggregated Stress
Teacher Beliefs		
Self-efficacy	–0.186***	–0.343***
Negative affect	0.331***	0.430***
Self-critical attitude	0.285***	0.418***
General Health	0.246***	0.358***
School Characteristics		
Support of Colleagues	–0.063*	–0.070**
Co-workers	–0.037	–0.076**
Management	–0.040	–0.077**
Student-Peer Relationship	–0.160***	–0.214***
Student Behavioral Values	–0.153***	–0.163***
Student Responsibility & Discipline	–0.190***	–0.191***
Parent & Community	–0.114***	–0.123***
Perception of Autonomy	–0.069*	–0.075*

*** $p < 0.001$; ** $p < 0.01$; * $p < 0.05$

stress, self-efficacy was negatively correlated with these variables. Yet the corresponding correlations between perceived school characteristics and aggregated incidence and aggregated stress were much weaker, with *Pearson r* ranging from –0.037 to –0.214.

Canonical Correlation between Various Sets of Teacher Perceptions

Several multivariate canonical correlation analyses were carried out to explore the relationship between various sets of variables (variate) for the Hong Kong teacher responses. Through employing this technique the analysis attempted to examine the degree to which one set of variables was accounted for by the other set of variables.

Incidence of Challenging Behavior Versus Teacher Stress

To begin this phase of the analysis, a correlation coefficient of .657 was computed between the aggregated teacher stress and the aggregated incidence. A canonical correlation analysis was then run between the set of incidences of student challenging behaviors and the set of associated teacher stress. A total of six significant canonical correlations were yielded with p values less than 0.001. Only the first function gave a significant share of variance between the two set of variables (canonical R (R_c) = 0.847, *Wilk's* λ = 0.007, $p < .001$). The high canonical R (0.847) suggested that teacher stress and incidence of challenging behaviors were strongly correlated with each other. The other five functions did not have a significant share of variance between the variates and their redundancies ranged from 4.1% to 7.3%.

The pattern of loadings for the first function is shown in Table 16.5. The incidences of against the grain and aggressive/hostile had high loadings on the incidence variate (i.e., 0.777 and 0.931), showing that these incidences were more strongly related to the teacher stress variate. The incidence of need a lot of attention/weak student had the lowest loading on the Incidence variate (−0.149), showing that it was very weakly linked to the teacher stress variate. Redundancy analysis showed that the Incidence Variate as a whole accounted for 29.3% of the variance of teacher stress variate.

Teacher Stress Versus Impact

Another canonical correlation was performed on the set of teacher stresses and the set of impacts of challenging behavior on teachers. It yield-

TABLE 16.5   Canonical Structure of the Variates of Behavior Incidence and Teacher Stress

Variates and Variables	Loadings	
Incidence Variate		
Against the Grain	−0.777	
Full of Activity/Easily Distractible	−0.668	
Need a lot of Attention/Weak Student	−0.149	
Easily Upset	−0.648	
Failure Syndrome/Excessively Perfectionistic	−0.255	
Aggressive/Hostile	−0.931	
% of Variance		0.404
Redundancy		0.290
Teacher Stress Variate		
Against the Grain	−0.731	
Full of Activity/Easily Distractible	−0.664	
Need a lot of Attention/Weak Student	−0.256	
Easily Upset	−0.679	
Failure Syndrome/Excessively Perfectionistic	−0.272	
Aggressive/Hostile	−0.936	
% of Variance		0.409
Redundancy		0.293
Canonical R		0.847

TABLE 16.6 Canonical Structure of the Variates of Teacher Stress and Impact on Teachers

Variates and Variables	Loadings	
Teacher Stress Variate		
Against the Grain	–0.935	
Full of Activity/Easily Distractible	–0.876	
Need a lot of Attention/Weak Student	–0.725	
Easily Upset	–0.787	
Failure Syndrome/Excessively Perfectionistic	–0.568	
Aggressive/Hostile	–0.831	
% of Variance		0.633
Redundancy		0.336
Impact Variate		
Disruption of teaching	–0.937	
Frustration working with parents	–0.583	
Loss of satisfaction from teaching	–0.862	
Self-doubt	–0.657	
Social distance between teacher & student	–0.807	
Student inspires and motivates teacher	–0.079	
% of Variance		0.508
Redundancy		0.269
Canonical R		0.728

ed two significant canonical correlations with canonical R = 0.728 (*Wilk's* λ = 0.397, $p < 0.001$) and 0.319 (*Wilk's* λ = 0.845, $p < 0.001$). Since the second function showed that only 10.2% (0.319^2) of the variance was shared between the two sets of variables, only the first function was analyzed (see Table 16.6). Results suggested that the impact on teachers was strongly related to teacher stress associated with challenging behaviors ($R_c = 0.728$). Redundancy analysis showed that 26.9% of the variance of the impact variate was accounted for by the teacher stress variate.

Within the Impact variate, relatively high loadings were found with the variables of disruption of teaching process (–0.937), loss of satisfaction from teaching (–0.862) and social distance between teacher and student (–0.807). The loading of student inspires and motivates teacher, however, was very small and insignificant. Within the teacher stress variate, all associated teacher stresses had moderate to high loadings on the variate, with the highest loading from against the grain (–0.935) and the lowest one from failure syndrome/excessively perfectionistic (–0.568).

Teacher Belief Versus Behavioral Incidence/Teacher Stress

The relationships between the set of teacher beliefs and (1) the set of incidence of challenging behaviors; and (2) the set of associated teacher stress were explored respectively. The first analysis yielded one significant canonical correlation of $R_c = 0.384$ (*Wilk's* $\lambda = 0.827$, $p < 0.001$), representing 14.7% overlapping variance for this pair of canonical variates. In the second analysis, one significant canonical correlation was also obtained, with $R_c = 0.506$ (*Wilk's* $\lambda = 0.720$, $p < 0.001$), representing 25.6% of variance shared across the two variates. The R_c values indicated that teacher beliefs correlated more strongly with teacher stress (0.506) than with incidence of challenging behaviors (0.384). The details of the two analyses are shown in Table 16.7.

In explaining the teacher belief variate, negative affect (loading = 0.907), played a slightly more important role than self-critical attitude (loading = 0.815) and self-efficacy (loading = –0.710) did. In the teacher stress variate, all the individual teacher stresses had high loadings with the highest loading from against the grain (0.937) and the lowest loading from failure syndrome/excessively perfectionistic (0.642). Redundancy analysis revealed that teacher belief variate explained 16.2% of the variance of teacher

TABLE 16.7 Canonical Structures of the Variates of Teacher Belief with Behavior Incidence and Teacher Stress

	First Analysis		Second Analysis	
	Belief vs. Incidence		Belief vs. Stress	
Variates and Variables	Loadings		Loadings	
Belief Variate				
Self-efficacy	–0.605		–0.710	
Negative affect	0.966		0.907	
Self-critical attitude	0.773		0.815	
% of Variance		0.632		0.664
Redundancy		0.093		0.170
Teacher Stress/Behavior Incidence Variate				
Against the grain	0.961		0.937	
Full of activity/easily distractible	0.608		0.872	
Need a lot of attention/weak student	0.515		0.754	
Easily upset	0.645		0.821	
Failure syndrome/excessively perfectionistic	0.602		0.642	
Aggressive/Hostile	0.759		0.712	
% of Variance		0.485		0.633
Redundancy		0.071		0.162
Canonical R		0.384		0.506

stress variate, while teacher stress variate explained 17.0% of the variance of teacher belief variate. To a lesser extent, teacher belief variate explained 7.1% of the variance of incidence variate, and incidence variate explained 9.3% of the variance of teacher belief variate.

Teacher Belief Versus Impact

The relationship between the set of teacher beliefs and the set of impacts on teachers was also looked into. All of the three canonical correlations obtained were significant, with $R_c = 0.629$ (*Wilk's* $\lambda = 0.509$, $p < 0.001$), 0.366 (*Wilk's* $\lambda = 0.841$, $p < 0.001$) and 0.168 (*Wilk's* $\lambda = 0.972$, $p < 0.001$) respectively. Only the first function was analyzed, since in the other two functions, the two sets of variables did not share a substantial amount of variance, that is, $0.366^2 = 13.3\%$ and $0.168^2 = 2.8\%$. The pattern of loadings of the two variates for the first function is shown in Table 16.8.

Results showed that self-efficacy, negative affect, and self-critical attitude had high and comparable loadings on the teacher belief variate, (0.806–0.824), showing that all these beliefs were to a great extent explained by this variate. For the impact variate, very high loadings (0.765–0.904) were found for self-doubt, social distance between teacher and student, loss of satisfaction from teaching, and disruption of teaching, and a moderate loading was found with the frustration in working with parents (0.553). Re-

TABLE 16.8 Canonical Structure of the Variates of Teacher Belief and Impact on Teachers

Variates and Variables	Loadings	
Teacher Belief Variate		
Self-efficacy	−0.806	
Negative affect	0.812	
Self-critical attitude	0.824	
% of Variance		0.663
Redundancy		0.262
Impact Variate		
Disruption of teaching	0.763	
Frustration working with parents	0.553	
Loss of satisfaction from teaching	0.781	
Self-doubt	0.904	
Social distance between teacher and student	0.884	
Student inspires and motivates teacher	−0.248	
% of Variance		0.527
Redundancy		0.208
Canonical R		0.629

dundancy analysis showed that teacher belief variate explained 20.8% of the variance of impact variate, while the impact variate explained 26.2% of the variance of teacher belief variate. In addition, a very weak relationship, yet in the other direction, existed between the variable of student inspires and motivate teacher and the teacher belief variate (–0.248).

School Characteristics Versus Behavioral Incidence/Teacher Stress/Impact

Canonical correlations were performed on school characteristics with the variates of (1) incidence of challenging behavior, (2) teacher stress, and (3) impact on teachers. Results indicated that they had only very weak correlations with each other. The corresponding canonical correlations were $R_c = 0.236$ for behavior incidence, $R_c = 0.249$ for teacher stress and $R_c = 0.338$ for impact on teachers. School characteristics were found to rarely explain the three teacher perceptions, as shown by the corresponding redundancies (i.e., 2.2%, 3.0% and 5.4%).

DISCUSSION

In this study we aimed to find out the incidences of various challenging student behaviors in the classrooms of Hong Kong primary schools and the associated teacher stresses. We also examined to what extent the kinds of stresses and impact on teachers were related to incidences of challenging behavior, teacher and school characteristics, and teacher beliefs in working with students with challenging behavior. We also compared the Hong Kong data with data obtained from six other countries.

Occurrence and Effects of Various Challenging Behaviors of Students

Full of activity/easily distractible ($M = 2.85$) was reported to be the most common challenging behavior and failure syndrome/perfectionistic ($M = 1.50$) the least common behavior of challenging students in Hong Kong classrooms. This set of most common and least common challenging behaviors was the same as in a study conducted in the Netherlands (Everaert & van der Wolf, 2005).

It appears that the individual challenging behaviors did not evoke stress to the same extent. For example, aggressive/hostile behavior, though relatively unpopular ($M = 2.15$), tended to exert a relatively high level of stress on teachers ($M = 2.13$), when compared with other challenging behaviors. The canonical correlation also showed that the incidence of aggressive/hostile behavior gave the greatest loading on incidence variate (–0.936) (see Table 16.5), suggesting that it was the most important behavior, among the six challenging behaviors, in explaining teacher stress. Needs a lot of attention/weak student was the second most common behavior ($M = 2.36$), yet it exerted relatively small stress on teachers ($M = 1.90$). The canonical correlation showed that the incidence of this behavior gave the smallest loading on the incidence variate (–0.256), suggesting that it was the least important behavior in accounting for teacher stress among various incidences of challenging behavior. The relative importance of the behavioral incidences of aggressive/hostile (–0.931) and against the grain (–0.777) in explaining teacher stress variate suggested that to reduce teacher stress, priority should be given to equipping teachers with the skills in handling students with these challenging behaviors.

Role of Teacher Belief in Working with Challenging Students

The three teacher beliefs in working with challenging students, namely self-efficacy, negative affect, and self-critical attitude were found to correlate moderately with both the aggregated teacher stress and various negative impacts on teachers (see Tables 16.7 and 16.8). The canonical correlation showed that 16.2% of the variance of teacher stress and 20.8% of the impacts on teachers can be explained by these teacher beliefs. Yet only 7.1% of the variance of behavior incidence can be explained by the teacher beliefs. This pattern suggested that teacher beliefs may be more relevant as a resource in managing/coping with stress, rather than a tool in screening challenging behaviors, that is, interpreting whether a behavior is a challenging one or not. Teacher beliefs may also be seen as moderating the effects of challenging student behaviors. Teachers with more negative beliefs seemed to be more susceptible, vulnerable, or *responsive* to challenging behaviors of students, and their stress may easily be evoked. Greene, Abidin, and Kmetz (1997) argued that "an individual's response to an event is a function of his or her affective and perceptual appraisal of the event and not merely the frequency of the event" (p. 241). It is likely that teachers with different strengths of belief may assign different meanings to a challenging behavior. Those with low self-efficacy, high negative affect, and high self-critical attitude may be more likely to interpret the challenging behavior as threatening. Using terms from Albert Ellis's rational emotive therapy (Ellis & Becker, 1982), challenging behaviors could be seen as the activating event (A), while teacher stress or impacts on teachers may be regarded as the emotional consequence (C), and self-efficacy, negative affect, and self-critical attitude can be seen as the belief system (B), which tell teachers about what was happening.

The direction of effects between teacher beliefs and teacher stress or impact on teachers can also be interpreted in the opposite direction; that is, an increased exposure to the stress associated with challenging behavior and an increased experience of negative impacts may result in an increase in negative thoughts among teachers. For example, the impact of disruption of teaching may lower the self-efficacy and increase the self-critical attitude and negative affect of teachers. Yoon (2002) argued that there exists a cyclic relationship between teacher belief and teacher stress/impacts on teachers. Teacher stress may increase the inappropriate display of negative affect, which may become a general tone in teachers' interactions with students and would more likely be perceived as adversarial by students. This experience of a negative teacher–student relationship may exacerbate teachers' stress level.

Factors Connected to Teacher Stress and Impacts on Teachers

It was found that teacher stress associated with students' challenging behaviors was highly correlated with teachers' perceived incidence of challenging behavior (see Table 16.5). This finding was consistent with a study by Boyle, Borg, Falzon, and Baglioni (1995) in which student misbehavior was found to be one of the two main factors that accounted for most of the variance in predicting teacher stress.

To a lesser extent, aggregated teacher stress was correlated with teachers' self-efficacy ($r = -0.186$), negative affect ($r = 0.331$), and self-critical attitude ($r = 0.285$). To an even lesser degree, aggregated teacher stress was correlated with the eight perceived school characteristics ($r = -0.070$ to -0.214) (see Table 16.4). Among the school characteristics, the student factors (i.e., student-peer relationships, student behavioral values, and student responsibility and discipline) were found to be slightly more important in predicting aggregated teacher stress than other school factors. The importance of student characteristics in predicting teacher stress was also noted in a study by Everaert and van der Wolf (2005).

The canonical correlation analyses also showed that the incidence of challenging behavior (redundancy = 0.293) was most important in explaining teacher stress, followed by teacher beliefs (redundancy = 0.162) and school characteristics (redundancy = 0.030). In explaining the impact on teachers, teacher beliefs accounted for 20.8% of the variance of impacts on teachers, while school characteristics only accounted for 5.4% of the variance of impacts on teachers. The above comparison suggested that teacher beliefs were more strongly associated with teacher stress and impacts on teachers than school characteristics were. Whether following the interpretation of the cyclic relationship between challenging behaviors and teacher beliefs (Yoon, 2002) or seeing teacher beliefs as moderating the effects of challenging behavior on teacher stress and impacts (Ellis & Becker, 1982), it suggested the crucial role of teacher beliefs in working with challenging students and the importance to strengthen these beliefs, which include self-efficacy, negative affect, and self-critical attitude.

In this study, male and female teachers did not differ in their perceived incidence and stress, contrary to earlier reports that female teachers found more challenging behavior and stress (Forlin, 2001; Everaert & van der Wolf, 2005).

Teacher Stress in Working with Challenging Students— Hong Kong and Beyond

The aggregated incidence of challenging behavior perceived by Hong Kong teachers ranked second highest ($M = 2.27$), the aggregated teacher stress ranked third highest ($M = 1.95$), and the impacts of the challenging students on teachers ranked highest on average among the seven countries in this study.

Yet the students in Hong Kong did not seem to be more challenging or difficult when compared to those in other countries. Hong Kong teachers reported that they spent 14% of their class time in maintaining classroom order, while teachers in other countries spent as much as 35% of their class time dealing with challenging student behavior. Hong Kong teachers estimated an average of 3.0 students with challenging behavior per class, and this figure was just comparable to those in other countries (i.e., 1.8 to 5.5 per class).

It is argued that the very negative beliefs of Hong Kong teachers may have made them more vulnerable to the student with challenging behaviors. Further, the fact that these teachers have to teach the largest number of students may have depleted their time and energy in attending to the challenging students. It was found in this study that Hong Kong teachers taught on average 5.3 classes in school, while their counterparts in other countries only manage 1.4–4.5 classes. In addition, the class size of Hong Kong primary schools was 32, while it was only 17.7 to 31.7 for the schools of other countries. These figures may explain why Hong Kong teachers spend the least time with the challenging student (i.e., 7.8 hours per week) compared to 13.1 to 24.7 hours per week for teachers from other countries. They may also account for the longest "relationship distance" of Hong Kong teachers from the challenging student (5.2 units), when compared to that of other countries (i.e., 3.9 to 5.1 units). As argued by Yoon (2002), the teacher–student relationship might be a factor contributing to teacher stress and negative impacts on teachers.

It was also speculated that the overall workload of teachers and the high expectations of various stakeholders on teachers have imposed further stress on teachers (Chan, 2006) and thus further depleted the mental and physical energy of teachers in coping with challenging students. While there were no data available to compare the workload of teachers across countries, an earlier study of Stevenson (1992) reported that Chinese parents had high expectation towards their children's education and were generally less satisfied with their children's schoolwork when compared to American parents.

That Hong Kong teachers were more vulnerable to challenging students may not have anything to do with their teaching experience. One-way ANOVA results suggested that the more experienced Hong Kong teachers (top 25%) did not differ from the less experienced ones (bottom 25%) in both aggregated stress and individual impacts except for self-doubt.

CONCLUSION

The high teacher stress, the very negative impacts of challenging students on teachers, and the very negative beliefs of Hong Kong teachers suggested that the conditions of these teachers leave much to be desired. Measures to improve teacher stress and beliefs may be introduced at the personal, school, and government levels. An implication for practice may consist of putting time and effort into increasing teachers' mental and physical stability. At the individual teacher level, diagnosis of teacher needs may be carried out by applying the instruments used in this study. Teacher beliefs may be enhanced via counseling and training by using, for example, cognitive behavioral therapy. Teachers would need to be equipped with the skills of working with challenging students, especially for the types of aggressive and antagonistic behaviors. Previously, Hastings and Bham (2003) suggested that methods for boosting teachers' self-efficacy might have beneficial effects in reducing the negative impact of student behavior on teachers. At the school level, there is a need to review the staff establishment and the teaching arrangement in school, such as class size and number of class taught by each teacher. Measures that help to improve student behavior and the relationships between teachers and students should be welcomed. At the government level, there is a need to review the implementation of education reforms, especially inclusive education. A recent development has been that the government has taken steps to reduce the class size in primary schools. These measures may be able to increase the job security of teachers and lower the pressure on teachers in the classroom.

To conclude the study, it needs to be pointed out that the stress of teachers does not only say something about their working conditions, but also about the learning environment of students. Teacher stress should not only be understood as a side effect of school reform, it should be seen as detrimental to the well-being of individuals in the education community, including teachers, students, and parents.

REFERENCES

Boyle, G. J., Borg, M. G., Falzon, J. M., & Baglioni, A. J. (Jr.) (1995). A structural model of the dimensions of teacher stress. *British Journal of Educational Psychology, 65*, 49–67.

Brown, J., Davis, S., & Johnson, E. (2002). *Teachers on teaching: A survey of the teaching profession*. London, UK: Market & Opinion Research International.

Caritas Hong Kong Youth and Community Office. (2010). *A survey report of the inclusive education in Hong Kong secondary schools*. Unpublished report. Hong Kong: Caritas. [In Chinese]

Chan, M. C. (2006). *A research study on Hong Kong teachers' stress: A preliminary analysis*. Hong Kong: Hong Kong Primary Education Research Association and Education Convergence. [In Chinese]

Cheng, Y. C. (2007). The future of Hong Kong education: Reform and instruction. Retrieved from http://www.ied.edu.hk/cric/new/doc/articles/4-8jul02.pdf [In Chinese]

City University of Hong Kong & Professional Teacher Union. (2006). 90% of teachers face 'much higher' pressure than five years ago. Retrieved from http://www.hkptu.org.hk/ptu/director/pubdep/ptunews/497/edu-talk.htm [In Chinese]

Democratic Alliance for Betterment of Hong Kong (DAB). (2002). *Hong Kong teacher stress survey*. Retrieved from http://www.dab.org.hk/UserFiles/Image/News%20centre/News/doc/2002/20021006poll.pdf [In Chinese]

Disability Discrimination Ordinance. (1997). Chapter 487. Retrieved from http://www.legislation.gov.hk/eng/home.htm

DAB & Hong Kong Federation of Education Workers. (2006). A survey on alleviating teacher workload and stress. Retrieved from http://www.dab.org.hk/UserFiles/Image/News%20centre/News/doc/2006/20060110poll.pdf [In Chinese]

Education Bureau (EDB). (2008). *Circular No. 9/2008—Learning Support Grant for Secondary Schools*. Retrieved from http://www.edb.gov.hk/FileManager/EN/Content_7434/edbc08009e.pdf

Education & Manpower Bureau. (2006). *Final report of the Committee on Teachers' Work*. Retrieved from http://www.legco.gov.hk/yr06-07/english/panels/ed/papers/ed0212cb2-1041-6-e.pdf

Ellis, A. & Becker, I. (1982). *A guide to personal happiness*. North Hollywood, CA: Wilshire Books.

Equal Opportunities Commission. (2001). *Disability Discrimination Ordinance: Code of Practice on Education*. Retrieved from http://www.eoc.org.hk/eoc/otherproject/eng/color/youthcorner/education/cop_edu/cop_edu_b.htm#_Toc514474796

Everaert, H. A. & van der Wolf, J. C. (2005). *Behaviorally challenging students and teacher stress.* Retrieved from http://www.educatie.onderzoek.hu.nl/~/media/sharepoint/Lectoraat%20Gedrag%20en%20Onderzoek%20in%20de%20Educatieve%20Praxis/2005/KG01_huisstijl.ashx

Forlin, C. (2001). Inclusion: Identifying potential stressors for regular class teachers. *Educational Research, 43*(3), 235–245.

Golembiewski, R. T., Munzenrider, R. F., & Carter, D. (1983). Phases of progressive burnout and their worksite covariants. *Journal of Applied Behavioral Science, 19,* 461–481.

Greene, R. W., Abidin, R. R., & Kmetz, C. (1997). The index of teaching stress: A measure of student-teacher compatibility. *Journal of School Psychology, (35)*3, 239–259.

Hastings R. P., & Bham, M. S. (2003). The relationship between student behaviour patterns and teacher burnout. *School Psychology International, 24*(1), 115–127.

Hong Kong Institute of Human Resource Management. (2004). Hong Kong employees tend to work longer hours. Retrieved from http://www.hkihrm.org/ihrm_eng/ih_pre_01.asp?id = 41

Hong Kong Mood Disorders Center. (2004). *Teacher stress and mood disorders survey (29/6/2004).* Retrieved from http://www.hmdc.med.cuhk.edu.hk/report/report19.html [In Chinese]

Jarvis, M. (2002). Teacher stress: A critical review of recent findings and suggestions for future research directions. *Stress News, 14*(1). Retrieved from http://www.isma.org.uk/stressnw/teachstress1.htm

Kyriacou, C. (1987). Teacher stress and burnout: An international review. *Educational Research, 29,* 146–152.

Smith, A., Brice, C., Collins, A., Matthews, V., & McNamara, R. (2000). *The scale of occupational stress: A further analysis of the impact of demographic factors and type of job* (Contract Research Report 311/2000). Sudbury, UK: Health and Safety Executive HSE Books.

Stevenson, H. W. (1992). *The learning gap: Why our schools are failing and what we can learn from Japanese and Chinese education.* New York, NY: Touchstone.

The Future of Hong Kong's Population. (2007, January). *Hong Kong Industrialist,* pp. 12–19.

Tsui, K. T., & Tse, C. Y. (2006). *Research report on the implementation of inclusive education in Hong Kong primary schools.* Hong Kong: Hong Kong Primary Education Research Association & Hong Kong Special Schools Council. [In Chinese]

Van der Wolf, K., & Everaert, H. A. (2003). Teacher stress, challenging parents and problem students. In S. Castelli, M. Mendel, & B. Ravn (Eds.), *School, family, and community partnership in a world of differences and changes* (pp. 135–146). Gdansk, Poland: University of Gdansk.

Yoon, J. S. (2002). Teacher characteristics as predictors of teacher-student relationships: Stress, negative affect and self-efficacy. *Social Behavior & Personality: An International Journal, 30*(5), 485–493.

CHAPTER 17

PREDICTORS OF ELEMENTARY TEACHERS' BURNOUT SYMPTOMS

The Role of Teacher's Personal Resources, Perceptions of Classroom Stress, and Disruption of Teaching

Christopher J. McCarthy
University of Texas at Austin

Richard Lambert
University of North Carolina at Charlotte

Megan O'Donnell
Arizona State University

Sara Villarreal and Lauren Melendres
University of Texas at Austin

International Perspectives on Teacher Stress, pages 333–355
Copyright © 2012 by Information Age Publishing
All rights of reproduction in any form reserved.

ABSTRACT

The role of personal coping resources, classroom demands, and disruption of teaching were examined as potential predictors of burnout symptoms in elementary school teachers. Participants included 263 teachers in North Carolina. Structural equation modeling was used to estimate constructs for the predictor variables (coping resources, classroom demands, and disruption of teaching) and to test whether classroom demands and disruptions mediate the relationship between coping resources and burnout symptoms. Support was not found for the mediational model, but a model in which each predictor construct was associated with burnout symptoms did show good fit. The results of this study may help researchers understand the factors that contribute to burnout in elementary school teachers.

While highly respected and valued as a profession, there are numerous factors that conspire against individuals who want to spend their careers as educators in K–12 schools. In the United States and many other countries, teaching is an occupation with low compensation compared to other professionals with similar levels of training (Gilroy, 2005). The typical workday of a teacher can also be extremely demanding—teachers often have very little "down time" at work and can spend much of their day isolated professionally (Goldstein & Noguera, 2006). This is not to say that teachers spend a great deal of time alone, as their days are full of time spent with students who have individual strengths and vulnerabilities and who can present unique challenges to teachers. Teachers must also contend with limited financial support whether they work in private or public schools, and many are forced to tap into their own salaries to pay for classroom supplies. Needless to say, the rise of national accountability standards has also added to the demand levels of teachers as well (Lambert & McCarthy, 2006).

Given such challenges, it is interesting to note Ingersoll's (2001) finding that teacher shortages are due not to a lack persons entering the field, but rather too many teachers leaving the field before retirement. It appears that while the demands of teaching are well known, it does not deter professionals from entering the field. The problem seems to arise later, after teachers have begun work in the profession.

When it comes to teacher stress and attrition, much attention has been paid in the literature to structural characteristics that impact teachers, such as salary, school financing, and accountability standards. However, McCarthy, Lambert, O'Donnell, and Melendres (2009) have argued that teachers' perceptions of their classroom demands and resources are often overlooked as a source of teacher stress. This neglect is particularly important to address given research in the stress and coping literature, in which the dominant models emphasize the critical role of perception (Lazarus & Folkman, 1984) and possession of adequate coping resources (Hobfoll,

1989). Research that addresses only the external demands that teachers face may be missing a critical element in understanding the factors that lead to burnout: teachers' individual perceptions of the resources and demands they contend with in their jobs (McCarthy et al., 2009).

It seems critical for researchers interested in strategies for preventing teachers stress, burnout, and attrition to better understand the role of teacher perceptions of their own unique demands and resources in the educational context. Therefore, in this study, the role of personal coping resources, classroom demands, and disruption of teaching were examined as potential predictors of burnout symptoms in elementary school teachers. Structural equation modeling was used to estimate constructs for the predictor variables (coping resources, classroom demands, and disruption of teaching) and, because of stress literature that will be reviewed next, to test for the possible mediational role of classroom demands and disruption between coping resources and burnout symptoms.

Elementary teachers were the focus of this study because, unlike middle and high school teachers, they work with a relatively intact classroom of students on a daily basis, at least in the United States. This allows for a meaningful analysis of teachers' resources and demands at the classroom level. Middle and high school teachers tend to specialize in a given subject area and have different a classroom of students every hour, making it considerably more difficult to make general conclusions about resources and demands at the classroom level.

In order to set the context for this study, we begin with an overview of public education in the United States. Given that research on stress and coping forms the theoretical basis for this study, a brief review of this literature as it pertains to the predictor variables in this study is presented next. This is followed by a rationale for examining burnout symptoms as the outcome variable for this study.

OVERVIEW OF PUBLIC EDUCATION IN THE UNITED STATES

Public education is available to all children in the United States, and educating children predominately lies in the hands of the state and local communities. Each state's public education system is divided into units called school districts, which can include a city or county. Admission to a public school is usually based on the school district where the child resides. Locally elected school boards oversee the administration of their school district and implement policy. Schools and colleges are established at state and local levels and are responsible for the daily management, funding, and policymaking of their own school. They develop their own curricula and determine requirements for enrollment and graduation. Additionally, schools and colleges can also be established by private organizations of all kinds.

Funding for public schools is heavily concentrated at the local level. This is particularly salient at the elementary and secondary level, where just over 91% of the funds will come from nonfederal sources (MSN Encarta, 2007). Therefore, public school systems in the United States rely on state funds and local property taxes to meet the majority of their school expenses. School districts vary from one district to another in available resources; thus, schools tend to reflect the educational values and financial capabilities of the communities in which they are located. States within the U.S. also vary in terms of the share of local education expenses that are paid by federal, state, and local governments. In North Carolina, the site for this study, the state government pays teacher and administrator salaries, local school systems pay for operational expenses, and local county or municipal governments pay for building construction. The federal government pays only for specific programs that are mostly designed to provide more funding to schools that serve children from low-income families.

There are four basic types of schools in the United States: pre-kindergarten, elementary, middle, and high schools lasting a total of 13 or 14 years of regular schooling. The school day differs, depending on each district, yet many schools run from 7:30 a.m. to 2:30 p.m., with various after-school programs such as sports and music available to the children. In most elementary schools (ages 5–11 years), teachers teach the same group of students for the entire day. In middle (ages 12–14 years) and high schools (ages 15–18 years), students change classes a number of times per day. Class sizes vary according to district, each school, and also by subject. Many elementary schools have class sizes of approximately 20, with middle and high school class sizes often exceeding this size. Because American schools are always looking to improve, a new trend is the implementation of year-round schooling; an alternative to traditional schedules. In districts in several states such as California, Florida, and Arizona, students are scheduled more frequent shorter breaks or "intercessions." Students still receive all major holidays and a summer break. In fact, students are spending the same number of days in class as they would for traditional schedules.

The U.S. Department of Education describes how the *No Child Left Behind* Act, signed in 2002, authorized the federal government to take a larger role in public education (U.S. Department of Education, 2007). The act requires schools to take more accountability for student performance and teacher standards through state testing programs. The aim is to close the gap in student achievement between majority and minority students. Since its implementation, the act has been a controversial one given its punitive nature. Schools in some states receive rewards for showing progress and while others may have their federal funds cut back for failing to demonstrate progress among their students. Each state has responded to these federal guidelines in its own way. Therefore, the exact structural character-istics of state and local accountability programs vary from state to state and by school system. What has remained constant across context is the central-ity of teacher perceptions of accountability programs and their association with teacher stress (Lambert & McCarthy, 2006).

A DEMAND–RESOURCE PERSPECTIVE ON STRESS AND COPING

Stress is widely viewed by the public as synonymous with life demands such as work pressures, family obligations, financial limitations, and everyday hassles (Lambert, McCarthy, O'Donnell, & Melendres, 2007). However, an impressive body of research has accumulated over the past several decades demonstrating that stress is actually the endpoint of a complex process that involves individual perceptions of both demands and resources (Sapolsky, 1998). Lazarus and Folkman (1984) were pioneers in suggesting a trans-actional model of stress, in which it is hypothesized that each of us cogni-tively weighs our perceived resources against our perceived demands when encountering a potentially demanding situation. As long as our resources seem at least roughly equal to the task, demands are viewed as challenges that can be met. However, if we perceive demands to outstrip our resources, leaving us unable to meet a demand, we are more likely to experience a stress reaction, which includes a range of physiological components includ-ing anxious feelings, increased heart rate, and in the long range, impaired physical health.

Hobfoll (1989) proposed a somewhat different perspective on the stress process in his conservation of resources model (COR). Hobfoll suggested stress results not from a subjective evaluation of demands and resources, but rather from the need to maintain and develop resources. In the COR model, therefore, stress results when resources such as social networks, material as-sets, and finances are threatened or lost. While the subjective weighing of demands and resources suggested by Folkman and Lazarus is not as central to Hobfoll's model, it is important to note that both theorists place a heavy emphasis on the role of resources in preventing or mitigating stress. It could be argued that the key to healthy living in both approaches is not necessarily reducing demands, but in developing and maintaining resources.

A central question addressed in this study, therefore, is the relationship of teachers' personal resources and perceived demands with symptoms of occupational burnout. Depending on teachers' available resources and perceived occupational demands, classroom situations could provoke a stressful reaction in one teacher while another teacher could view the same situation as unimportant or even as a welcome event. Such differences result from both perceptions of the nature of one's professional demands and individual differences in the resources one has for coping with such demands (McCarthy et al., 2009).

Three specific constructs were used in the present study as predictors of burnout symptoms. First, classroom-specific demands of elementary school teachers were assessed using the Classroom Appraisal of Resources and Demands (CARD, school age version; Lambert, McCarthy, & Abbott-Shim, 2001). This measure assesses the teachers' perception of the elementary classroom environment and the material resources available to teachers to meet these demands. In previous research using the CARD, Lambert, O'Donnell et al. (2006) found that teachers' perceptions of stress in the classroom were related to their teaching in classrooms with higher numbers of children with problem behaviors.

Teachers' psychological coping resources were also examined as potential predictors of burnout symptoms in this study. The identification of resources useful for preventing stress used in this study was based on a taxonomy suggested by Matheny, Aycock, Pugh, Curlette, and Canella (1986). These authors differentiate types of psychological coping resources based on whether they are most useful for preventing stress or combating stress after it has already occurred. Following Lazarus and Folkman's (1984) transactional framework, combative coping resources are those drawn upon after a threatening event or circumstance has occurred that has the potential to cause harm if not coped with successfully.

Skills associated with combative coping include the ability to self-disclose, lowering emotional arousal through relaxation procedures, and using problem-solving skills (McCarthy et al., 2009). Preventive coping resources allow the individual to recognize and minimize excessive demand levels to ward off the stress response (for a further review, see McCarthy, Lambert, Beard, & Dematatis, 2002). McCarthy et al. (2009) found that teachers' preventive coping resources were significant negative predictors of burnout symptoms.

The prevalence of children with problem behaviors in the classroom has been associated with teacher's perception of occupational stress (Lambert, O'Donnell et al., 2006; Lambert et al., 2007). Problem behavior can be difficult in the classroom because it often requires the teacher to use behavior management strategies that can take time away from teaching other students. Disruptive behavior can stem from being challenged by children who are fundamentally not interested in the material being offered by school (Kloska & Ramasut, 1985). Unmotivated students' behavioral problems are one of the leading causes and sources for stress among teachers. Research further suggests that because teachers can have success with motivated students, when problems occur in the classroom with the unmotivated students, it can lead to an increase in their perceived levels of stress (Kloska & Ramasut, 1985). Apparently, as teachers view it, the work they are achieving with motivated students is undermined by the unmotivated students' vocal disruptions. Other research not only focuses on teacher perceptions of stress but also on teacher capabilities in coping with classroom behavior problems. In a study concentrating on high school students in the Netherlands, researchers found that teachers' perceived competence in coping with disruptive student behavior was negatively associated with having a detached attitude towards students known as depersonalization. Such competence beliefs were also negatively related to teachers' self-evaluation of lack of professional accomplishment (Evers, Tomic, & Brouwers, 2004). Other research suggests that behavior problems can lead to teacher stress because it places accountability on the teacher's abilities to manage classrooms. Disruptive behavior can be attributed to a teachers' inability to establish order or to a lack of professionalism (Verkuyten, 2002).

OCCUPATIONAL BURNOUT

Occupational burnout was used as an outcome variable in this study because it is a natural endpoint of the stress process. It is often defined as a loss of idealism and enthusiasm for work (Matheny, Gfroerer, & Harris, 2000). Maslach and Jackson (1981) have developed the most widely accepted definition of burnout, and Maslach and Schaufeli (1993) developed the Maslach Burnout Inventory (MBI), which was used in over 90% of research on the topic (Hastings, Horne, & Mitchell, 2004; Schaufeli & Enzmann, 1998). The MBI assesses three dimensions of burnout: emotional exhaustion, depersonalization, and personal accomplishment (Maslach, Schaufeli, & Leiter, 2001).

Emotional exhaustion (EE) refers to feelings of exhaustion and an inability to cope with life demands and is perhaps the most central symptom of burnout (Maslach et al., 2001). However, Maslach et al. note that while important, EE alone is insufficient as a criterion for burnout. Two other components of burnout are depersonalization (DP) and decreased personal accomplishment (PA). The former construct refers to the development of callous or cynical attitudes towards others, and the latter refers lowered feelings of competence and personal achievement in the workplace.

The significance of burnout as a threat to teachers' wellbeing is perhaps best reflected in the fact that they represent the largest homogenous group of workers studied in the burnout literature. Nearly one fourth (22%) of all burnout research has been conducted with teachers, according to Schaufeli and Enzmann (1998). This research has revealed some of the contributing factors to occupational burnout. For instance, LeCompte and Dworkin

(1991) noted a lack of control in defining professional roles as a contributor to occupational burnout. Others have identified inconsistent professional roles expectations as major sources of physical and mental exhaustion for educators (Brown & Ralph, 1998; Bullough & Baughman, 1997; Esteve, 2000; Troman & Woods, 2001).

GOALS OF THE CURRENT STUDY

As suggested by McCarthy et al. (2009), one of the reasons that stress and burnout among elementary teachers is still not well understood is that too much emphasis may have been placed on sources of external demands, without a recognition that many of the stressors faced by teachers today involve a strong perceptual component having to do with both perceptions of demands and resources for coping with such demands. Thus, the first research question addressed in this study is whether constructs with adequate measurement properties can be found using structural equation modeling (SEM) for each of these measures—perceived demands, resources, and burnout used. The second research question builds on previous work and asks whether the relationship of teachers' preventive coping resources to burnout is mediated by their perceptions of classroom demands generally and disruptions to teachers' ability to teach in particular. This question was based on suggestions in the stress and coping literature that both resources and demands are predictive of whether events will be perceived as stressors and is illustrated in Figure 17.1. A third research-related question examines the relative predictive strength of preventive coping resources, classroom demands, and disruption of teaching in relation to teachers' burnout symptoms.

As was noted previously, specific classroom demands that are hypothesized to contribute to elementary teachers' burnout symptoms were assessed using the demands scale of the CARD (Lambert et al., 2001), and disruptions

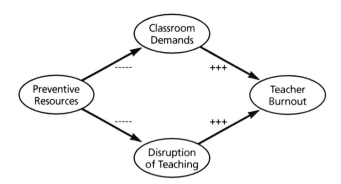

Figure 17.1 Proposed model of teacher burnout.

of teaching were measured using selected scales from the Standard Questionnaire (SQ; Everaert, this volume). Scales from the Preventive Resources Inventory (PRI; McCarthy et al., 2002) were used as a measure of teachers' psychological coping resources. Burnout symptoms were measured by the Maslach Burnout Inventory (MBI; Maslach, Jackson, & Leiter, 1996).

METHOD

Participants

The data for this study were collected from teachers ($N = 521$) working in 16 elementary schools within one county in the southeastern United States. The participating schools are located in both urban and suburban locations and serve a demographically diverse student population. Some schools in the sample serve high concentrations of children living in poverty. The present study is based on a subset of this larger sample (see McCarthy et al., 2009) that participated in the international study on teacher stress that is highlighted in the chapters of this book. For data collection in the United States, we added the CARD, PRI, and MBI instruments to the survey packets for a subset of the teachers, and it is this sample that is used for these analyses. The SQ questionnaire used in the current study comprised the core of common measures across all countries in the first section of this book.

Teachers in this sample ($N = 263$) had an average of 12.97 years of experience in the profession (SD = 9.43). Their experience levels ranged from less than one year to a maximum of 37 years, and 8.2% of the sample was in their first year of teaching. The teachers had worked at their current school for an average of 7.19 years (SD = 7.30). Teachers' years of experience at their current school ranged from less than one year to as high as 34 years, and 19.6% of the sample was in their first year at their current school. The sample included 3.3% males and 96.7% females. The survey participants reported having the following degrees: bachelor's degree (70.1%) and master's degree (29.9%). The average age of the teachers was 38.48 years (SD = 10.96).

Procedures

Data collection took place during the spring of one academic year. The surveys were administered at staff meetings. The participants were given the option of returning the surveys to the researchers during the meeting or to mail them to the university using a business reply envelope that was provided.

This method ensured anonymity and confidentiality. In every participating school, the researchers obtained a 100% or nearly 100% cooperation rate among teachers who attended the staff meetings. In the cases where teachers did not return surveys during the meeting, some business reply envelopes were returned to the researchers with completed surveys. Blank copies of the survey packet along with business reply envelopes were left with the school secretaries to distribute in the mailboxes of those teachers who did not attend the staff meetings. However, the researchers did not obtain exact information about the size of the staff at each school nor the attendance rates at the meetings. Therefore, the exact response rates could not be determined, and this sample can only be considered one of convenience.

Due to concerns related to confidentiality and anonymity, the researchers choose not to ask the participants to report their grade level or ethnicity. Within many elementary schools the combination of ethnicity and grade level can completely identify an individual. The researchers obtained the ethnic composition of the staff from each school, and due to the high cooperation rates, estimated the ethnicity of the participants as follows: European American (90.1%), African American (1.8%), Hispanic (0.5%), and other (7.5%).

Measures

Classroom Appraisal of Resources and Demands (CARD; Lambert et al., 2001)

The CARD assesses teacher stress by examining perceptions of both classroom demands and resources provided by schools to meet these demands. Lambert, McCarthy et al. (2006) developed items based on both a review of the literature concerning stress among teachers of young children and interviews with teachers and administrators.

The measure is divided into demands section and a resources section. The demands scale consists of 35 items that are rated according to the severity of demands associated with different aspects of the classroom environment. Responses are provided using a five-point Likert scale that ranged from 1, "not demanding," to 5, "extremely demanding." The resources section has 30 items and asks respondents to rate the helpfulness of various administrator-provided resources. A five-point Likert scale was used that ranged from 1, "very unhelpful," to 5, "very helpful." McCarthy et al. (2009) found a relatively low degree of correlation between the scales ($r = -.208$), suggesting that both scales are conceptually distinct.

McCarthy et al. (2009) reviewed previous research using the CARD, specifically Lambert et al.'s (2007) use of the elementary version of the CARD that demonstrated sample-specific reliability evidence for the demands scale score information (a = .92, .93 for this sample) and the resources scale score information (a = .95). Lambert et al. also reported factor analysis results that helped define the construct validity of the CARD, and criterion validity was demonstrated by associations in the expected direction between CARD scale scores and the classroom level number of children with problem behaviors and learning disabilities.

These analyses were replicated using the data from the present study and questions from the SQ (P2dq10b, P2dq10g; for more details on this measure see Huub, this volume). Specifically, we created subgroups of teachers for whom resources were equal to demands, demands were greater than resources, and vice versa. There was a statistically significant difference between these groups and teacher reports of the number of boys in the classroom who display challenging behaviors that are similar to the behaviors of the most challenging student ($F_{(2,175)} = 12.10$, $p < .01$). Specifically, the resources greater than demands group reported fewer such boys on average (Mean = 1.85, SD = 1.61) than did the demands equal to resources group (Mean = 2.91, SD = 2.00) or the demands greater than resources group (Mean = 3.23, SD = 1.79). A similar pattern was observed regarding the number of girls in the classroom who display behaviors that are similar to those of the most challenging student ($F_{(2,158)} = 3.89$, $p = .02$). Specifically, the resources greater than demands group reported fewer such girls on average (Mean = .88, SD = 1.06) than did the demands equal to resources group (Mean = 1.27, SD = 1.94) or the demands greater than resources group (Mean = 1.63, SD = 1.75).In another previous study, Lambert, Kusherman, O'Donnell, and McCarthy (2006) reported similar reliability and validity evidence was demonstrated for a preschool version of the CARD. The subscales of the demands section of the CARD were used in this analysis and are listed along with their Cronbach's alpha values from this sample: other student related demands (.85), children with problem behaviors (.93), administrative demands (.89), and availability of instructional materials (.89). For a more complete description of validity evidence for the CARD, see Lambert, McCarthy, O'Donnell, and Wang (2009).

Preventive Resources Inventory
(PRI; McCarthy et al., 2002)

The PRI was used to assess participants' preventive coping resources. The measure contains 83 items and uses a five point Likert-like scale ranging from "strongly disagree" to "strongly agree," with "neutral" as a midpoint score. The items ask respondents about specific personal habits relating to the prevention of stress. The PRI contains a total score scale, used in the current study, which is comprised of al the items from the five scale scores on the PRI that measure the following: *perceived control*, which refers to beliefs that one can cope successfully with life demands; *maintaining perspective*, which assesses attitudes and beliefs that put life events into a context that keeps stress-produced emotions at manageable levels; *social re-sourcefulness*, the ability to draw upon a social network of caring others who can act as a buffer against stress; *self-acceptance*, the degree to which one can accept and overcome personal shortcomings and limitations; and *scanning*, which measures one's perceived ability to recognize, anticipate, and plan for demands and potential stressors. The preventive resources total score from the PRI also includes additional items not on these scales that relate to a generalized sense of one's ability to prevent stress.

Validity evidence for the use of PRI scores has been demonstrated in previous research (McCarthy et al., 2002; Lambert, McCarthy, Gilbert, Sebree, & Steinley-Bumgarner, 2006). McCarthy et al. (2002) found sample-specific evidence for the construct validity of the PRI, and correlations in the expected direction with other existing measures of stress and coping offered evidence of concurrent validity. Lambert, McCarthy et al. (2006) used a confirmatory factor analysis to further support the factor structure and construct validity of the measure and also found statistically significant group differences between respondents with known and varying levels of a variety of psychological complaints and symptoms. Concurrent validity was also demonstrated with correlations in the expected directions between the PRI and measures of psychological stress and personality characteristics.

The scales, along with the Cronbach's alphas from previous research (McCarthy et al., 2002) and this sample respectively, are perceived control (.91/.91), maintaining perspective (.87/.88), social resourcefulness (.87/.84), self-acceptance (.718/.83), and the total preventive resources score (.95/.97).

Standard Questionnaire (SQ)

The SQ was developed (Everaert, this volume) to access teacher perceptions of different types of demanding student behavior and the stress teachers report as associated with these behaviors. The measure focuses on the subjective views of teachers regarding the interaction between students and teachers in the context of normal daily classroom activities. By soliciting perceptions of the most difficult children in an individual teacher's classroom, the measure is designed to assess a specific kind of stressor teachers may experience in their workplace. Each teacher is asked to answer a series of questions about the *incidence* of specific students' behaviors and a series of questions how much *stress* is associated with each of the same behaviors. The measure also includes several scales that solicit teacher ratings regarding the extent to which specific student behaviors *disrupt the teaching process.*

Maslach Burnout Inventory–Educators Survey
(MBI-ES; Maslach et al., 1996)

The MBI–Educators Survey version (hereafter referred to as MBI) was used to assess burnout symptoms in this study. Respondents indicate their level of agreement with various statements about feelings related to their jobs. The only modification of the Educators' Survey version of the MBI is that items refer to "students" instead of "recipients" (Maslach et al.). The MBI consists of 22 items and has three scales: emotional exhaustion (EE, 9 items), depersonalization (DP, 5 items), and professional accomplishment (PA, 8 items). The EE scale measures how much teachers feel emotionally overextended and exhausted by their work; the DP scale measures interactions with students that could be characterized as unfeeling and impersonal; and the PA subscale measures how much the teacher feels a loss of personal effectiveness and goal attainment. Items on the MBI are rated using a 7-point frequency scale ranging from 0 = "never" to 6 = "every day." For both the MBI-EE and MBI-DP scales, higher scores refer to higher levels of experienced burnout. For ease of interpretation for this study, scores on the MBI-PA scale were reverse coded so that higher scores correspond to higher degrees of experienced burnout (i.e., reduced personal accomplishment).

As was noted previously, the MBI is the most often used measure of burnout, and considerable support has been found for its psychometric properties (Maslach et al., 2001). The Maslach Burnout Inventory manual (Maslach et al., 1996) reviews research conducted on the MBI in many countries and the fact that several studies have supported the validity of the three-dimensional structure of the measure.

Maslach, Jackson, and Leiter (1997) reviewed research on the validity and reliability of the MBI-ES used in this study and reported Cronbach's alphas ranging from .88 to .90 for EE, .74 to .76 for DP, and .72 to .76 for PA. These values are similar to findings for the general version of the MBI. The overall Cronbach's alpha for the MBI total scale score with this study was .91, while values of .90, .68, and .75 were found for the EE, DP, and PA subscales, respectively.

Analyses

Structural equation modeling (SEM) was used to test the research questions. A covariance matrix was created for the analysis by estimating each point in the matrix using the available data for the each unique pair of measures. The values in the matrix were based on from 187 teachers to 393 teachers. As outlined earlier, a total of 393 teachers completed the CARD, MBI, and PRI and all points in the covariance matrix based on pairs of scale scores from these measures are based on this sample size. A total of 187 teachers completed all four measures including the SQ. Therefore, all points in the covariance matrix that involved scale scores from the SQ were based on 187 teachers.

As part of the exploratory analyses that were conducted prior to testing the proposed models, the correlations between all of the scale scores from the various measures were examined. The scale scores from the SQ were examined for their correlations both with each other and with the teacher burnout scores from the MBI. There were no substantial relationships between the *incidence* and *stress* subscales and any of the scale scores from the CARD, MBI, or PRI. Almost all of these correlations were between –.10 and .10. Only the SQ scales scores regarding *disruption to the teaching process* were found to be related to reported burnout symptoms and/or to each other in coherent way. Therefore, these scale scores from the SQ were used to form the disruption of teaching latent variable for both the measurement and structural models, reported along with Cronbach's alphas for this sample: The disruption of the teaching process (.88), loss of satisfaction from teaching (.88), and student teacher distance (.75).

SEM was used to estimate latent constructs for each of the predictor variables (coping resources, classroom demands, and disruption of teaching). Measurement models were evaluated for each construct prior to estimation of the structural model. Four scale scores from the PRI were used to estimate the preventive resources construct: self-acceptance, perceived control, maintaining perspective, and social resourcefulness. The four classroom demands scales from the CARD were used to measure the construct of classroom demands: other student related demands, children with problem behaviors, administrative demands, and lack of instructional resources. Finally, the construct of teacher burnout was estimated with the three scales from the MBI: EE, DP, and PA.

For each construct, the scale scores were modeled as the observed scores. In this way the scale scores served as item parcels. The decision was made not to model individual item responses as observed scores, as the items from all of the instruments use Likert scales and as such yield distributions of scores that are coarsely classified and often non-normally distributed. The distributions of scale means for all of the observed variables in the model were distributed approximately normally and included many more values than would the item distributions. Furthermore, previous factor analytic research has demonstrated the unidimensionality of the scale scores for all of the measures. Item parcels have been shown to yield better fit statistics and less bias in estimation of structural parameters than does the use of items as observed variables when the parcels are unidimensional and approximately normally distributed (Bandalos, 2002), conditions that were met in this study.

Following estimation of the measurement model, the model presented in Figure 17.1 was tested in which disruption of teaching and classroom demands were hypothesized to mediate the relationship between Preventive Resources and Burnout. The theoretically expected directionality of each proposed relationship is indicated on the figure by + and – signs. We employed the method for testing mediational models using SEM proposed by Holmbeck (1997). This method involves three steps and requires that a relationship between the antecedent latent variable, in this case preventive resources, and the outcome latent variable, in this case teacher burnout, first be established. Second, the proposed mediators are added to the model. The relationships between the antecedent latent variable and the latent mediators are tested along with the relationships between the mediators and the outcome latent variable without estimating the direct path from antecedent to outcome and all need to be statistically significant and of reasonably interpretable magnitude. Third, a model is tested in which the direct path from the antecedent latent variable to the outcome latent variable is reintroduced in order to determine if it has dropped to zero or been substantially reduced in magnitude given the presence of the mediators.

RESULTS

In the first structural model tested (See Figure 17.2), the direct path from the antecedent variable, preventive resources, to the latent outcome, teacher burnout, was estimated to be $-.46$ ($p < .001$), meeting the first criterion for a mediational model. Second, the path coefficients from preventive resources to the mediators were estimated to be $-.17$ ($p < .05$) for classroom demands and $-.13$ ($p > .05$) for disruption of teaching. These values are small in magnitude and only statistically significant for classroom demands. The path coefficient from classroom demands to teacher burnout was estimated to be .45 ($p < .001$) while the path coefficient from disruption of teaching to teacher burnout was estimated to be .49 ($p < .001$), both moderate in magnitude and statistically significant. Therefore, the second criterion for mediation was only partially met. In the third model, the direct path from preventive resources to teacher burnout was reintroduced into the model, and it was not found to have been substantially reduced ($-.37$, $p < .001$) from the first model ($-.46$, $p < .001$). Therefore the third criterion for mediation was not met. The fit statistics for all three models are reported in Table 17.1, and all indicate good fit.

Although evidence was not found to support the proposed mediational model, moderately strong relationships were found between the latent outcome, teacher burnout, and the mediator and antecedent latent variables. Therefore, a fourth model was tested in which the mediational pathways were dropped and all three variables were tested as directly relating to teacher burnout. This model is reported in Figure 17.3. The coefficients for the pathways to teacher burnout from all three latent variables were found to be in the expected directions, moderately large, and statistically significant ($p < .001$): classroom demands (.37), preventive resources ($-.37$), and

Model I

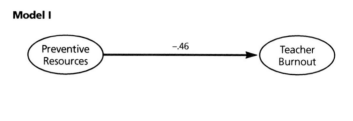

Model II

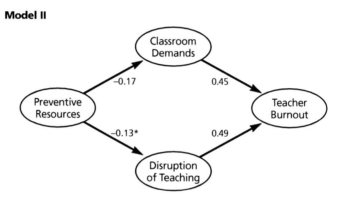

Model III

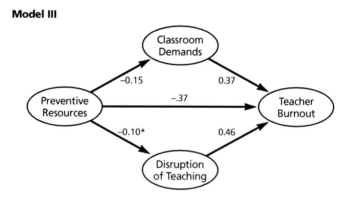

Figure 17.2 Results of testing the proposed meditational models.

disruption of teaching (.47). As can be seen in Table 17.1, the fit statistics remained almost exactly the same for this model as were found for the third model, indicating as expected that the mediational pathways did not contribute to the overall fit of the data to the model.

It should be noted that when the measurement model was tested, two correlated errors emerged as aiding overall fit. Within the preventive resources latent variable, the errors of maintaining perspective and social re-

TABLE 17.1 Model Fit Statistics

Model	χ^2	df	Ratio	GFI	AGFI	NFI	NNFI	CFI	RMSEA	90% LL	90% UL
I	20.22	12	1.69	0.98	0.95	0.99	0.99	0.99	0.05	0.00	0.09
II	205.62	71	2.90	0.90	0.85	0.92	0.93	0.94	0.09	0.07	0.10
III	165.04	70	2.36	0.92	0.88	0.94	0.95	0.96	0.07	0.06	0.09
IV	165.09	69	2.39	0.92	0.87	0.94	0.95	0.96	0.07	0.06	0.09

Note: GFI = Goodness of Fit; AGFI = Adjusted Goodness of Fit; NFI = Normed Fit Index; NNFI = Non-Normed Fit Index; CFI = Comparative Fit Index; RMSEA = Root Mean Square Error of Approximation

sourcefulness were negatively correlated, and this pathway was retained in all four models. This correlated error term and was estimated to be –.09 and statistically significant in all four models. Within the classroom demands latent construct, the errors of children with problem behaviors and other student-related demands were positively correlated, and this pathway was retained in all models where it applied. This correlated error term and was estimated to be .29 (Model II), .31 (Model III), and .31 (Model IV) and statistically significant in all three models.

DISCUSSION

Teachers face many demands in the classroom, but stress researchers believe it is also important to understand how coping resources contribute to the stress equation (Matheny et al., 1986; Sapolsky, 1998). Understanding the factors that contribute to teacher stress, and ultimately burnout, is essential, given Ingersoll's (2001) finding that teacher shortages are caused in part by a "revolving door" of professionals who enter the field only to leave before retirement. A potential contribution of this study is that teacher's preventive coping resources, classroom demands, and classroom disruptions were found to be statistically significant predictors of burnout symptoms in elementary teachers. In order to further examine these findings, the measurement models used to establish each construct will first be discussed, followed by a review of the results for the mediation model tested and the follow-up analysis using preventive resources, classroom demands, and classroom disruptions as predictors of teacher burnout symptoms.

The scales with the largest coefficients in the measurement models developed for this study shed some light on which scales seem most important for measuring each construct. First, with respect to classroom demands, it was the administrative demands scale from the CARD with the highest loading (see Figure 17.3). If we are to better understand the factors that

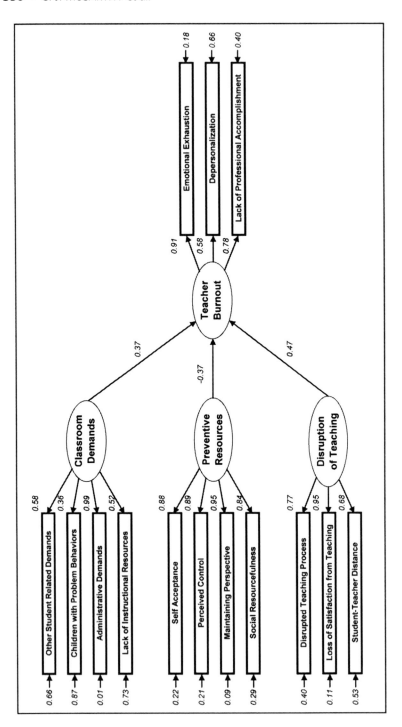

Figure 17.3 Final model of teacher burnout, Model IV.

lead to teacher burnout, it may be worth considering that administrative obligations such as keeping up with paperwork, policy issues, and testing could represent an obstacle to teachers' work satisfaction (Lambert & McCarthy, 2006). While this finding may represent common sense (i.e., who would be surprised by the finding that teachers do not like paperwork?), when compared to the other factors that load on the classroom demands construct (lack of instructional resources, dealing with student problem behaviors), alleviating teachers' administrative burden could represent an area in which it is feasible to intervene, perhaps through hiring extra administrative personnel or streamlining bureaucracies.

The scale with the largest coefficient for the preventive resources construct was maintaining perspective—in other words, teachers who are able to avoid stress by keeping life demands in perspective are likely more able to cope preventively and could be less vulnerable to burnout symptoms. Given the importance of subjective evaluations in transactional models of stress (Sapolsky, 1998), this finding might suggest the importance of teachers having professional supports and outlets for their concerns that would enable them to keep demands in perspective. Interestingly for the present study, the scale with the highest loading on disruption of teaching was the loss of satisfaction from teaching scale, which supports the overall goal of the study: Teaching effectiveness is degraded when teachers are unhappy. Finally, the finding that emotional exhaustion was the highest loading construct on teacher burnout was not surprising given that Maslach et al. (1996) suggested that EE is the most obvious and central manifestation of burnout.

This study tested disruption of teaching and classroom demands as possible mediators between preventive resources and burnout symptoms because it was assumed, given transactional models of stress, that having greater resources might enable teachers to perceive their classroom as less demanding and would also allow teachers to experience fewer disruptions. As can be seen in Figure 17.2, the test of mediation was not supported, but each of these constructs was found to predict teacher burnout with similar levels of association (see Figure 17.3). Teachers with better preventive coping resources did experience lower levels of burnout, but possession of greater resources did not seem to lead to perceiving the classroom as less demanding or as having fewer disruptions of the teaching process. It appears, at least within the context of the few models tested in this study, that each of these factors operated more or less independently as contributors to burnout symptoms. While interesting, these results do not necessarily contradict the central prediction of authors like Folkman and Lazarus (1984) that stress results from a perceived imbalance between demands and resources. In other research, McCarthy et al. (2009) and Lambert et al. (2007) have tested Folkman and Lazarus' (1984) prediction by creating difference scores between the resources and demands scales of the CARD and found support for transactional theories.

Both the latent variable related to classroom demands and the latent variable in the models that measured the disruption of the teaching process were moderately related to teacher burnout. However, neither the scale scores from the SQ that capture either the incidence of challenging behavior from the most challenging student nor the scale scores that measure the stress related to this behavior were related to burnout. Taken together, these finding suggest that a teacher's perceptions of the entire classroom as a whole are more predictive of burnout than are the perceptions of individual children who exhibit challenging behaviors. The teacher's perceptions of these children may only impact burnout when these children are disrupting the teaching process with their behaviors.

Limitations

This study had several limitations. First, it is important to note that a sample of convenience was used. The generalizability of the study is also limited by the fact that only one geographic region was represented in the sample. It is certainly possible that a more diverse sample of schools, and teachers, would have led to different findings. Further, the data for this study were collected using self-report measures and since the analyses were correlational, caution should be exercised in making any causal inferences. However, McCarthy et al. (2009) suggested that since transactional models of stress emphasize role of the cognitive process by which *perceived* demands are weighed against *perceived* resources, self-report data is critical to an understanding of teacher stress and an appropriate data collection strategy given the nature of the research questions.

Future Research

It is important to note that this research focused on only one specific pattern of mediation effects, along with the direct effects of coping and classroom conditions on burnout. Moderating effects were not included. In previous research, the additive effects of teacher perceptions of both classroom demands and resources were considered (Lambert, O'Donnell et al., 2006, Lambert et al., 2007) in order to classify teachers into three stress conditions: demands greater than resources (the stress condition), resources equal to demands, and resources greater than demands. It is possible that the relationships between latent constructs investigated in this study may functional differently for these three subgroups of teachers. For example, the relationship between coping resources and disruption of teaching may be stronger for teachers who are not experiencing occupational stress and weaker for those experiencing stress. In this sense, teacher stress condition could serve as a moderator between coping resources and other predictors of burnout. It will be useful to examine the potential moderator effects of stress condition in future research.

In addition, future research that includes both observational and interview data that can supplement the survey information used in this study may advance the understanding of teacher stress examined in this study. While the MBI-ES has been widely studied, future research using measures such as the SQ, CARD, and PRI will be most useful if reliability and validity evidence can be established in a variety of educational contexts. Additional studies will be necessary to examine the construct validity of these measures, particularly by using them along with other indicators of teacher wellness. Future research efforts should also extend this work with a larger and more diverse sample of teachers and schools.

AUTHOR NOTE

Partial funding for this study was provided by the United States Department of Education and the Hogeschool, Utrecht in the Netherlands.

REFERENCES

Bandalos, D. (2002). The effects of item parceling on goodness-of-fit and parameter estimate bias in structural equation modeling. *Structural Equation Modeling, 9*(1), 78–102.

Brown, M., & Ralph, S. (1998). The identification of stress in teachers. In J. Dunham & V. Varma (Eds.), *Stress in teachers: Past, present and future* (pp. 37–56). London, UK: Whurr Publishers.

Bullough, Jr., R. V., & Baughman, K. (1997). *"First-year Teacher" Eight Years Later: An inquiry into teacher development.* New York, NY: Teachers College Press.

Esteve, J. M. (2000). The transformation of the teachers' role at the end of the twentieth century: new challenges for the future. *Educational Review, 5,* 197–207.

Evers, J.G. E, Tomic, W., & Brouwers, A. (2004). Burnout among teachers students' and teachers' perceptions compared. *School Psychology International,* 25, 131–148

Gilroy, P. (2005). The commercialization of teacher education: teacher education in the marketplace. *Journal of Education for Teaching, 31,* 275–277.

Goldstein, J., & Noguera, P. A. (2006). A thoughtful approach to teacher evaluation. *Educational Leadership, 63,* 31–37.

Hastings, R.P., Horne, S., & Mitchell, G. (2004). Burnout in direct care staff in intellectual disability services: a factor analytic study of the Maslach Burnout Inventory. *Journal of Intellectual Disability Research, 48,* 268–273.

Hobfoll, S. E. (1989). Conservation of resources: A new attempt at conceptualizing stress. *American Psychologist, 44*, 513–524.

Holmbeck, G. (1997). Toward terminological, conceptual, and statistical clarity in the study of mediators and moderators: Examples form the child-clinical and pediatric psychology literatures. *Journal of Consulting and Clinical Psychology, 65*(4), 599–610.

Ingersoll, R. M. (2001). Teacher turnover and teacher shortages: An organizational analysis. *American Educational Research Journal, 38*, 499–534.

Kloska, A., & Ramasut, A. (1985). Teacher stress. *Maladjustment and Therapeutic Education,* 3, 19–26

Lambert, R. G., & McCarthy, C. J. (Eds.). (2006). *Understanding teacher stress in an era of accountability.* (Vol. III). Greenwich, CT: Information Age Publishing.

Lambert, R. G., McCarthy, & Abbott-Shim, M. (2001). *Classroom appraisal of resources and demands, school-age version.* Atlanta, GA: Head Start Quality Research Center.

Lambert, R. G., McCarthy, C. J., Gilbert, T., Sebree, M., & Steinley-Bumgarner, M. (2006). Validity evidence for the use of the Preventive Resources Inventory with college students *Measurement and Evaluation in Counseling and Development, 39,* 66–83.

Lambert, R. G., McCarthy, C. J., O'Donnell, M., & Melendres, L. (2007). Teacher Stress and Classroom Structural Characteristics in Elementary Settings. In Gates, G. (Ed.). (Vol. IV). Greenwich, Connecticut: Information Age Publishing, Inc. *Research on Stress and Coping in Education.*

Lambert, R., McCarthy, C., O'Donnell, M., & Wang, C. (2009). Measuring elementary teacher stress and coping in the classroom: Validity evidence for the Classroom Appraisal of Resources and Demands, *Psychology in the Schools, 46*(10), 973–988.

Lambert, R., O'Donnell, M., Kusherman, J., & McCarthy, C. (2006). Teacher stress and classroom structural characteristics in preschool settings. In R. Lambert and C. McCarthy (Eds.), *Understanding teacher stress in an age of accountability* (pp. 105–120). Greenwich, CT: Information Age Publishing.

Lazarus, R. S., & Folkman, S. (1984). *Stress, appraisal, and coping.* New York, NY: Springer.

LeCompte, M. D., & Dworkin, A. G. (1991). *Giving up on school: Student dropouts and teacher burnouts.* Newbury Park, CA: Corwin Press.

Maslach, C. & Jackson, S. E. (1981). The measurement of experienced burnout. *Journal of Occupational Behavior, 2,* 99–113.

Maslach, C., Jackson, S. E., Leiter, M. P. (1997). Maslach Burnout Inventory (3rd ed.). In C P. Zalaquett & R. J. Wood (Eds.), *Evaluating stress: A book of resources* (pp. 191–218). Lanham, MD: Scarecrow Press.

Maslach, C., Jackson, S. E., & Leiter, M. P. (1997). Maslach Burnout Inventory (3rd ed.). *Evaluating Stress: A Book of Resources. 1,* 191–218.

Maslach, C. & Schaufeli, W. B. (1993). Historical and conceptual development of burnout. In C. Maslach, W. B. Schaufeli, & T. Marek (Eds.), *Professional burnout: Recent developments in theory and research* (pp. 1–16). Washington, DC: Taylor & Francis.

Maslach, C., Schaufeli, W.B., & Leiter, M.P. (2001). Job burnout. *Annual Review of Psychology, 52,* 397–422.

Matheny, K. B., Aycock, D. W., Pugh, J. L., Curlette, W. L., & Canella, K. A. (1986). Stress coping: A qualitative and quantitative synthesis with implications for treatment. *The Counseling Psychologist, 14*(4), 499–549.

Matheny, K. B., Gfroerer, C. A., & Harris, K. (2000). Work stress, burnout, and coping at the turn of the century: An Adlerian perspective. *Journal of Individual Psychology, 56*(1), 74–87.

McCarthy, C. J., Lambert, R. G., Beard, L. M., & Dematatis, A. P. (2002). Factor structure of the Preventive Resources Inventory and its relationship to existing measures of stress and coping. In G. S. Gates, M. Wolverton, & W. H. Gmelch (Eds.), *Research on stress and coping in education* (pp. 3–37). Greenwich, CT: Information Age.

McCarthy, C. J., Lambert, R. G., O'Donnell, M. & Melendres, L. (2009). Relationship of elementary teachers' experience, perceived demands, and coping resources to burnout symptoms. *Elementary School Journal, 109*, 1–19.

MSN Encarta. (2007). Public education in the United States. Retrieved from http://encarta.msn.com/encyclopedia_761571491_2/Public_Education_in_the_United_States.html

No Child Left Behind Act of 2001, Pub. L. No. 107-110, $ 2204 (2002).

Sapolsky, R. M. (1998). *Why zebras don't get ulcers: An updated guide to stress, stress-related diseases, and coping.* New York, NY: W. H. Freeman.

Schaufeli, W. B., & Enzmann, D. (1998). *The burnout component to study and practice.* London, UK: Taylor & Francis.

Troman, G. & Woods, P. (2001). *Primary Teachers' Stress.* New York, NY: Routledge/Falmer.

U.S. Department of Education. (2007). The *No Child Left Behind* Act. Retrieved from http://www.ed.gov/index.jhtml

Verkuyten, V. (2002). Making teachers accountable for student disruptive classroom behavior. *British Journal of Sociology of Education, 23*, 107–122.

CHAPTER 18

CONSIDERATION FOR A GLOBAL APPROACH TO UNDERSTANDING AND PREVENTING TEACHER STRESS

Christopher McCarthy, Ryan Douglas, and Monique Shah Kulkarni
University of Texas at Austin

ABSTRACT

This chapter argues for a need to link teacher stress research to the general stress literature. Stress has historically been conceptualized in one of three ways: as an external demand, as a transaction between the person and environment, or as a threat to resources. Research presented in this book can be understood in terms of one or more of these models, and it is argued that future scholarship on teacher stress be explicitly connected to existing theories of stress and coping. Because teacher stress is likely to be increasingly viewed as an international phenomenon, this chapter concludes by reviewing how literature on globalization and international psychology informs this topic.

International Perspectives on Teacher Stress, pages 357–369

The contributions in this volume offer a wide range of perspectives on ways to understand, research, and prevent teacher stress. A major premise of this book is that it is essential to take an international perspective on this topic, given the increasing globalization of culture, commerce, and the exchange of knowledge. Many of today's teachers, across various national boundaries, are preparing their students to work in a global marketplace. This will likely continue to affect what teachers do in the classroom, including what they teach, how they teach, and what expectations will be in place for them and their students.

In providing a conclusion to this volume, we feel it is important to grapple with the complexity of concepts and ideas that are inherent in stress research. Anyone reading this volume will see how many different constructs fall under the stress umbrella. While this makes for a rich area of research, it can also create a Tower of Babel situation in which researchers are not speaking a common language. To help address this issue, we review how the various contributions in this volume are connected to a few dominant perspectives on stress and coping. This is important because of the many different literatures involved in teacher wellbeing and the ambiguities inherent in our understanding of stress. Researchers can make an important contribution to the literature by clearly situating their work with teachers in the existing stress literature and suggesting how their findings can expand our models and understanding of stress. We will conclude this chapter by identifying how globalization and international psychology provide important avenues of understanding for teacher stress.

MODELS OF STRESS AND COPING

Before considering how best to help teachers reduce stress, we must first have a clear understanding of how stress is conceptualized. This can be difficult, as stress is a widely studied but poorly understood phenomenon. In an attempt to summarize the stress literature, Matheny, Aycock, Pugh, Curlette, and Canella (1986) conducted a meta-analysis of stress interventions. They found evidence that stress interventions were as effective as other forms of counseling (cf. Smith & Glass, 1977). While these results were encouraging for stress researchers, Matheny et al. (1986) also noted a disturbing lack of consistency in definitions of what constitutes stress—in other words, different theorists have different understandings of what stress is, when it occurs, and what needs to happen in order to reduce it.

More recently, Hobfoll, Schwarzer, and Chon (1998) described stress as the most widely studied phenomenon in psychology, noting that a keyword search they conducted since 1984 retrieved 29,000 papers for just the terms stress and coping. This led Hobfoll et al. to conclude that it was no longer feasible, even at the time of their publication more than a decade ago, to summarize the enormous body of research on stress. Hobfoll and colleagues also noted some major ways in which stress is conceptualized and provided a review of the major models of stress as they pertained to health research. Since their contribution, many new studies have been added to the stress literature. In the ensuing years it could be argued that not only has stress research continued to burgeon, but also that a variety of similar interventions under such names as mind-body health, mindfulness, and wellness have continued to expand.

Hobfoll (1989) described three major models of stress as most influential, and we believe elements of one or more of these three perspectives can be meaningfully applied to the teacher studies in this volume. The ultimate goal of doing so is to broaden our understanding of stress in general and how stress models can be applied to understanding teacher stress. The three theories are: a stimulus (or environmental) perspective, a transactional (or cognitive) perspective, and a resource perspective. Each approach has a long and substantive tradition in the psychology of stress.

Stimulus Perspectives on Stress

This perspective conceptualizes stress as an external event, or stimulus, which causes a physiological reaction in the individual (Hobfoll, 1989). Accordingly, stress is mainly viewed as any event or circumstance that produces the physiology of a stress response. Threats to one's wellbeing, relationships, finances, and reputation are examples of events that can potentially trigger the stress response. Models of stress that focus mainly on external stimuli as causes of the stress response (i.e., Holmes & Rahe, 1967; Selye, 1956) were among the earliest to appear in the stress literature and helped make a connection between external events and the resultant physiological toll such events can take. Such models advanced our understanding of mind–body connections but tended to focus mainly on the objective characteristics of environmental circumstances as the main cause of stress.

Transactional Models of Stress

Lazarus and Folkman's (1984) transactional theory of stress is still the most dominant theory today and posits that stress results from a dynamic transaction between the environment (demands) and one's ability to cope with demands (resources). The transaction of demands and resources is mediated by cognitive appraisals of events and resources, and thus it is also referred to as a cognitive theory of stress.

This perspective presents a comprehensive model of stress and coping, which is triggered by the awareness of life demands, followed by an appraisal of the demand's potential for harm, and then an appraisal of the sufficiency of one's resources for coping (for a review, see McCarthy, Lambert, Beard, & Dematatis, 2002). Events that are appraised by an individual as outweighing available coping resources will be perceived as stressors, triggering the stress response and activating the use of coping strategies for ameliorating or eliminating the stressor. Long-term stressors can result in stress symptoms, such as anxiety or depression, and health problems.

Resource Models of Stress

Resource theories of stress emphasize that stress results from an actual, or threatened, loss of resources (Hobfoll, 1989). Hobfoll's (1989) conservation of resources (COR) model is the dominant perspective in this tradition, and he maintains that COR bridges a gap that exists between environmental and cognitive models of stress. In Hobfoll's view, this gap exists because stress is not strictly environmental or perceptual—as Hobfoll (1989) described the COR model, stress is

> defined as a reaction to the environment in which there is (a) the threat of a net loss of resources, (b) the net loss of resources, or (c) a lack of resource gain following the investment of resources. Both perceived and actual loss or lack of gain are envisaged as sufficient for producing stress. Resources, then, are the single unit necessary for understanding stress. (p. 516)

Hobfoll (1989) argued that COR theory addresses a gap in stimulus models of stress in that external demands alone do not determine stress, and that resources must be taken into account. Hobfoll also viewed COR as being more parsimonious than transactional models that posit the importance of appraisals of demands and resources without a clear definition of either construct. According to Hobfoll, COR theory allows for the role of cognitive appraisals, but puts the emphasis where it belongs, on the central construct of resources. Hobfoll et al. (1998) did note that definitions of what resources are, and which are most important in coping, vary widely from theorist to theorist and can include psychological resources (self-efficacy, interpersonal skills) and other types of resources such as social support or even material assets such as finances.

An example of the difference between COR theory and transactional models of stress can be demonstrated in the case of a teacher who, in a time of declining school budgets, loses a long-time teacher's aide for her/his classroom. Transactional models suggest that as long as teachers perceive themselves as having sufficient resources to manage classroom demands, they will not feel stressed by the event. Hobfoll's COR model, however, suggests that even if a teacher has the resources to manage classroom demands, she or he may still feel stressed because the loss of an aide represents a loss of resources. As this example hopefully illustrates, the two models do not necessary suggest different outcomes in a given situation, but they do provide a different lens on the subject of stress. Interested readers are referred to Hobfoll (1989) for a more complete discussion of COR theory.

Following our brief review of models of stress, we will now consider how each of the chapters in the first part of this volume inform one or more of the traditions described above: environmental, cognitive, or resource. Our goal in doing so is to explicitly link each of the studies in this volume to the larger stress field with the goal of creating more consistency in how we understand teacher stress. A variety of methods and constructs were used to study teacher stress in different nations. However, this very richness and complexity can make it more challenging to translate into practical and effective ways to reduce teacher stress. It is hoped that by connecting each study to the traditions of stress research, the implications of each study, and the volume as a whole, will be enhanced.

MODELS OF STRESS REPRESENTED IN PART 1

Part 1 of this volume can be considered multimethod and multinational in that a number of different methodologies and teacher nationalities are represented. Because of this complexity, most of the studies do not fit neatly into one of the three stress models identified previously.

One example that does seem to clearly reside in the stimulus tradition, Baran's chapter, "The Impact of Cultural Values, Country Characteristics, and Educational Reform on Teacher Stress Levels in Norway," provides important context information about events in Norway that impact teacher stress. In addition, Gokalp's chapter on "Effects of Stress on Teacher Decision Making" also represents this tradition by focusing on how stress impacts teachers' decisions about how to handle problematic student behaviors. Both contributions demonstrate the importance of environmental factors in teacher stress, and even though more recent models of stress emphasize coping resources as equal in importance to events, they serve as reminders of the importance of the environmental context in teacher stress.

Part 2 of this volume also includes a number of attempts to explicitly test Folkman and Lazarus' transactional model of stress. Erktin and Kisa's chapter, "Elementary Level Mathematics Teachers' Stress at a Time of Curriculum Reform in Turkey," operationalized many components of Folkman and Lazarus' model in their study and found some support for this theoretical perspective. Lambert, McCarthy, McCarthy, Crowe, and Fisher, in

"Assessment of Teacher Demands and Resources: Relationship to Stress, Classroom Structural Characteristics, Job Satisfaction, and Turnover," also tested specific hypothesis of transactional models of stress with a measure that attempts to directly test teachers appraisals of demands and resources in the classroom (the Classroom Assessment of Demands and Resources). Support was found for the prediction that teachers who appraised demands as outstripping resources were less satisfied and more likely to be thinking about leaving the profession.

Finally, Gates and Dean's chapter, "Washington State Elementary Teachers' Stress: The Importance of Occupational Commitment," could also be primarily situated in the transactional tradition, as they found teacher personality variables (professional commitment and locus of control) to moderate perceived stress. Each of these studies represents the potential importance of understanding teacher stress through a transactional lens. Further, the studies also show that to adequately test transactional models, construct-relevant measures and analyses need to be employed.

A number of contributions seem most consistent with a resource perspective of teacher stress. Singleton, Shue, and Smith's chapter, "Effects of Collaborative Problem Solving on Stress, Burnout, and Coping Resources in Early Childhood Special Educators," describes an intervention study aimed at decreasing stress and building coping resources. They used a mixed-methods approach to demonstrate that the goals of this intervention were achieved. Kokkinos, Stavropoulos, and Davazoglou's chapter, "Student Teachers' Epistemological Beliefs, Conceptions About Teaching and Learning and Perceived Stress During Practicum: Are They Related?" also focused on a type of teacher resource, namely their ideas about knowledge and pedagogy. As predicted, they found relationships between these resources and stress during a teaching practicum. Finally, Carson, Tsouloupas, and Barber's chapter, "Burnout and Coping Strategies Across Primary and Secondary Public Schoolteachers," is a fitting way to end this review of stress models, in that it draws heavily from each of the three stress traditions. However, because it focuses on teachers' coping strategies, it could be considered most representative of the resource approach to understanding stress.

MODELS OF STRESS REPRESENTED IN PART 2
OF THIS VOLUME

Part two of this book used a mono-method, multinational approach to studying teacher stress, which was accomplished through different researchers using the same measure in different countries. The measure contained in Everaert's chapter, "Measuring the Perceived Incidence of Challenging Student Behavior: The Development of the Utrecht Challenging Student Questionnaire for Teachers (UCSQT)," describes the UCSQT as assessing "the incidence of teachers' daily interaction with the most challenging student in their classroom, and the hindrance that this becomes for them" (p. 2). This definition of the measure indicates that the research is mainly operating from a stimulus perspective, conceptualizing stress as an external event (demands caused by a challenging student), which potentially produces stress for the teacher. However, as Everaert makes clear, challenging student behavior is assessed according to teachers' perceptions of students, not objective indicators of student actions, thus introducing a perceptual element consistent with transactional models of stress. While evidence is reported for an interpretable factor structure for the measure, Everaert notes that teacher resources were not taken into account with the measure. Therefore, it does not directly test transactional or COR perspectives on stress.

Following Everaert's work, Castelli, Pepe, and Adimando's chapter, "A Mixed Methods Study of the Responses to Two Open Ended Questions Regarding Stress in the Classroom from a Sample of Italian Teachers" attempted to better understand teacher responses to specific items on the UCSQT. Castelli et al's study provides a rich structure for understanding the cultural relevance of items on the UCSQT, and the analysis itself operates mainly from a stimulus perspective on stress as well.

Volochkov and Popov's chapter, "Stress in Teacher–Student Interactions and Teacher Activeness as a Positive Coping Resource," presented research with teachers in the Perm region of Russia and included the UCSQT. While this emphasis would clearly situate the study in the realm of stimulus models of stress, Volochkov and Popov do note in their chapter that environment is only a potential influence on teacher–student interactions. Accordingly, their chapter introduces a construct with a rich history in the literature of Russian psychology: teacher activeness. This construct assesses "a quality of the subject's volitional interactions within a concrete sphere of being... including their choices (and the underlying processes) in what to say or how to respond to students displaying challenging behavior in the classroom" (p. 6). Teacher activeness may therefore be consistent with Hobfoll's (1989) COR model in that it incorporates teachers' activeness as a resource. Similarly, Pang and Tao's chapter on "Teacher Stress in Working with Behavioral Problems of Students in Hong Kong" studies both external events (challenging students) and teachers' resources (self-efficacy, negative affect, and attitudes).

McCarthy, Lambert, O'Donnell, Villarreal, and Melendres' chapter, "Predictors of Elementary Teachers' Burnout Symptoms: The Role of Teachers' Personal Resources, Perceptions of Classroom Stress, and Disruption of Teaching," attempted to explicitly use transactional models of stress with teachers from the United States by using structural equation modeling to test whether classroom demands and disruptions mediated the relationship between coping resources and burnout symptoms, as Folkman and Lazarus (1984) would predict. While support for the meditational model was not found, support was found for a model in which each predictor construct was associated with burnout symptoms. This relationship might provide support for Hobfoll's COR model in that resources were connected to stress symptoms (burnout).

Our review of the contributions in the second section of this volume suggests the potential utility of using a mono-method, multinational approach to understanding teacher stress. Each study utilized a common measure, allowing for a direct comparison of findings across different nations. As we have attempted to show in this review, the contributions varied in the extent to which different theories of stress were incorporated. Since all of the studies in this section used the UCSQT, a measure of challenging student behavior, it could be argued that each represented the environmental approach to understanding stress. However, many of the studies incorporated teacher resources, and thus included elements of COR theory. McCarthy et al.'s study was the only one that seemed to attempt to directly test Lazarus and Folkman's (1984) transactional model, although empirical evidence was not found to support it.

In conclusion to this section, research on teachers using each of the three stress paradigms can make important contributions. We need to understand external factors that cause teachers stress, what types of resources teachers need to be effective in their work, and how teacher perceptions influence the stress process. Connecting teacher research to existing models of stress is particularly important given the nexus of factors that pertain to teacher stress research. Teacher research resides at the intersection of many roads of academic inquiry: educational policy, worker wellness, accountability standards, and health psychology, to name a few. Research in these various areas can become compartmentalized unless it is integrated into the larger body of literature on teacher stress. For example, teachers are widely represented in burnout research (Schaufeli & Enzmann, 1998), but many times burnout is treated as a topic unto itself, without reference to stress theory (McCarthy, Lambert, O'Donnell, & Melendres, 2009). Understanding the perceptual nature of this process also seems valuable. Situating research within one or more of these frameworks and explicitly connecting study findings to these models may help us make more rapid progress in synthesizing and communicating the findings of studies conducted across the globe.

GLOBALIZATION, TEACHING, AND STRESS

When considering teacher stress internationally, it is important to examine teacher demands and resources within the context of globalization. The recent international psychology movement offers perspectives that can be helpful in the context of teacher stress. International psychology highlights the importance of understanding psychological constructs in an international context in order to make psychological knowledge more cross-culturally applicable (Stevens & Wedding, 2004). It promotes sharing the perspectives of psychologists from different backgrounds on similar issues, as well as utilizing psychological knowledge to assist policymakers across nations and cultures. A goal of international psychology is to contribute to a multidisciplinary approach to solving global problems (Stevens & Wedding, 2004). This perspective is important because teacher stress is a psychological issue that is important across cultures and impacted by global change. An international understanding of teacher stress is useful in policymaking and in furthering scientific knowledge, especially as the impact of globalization on education increases.

While the perspectives presented in this book do not directly engage the issue of globalization and teacher stress, globalization is certainly in the background of many stressors that teachers face. Globalization has had a significant, though often indirect, effect on education in ways that can contribute to stress. Before we discuss some of the ways that globalization impacts teacher stress, it is important to describe globalization and its role in educational settings. Globalization is a multifaceted concept that impacts a wide range of disciplines. An all-encompassing definition of such a concept is impossible, but some ways of understanding globalization are useful to understand its impact on stress.

Weber (2007) stated that "globalization refers to the increasing social, economic, financial, cultural, and technological integration of different countries and regions, especially in recent decades" (p. 280). This definition of globalization implies an increasing degree of interdependence among cultures, nations, and individuals in order to meet goals such as economic and social stability. It also speaks to the increasing technological change that facilitates so much of this growth. However, other definitions of globalization highlight that this interconnectedness and increasing economic relationships between nations often comes at a cost—events in one region may have an increased impact on another region that can be negative (Merriman & Nicoletti, 2008). For instance, reforms in one region may have a direct impact on the economy of another region, which impacts educational needs.

Both ways of understanding the phenomenon of globalization, as either increased integration or as creating a cost, have implications for educators. Teachers' roles can be impacted by the need for greater integration with other cultures, which changes curricula, educational values, and other aspects of teaching; however, teachers' roles can also be impacted by the effects of economic or social changes in other regions or nations that in the past might not have been relevant to their educational setting. Globalization can serve as a background factor influencing teacher stress in that cultural change may result in role confusion for teachers or stress due to increased need for teacher accountability among other globalization-related stressors.

HOW GLOBALIZATION IMPACTS TEACHER STRESS

It is beyond the scope of this chapter to describe all the ways in which globalization contributes to stress for teachers, but we will address some implications of globalization for international teacher stress. Some prominent aspects of globalization in education include curriculum revisions, changes in the distribution of power given to various stakeholders in educational systems, a rapid rate of change that requires greater teacher flexibility, and an increase in the amount of multicultural knowledge needed to be an effective educator.

Many of these changes can have a positive effect on education, but they can also increase teacher stress, especially when resources needed to cope with these changes become less available to teachers. An example in the United States is that as a result of current financial and political issues, teachers' salaries, benefits, and school district resources have been impacted by budget shortfalls. In such a climate it may be more difficult for teachers to access the resources they need to meet the demands they face to provide education that helps students participate in an increasingly interconnected world. In the following paragraphs we will elaborate on some of the globalization-related challenges that place demands on teachers.

One important way that globalization impacts teachers is through an increased rate of social, technological, and scientific change that creates greater demands in the form of knowledge and technological abilities needed to instruct students. These rapid changes can increase demands on teachers by adding more training requirements and increasing the expectations of administrators and parents. While in many ways these changes are positive for educators, De Vogli (2004) suggested that for some individuals this rapid rate of change could erode their sense of purpose or familiarity with their role. For teachers, the change inherent in globalization may lead to stress stemming from feeling undervalued or unsure of their role as teacher.

The rate of change can also put pressure on teachers to meet demands viewed as necessary in global markets, regardless of whether the teacher views such demands necessary in their classroom. These may include emphasis on math and science over other disciplines or changes in educational policies based on the current needs of the workforce. One example of this is an increased demand on teachers to prepare students for jobs that are projected to be available in the future based on current market trends. However, since there is not agreement on how current job market trends should be interpreted, teachers' roles in this preparation process may not always be clear. So while increasing expectations on educators serves an important role in education, such demands may also contribute to teacher stress.

Another area that is affected by globalization is the content of curricula. Teacher stress and curriculum changes are addressed in this volume by research from two countries: Baran (Norway) and Erktin and Kısa (Turkey). Changes in curriculum influenced by globalization occur for a variety of reasons, including the need to increase multicultural components in education, the need to help students become more competitive with international peers, and the need to educate students about systems that are intertwined with their nation's economic, political, or cultural interests. Further, teachers may be called upon then to educate students about the history and culture of nations that are important trade partners so that students will be able to engage in cultural and economic exchange.

Though changes in curriculum may be necessary and useful, as research in this volume has indicated, such reform can contribute to teacher stress when teachers do not have the resources to cope with the new demands. This broadening of content may place a strain on teachers when time is limited to cover these topics or when teachers do not receive enough administrative support to enact curriculum changes. It is important then that we have a better understanding of how to promote adaptation to these changes through bolstering teachers' resources.

Globalization also has an effect on teachers' roles in the classroom, which can impact teachers' autonomy and confidence. One example of this is the increasing presence of curricula shaped by standardized tests. Influenced by the perceived need to stay competitive in global markets, many schools in the United States have placed greater emphasis on standardized testing as a way to measure the quality of schools and teachers. Emphasis has been placed on performance on these tests as being poor relative to other nations with different educational systems. Because of these concerns, curricula and the amount of time spent on various instructional activities have been altered in order to make U.S. students more competitive with international students. However, in many cases these changes have led to less autonomy for the teacher, as evidenced by less control over the content that they teach, the amount of time spent reviewing certain materials, and how to present certain concepts to their students. This loss of autonomy can contribute to a sense of devaluation and lowered morale in teachers that increases stress (Mathison & Freeman, 2006).

These are just a few ways that changes related to globalization impact teacher stress. It is important to note that while some examples given have focused on the U.S., teachers face similar issues around the world. As suggested by the international psychology literature, it is important to understand the demands placed on teachers in the context of their own cultural and political context. For instance, Waks (2003) has pointed out that in many European countries, curricula have become less centralized and more local as opposed to the opposite trend in the U.S. While this represents a different impact of globalization than that faced by teachers in the U.S., it is still a changing trend that places demand on teachers. Coping with these demands is shaped by the specific context in which teachers work. While meeting these demands may increasingly be a challenge, it is vital that communities, school systems, and governments help teachers obtain the resources they need to meet the increasing demands of the teaching profession.

The theories reviewed in this section and the impact of globalization on teacher stress can serve as a useful context in which to consider specific situations that teachers face. Our hope is that as more research on international teacher stress is conducted, researchers will consider how specific theoretical or contextual factors influence their studies. Taking these considerations into account can lead to more meaningful research on international teacher stress and more theoretical advancements that can help guide future research.

REFERENCES

De Vogli, R. (2004). *Change, psychosocial stress and health in an era of globalization.* Unpublished Manuscript.

Hobfoll, S. E. (1989). Conservation of resources: A new attempt at conceptualizing stress. *American Psychologist, 44,* 513–524.

Hobfoll, S. E., Schwarzer, R., & Chon, K. K. (1998). Disentangling the stress labyrinth: Interpreting the meaning of the term stress as it is studied in health context. *Anxiety, Stress, and Coping, 11,* 181–212.

Holmes, T. H., & Rahe, R. H. (1967). The social readjustment rating scale. *Journal of Psychosomatic Research, 11,* 213–218.

Lazarus, R. S., & Folkman, S. (1984). *Stress, appraisal, and coping.* New York, NY: Springer.

Matheny, K. B., Aycock, D. W., Pugh, J. L., Curlette, W. L., & Canella, K. A. (1986). Stress coping: A qualitative and quantitative synthesis with implications for treatment. *The Counseling Psychologist, 14*(4), 499–549.

Mathison, S., & Freeman, M. (2006). Teacher stress and high stakes testing: How using one measure of academic success leads to multiple teacher stressors. In R. Lambert & C. McCarthy (Eds.), *Understanding teacher stress in an age of accountability* (pp. 43–63). Greenwich, CT: Information Age Publishing.

McCarthy, C. J., Lambert, R. G., Beard, L. M., & Dematatis, A. P. (2002). Factor structure of the Preventive Resources Inventory and its relationship to existing measures of stress and coping. In G. S. Gates, M. Wolverton, & W. H. Gmelch (Eds.), *Research on stress and coping in education* (pp. 3–37). Greenwich, CT: Information Age.

McCarthy, C. J., Lambert, R. G., O'Donnell, M., & Melendres, L. T. (2009). The relation of elementary teachers' experience, stress, and coping resources to burnout symptoms. *The Elementary School Journal, 109*, 282–300.

Merriman, W., & Nicoletti, A. (2008). Globalization and American education. *The Educational Forum, 72*(1), 8–22.

Schaufeli, W. B., & Enzmann, D. (1998). *The burnout component to study and practice.* London, UK: Taylor & Francis.

Selye, H. (1956). *The stress of life.* New York, NY: McGraw-Hill.

Smith, M. L., & Glass, G. V. (1977). Meta-analysis of psychotherapy outcome studies. *American Psychologist, 32*(9), 752–760.

Stevens, M. J., & Wedding, D. (2004). International psychology: An overview. In M. J. Stevens, & D. Wedding (Eds.), *Handbook of international psychology* (pp. 1–21). New York, NY: Brunner-Routledge.

Waks, L. J. (2003). How globalization can cause fundamental curriculum change: An American perspective. *Journal of Educational Change 4*(4), 383–418.

Weber, E. (2007). Globalization, "glocal" development, and teachers' work: A research agenda. *Review of Educational Research, 77*, 279–309.

ABOUT THE CONTRIBUTORS

Loredana Addimando received her PhD in social psychology at the University of Milano-Bicocca. A chartered psychologist, she teaches vocational guidance in the Department of Educational Sciences—University of Verona, Italy. Her research interests include parental involvement, occupational issues about teachers' workplace (i.e., stress management, effective communication, and active management of parents), and students' challenging behaviors.

Mette L. Baran received her EdD in administrative leadership and supervision from De Paul University in Chicago, Illinois. She is an assistant professor in the doctoral program in leadership studies at Cardinal Stritch University in Milwaukee. She has an extensive background in higher education serving as faculty of business, director of development, director of education, campus director, and program director. In addition, she is an international business consultant. Dr. Baran teaches research methods courses in addition to courses in leadership and learning. Dr. Baran's publications include articles in the areas of service learning, academic achievement, student attitudes toward school, looping, relationship building, and teaching multi-methodology research strategies. Dr. Baran serves on the board of trustees of Robert Morris University of Illinois. In addition she is a board member of various not-for-profit organizations.

Larissa K. Barber, PhD, is an assistant professor in the department of psychology at Northern Illinois University. She is a member of the graduate faculty for the social/industrial–organizational psychology program, and publishes

International Perspectives on Teacher Stress, pages 371–377
Copyright © 2012 by Information Age Publishing
All rights of reproduction in any form reserved.

research in the areas of self-regulation, occupational health risk factors and outcomes (i.e, sleep, stress and burnout), work-life issues, and personality.

Russell L. Carson, PhD, is an assistant professor in the Department of Kinesiology at Louisiana State University in Baton Rouge, LA. His research focuses on the psychological processes (motivation, stress, burnout) of teachers, and typically includes mixed methodologies and real-time technologies. His work has been funded by the Robert Wood Johnson Foundation, The Spencer Foundation and the National Association for Sport and Physical Education. He has served as the program chair for the Stress and Coping in Education Special Interest Group of the American Educational Research Association.

Stefano Castelli (MA, PhD) is a professor of work and organizational psychology at the University of Milano-Bicocca, where he also serves in the board of directors. President of the European Research Network about Parents in Education (ERNAPE), he is founder and editor in chief of the International Journal about Parents in Education.

Betsy Crowe is a PhD student in the Department of Educational Psychology at the University of Texas at Austin. Her research interests include stress, social support, and health in underserved populations.

Aggeliki Davazoglou is a professor of special educational needs at the Department of Primary Education, Democritus University of Thrace, Greece. Her research interests focus on teacher training, home–school relations, and social and emotional development of gifted children.

Effie Dean is a graduate of the educational leadership doctoral program at Washington State University.

Ryan P. Douglas, Med, is a counseling psychology PhD student at the University of Texas at Austin. His research interests include meaning-focused and religious coping, grief and loss, and attachment.

Emine Erktin is a professor in the department of primary education at Bogazici University of Istanbul, Turkey. Her research interests include stress and coping in educational contexts, math education, metacognition, and self-regulation. She is a member of the Stress and Coping Special Interest Group of the American Educational Research Association. She is also a member and the Turkish national representative of the Stress and Anxiety Research Society (STAR).

Huub A. Everaert is an associate professor in the department of educational leadership at HU University of Applied Sciences Utrecht. His main research interests are demography of slavery, methodology, data management, and applied statistics in education. He is a member of the Stress and Coping Special Interest Group of the American Educational Research Association.

Molly H. Fisher is an assistant professor of mathematics education in the department of STEM education at the University of Kentucky, where she also serves as the co-director of the P20 STEM Innovation lab. Her research interests include secondary teacher retention and supporting new teachers as well as the professional noticing of pre-service elementary teachers.

Gordon Gates is associate professor of educational leadership at Washington State University. His research focuses on leadership practices and processes as suffused with and constituted by emotion work. He is particularly interested in stress and coping with conflict and change in institutions of learning. Currently, he is investigating how educators adapt to reform with the goal of understanding organizational reliability and the resilience of leaders in managing uncertainty, preventing mishaps, and improving safety.

Gokce Gokalp completed her Ph.D. with an emphasis in Educational Psychology at the USC Rossier School of Education. She is now an assistant professor in the Department of Educational Sciences at the Middle East Technical University in Ankara, Turkey. Her research interests include effects of stress on cognitive processes of teachers such as decision making and classroom management, and use of simulations in teacher training.

Michele R. Guzmán is Assistant Director of Research and Evaluation at the Hogg Foundation for Mental Health, which is part of The University of Texas at Austin's Division of Diversity and Community Engagement. Michele is also a Clinical Associate Professor in the Department of Educational Psychology. In the past, her primary areas of teaching and research interest have been multicultural counseling, ethnic and racial identity development, and multicultural competencies. Prior to joining the Hogg Foundation full time, where Michele works on grant programs related to mental health provider workforce issues, she conducted diversity education workshops both on and off campus to various audience including police officers and school administrators. Michele received her Ph.D. in Counseling Psychology from the University at Albany, State University of New York, and her bachelor's degree in Psychology from Vassar College.

Sonia Hart is a doctoral student in the department of educational psychology at the University of Texas at Austin. Her research interests include stress, resilience, and non-traditional coping mechanisms in minority populations. She has also begun researching interdisciplinary methodology and practice in the social services.

Zahid Kisa is a PhD student in the learning sciences and policy program at the University of Pittsburgh and working in Learning Research Development Center as a graduate student researcher. His research interests include the improvement of teaching and the policies, systems, and supports that aid teachers in employing high-quality instruction.

Constantinos M. Kokkinos is an associate professor of educational psychology in the department of primary education, Democritus University of Thrace, Greece. His research interests are in the areas of children's disruptive and antisocial behaviors, classroom psychosocial climate, psychological assessment, and teachers' stress and burnout. He is a member of the Stress and Coping Special Interest Group of the American Educational Research Association.

Monique Shah Kulkarni is a doctoral candidate in counseling psychology at the University of Texas at Austin. Her expected date of graduation is August 2012. Her research interests are in the areas of religious coping, multicultural competency, and mental health stigma in the South Asian community.

Richard G. Lambert is a professor in the department of educational leadership at the University of North Carolina at Charlotte where he also serves as the director of the Center for Educational Measurement and Evaluation. His research interests include stress and coping in educational contexts, applied statistics, and evaluating the quality of programs for young children. He is a member of the Stress and Coping Special Interest Group of the American Educational Research Association.

Christopher J. McCarthy is a professor in the department of educational psychology at the University of Texas at Austin. His research interests include stress and coping in educational contexts, group counseling, and health and wellness. He is a member of the Stress and Coping Special Interest Group of the American Educational Research Association, and has served as its chair and program chair.

Colleen J McCarthy is a doctoral student in counseling psychology at the University of Oregon. She holds a masters degree in counselor education from the University of Texas at Austin. Her research interests include career counseling with underrepresented populations and stress in educational contexts.

Lauren T. Melendres received her PhD in counseling psychology at the University of Texas at Austin. She is currently a post-doctoral psychology fellow at the James J. Peters VA Medical Center in New York, NY. She is involved in treatment research for veterans with high-risk suicidal behavior. Other research interests include performance anxiety in academic and sports contexts and related interventions, including mindfulness-based interventions.

Megan O'Donnell is a doctoral student in the family and human development program at Arizona State University (ASU). She teaches statistics at ASU and also works as a research associate within the Prevention Research Center. Her research interests include cultural-related stress, coping, and acculturation processes in Mexican American adolescents.

I-Wah Pang is an associate dean in the faculty of education studies at the Hong Kong Institute of Education. His research interests include parent involvement, teacher stress, and school governance. He has extensive experience in developing and managing teacher education programs, both pre-service and in-service. Besides courses of parent involvement, he also taught work psychology of teachers and happiness studies.

Alessandro Pepe is an adjunct professor of human resource management in the department of psychology of the University of Milano–Bicocca (Italy). His research interests focus on the organizational aspects of teachers' work, strategies to improve communication between parents and schools, applied mixed-methods research design, and bibliometrics. He is currently editor of the *International Journal About Parents in Education* and data analysis consultant.

Alexey Popov is a senior lecturer in the department of psychology at Perm State Pedagogical University (Perm, Russia). His research interests include psychometrics, judgment heuristics, experimental research of decision making, and coping resources. He also works in the sphere of designing expert systems to model expert decision making under uncertainty.

Jenson Reiser is a doctoral student in counseling psychology at the University of Texas at Austin. She spent five years teaching and supporting teachers in low-income New York City classrooms. Her research interests include educator stress, LGBTQ counseling, and mental health in low-income communities.

Jennifer L. Singleton is a special education teacher in Charlotte, North Carolina. She has a bachelor's degree in special education: moderate to severe disabilities from the University of Kentucky and a master's degree in early childhood education from the University of North Carolina at Charlotte. Her current research includes stress and coping among early childhood special educators.

George Stavropoulos, BEd, MEd, is a primary school teacher in Greece. His research interests include student teacher stress and epistemological beliefs during their training.

Pamela L. Shue is an assistant professor in the Department of Special Education and Child Development at the University of North Carolina at Charlotte. Her research interests include universal prekindergarten, enhancing the quality of programs that serve families and children in poverty and English language learners, as well as literacy and language development and education. She is a member of the Literacy Development in Young Children Special Interest Group of the International Reading Association and Early Education and Child Development Special Interest Group of the American Educational Research Association.

JaneDiane Smith is an associate professor in the department of special education and child development at the University of North Carolina at Charlotte. Her research interests focus on the role of early intervention (EI)/early childhood special education (ECSE) for young children with disabilities (or at-risk of developmental delays) and their families as well as interdisciplinary personnel preparation.

Sau Wai Tao is a senior research assistant at the Hong Kong Institute of Education. She has supported research projects on various areas in education including inclusive education, IT in education, teacher stress, and school evaluation.

Costas N. Tsouloupas, PhD, is a lecturer in the Department of Life and Health Sciences at the University of Nicosia in Cyprus. His Research interests include teacher cognitive appraisals/regulation of emotion, teacher adverse outcomes, and teacher efficacy towards job-related stressors. He is a member of the Stress and Coping Special Interest Group of the American Educational Research Association.

Annette Ullrich is a professor in the department of social work at Baden-Württemberg Cooperative State University Stuttgart. Her research interests include stress and coping in educational contexts. She is a member of the Stress and Anxiety Research Association and the American Educational Research Association.

Sara A. Villarreal received her PhD in counseling psychology at the University of Texas at Austin in 2011. Following internship training at Bay Pines VA, she joined the U.S. Public Health Service and was commissioned in 2012. She is currently completing her post-doctoral fellowship at the San Antonio Military Medical Center/Ft. Sam Houston, with a focus on trauma.

Andrey Volochkov is a professor in the department of psychology at Perm State Pedagogical University (Perm, Russia). His research interests lie in the area of agency, locus of control, self-determination, and "activeness" as an integral coping resource. He works on developing his theory of activeness as well as a series of questionnaires to measure coping resources in students, teachers, policemen, and some other groups of professionals.

Andreas Zimber is a professor in the department of applied psychology at the SRH-University of Applied Psychology at Heidelberg. His research interests focus on the psychology of occupational health and health promotion, on the association between leadership and health, and on mental health and health care system issues. He developed several intervention programs in order to improve individual skills relevant for occupational health.